YAY! ☆ HAYATE THE COMBAT BUTLER VOLUME TWO IS OUT NOW...!!
YAHOO...!!
AGENT
IT'S YOU, AGAIN...
SO, NOW THAT WE'RE ON VOLUME TWO, WHAT'S IT LIKE FOR YOU?
ON THE FRONT COVER, I SEE OJÔ-SAMA SEEMS OFFENDED THAT THE SUNFLOWERS ARE TALLER THAN SHE IS...
SHUT UP, BALDY!!
GRRR
WELL, IT SEEMS THE GENERAL PUBLIC IS SAYING VOLUME ONE WAS A GOOD SELLER...
Seriously, how rude of her to talk to a priestess that way...
...
Not again...
TO BE HONEST...
...IT'S ONLY BECAUSE NOT MANY COPIES WERE PRINTED IN THE FIRST PLACE...
Ah! A shooting star!
IN ORDER TO GAIN TRUE POPULARITY...
...OUR HEROINE NEEDS TO BEAR MORE RESPONSIBILITY FOR HELPING OUT...
EH?!
B...BARE MORE?! THAT'S CRAZY! GOING FOR CHEAP SEX APPEAL COULD CAUSE A BIG DROP IN POPULARITY!!
DON'T WORRY! ♥
ACTUALLY, POPULARITY HAS NOTHING TO DO WITH IT...
HEH HEH HEH HEH
THE ARTIST SIMPLY WANTS TO DRAW MORE NUDITY...
PUFF
THAT'S EVEN WORSE!!
STONE OF SELF-REFLECTION
WHUNCH

And, as expected, there's no nudity...

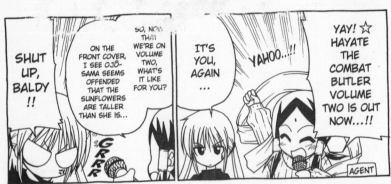

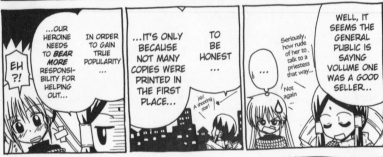

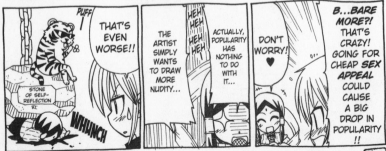

HAYATE THE COMBAT BUTLER
VOL. 2

STORY AND ART BY
KENJIRO HATA

English Adaptation/Mark Giambruno
Translation/Yuki Yoshioka & Cindy H. Yamauchi
Touch-up Art & Lettering/Freeman Wong
Design/Yukiko Whitley
Editor/Kit Fox

Editor in Chief, Books/Alvin Lu
Editor in Chief, Magazines/Marc Weidenbaum
VP, Publishing Licensing/Rika Inouye
VP, Sales & Product Marketing/Gonzalo Ferreyra
VP, Creative/Linda Espinosa
Publisher/Hyoe Narita

Printed in Canada

Published by VIZ Media, LLC
P.O. Box 77010
San Francisco, CA 94107

10 9 8 7 6 5 4 3 2
First printing, February 2007
Second printing, August 2008

RATED T FOR TEEN

PARENTAL ADVISORY
HAYATE THE COMBAT BUTLER is rated T+ for Older Teen and is recommended for ages 16 and up. This volume contains strong language, realistic and fantasy violence, and crude humor.

ratings.viz.com

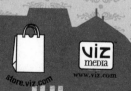

Hayate the Combat Butler

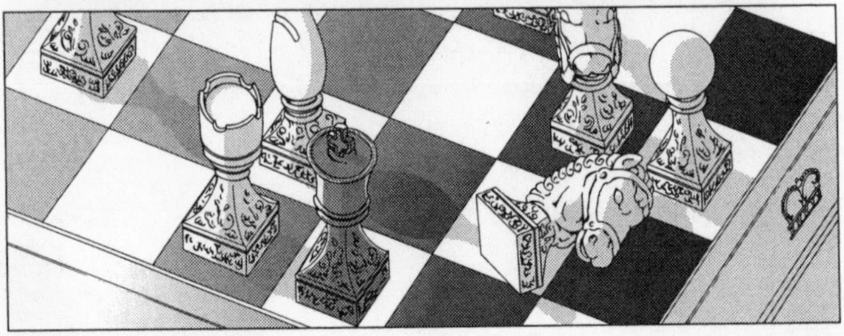

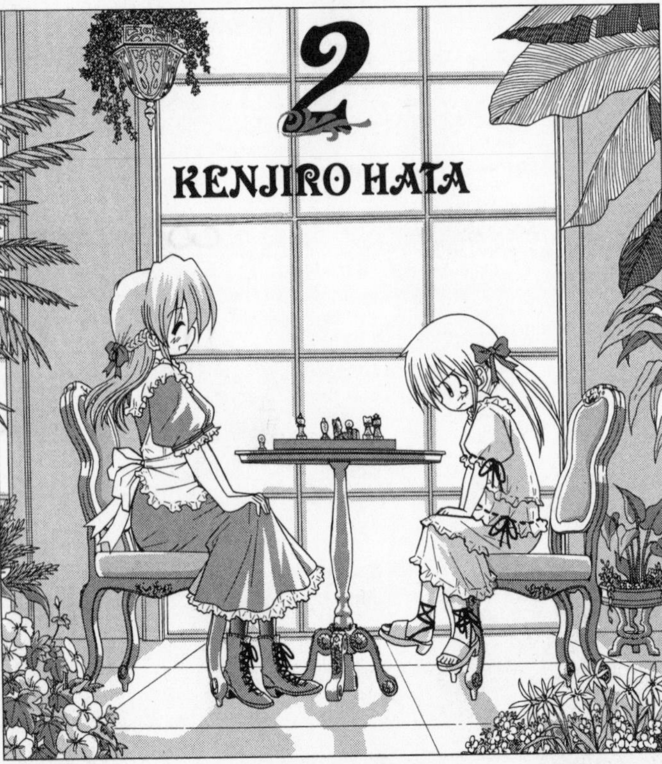
2
KENJIRO HATA

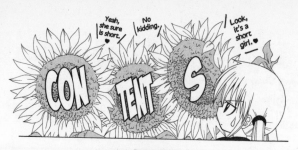

Look, it's a short girl.♥
No kidding.
Yeah, she sure is short.♥
CON TENT S

Episode 1: "In the Wee Hours of a Full Moon Night, Roasting, Smashing and Grinding Them to Powder"

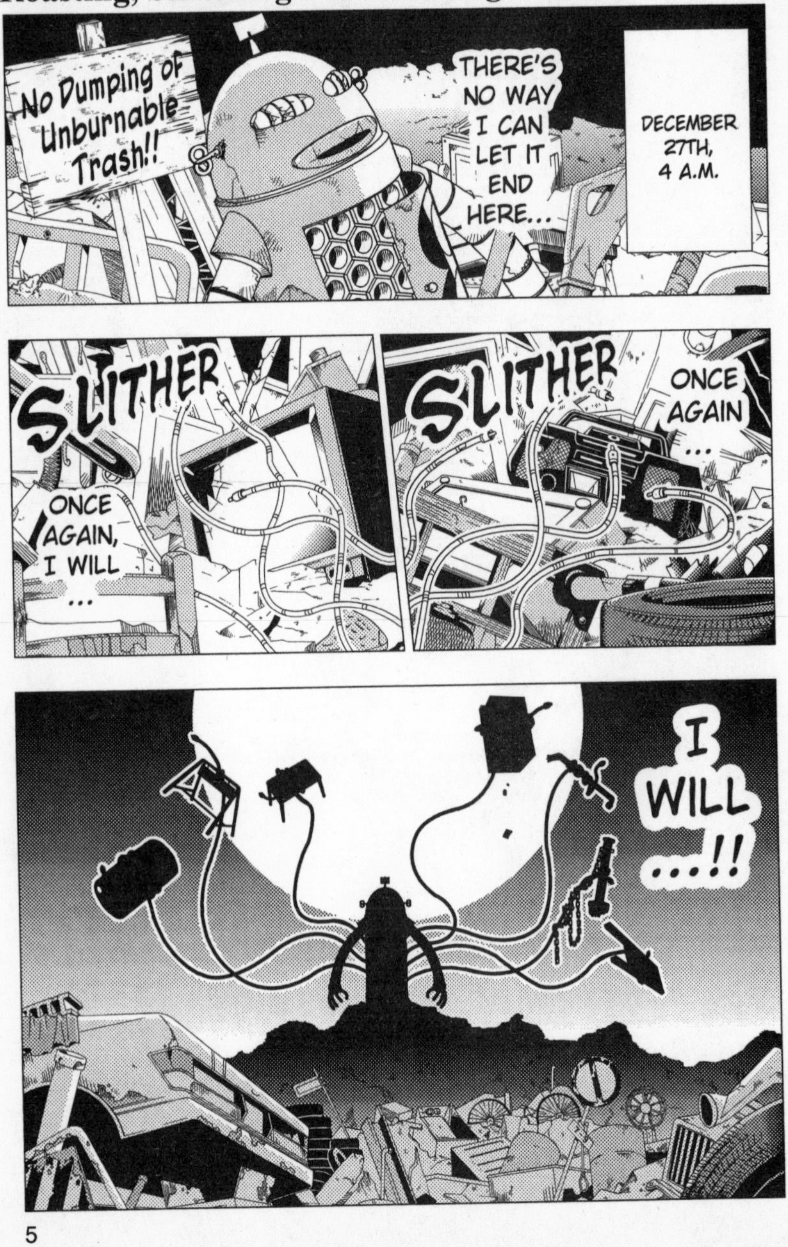
DECEMBER 27TH, 4 A.M.
THERE'S NO WAY I CAN LET IT END HERE...
No Dumping of Unburnable Trash!!
ONCE AGAIN ...
SLITHER
SLITHER
ONCE AGAIN, I WILL ...
I WILL ...!!

Episode 1: "In the Wee Hours of a Full Moon Night, Roasting, Smashing and Grinding Them to Powder"

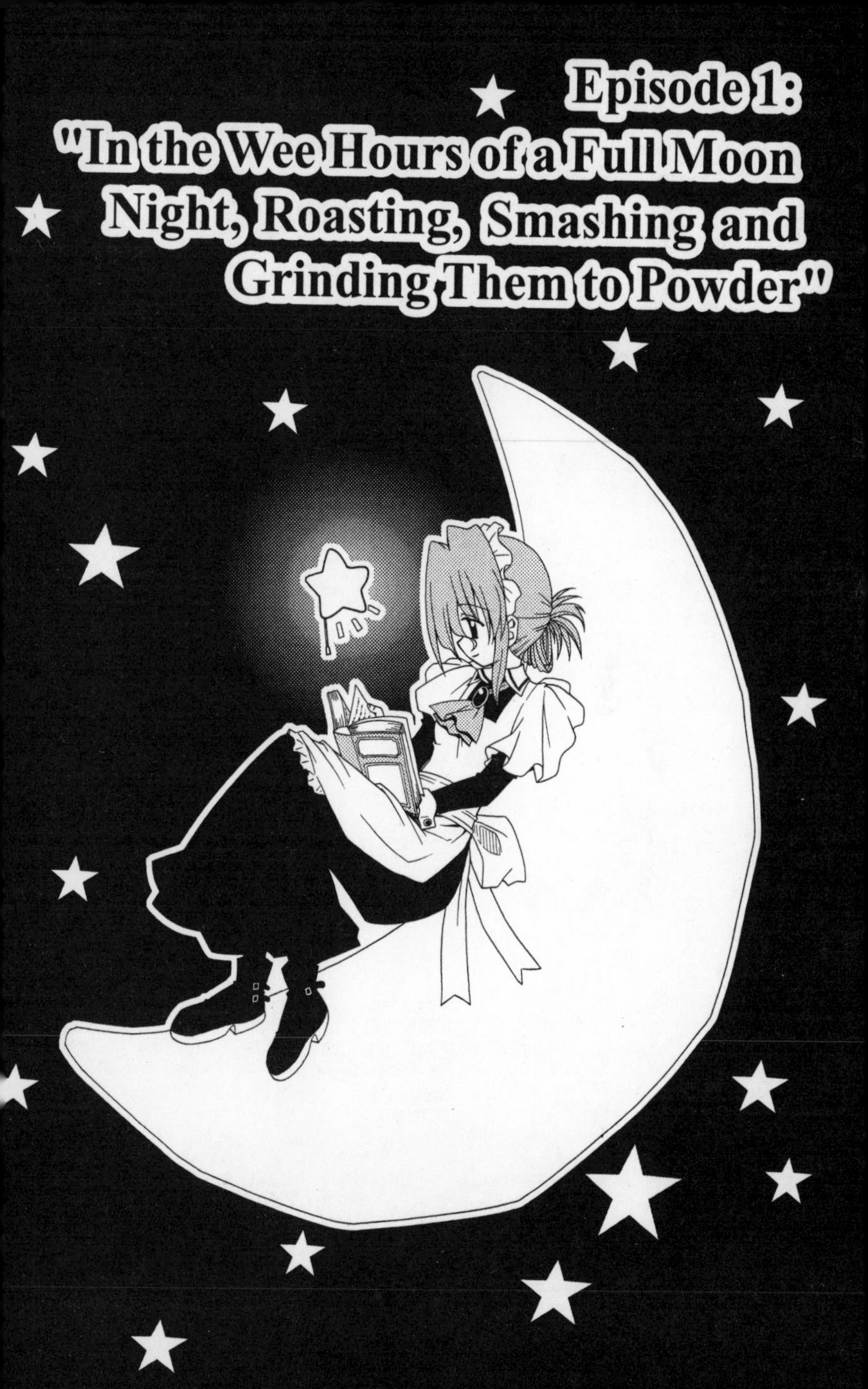

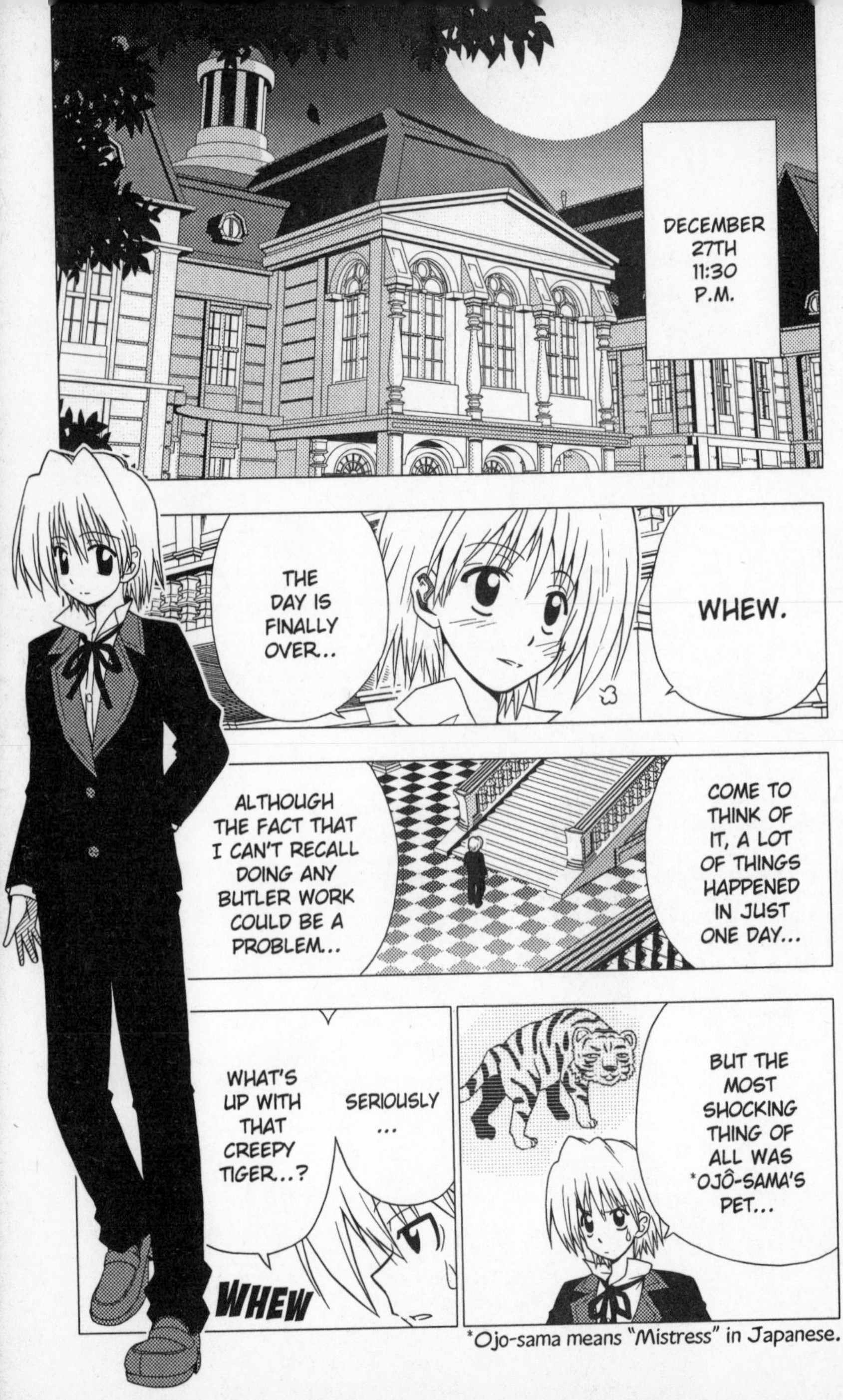
DECEMBER 27TH 11:30 P.M.
WHEW.
THE DAY IS FINALLY OVER...
COME TO THINK OF IT, A LOT OF THINGS HAPPENED IN JUST ONE DAY...
ALTHOUGH THE FACT THAT I CAN'T RECALL DOING ANY BUTLER WORK COULD BE A PROBLEM...
BUT THE MOST SHOCKING THING OF ALL WAS *OJÔ-SAMA'S PET...
SERIOUSLY...
WHAT'S UP WITH THAT CREEPY TIGER...?
WHEW

*Ojo-sama means "Mistress" in Japanese.

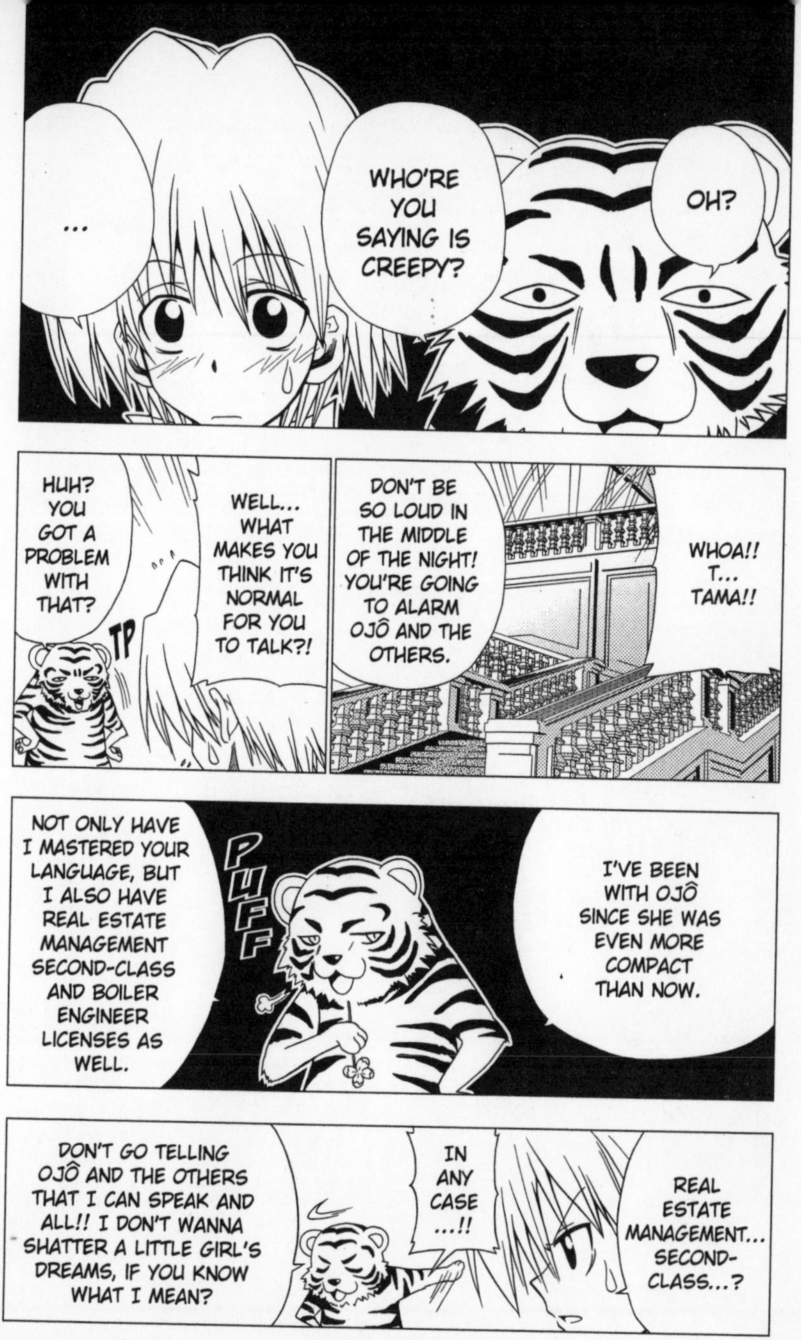
OH?
WHO'RE YOU SAYING IS CREEPY?
...
WHOA!! T... TAMA!!
DON'T BE SO LOUD IN THE MIDDLE OF THE NIGHT! YOU'RE GOING TO ALARM OJÔ AND THE OTHERS.
WELL... WHAT MAKES YOU THINK IT'S NORMAL FOR YOU TO TALK?!
HUH? YOU GOT A PROBLEM WITH THAT?
TP
I'VE BEEN WITH OJÔ SINCE SHE WAS EVEN MORE COMPACT THAN NOW.
PUFF
NOT ONLY HAVE I MASTERED YOUR LANGUAGE, BUT I ALSO HAVE REAL ESTATE MANAGEMENT SECOND-CLASS AND BOILER ENGINEER LICENSES AS WELL.
REAL ESTATE MANAGEMENT... SECOND-CLASS...?
IN ANY CASE ...!!
DON'T GO TELLING OJÔ AND THE OTHERS THAT I CAN SPEAK AND ALL!! I DON'T WANNA SHATTER A LITTLE GIRL'S DREAMS, IF YOU KNOW WHAT I MEAN?

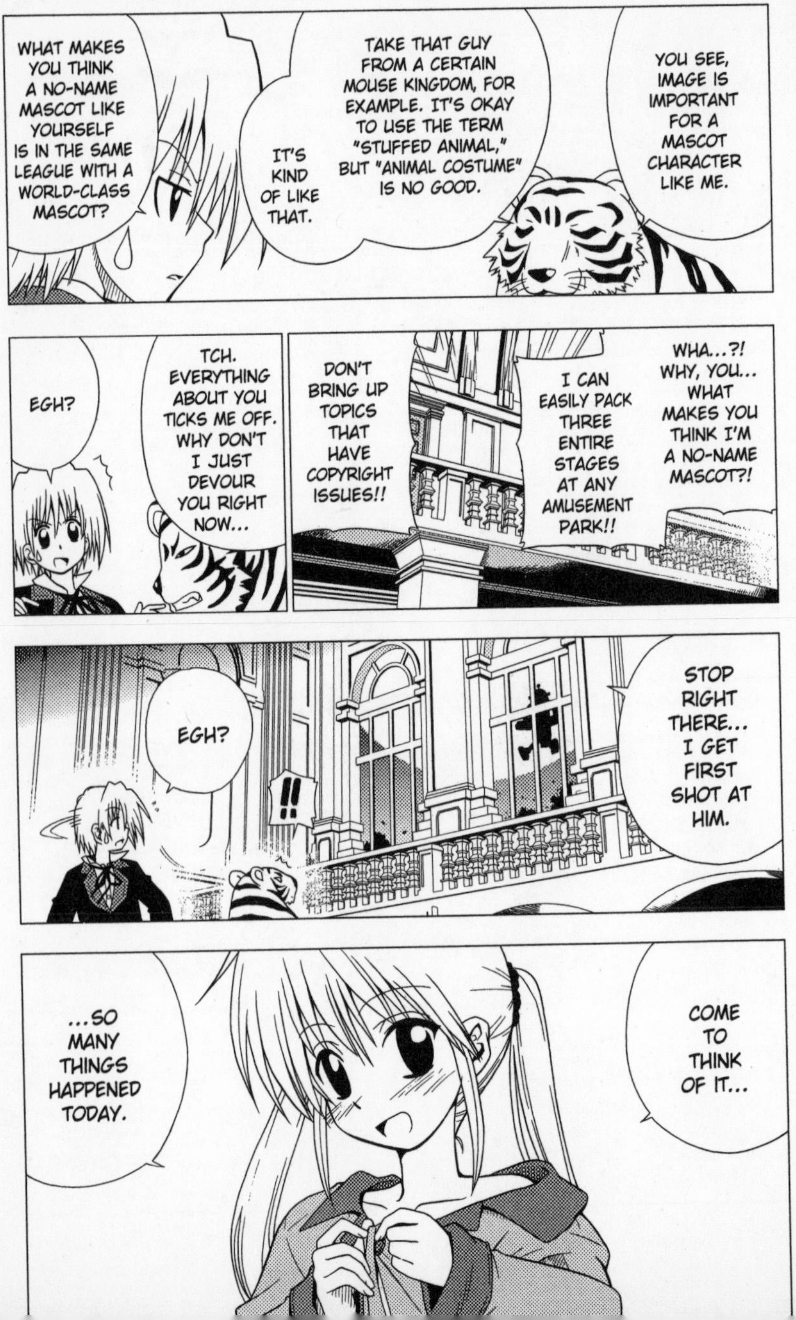
YOU SEE, IMAGE IS IMPORTANT FOR A MASCOT CHARACTER LIKE ME.
TAKE THAT GUY FROM A CERTAIN MOUSE KINGDOM, FOR EXAMPLE. IT'S OKAY TO USE THE TERM "STUFFED ANIMAL," BUT "ANIMAL COSTUME" IS NO GOOD.
IT'S KIND OF LIKE THAT.
WHAT MAKES YOU THINK A NO-NAME MASCOT LIKE YOURSELF IS IN THE SAME LEAGUE WITH A WORLD-CLASS MASCOT?
WHA...?! WHY, YOU... WHAT MAKES YOU THINK I'M A NO-NAME MASCOT?!
I CAN EASILY PACK THREE ENTIRE STAGES AT ANY AMUSEMENT PARK!!
DON'T BRING UP TOPICS THAT HAVE COPYRIGHT ISSUES!!
TCH. EVERYTHING ABOUT YOU TICKS ME OFF. WHY DON'T I JUST DEVOUR YOU RIGHT NOW...
EGH?
STOP RIGHT THERE... I GET FIRST SHOT AT HIM.
!!
EGH?
COME TO THINK OF IT...
...SO MANY THINGS HAPPENED TODAY.

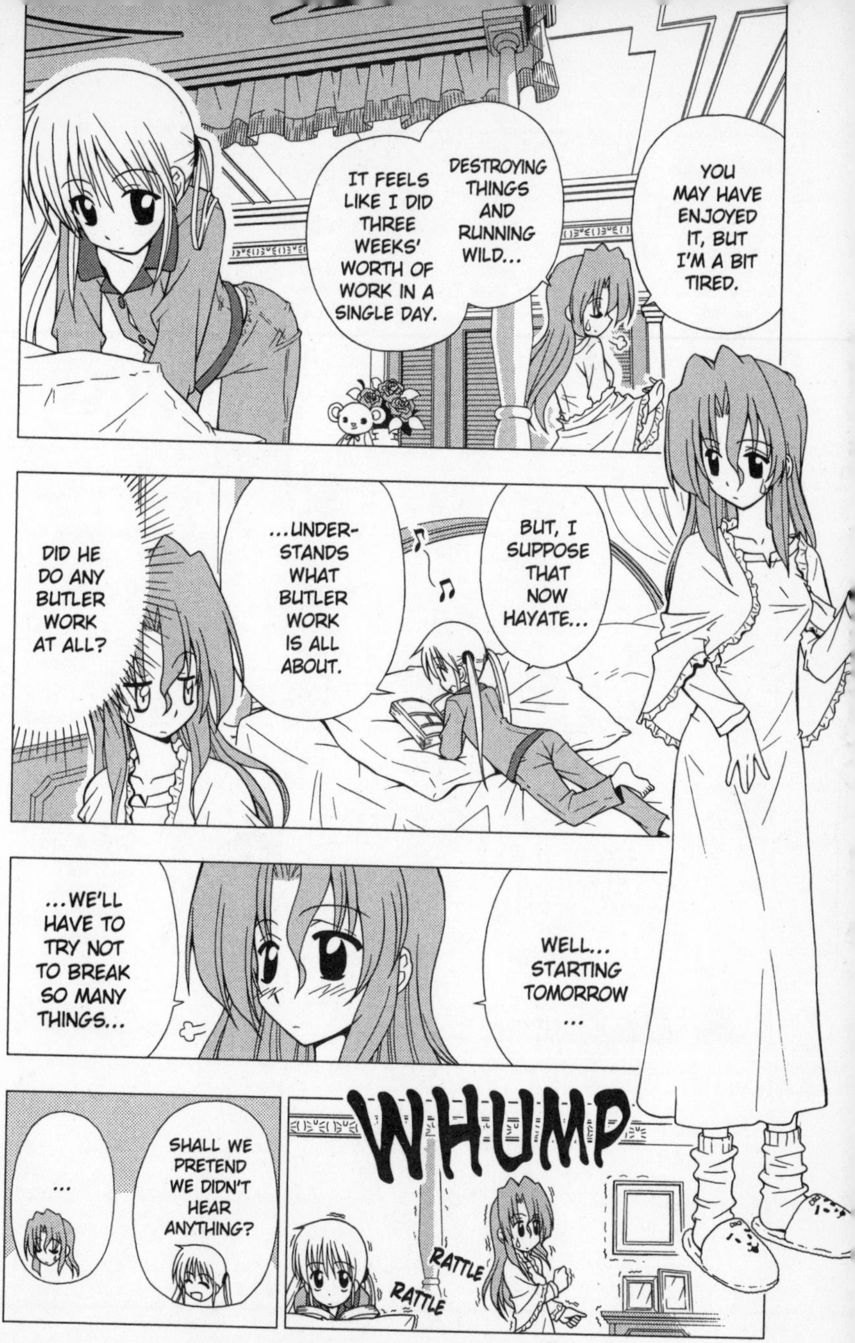
YOU MAY HAVE ENJOYED IT, BUT I'M A BIT TIRED.
DESTROYING THINGS AND RUNNING WILD...
IT FEELS LIKE I DID THREE WEEKS' WORTH OF WORK IN A SINGLE DAY.
BUT, I SUPPOSE THAT NOW HAYATE...
...UNDER-STANDS WHAT BUTLER WORK IS ALL ABOUT.
DID HE DO ANY BUTLER WORK AT ALL?
WELL... STARTING TOMORROW...
...WE'LL HAVE TO TRY NOT TO BREAK SO MANY THINGS...
WHUMP
RATTLE
RATTLE
SHALL WE PRETEND WE DIDN'T HEAR ANYTHING?
...

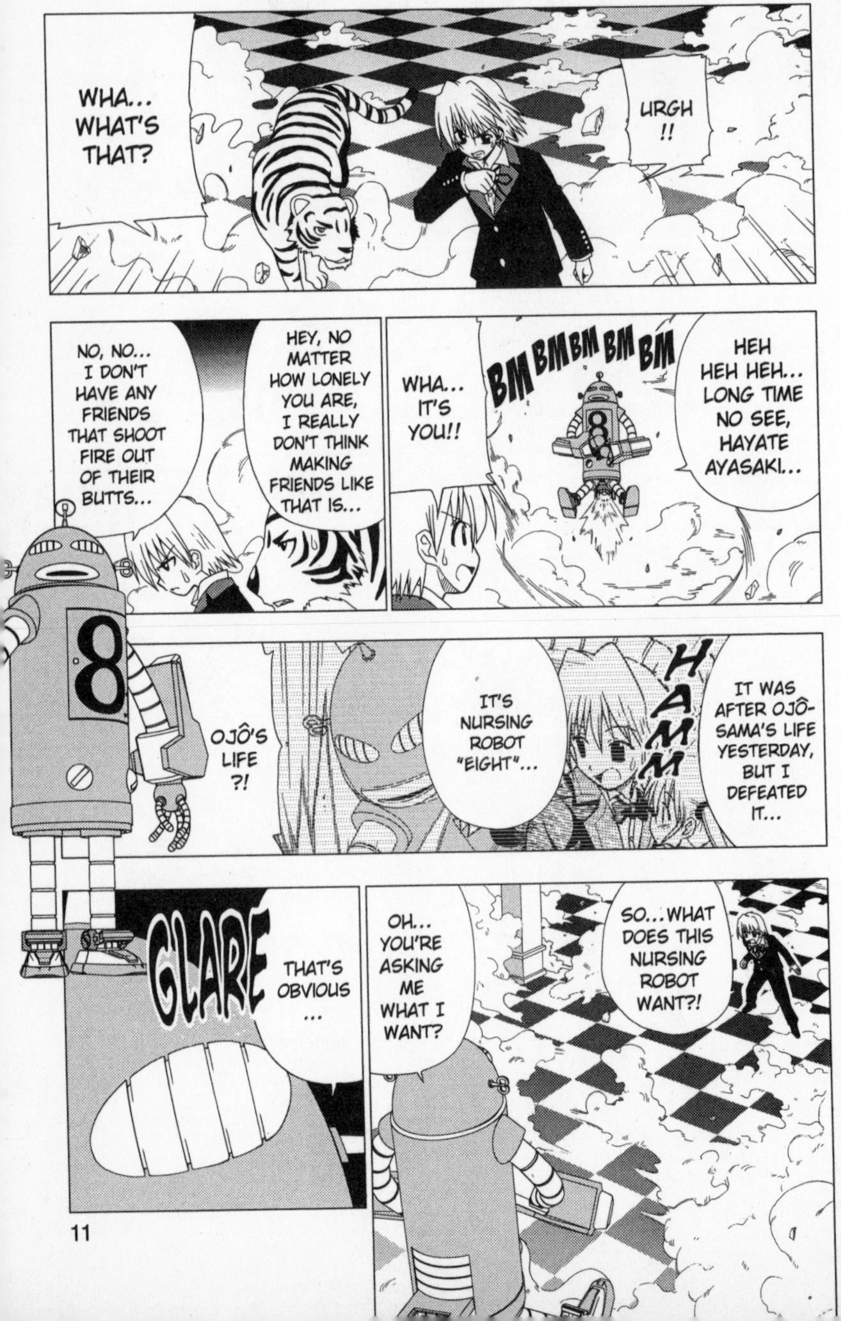
URGH!!
WHA... WHAT'S THAT?
HEH HEH HEH... LONG TIME NO SEE, HAYATE AYASAKI...
BM BMBM BM BM BM
WHA... IT'S YOU!!
HEY, NO MATTER HOW LONELY YOU ARE, I REALLY DON'T THINK MAKING FRIENDS LIKE THAT IS...
NO, NO... I DON'T HAVE ANY FRIENDS THAT SHOOT FIRE OUT OF THEIR BUTTS...
IT WAS AFTER OJÔ-SAMA'S LIFE YESTERDAY, BUT I DEFEATED IT...
HAMM
IT'S NURSING ROBOT "EIGHT"...
OJÔ'S LIFE?!
SO...WHAT DOES THIS NURSING ROBOT WANT?!
OH... YOU'RE ASKING ME WHAT I WANT?
THAT'S OBVIOUS...
GLARE

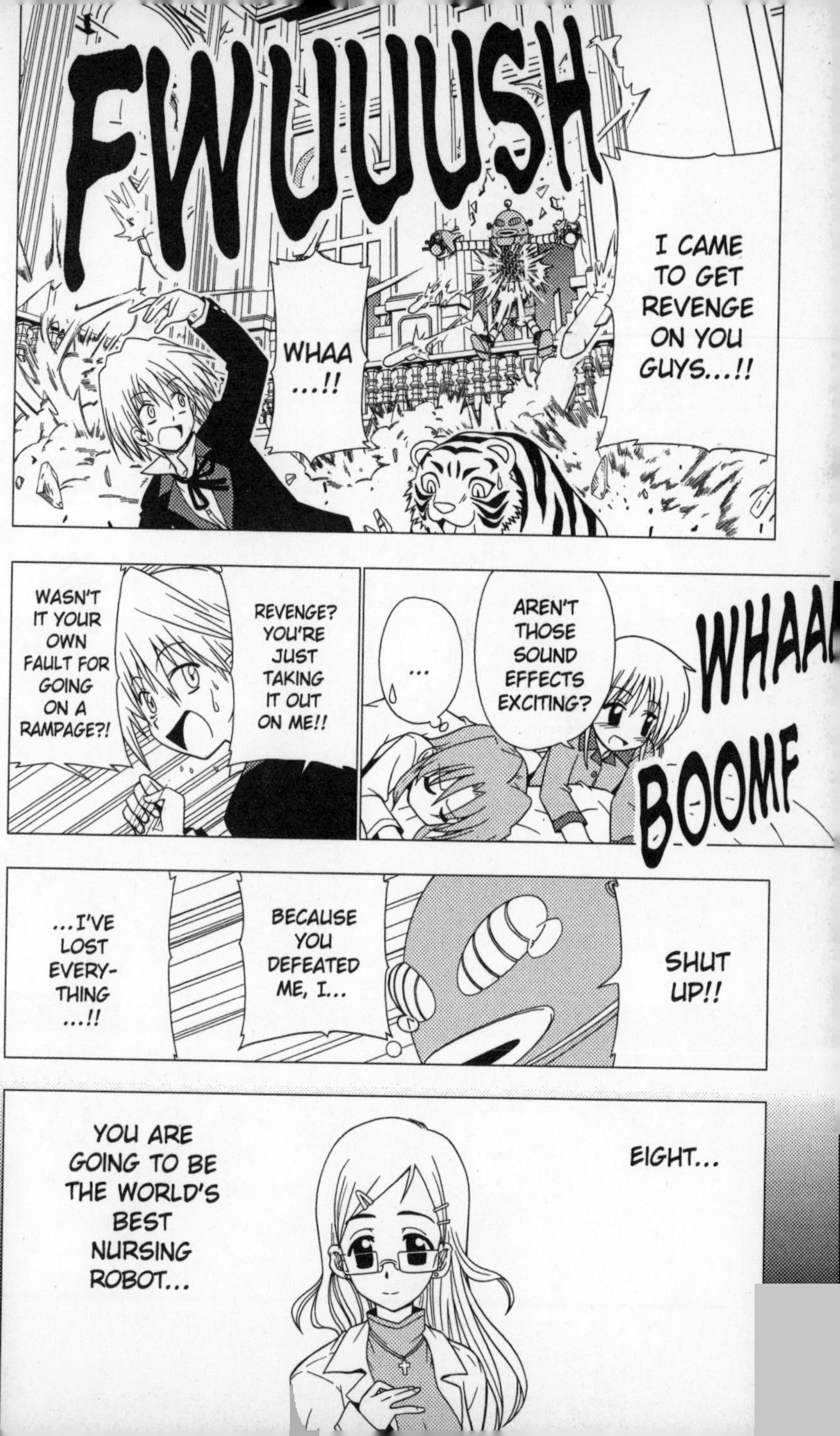
FWUUUSH
I CAME TO GET REVENGE ON YOU GUYS...!!
WHAA ...!!
WHAA
BOOMF
AREN'T THOSE SOUND EFFECTS EXCITING?
...
REVENGE? YOU'RE JUST TAKING IT OUT ON ME!!
WASN'T IT YOUR OWN FAULT FOR GOING ON A RAMPAGE?!
SHUT UP!!
BECAUSE YOU DEFEATED ME, I...
...I'VE LOST EVERY-THING ...!!
EIGHT...
YOU ARE GOING TO BE THE WORLD'S BEST NURSING ROBOT...

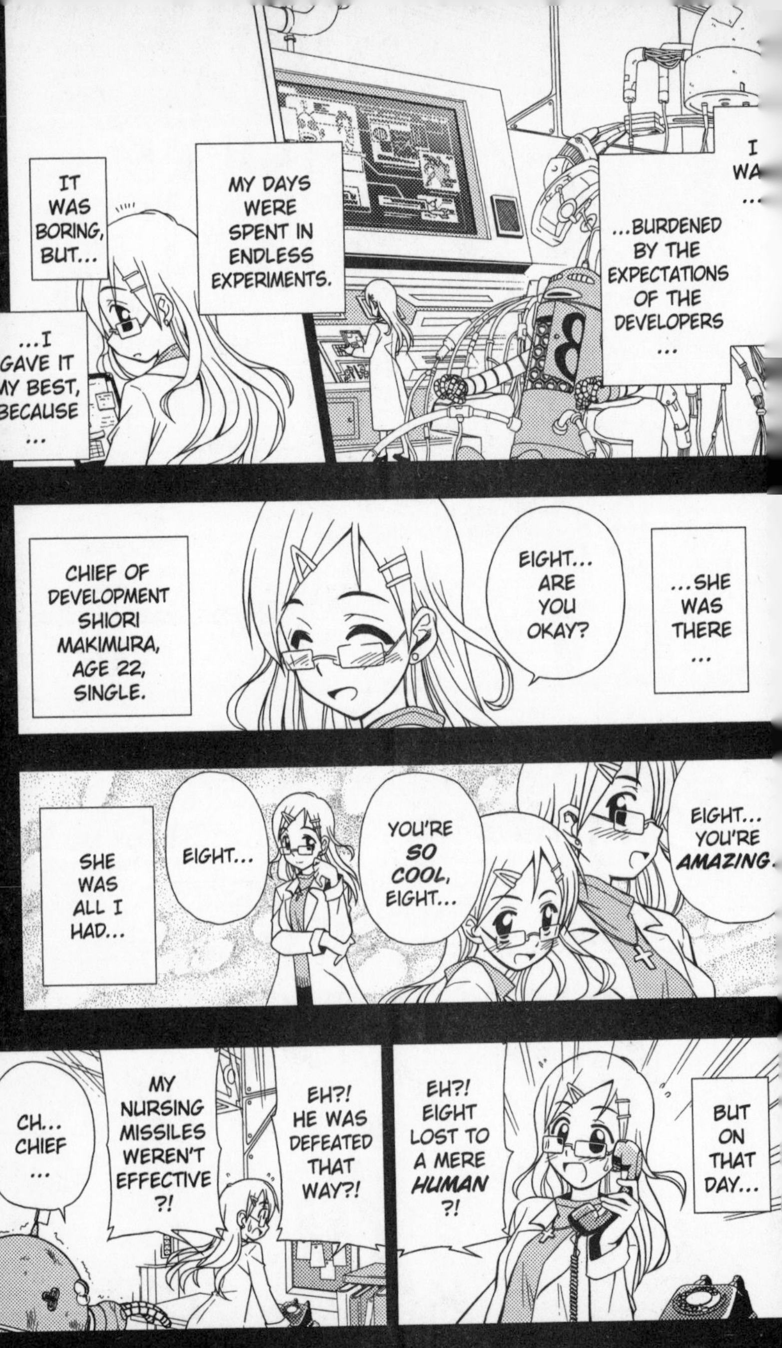
I WA...
...BURDENED BY THE EXPECTATIONS OF THE DEVELOPERS...
MY DAYS WERE SPENT IN ENDLESS EXPERIMENTS.
IT WAS BORING, BUT...
...I GAVE IT MY BEST, BECAUSE...
...SHE WAS THERE...
EIGHT... ARE YOU OKAY?
CHIEF OF DEVELOPMENT SHIORI MAKIMURA, AGE 22, SINGLE.
EIGHT... YOU'RE AMAZING.
YOU'RE SO COOL, EIGHT...
EIGHT...
SHE WAS ALL I HAD...
BUT ON THAT DAY...
EH?! EIGHT LOST TO A MERE HUMAN?!
EH?! HE WAS DEFEATED THAT WAY?!
MY NURSING MISSILES WEREN'T EFFECTIVE?!
CH... CHIEF...

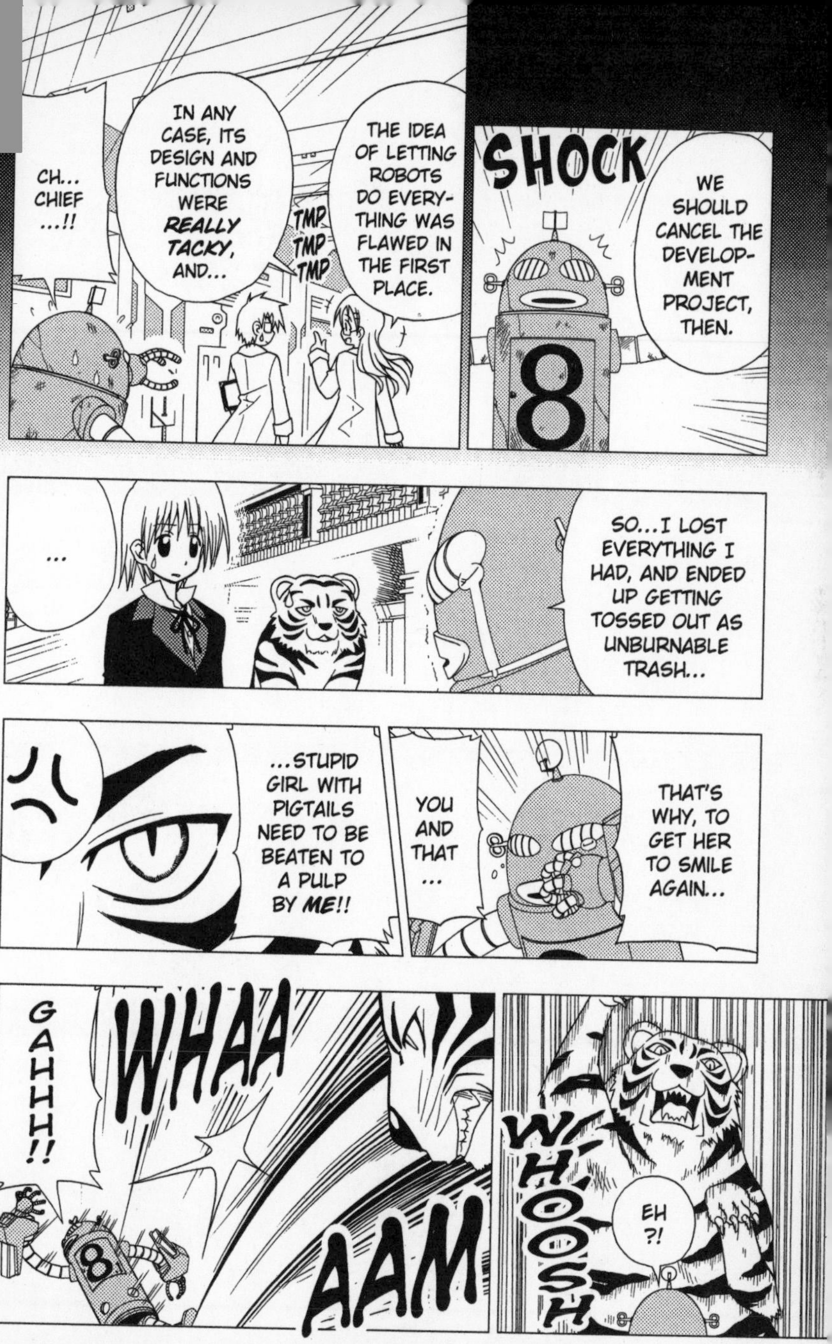
SHOCK
WE SHOULD CANCEL THE DEVELOPMENT PROJECT, THEN.
THE IDEA OF LETTING ROBOTS DO EVERYTHING WAS FLAWED IN THE FIRST PLACE.
TMP TMP TMP
IN ANY CASE, ITS DESIGN AND FUNCTIONS WERE *REALLY TACKY*, AND...
CH... CHIEF ...!!
SO...I LOST EVERYTHING I HAD, AND ENDED UP GETTING TOSSED OUT AS UNBURNABLE TRASH...
...
THAT'S WHY, TO GET HER TO SMILE AGAIN...
YOU AND THAT ...
...STUPID GIRL WITH PIGTAILS NEED TO BE BEATEN TO A PULP BY *ME*!!
WHOOSH
EH ?!
WHAA
AAM
GAHHH!!

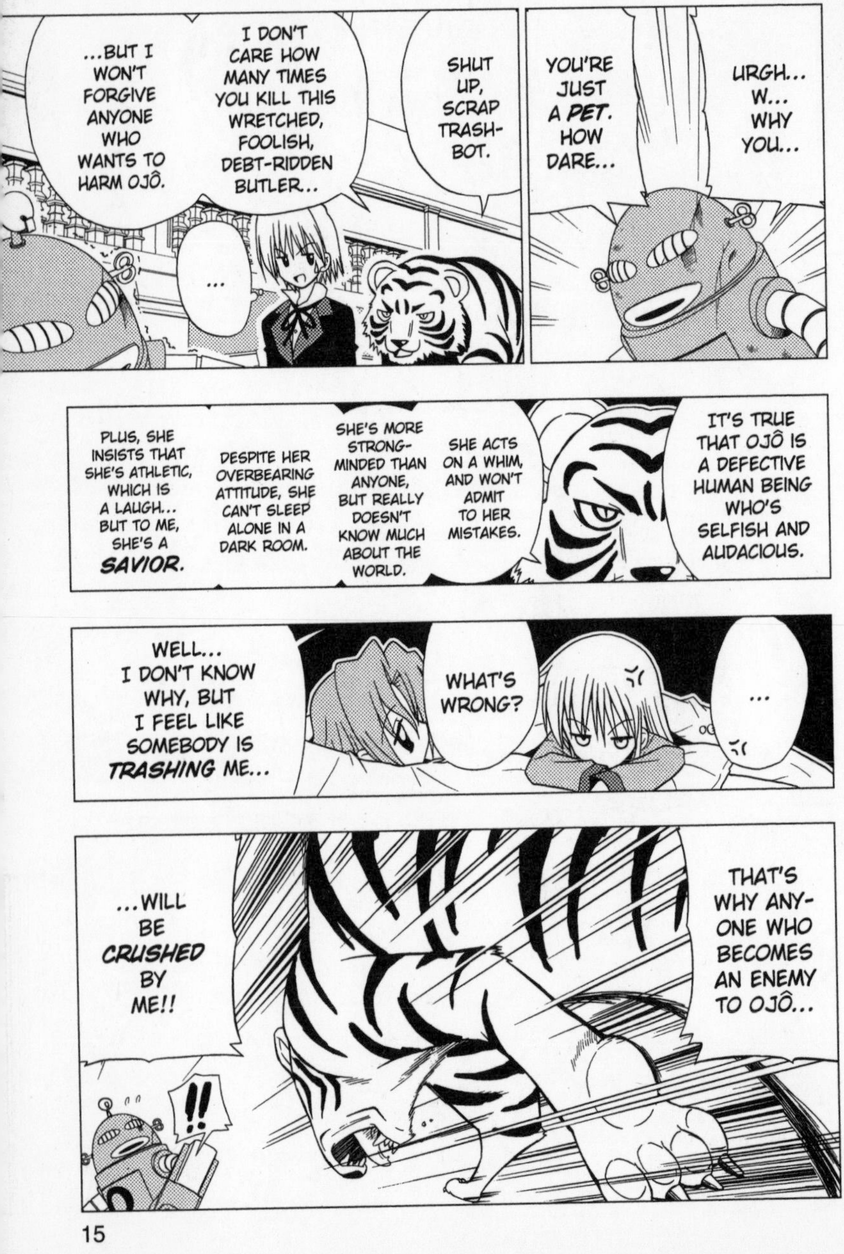
URGH... W... WHY YOU...
YOU'RE JUST A PET. HOW DARE...
SHUT UP, SCRAP TRASH-BOT.
I DON'T CARE HOW MANY TIMES YOU KILL THIS WRETCHED, FOOLISH, DEBT-RIDDEN BUTLER...
...
...BUT I WON'T FORGIVE ANYONE WHO WANTS TO HARM OJÔ.
IT'S TRUE THAT OJÔ IS A DEFECTIVE HUMAN BEING WHO'S SELFISH AND AUDACIOUS.
SHE ACTS ON A WHIM, AND WON'T ADMIT TO HER MISTAKES.
SHE'S MORE STRONG-MINDED THAN ANYONE, BUT REALLY DOESN'T KNOW MUCH ABOUT THE WORLD.
DESPITE HER OVERBEARING ATTITUDE, SHE CAN'T SLEEP ALONE IN A DARK ROOM.
PLUS, SHE INSISTS THAT SHE'S ATHLETIC, WHICH IS A LAUGH... BUT TO ME, SHE'S A SAVIOR.
...
WHAT'S WRONG?
WELL... I DON'T KNOW WHY, BUT I FEEL LIKE SOMEBODY IS TRASHING ME...
THAT'S WHY ANY-ONE WHO BECOMES AN ENEMY TO OJÔ...
...WILL BE CRUSHED BY ME!!
!!

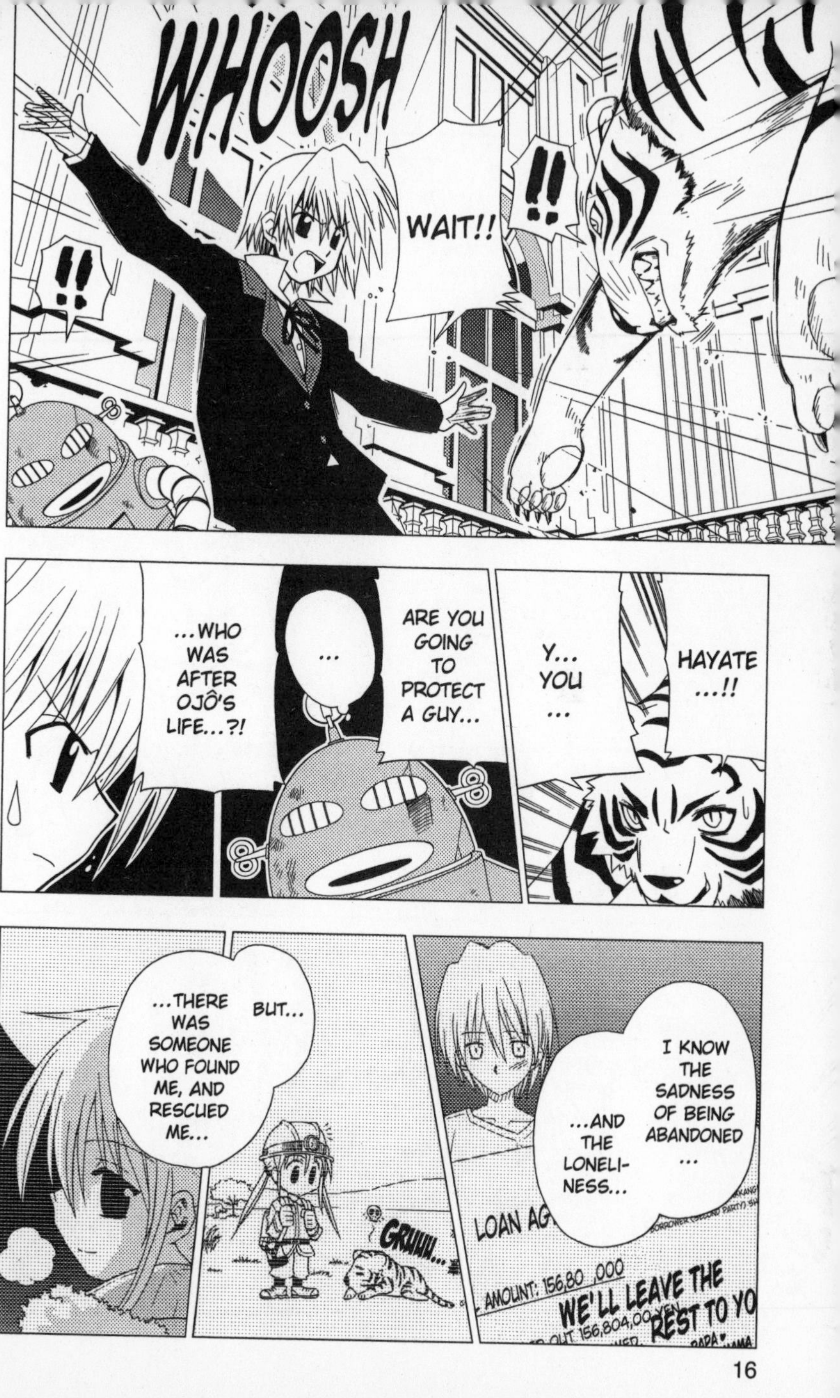
WHOOSH
!!
WAIT!!
!!
HAYATE ...!!
Y... YOU ...
ARE YOU GOING TO PROTECT A GUY...
...
...WHO WAS AFTER OJÔ'S LIFE...?!
I KNOW THE SADNESS OF BEING ABANDONED ...
...AND THE LONELI-NESS...
LOAN AG
AMOUNT: 156,80 ,000
WE'LL LEAVE THE REST TO YO
BUT...
GRUUU...
...THERE WAS SOMEONE WHO FOUND ME, AND RESCUED ME...

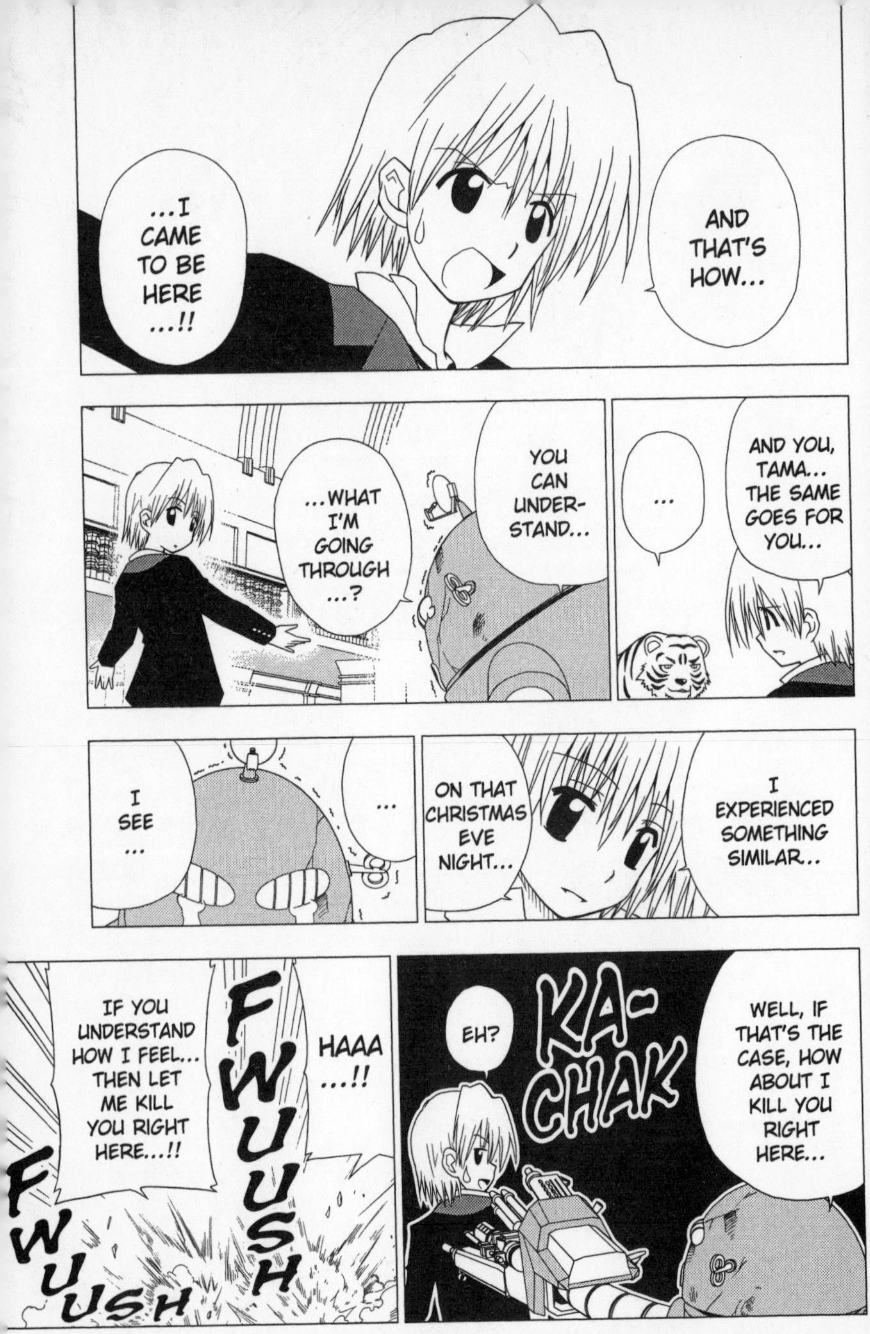
AND THAT'S HOW...
...I CAME TO BE HERE...!!
AND YOU, TAMA... THE SAME GOES FOR YOU...
...
YOU CAN UNDER-STAND...
...WHAT I'M GOING THROUGH...?
I EXPERIENCED SOMETHING SIMILAR...
ON THAT CHRISTMAS EVE NIGHT...
...
I SEE...
WELL, IF THAT'S THE CASE, HOW ABOUT I KILL YOU RIGHT HERE...
KA-CHAK
EH?
HAAA...!!
FWUUSH
IF YOU UNDERSTAND HOW I FEEL... THEN LET ME KILL YOU RIGHT HERE...!!
FWUUSH

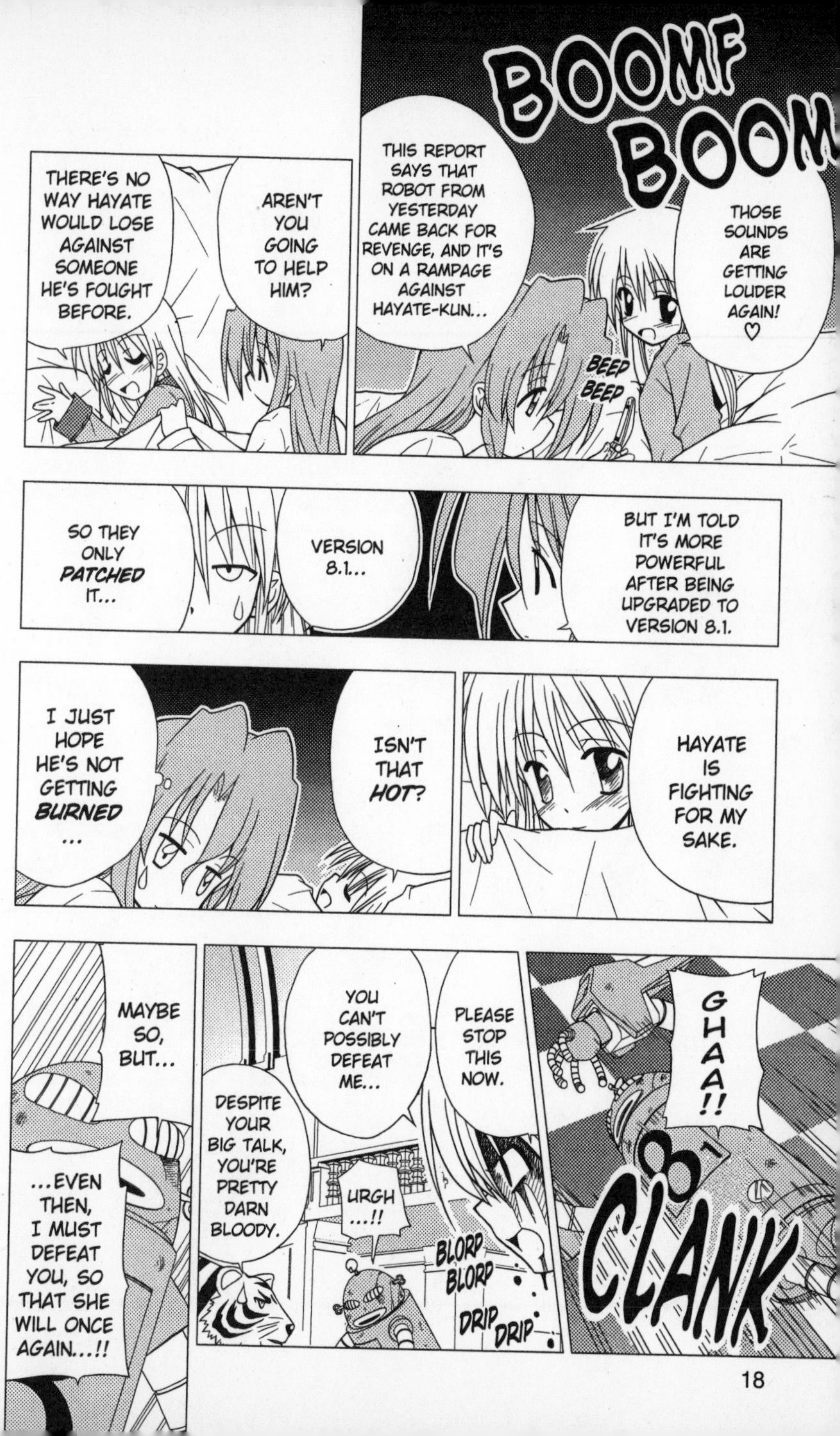
BOOMF
BOOM
THOSE SOUNDS ARE GETTING LOUDER AGAIN! ♡
THIS REPORT SAYS THAT ROBOT FROM YESTERDAY CAME BACK FOR REVENGE, AND IT'S ON A RAMPAGE AGAINST HAYATE-KUN...
BEEP BEEP
AREN'T YOU GOING TO HELP HIM?
THERE'S NO WAY HAYATE WOULD LOSE AGAINST SOMEONE HE'S FOUGHT BEFORE.
BUT I'M TOLD IT'S MORE POWERFUL AFTER BEING UPGRADED TO VERSION 8.1.
VERSION 8.1...
SO THEY ONLY *PATCHED* IT...
HAYATE IS FIGHTING FOR MY SAKE.
ISN'T THAT *HOT*?
I JUST HOPE HE'S NOT GETTING *BURNED* ...
GHAA!!
CLANK
PLEASE STOP THIS NOW.
YOU CAN'T POSSIBLY DEFEAT ME...
DESPITE YOUR BIG TALK, YOU'RE PRETTY DARN BLOODY.
URGH ...!!
BLORP BLORP
DRIP DRIP
MAYBE SO, BUT...
...EVEN THEN, I MUST DEFEAT YOU, SO THAT SHE WILL ONCE AGAIN...!!

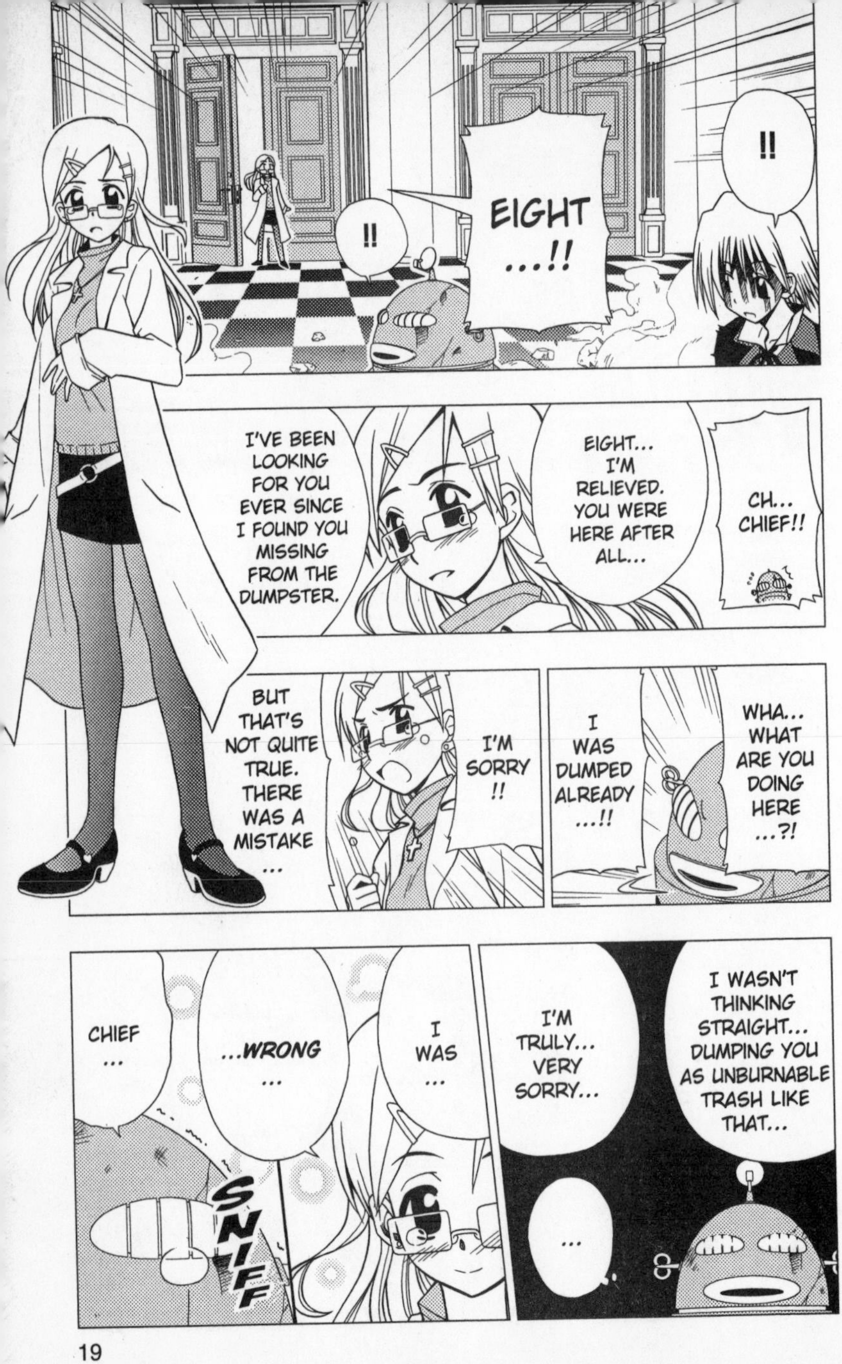
!!
EIGHT ...!!
!!
CH... CHIEF!!
EIGHT... I'M RELIEVED. YOU WERE HERE AFTER ALL...
I'VE BEEN LOOKING FOR YOU EVER SINCE I FOUND YOU MISSING FROM THE DUMPSTER.
WHA... WHAT ARE YOU DOING HERE ...?!
I WAS DUMPED ALREADY ...!!
I'M SORRY !!
BUT THAT'S NOT QUITE TRUE. THERE WAS A MISTAKE ...
I WASN'T THINKING STRAIGHT... DUMPING YOU AS UNBURNABLE TRASH LIKE THAT...
I'M TRULY... VERY SORRY...
...
I WAS ...
...WRONG ...
CHIEF ...
SNIFF

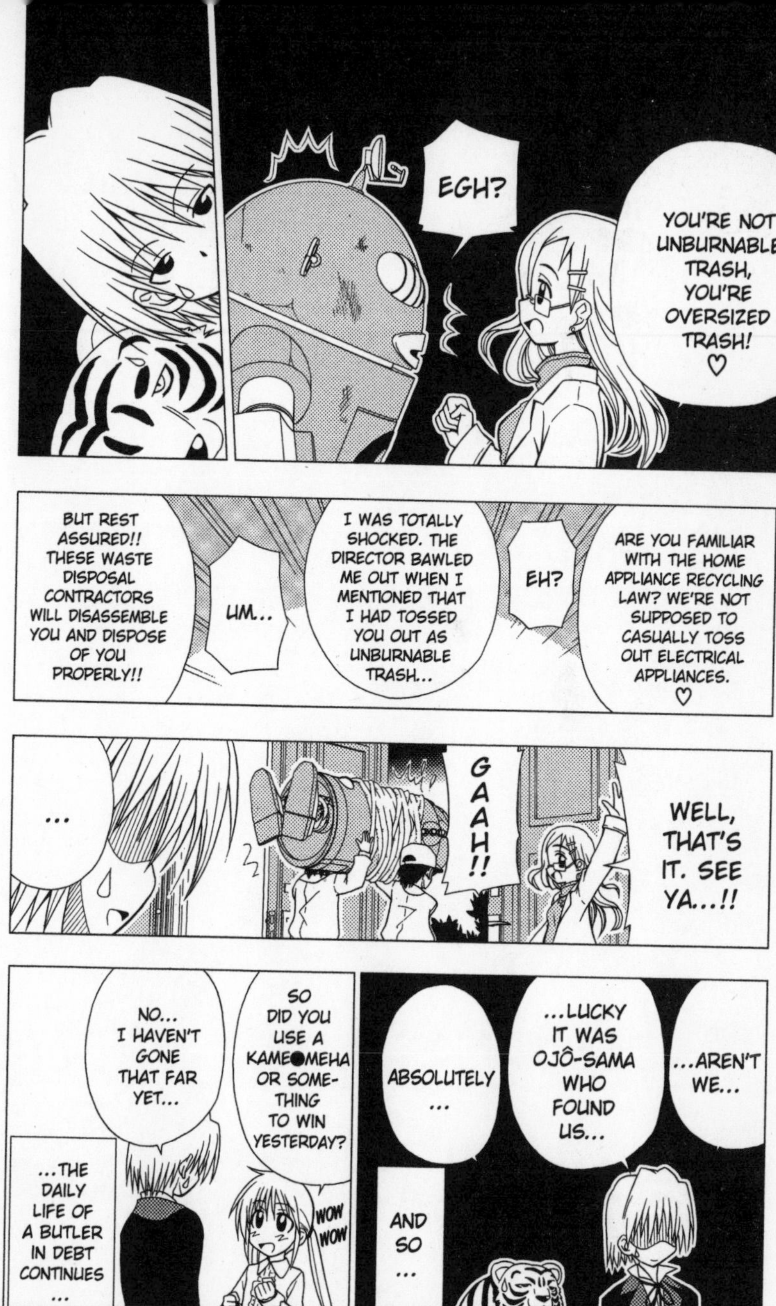
YOU'RE NOT UNBURNABLE TRASH, YOU'RE OVERSIZED TRASH! ♡
EGH?
ARE YOU FAMILIAR WITH THE HOME APPLIANCE RECYCLING LAW? WE'RE NOT SUPPOSED TO CASUALLY TOSS OUT ELECTRICAL APPLIANCES. ♡
EH?
I WAS TOTALLY SHOCKED. THE DIRECTOR BAWLED ME OUT WHEN I MENTIONED THAT I HAD TOSSED YOU OUT AS UNBURNABLE TRASH...
UM...
BUT REST ASSURED!! THESE WASTE DISPOSAL CONTRACTORS WILL DISASSEMBLE YOU AND DISPOSE OF YOU PROPERLY!!
WELL, THAT'S IT. SEE YA...!!
GAAH!!
...
...AREN'T WE...
...LUCKY IT WAS OJÔ-SAMA WHO FOUND US...
ABSOLUTELY...
AND SO...
SO DID YOU USE A KAME●MEHA OR SOME-THING TO WIN YESTERDAY?
WOW WOW
NO... I HAVEN'T GONE THAT FAR YET...
...THE DAILY LIFE OF A BUTLER IN DEBT CONTINUES...

Episode 2: "The Mystery of Men Playing Shogi All the Time at the Foot of the Tsutenkaku Tower"

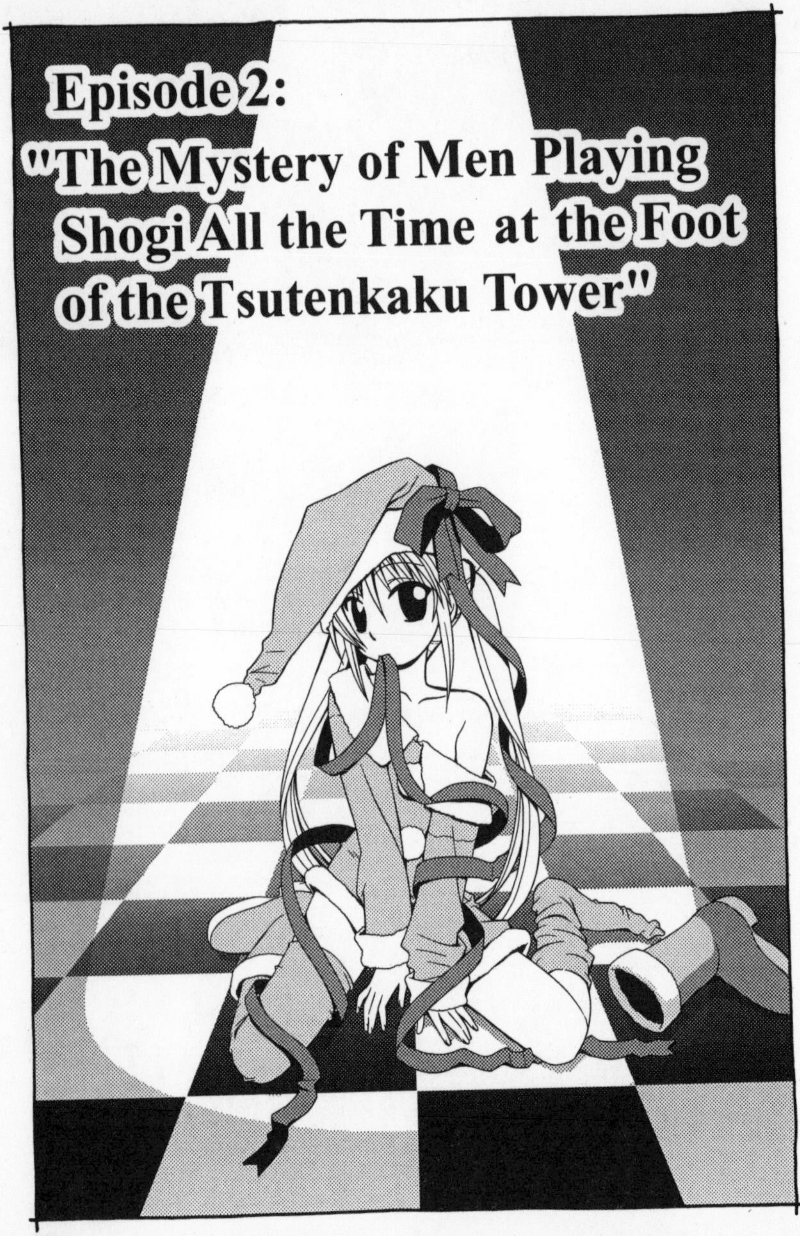

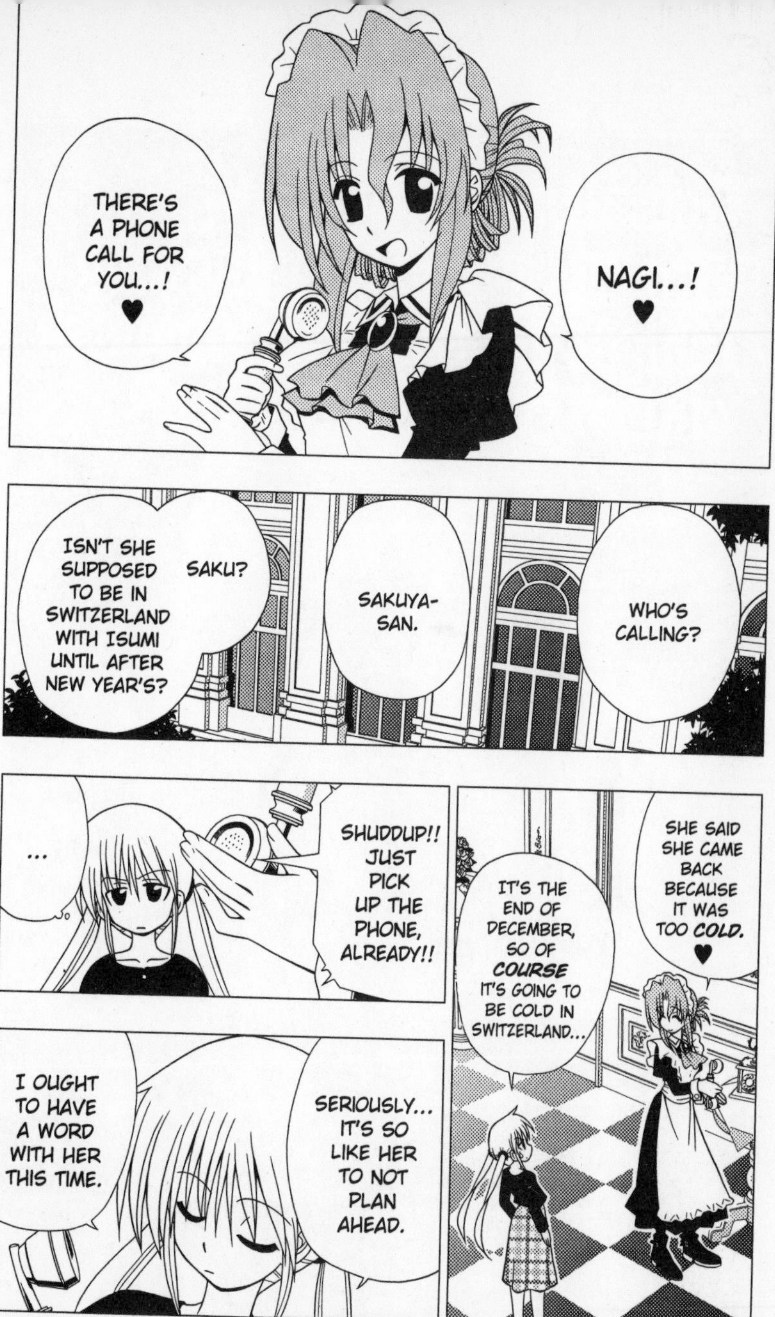
NAGI...! ♥
THERE'S A PHONE CALL FOR YOU...! ♥
WHO'S CALLING?
SAKUYA-SAN.
SAKU?
ISN'T SHE SUPPOSED TO BE IN SWITZERLAND WITH ISUMI UNTIL AFTER NEW YEAR'S?
SHE SAID SHE CAME BACK BECAUSE IT WAS TOO COLD. ♥
IT'S THE END OF DECEMBER, SO OF COURSE IT'S GOING TO BE COLD IN SWITZERLAND...
SHUDDUP!! JUST PICK UP THE PHONE, ALREADY!!
...
SERIOUSLY... IT'S SO LIKE HER TO NOT PLAN AHEAD.
I OUGHT TO HAVE A WORD WITH HER THIS TIME.

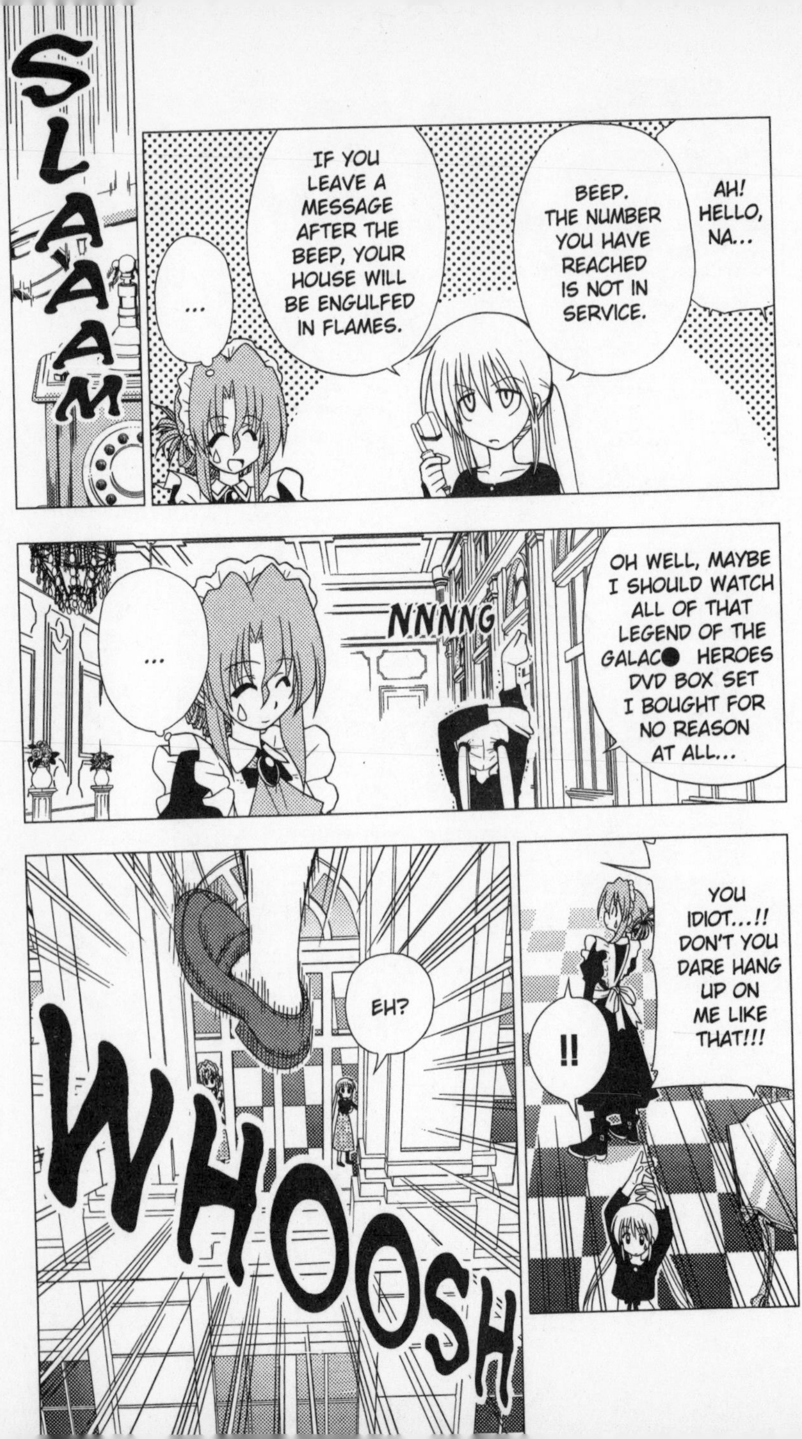
AH! HELLO, NA...
BEEP. THE NUMBER YOU HAVE REACHED IS NOT IN SERVICE.
IF YOU LEAVE A MESSAGE AFTER THE BEEP, YOUR HOUSE WILL BE ENGULFED IN FLAMES.
...
SLAAAAM
OH WELL, MAYBE I SHOULD WATCH ALL OF THAT LEGEND OF THE GALAC● HEROES DVD BOX SET I BOUGHT FOR NO REASON AT ALL...
NNNNG
...
YOU IDIOT...!! DON'T YOU DARE HANG UP ON ME LIKE THAT!!!
!!
EH?
WHOOSH

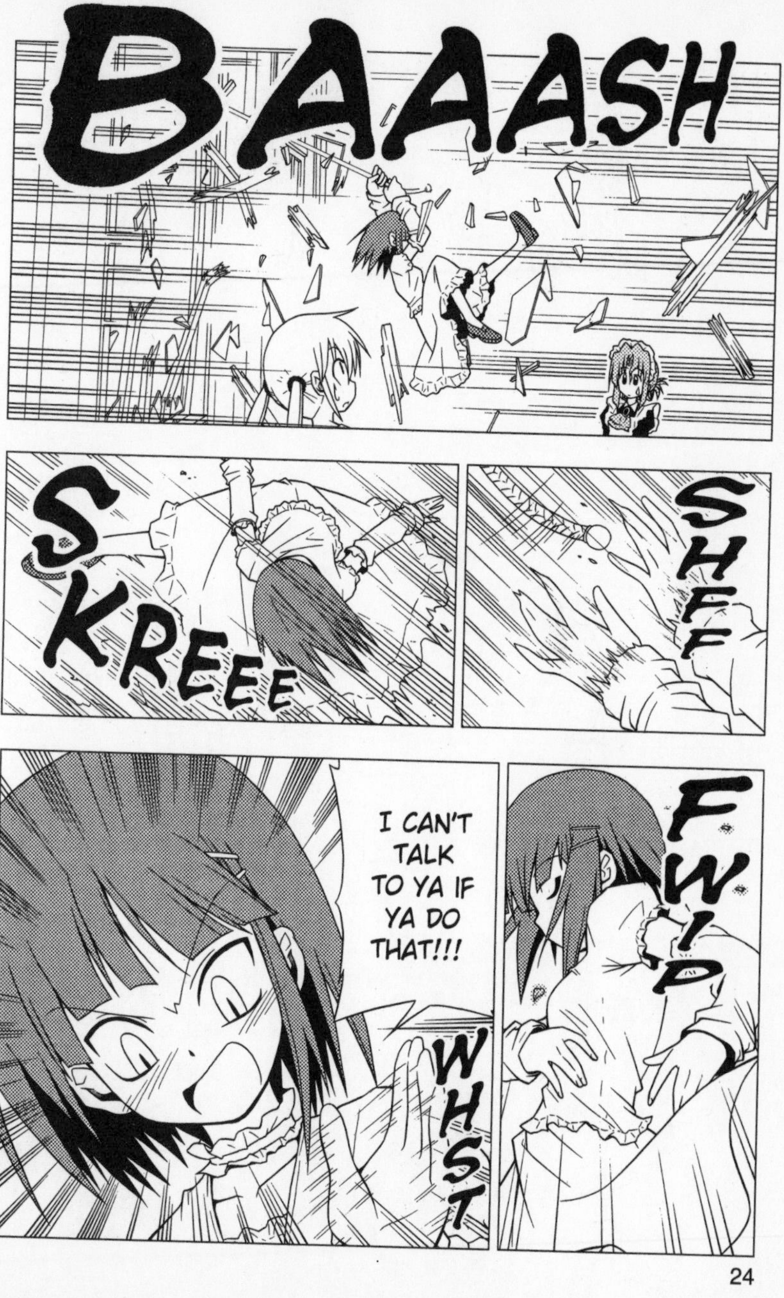
BAAASH
SHFF
SKREEE
FWIP
I CAN'T TALK TO YA IF YA DO THAT!!!
WHST

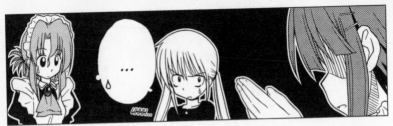

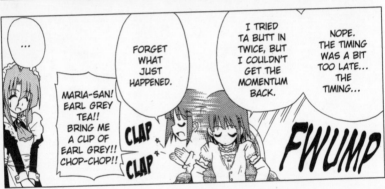

...
UHHH...
NOPE. THE TIMING WAS A BIT TOO LATE... THE TIMING...
I TRIED TA BUTT IN TWICE, BUT I COULDN'T GET THE MOMENTUM BACK.
FWUMP
FORGET WHAT JUST HAPPENED.
CLAP
CLAP
MARIA-SAN! EARL GREY TEA!! BRING ME A CUP OF EARL GREY!! CHOP-CHOP!!
...
SPLOOSH
...
THAT'S HOT!! SERIOUSLY HOT!!
THAT'S BOILING HOT WATER!! BOILING !!!
IF YA DON'T COOL IT OFF A BIT, IT MAKES IT HARD FOR ME TO "COUNTER" YER ACTIONS!! SERIOUSLY!!
ROLL ROLL
ROLL ROLL
DON'T WORRY, YOU'RE COUNTERING ENOUGH. AND FEEL FREE TO DROP DEAD WHILE YOU'RE AT IT.

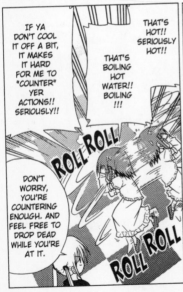

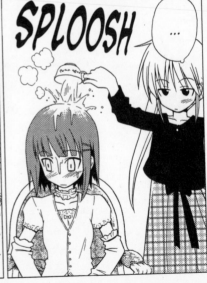

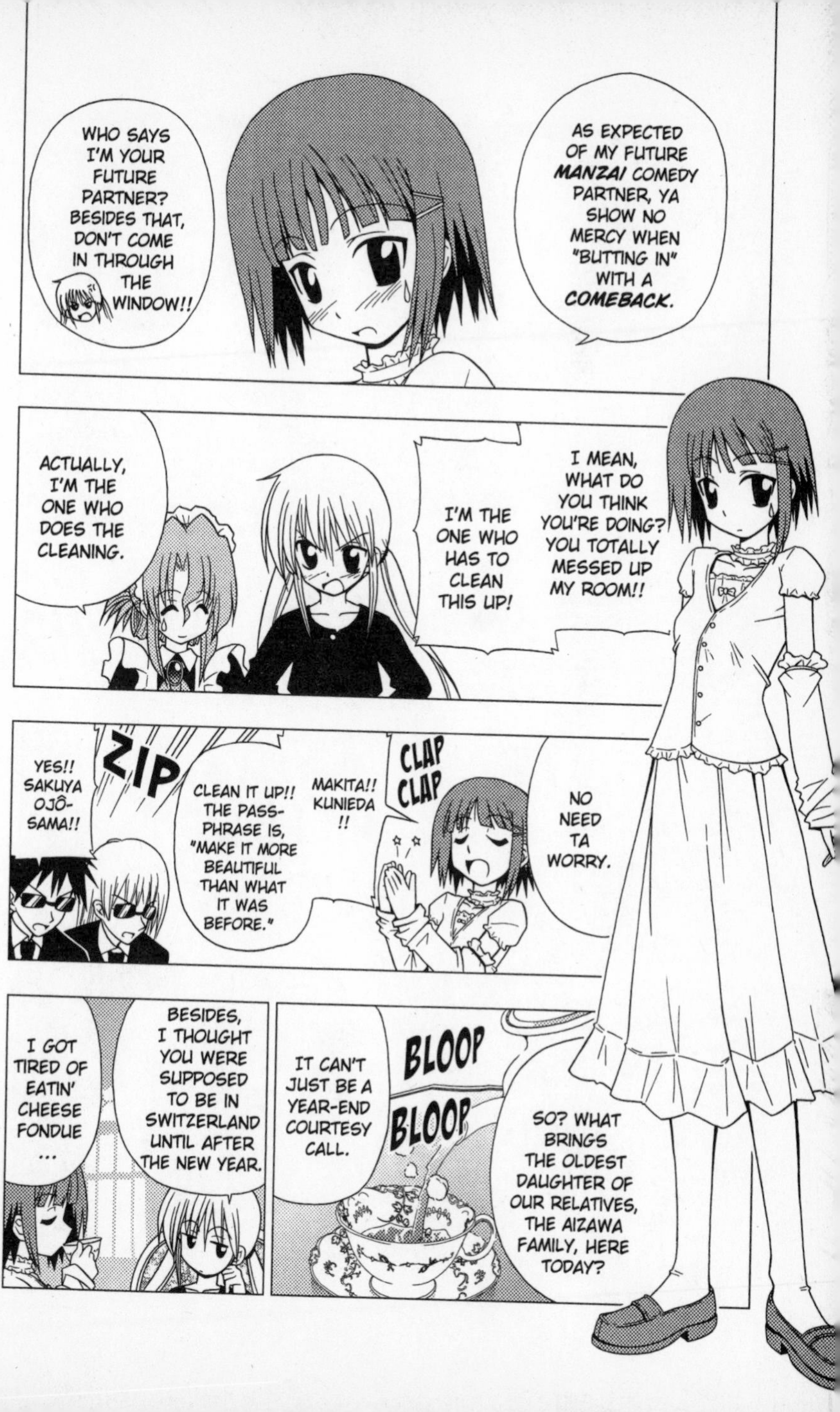
AS EXPECTED OF MY FUTURE *MANZAI* COMEDY PARTNER, YA SHOW NO MERCY WHEN "BUTTING IN" WITH A **COMEBACK**.
WHO SAYS I'M YOUR FUTURE PARTNER? BESIDES THAT, DON'T COME IN THROUGH THE WINDOW!!
I MEAN, WHAT DO YOU THINK YOU'RE DOING? YOU TOTALLY MESSED UP MY ROOM!!
I'M THE ONE WHO HAS TO CLEAN THIS UP!
ACTUALLY, I'M THE ONE WHO DOES THE CLEANING.
NO NEED TA WORRY.
CLAP CLAP
MAKITA!! KUNIEDA!!
CLEAN IT UP!! THE PASS-PHRASE IS, "MAKE IT MORE BEAUTIFUL THAN WHAT IT WAS BEFORE."
ZIP
YES!! SAKUYA OJÔ-SAMA!!
SO? WHAT BRINGS THE OLDEST DAUGHTER OF OUR RELATIVES, THE AIZAWA FAMILY, HERE TODAY?
BLOOP
BLOOP
IT CAN'T JUST BE A YEAR-END COURTESY CALL.
BESIDES, I THOUGHT YOU WERE SUPPOSED TO BE IN SWITZERLAND UNTIL AFTER THE NEW YEAR.
I GOT TIRED OF EATIN' CHEESE FONDUE ...

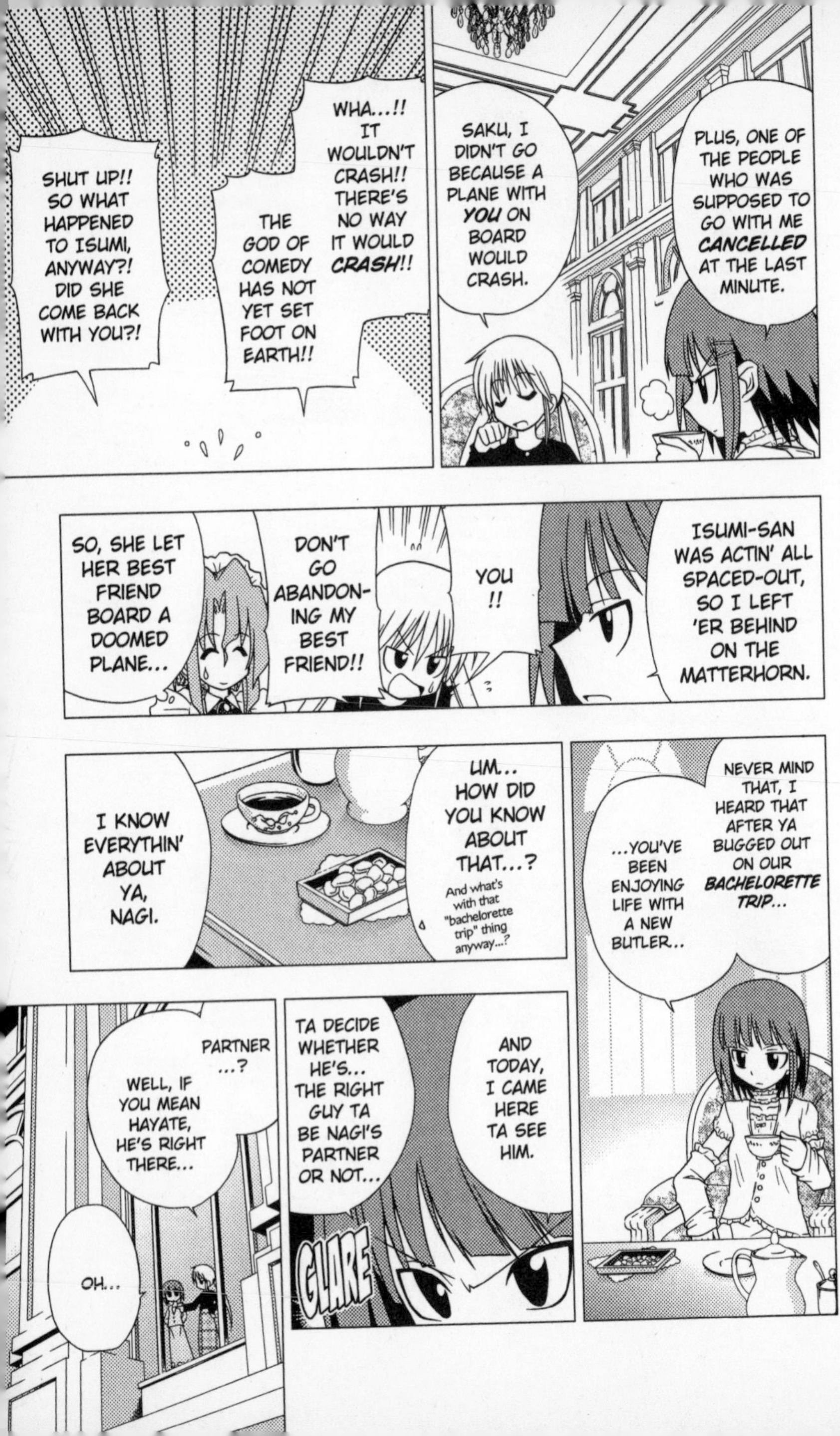
PLUS, ONE OF THE PEOPLE WHO WAS SUPPOSED TO GO WITH ME CANCELLED AT THE LAST MINUTE.
SAKU, I DIDN'T GO BECAUSE A PLANE WITH YOU ON BOARD WOULD CRASH.
WHA...!! IT WOULDN'T CRASH!! THERE'S NO WAY IT WOULD CRASH!!
THE GOD OF COMEDY HAS NOT YET SET FOOT ON EARTH!!
SHUT UP!! SO WHAT HAPPENED TO ISUMI, ANYWAY?! DID SHE COME BACK WITH YOU?!
ISUMI-SAN WAS ACTIN' ALL SPACED-OUT, SO I LEFT 'ER BEHIND ON THE MATTERHORN.
YOU !!
DON'T GO ABANDONING MY BEST FRIEND!!
SO, SHE LET HER BEST FRIEND BOARD A DOOMED PLANE...
NEVER MIND THAT, I HEARD THAT AFTER YA BUGGED OUT ON OUR BACHELORETTE TRIP...
...YOU'VE BEEN ENJOYING LIFE WITH A NEW BUTLER...
UM... HOW DID YOU KNOW ABOUT THAT...?
And what's with that "bachelorette trip" thing anyway...?
I KNOW EVERYTHIN' ABOUT YA, NAGI.
AND TODAY, I CAME HERE TA SEE HIM.
TA DECIDE WHETHER HE'S... THE RIGHT GUY TA BE NAGI'S PARTNER OR NOT...
GLARE
PARTNER ...?
WELL, IF YOU MEAN HAYATE, HE'S RIGHT THERE...
OH...

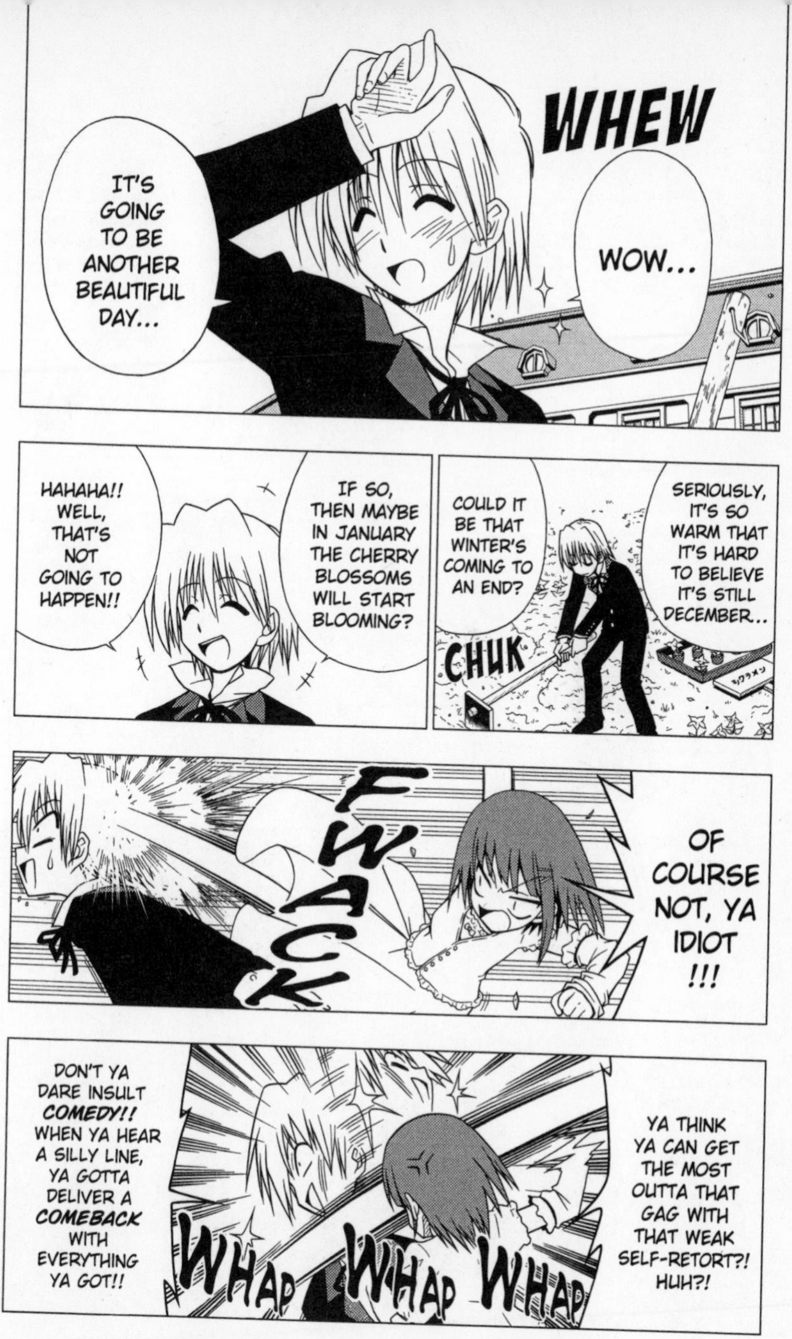
WHEW
WOW...
IT'S GOING TO BE ANOTHER BEAUTIFUL DAY...
SERIOUSLY, IT'S SO WARM THAT IT'S HARD TO BELIEVE IT'S STILL DECEMBER...
COULD IT BE THAT WINTER'S COMING TO AN END?
CHUK
IF SO, THEN MAYBE IN JANUARY THE CHERRY BLOSSOMS WILL START BLOOMING?
HAHAHA!! WELL, THAT'S NOT GOING TO HAPPEN!!
OF COURSE NOT, YA IDIOT!!!
FWACK
YA THINK YA CAN GET THE MOST OUTTA THAT GAG WITH THAT WEAK SELF-RETORT?! HUH?!
DON'T YA DARE INSULT COMEDY!! WHEN YA HEAR A SILLY LINE, YA GOTTA DELIVER A COMEBACK WITH EVERYTHING YA GOT!!
WHAP WHAP WHAP

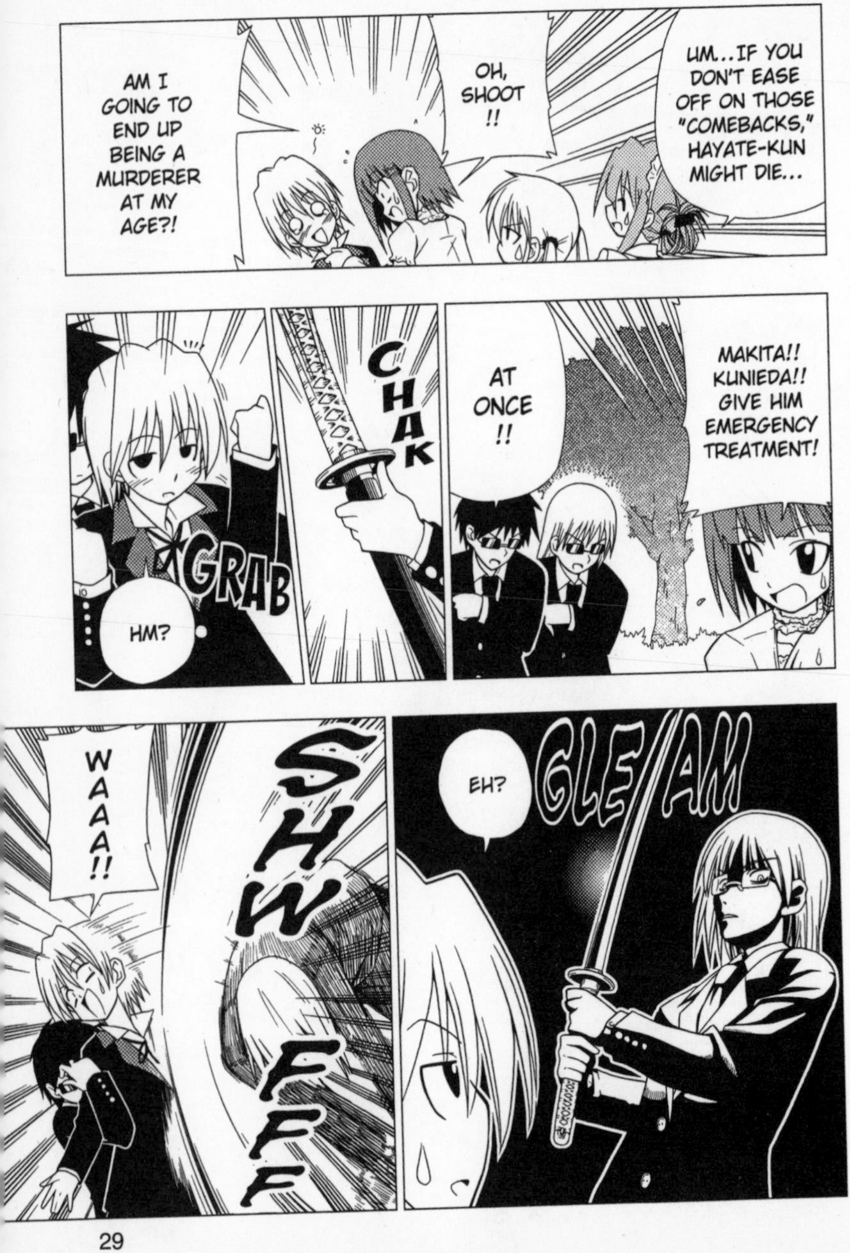
UM...IF YOU DON'T EASE OFF ON THOSE "COMEBACKS," HAYATE-KUN MIGHT DIE...
OH, SHOOT !!
AM I GOING TO END UP BEING A MURDERER AT MY AGE?!
MAKITA!! KUNIEDA!! GIVE HIM EMERGENCY TREATMENT!
AT ONCE !!
CHAK
GRAB
HM?
GLEAM
EH?
SHWFFF
WAAAA!!

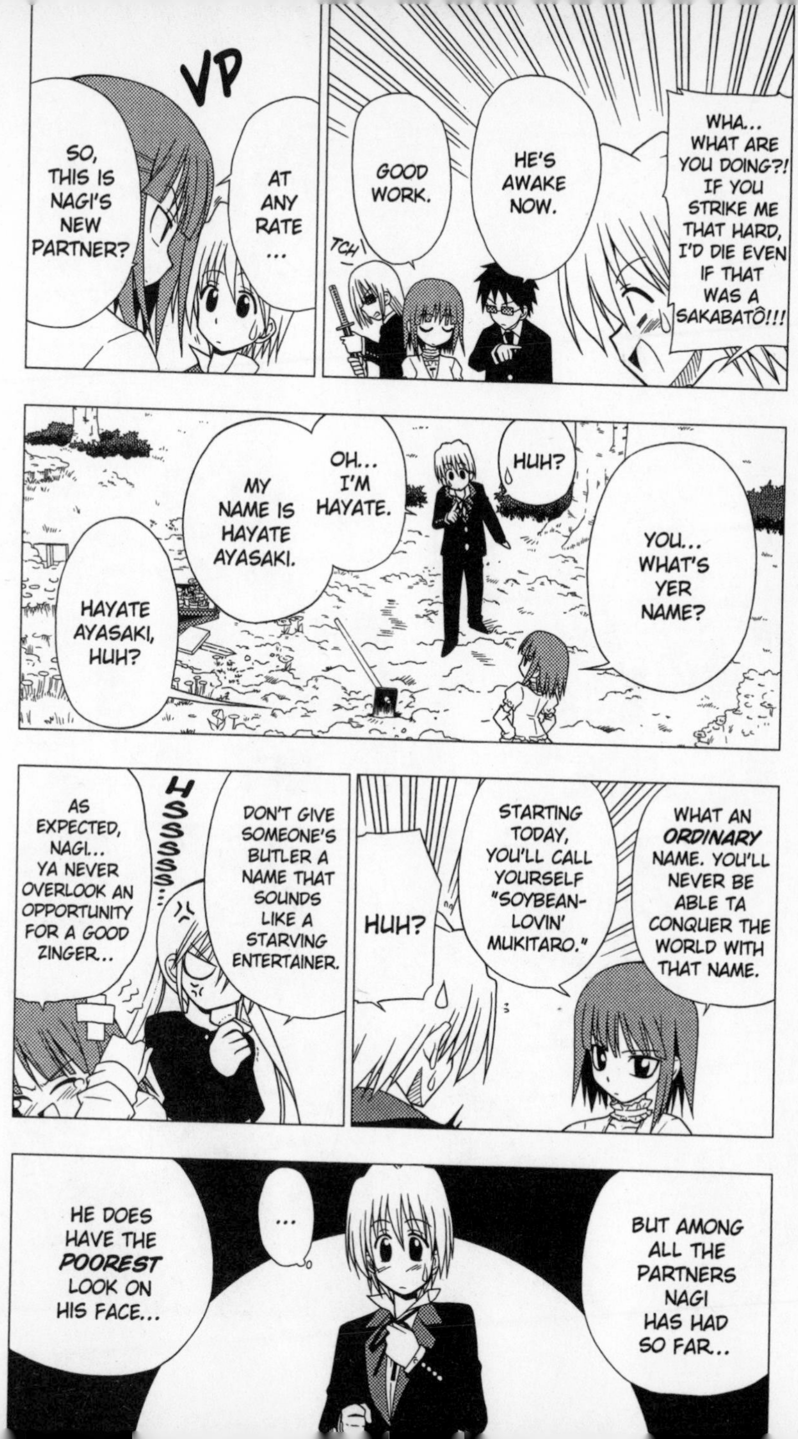
WHA... WHAT ARE YOU DOING?! IF YOU STRIKE ME THAT HARD, I'D DIE EVEN IF THAT WAS A SAKABATÔ!!!
HE'S AWAKE NOW.
GOOD WORK.
TCH
VP
AT ANY RATE ...
SO, THIS IS NAGI'S NEW PARTNER?
YOU... WHAT'S YER NAME?
HUH?
OH... I'M HAYATE.
MY NAME IS HAYATE AYASAKI.
HAYATE AYASAKI, HUH?
WHAT AN ***ORDINARY*** NAME. YOU'LL NEVER BE ABLE TA CONQUER THE WORLD WITH THAT NAME.
STARTING TODAY, YOU'LL CALL YOURSELF "SOYBEAN-LOVIN' MUKITARO."
HUH?
DON'T GIVE SOMEONE'S BUTLER A NAME THAT SOUNDS LIKE A STARVING ENTERTAINER.
HSSSSS...
AS EXPECTED, NAGI... YA NEVER OVERLOOK AN OPPORTUNITY FOR A GOOD ZINGER...
BUT AMONG ALL THE PARTNERS NAGI HAS HAD SO FAR..
...
HE DOES HAVE THE ***POOREST*** LOOK ON HIS FACE...

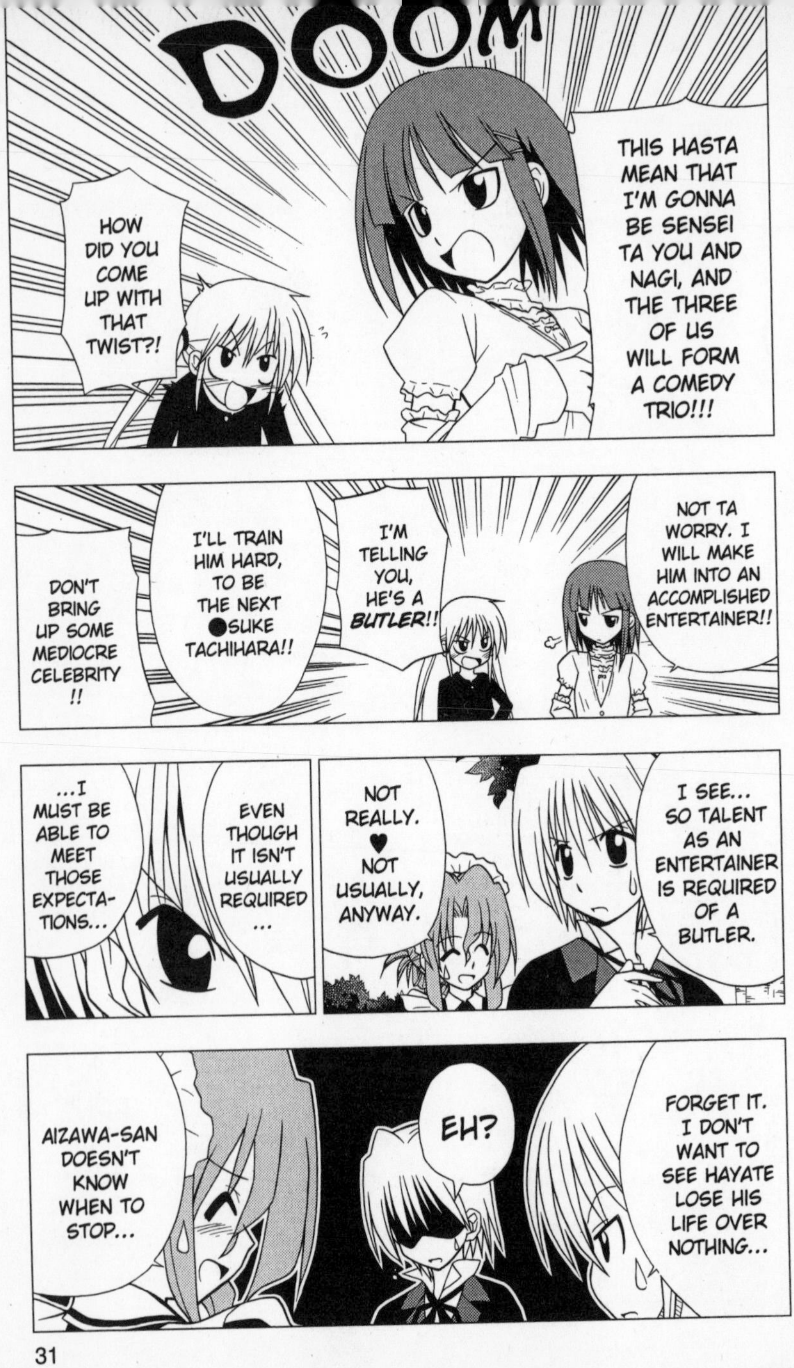
DOOM
THIS HASTA MEAN THAT I'M GONNA BE SENSEI TA YOU AND NAGI, AND THE THREE OF US WILL FORM A COMEDY TRIO!!!
HOW DID YOU COME UP WITH THAT TWIST?!
NOT TA WORRY. I WILL MAKE HIM INTO AN ACCOMPLISHED ENTERTAINER!!
I'M TELLING YOU, HE'S A *BUTLER*!!
I'LL TRAIN HIM HARD, TO BE THE NEXT ●SUKE TACHIHARA!!
DON'T BRING UP SOME MEDIOCRE CELEBRITY!!
I SEE... SO TALENT AS AN ENTERTAINER IS REQUIRED OF A BUTLER.
NOT REALLY. ♥ NOT USUALLY, ANYWAY.
EVEN THOUGH IT ISN'T USUALLY REQUIRED...
...I MUST BE ABLE TO MEET THOSE EXPECTA-TIONS...
FORGET IT. I DON'T WANT TO SEE HAYATE LOSE HIS LIFE OVER NOTHING...
EH?
AIZAWA-SAN DOESN'T KNOW WHEN TO STOP...

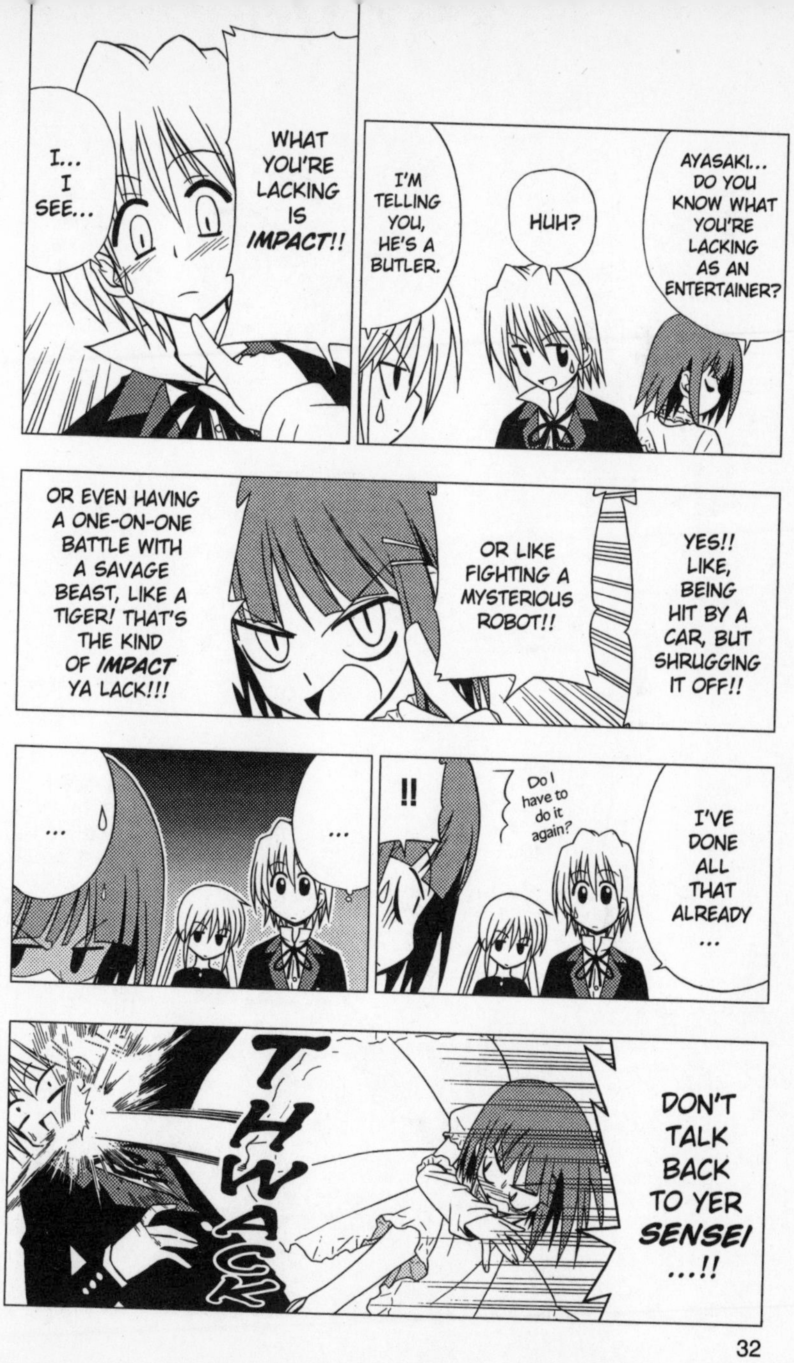
AYASAKI... DO YOU KNOW WHAT YOU'RE LACKING AS AN ENTERTAINER?
HUH?
I'M TELLING YOU, HE'S A BUTLER.
WHAT YOU'RE LACKING IS *IMPACT*!!
I... I SEE...
YES!! LIKE, BEING HIT BY A CAR, BUT SHRUGGING IT OFF!!
OR LIKE FIGHTING A MYSTERIOUS ROBOT!!
OR EVEN HAVING A ONE-ON-ONE BATTLE WITH A SAVAGE BEAST, LIKE A TIGER! THAT'S THE KIND OF *IMPACT* YA LACK!!!
I'VE DONE ALL THAT ALREADY...
Do I have to do it again?
!!
...
...
DON'T TALK BACK TO YER *SENSEI*...!!
THWACK

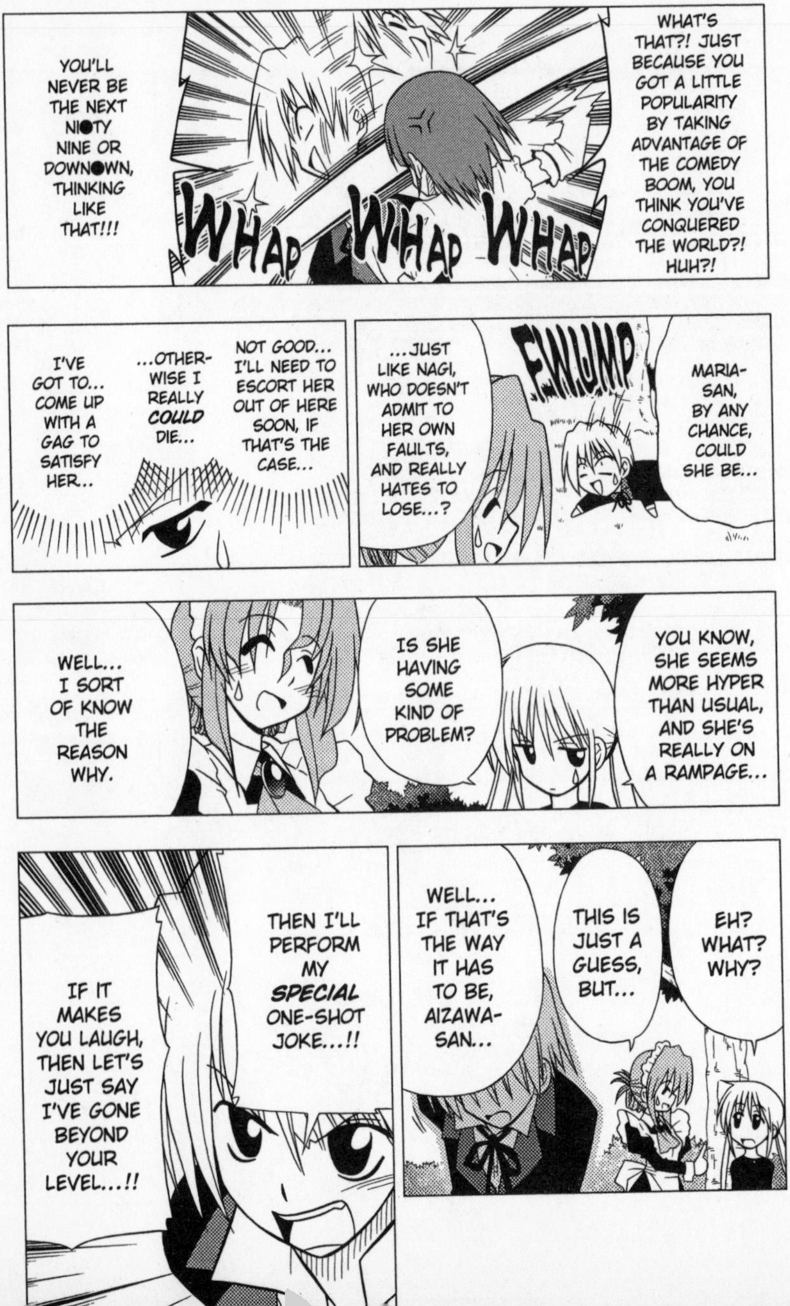
WHAT'S THAT?! JUST BECAUSE YOU GOT A LITTLE POPULARITY BY TAKING ADVANTAGE OF THE COMEDY BOOM, YOU THINK YOU'VE CONQUERED THE WORLD?! HUH?!
YOU'LL NEVER BE THE NEXT NI●TY NINE OR DOWN●WN, THINKING LIKE THAT!!!
WHAP WHAP WHAP
MARIA-SAN, BY ANY CHANCE, COULD SHE BE...
FWUMP
...JUST LIKE NAGI, WHO DOESN'T ADMIT TO HER OWN FAULTS, AND REALLY HATES TO LOSE...?
NOT GOOD... I'LL NEED TO ESCORT HER OUT OF HERE SOON, IF THAT'S THE CASE...
...OTHERWISE I REALLY *COULD* DIE...
I'VE GOT TO... COME UP WITH A GAG TO SATISFY HER...
YOU KNOW, SHE SEEMS MORE HYPER THAN USUAL, AND SHE'S REALLY ON A RAMPAGE...
IS SHE HAVING SOME KIND OF PROBLEM?
WELL... I SORT OF KNOW THE REASON WHY.
EH? WHAT? WHY?
THIS IS JUST A GUESS, BUT...
WELL... IF THAT'S THE WAY IT HAS TO BE, AIZAWA-SAN...
THEN I'LL PERFORM MY *SPECIAL* ONE-SHOT JOKE...!!
IF IT MAKES YOU LAUGH, THEN LET'S JUST SAY I'VE GONE BEYOND YOUR LEVEL...!!

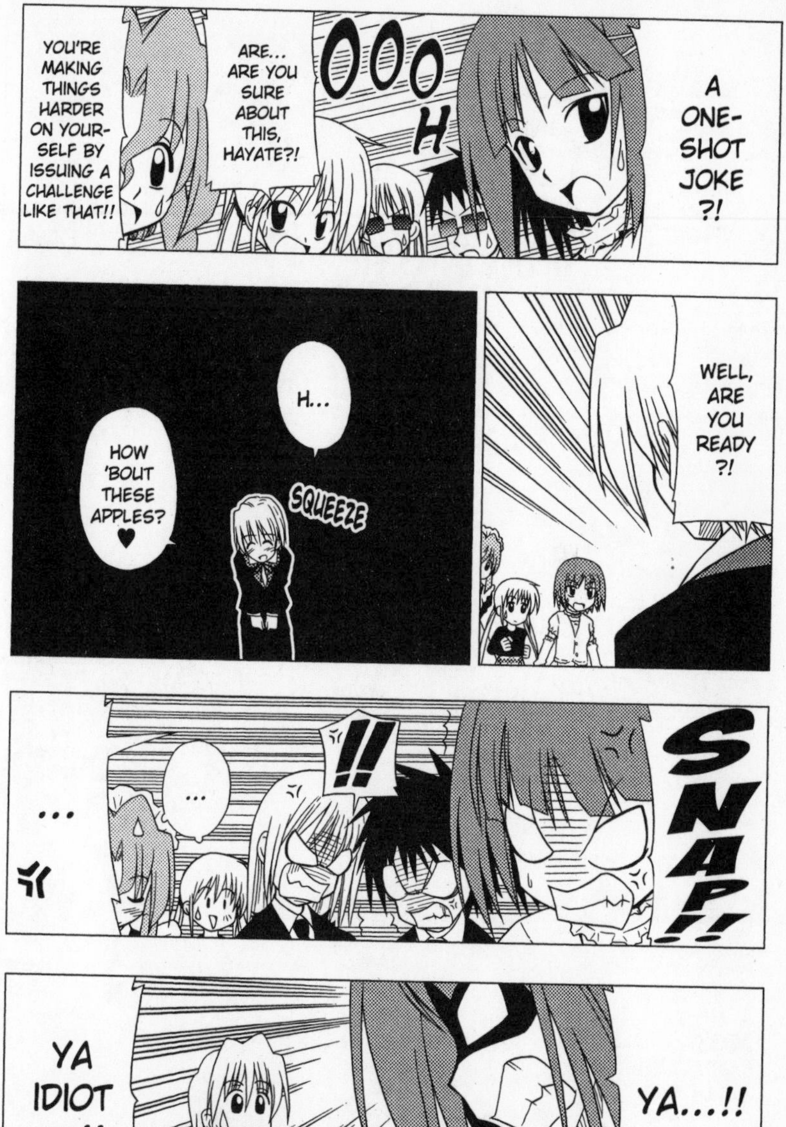
A ONE-SHOT JOKE?!
OOOH
ARE... ARE YOU SURE ABOUT THIS, HAYATE?!
YOU'RE MAKING THINGS HARDER ON YOURSELF BY ISSUING A CHALLENGE LIKE THAT!!
WELL, ARE YOU READY?!
H...
SQUEEZE
HOW 'BOUT THESE APPLES? ♥
SNAP!!
!!
...
...
YA...!!
YA IDIOT...!!

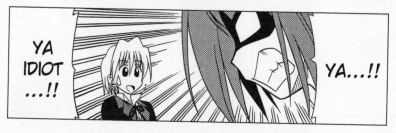

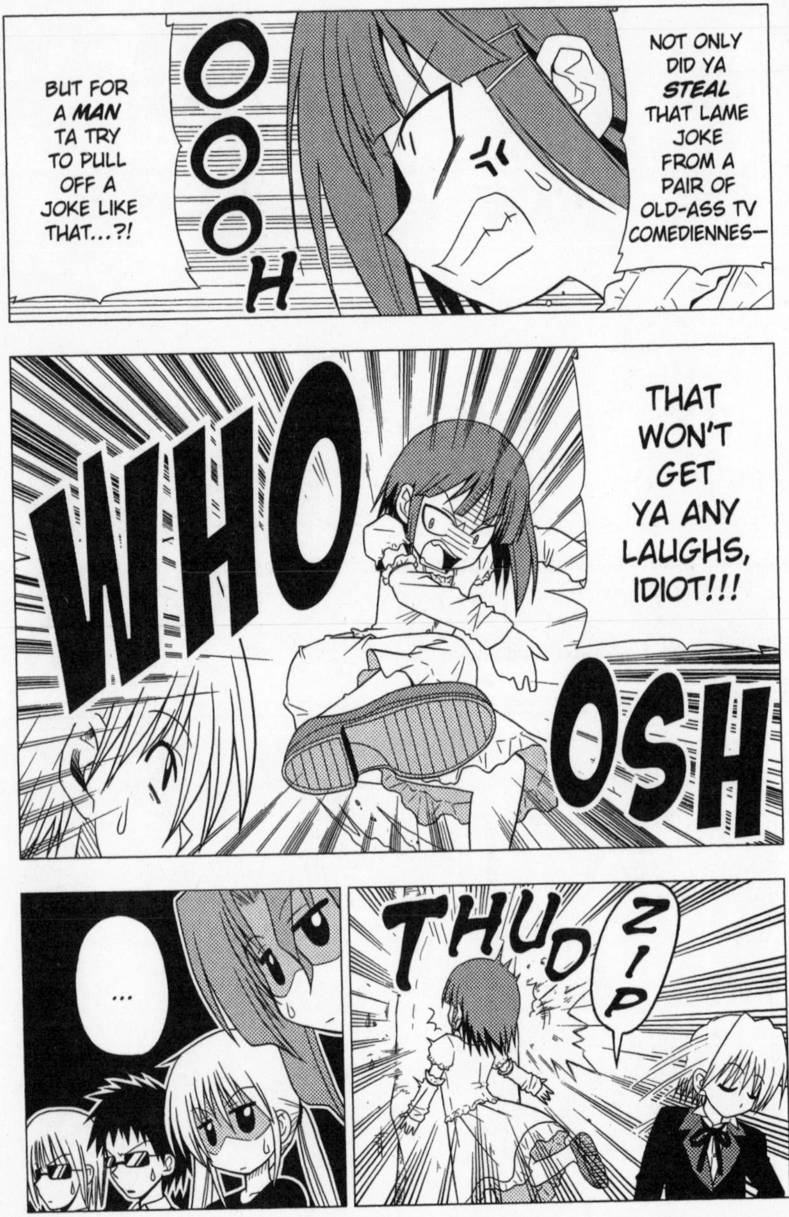
NOT ONLY DID YA STEAL THAT LAME JOKE FROM A PAIR OF OLD-ASS TV COMEDIENNES—
OOOOH
BUT FOR A MAN TA TRY TO PULL OFF A JOKE LIKE THAT...?!
THAT WON'T GET YA ANY LAUGHS, IDIOT!!!
WHOOSH
ZIP
THUD
...

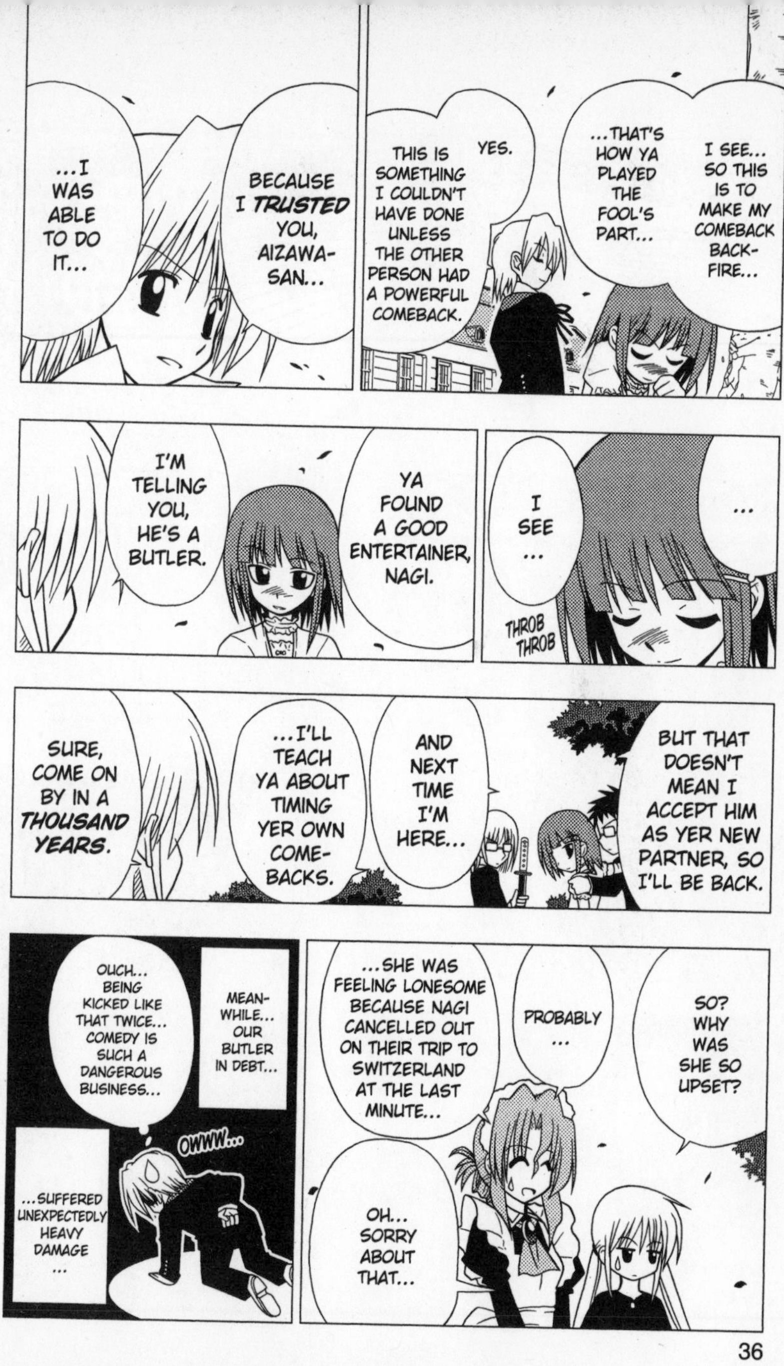
I SEE... SO THIS IS TO MAKE MY COMEBACK BACK-FIRE...
...THAT'S HOW YA PLAYED THE FOOL'S PART...
YES.
THIS IS SOMETHING I COULDN'T HAVE DONE UNLESS THE OTHER PERSON HAD A POWERFUL COMEBACK.
BECAUSE I *TRUSTED* YOU, AIZAWA-SAN...
...I WAS ABLE TO DO IT...
...
I SEE ...
THROB THROB
YA FOUND A GOOD ENTERTAINER, NAGI.
I'M TELLING YOU, HE'S A BUTLER.
BUT THAT DOESN'T MEAN I ACCEPT HIM AS YER NEW PARTNER, SO I'LL BE BACK.
AND NEXT TIME I'M HERE...
...I'LL TEACH YA ABOUT TIMING YER OWN COME-BACKS.
SURE, COME ON BY IN A *THOUSAND YEARS*.
SO? WHY WAS SHE SO UPSET?
PROBABLY ...
...SHE WAS FEELING LONESOME BECAUSE NAGI CANCELLED OUT ON THEIR TRIP TO SWITZERLAND AT THE LAST MINUTE...
OH... SORRY ABOUT THAT...
MEAN-WHILE... OUR BUTLER IN DEBT...
OUCH... BEING KICKED LIKE THAT TWICE... COMEDY IS SUCH A DANGEROUS BUSINESS...
OWWW...
...SUFFERED UNEXPECTEDLY HEAVY DAMAGE ...

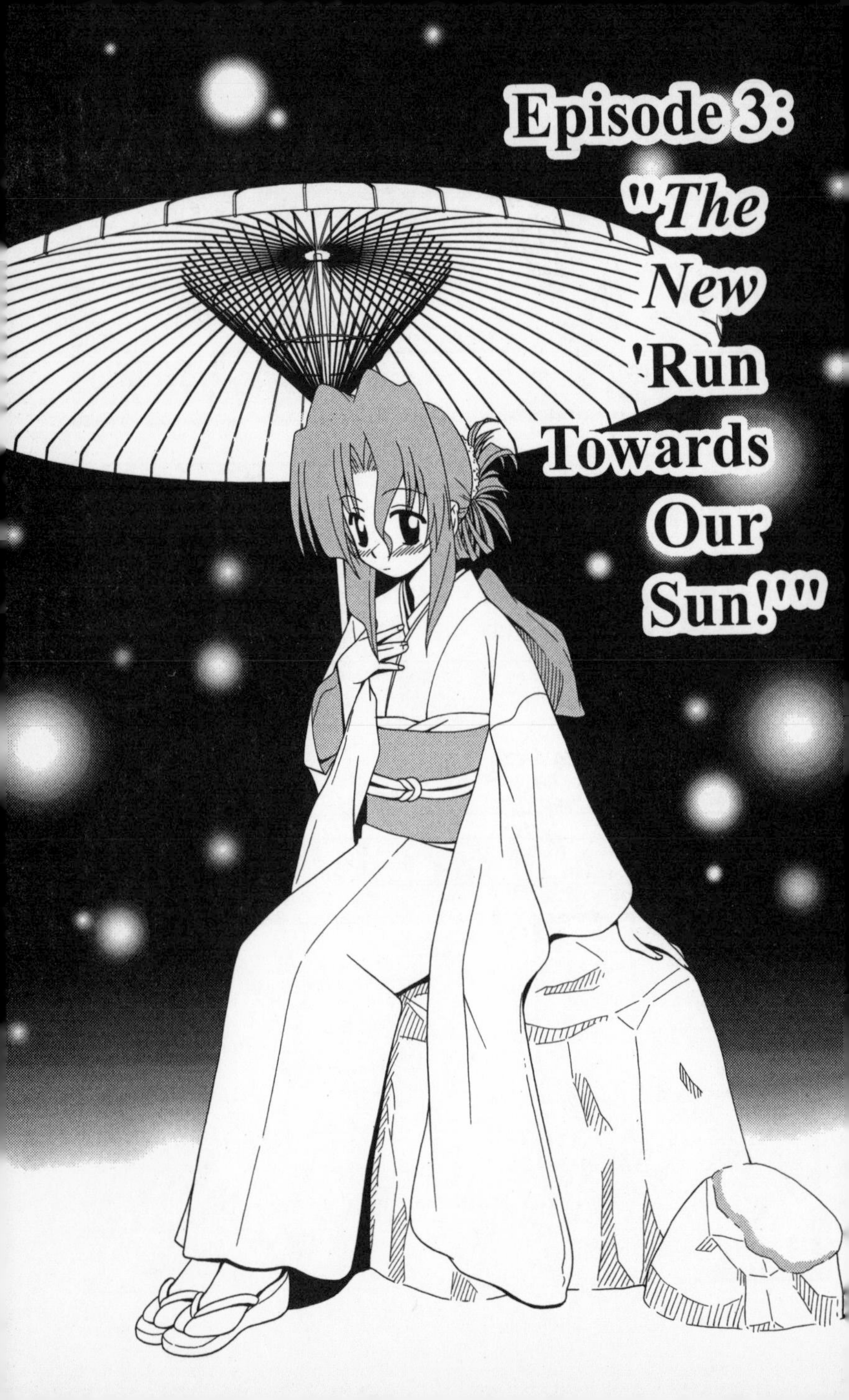
Episode 3: "The New 'Run Towards Our Sun!'"

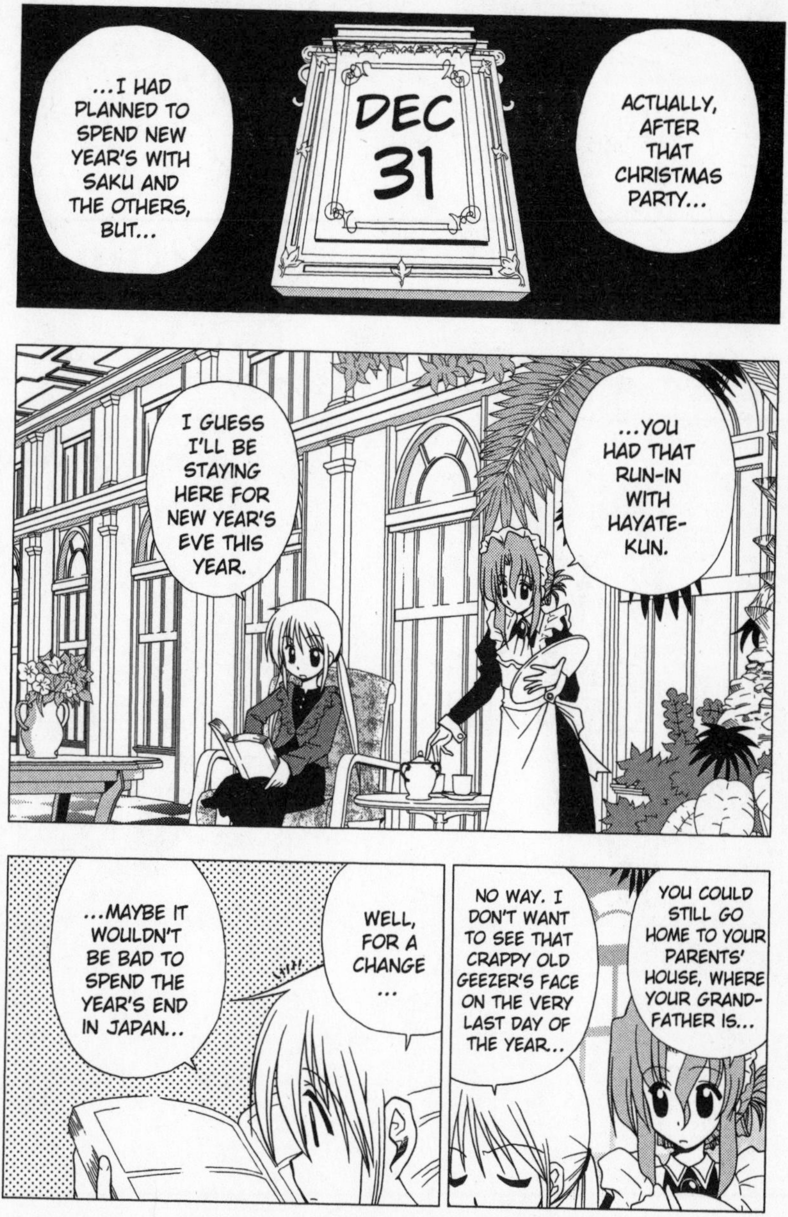
ACTUALLY, AFTER THAT CHRISTMAS PARTY...
DEC 31
...I HAD PLANNED TO SPEND NEW YEAR'S WITH SAKU AND THE OTHERS, BUT...
...YOU HAD THAT RUN-IN WITH HAYATE-KUN.
I GUESS I'LL BE STAYING HERE FOR NEW YEAR'S EVE THIS YEAR.
YOU COULD STILL GO HOME TO YOUR PARENTS' HOUSE, WHERE YOUR GRAND-FATHER IS...
NO WAY. I DON'T WANT TO SEE THAT CRAPPY OLD GEEZER'S FACE ON THE VERY LAST DAY OF THE YEAR...
WELL, FOR A CHANGE ...
...MAYBE IT WOULDN'T BE BAD TO SPEND THE YEAR'S END IN JAPAN...

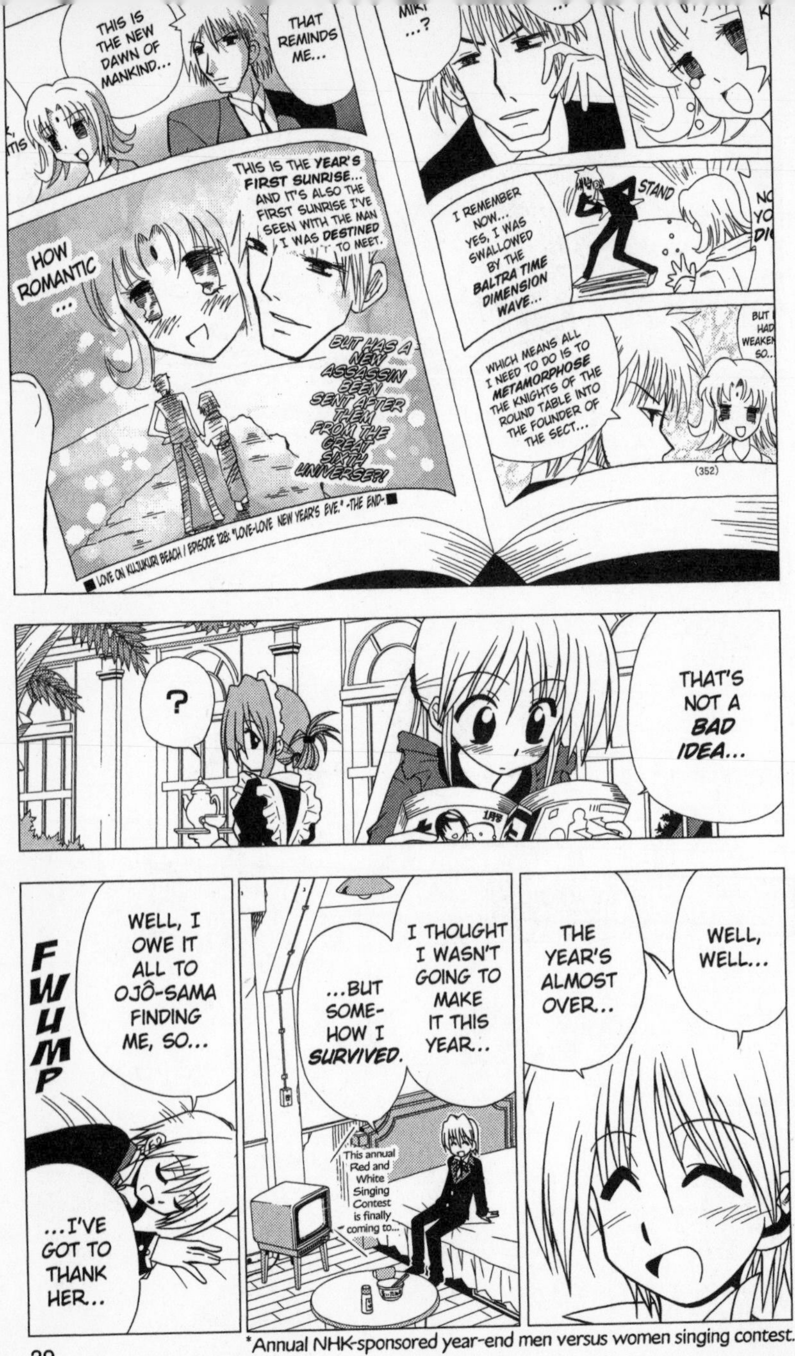
I REMEMBER NOW... YES, I WAS SWALLOWED BY THE BALTRA TIME DIMENSION WAVE...
STAND
WHICH MEANS ALL I NEED TO DO IS TO METAMORPHOSE THE KNIGHTS OF THE ROUND TABLE INTO THE FOUNDER OF THE SECT...
(352)
THAT REMINDS ME...
THIS IS THE NEW DAWN OF MANKIND...
THIS IS THE YEAR'S FIRST SUNRISE... AND IT'S ALSO THE FIRST SUNRISE I'VE SEEN WITH THE MAN I WAS DESTINED TO MEET.
HOW ROMANTIC...
BUT HAS A NEW ASSASSIN BEEN SENT AFTER THEM FROM THE GREAT SIXTH UNIVERSE?!
LOVE ON KUJUKURI BEACH / EPISODE 128: "LOVE-LOVE NEW YEAR'S EVE." -THE END-
THAT'S NOT A BAD IDEA...
?
WELL, WELL...
THE YEAR'S ALMOST OVER..
I THOUGHT I WASN'T GOING TO MAKE IT THIS YEAR..
...BUT SOMEHOW I SURVIVED.
This annual Red and White Singing Contest is finally coming to...
WELL, I OWE IT ALL TO OJÔ-SAMA FINDING ME, SO...
FWUMP
...I'VE GOT TO THANK HER..

*Annual NHK-sponsored year-end men versus women singing contest.

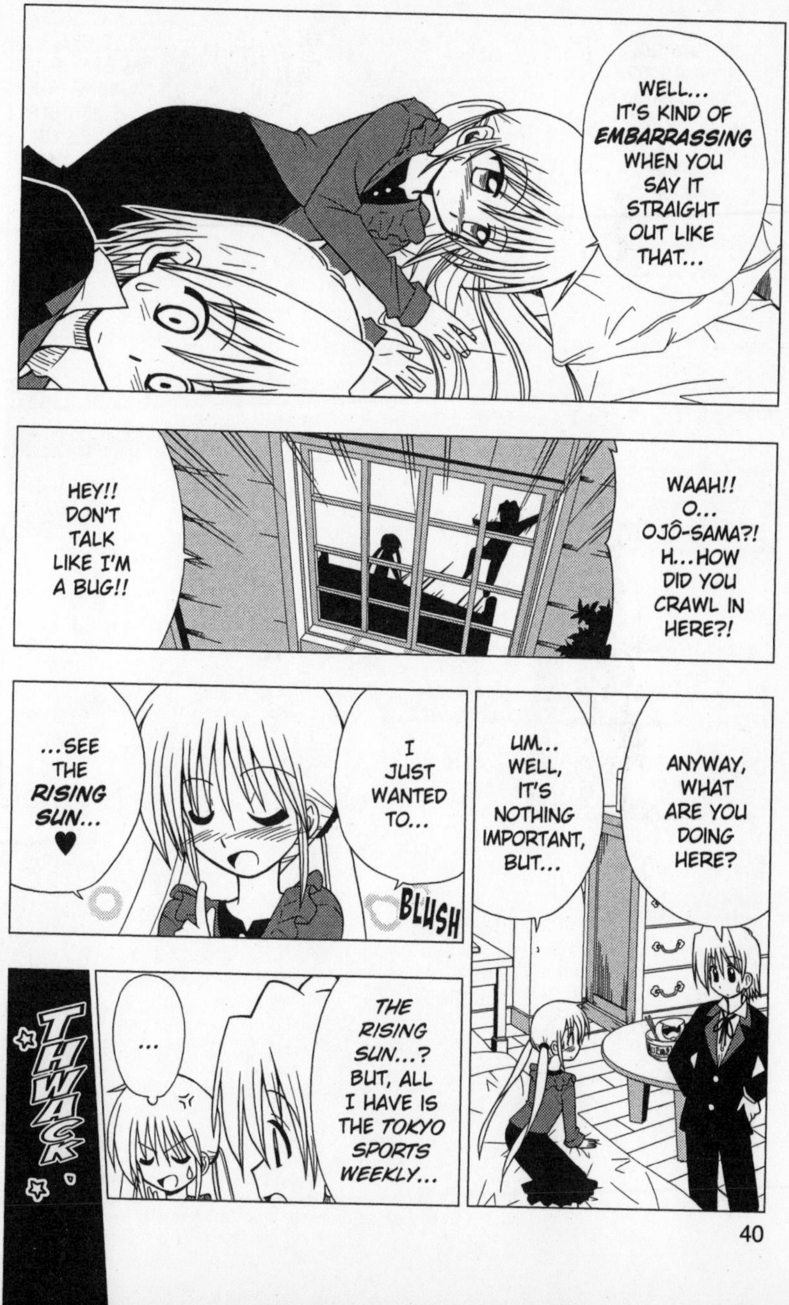
WELL... IT'S KIND OF EMBARRASSING WHEN YOU SAY IT STRAIGHT OUT LIKE THAT...
WAAH!! O... OJÔ-SAMA?! H...HOW DID YOU CRAWL IN HERE?!
HEY!! DON'T TALK LIKE I'M A BUG!!
ANYWAY, WHAT ARE YOU DOING HERE?
UM.. WELL, IT'S NOTHING IMPORTANT, BUT...
I JUST WANTED TO...
BLUSH
...SEE THE RISING SUN... ♥
THE RISING SUN...? BUT, ALL I HAVE IS THE TOKYO SPORTS WEEKLY...
...
THWACK

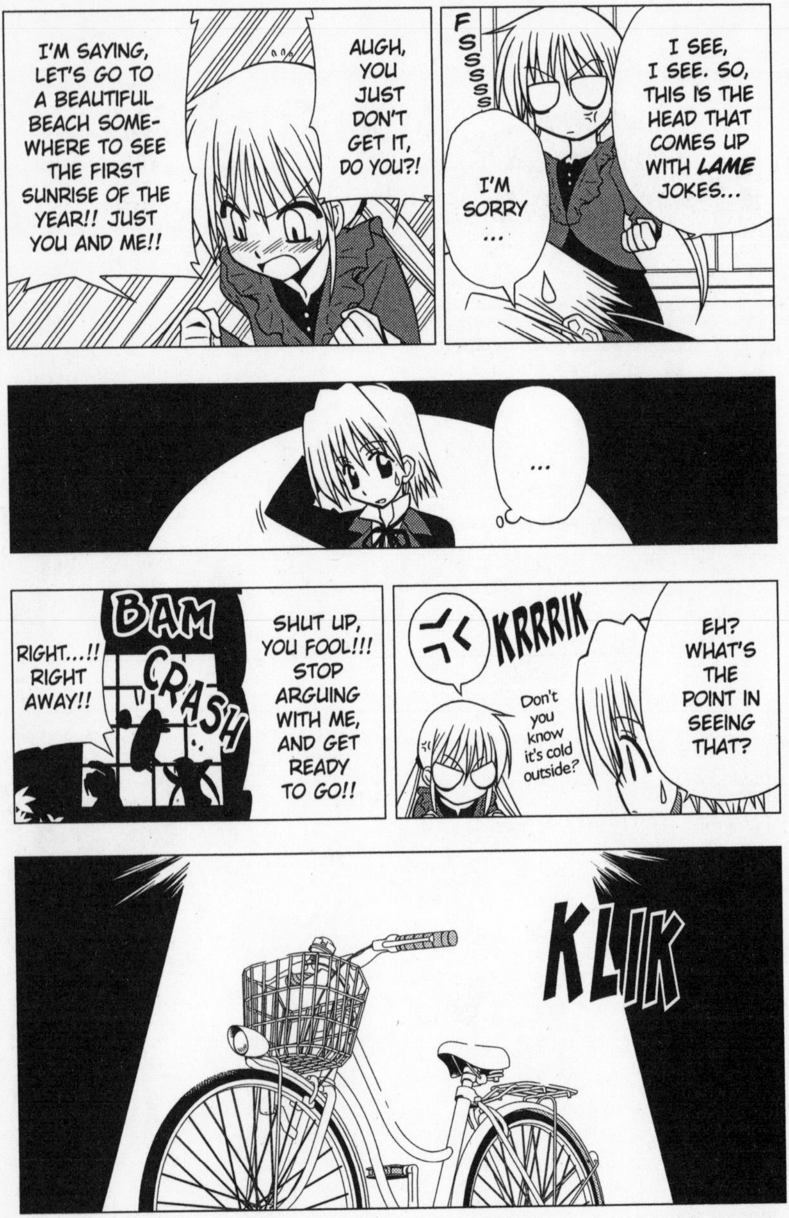
I SEE, I SEE. SO, THIS IS THE HEAD THAT COMES UP WITH **LAME** JOKES...
FSSSSS
I'M SORRY...
AUGH, YOU JUST DON'T GET IT, DO YOU?!
I'M SAYING, LET'S GO TO A BEAUTIFUL BEACH SOME-WHERE TO SEE THE FIRST SUNRISE OF THE YEAR!! JUST YOU AND ME!!
...
EH? WHAT'S THE POINT IN SEEING THAT?
KRRRIK
Don't you know it's cold outside?
SHUT UP, YOU FOOL!!! STOP ARGUING WITH ME, AND GET READY TO GO!!
BAM
CRASH
RIGHT...!! RIGHT AWAY!!
KLIK

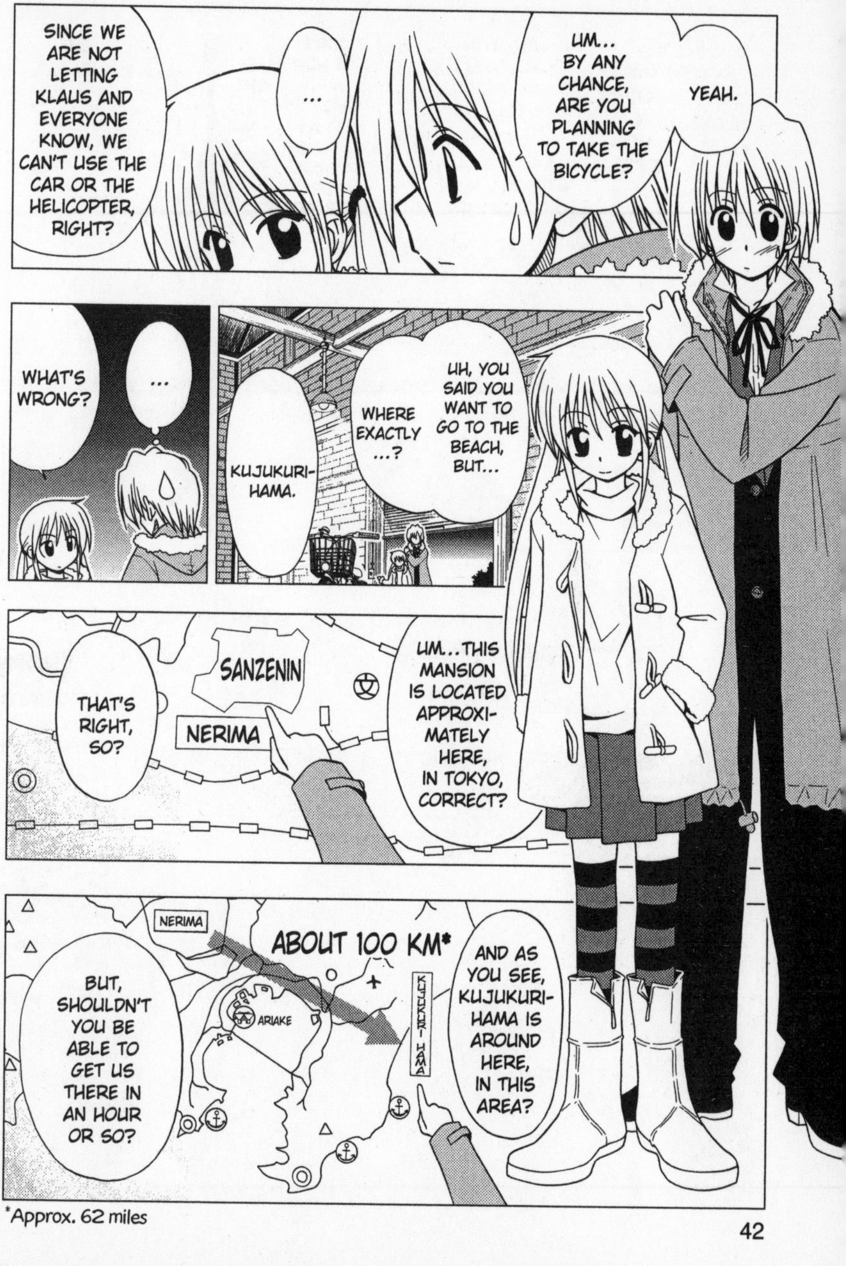
YEAH.
UM... BY ANY CHANCE, ARE YOU PLANNING TO TAKE THE BICYCLE?
...
SINCE WE ARE NOT LETTING KLAUS AND EVERYONE KNOW, WE CAN'T USE THE CAR OR THE HELICOPTER, RIGHT?
UH, YOU SAID YOU WANT TO GO TO THE BEACH, BUT...
WHERE EXACTLY ...?
KUJUKURI-HAMA.
...
WHAT'S WRONG?
UM...THIS MANSION IS LOCATED APPROXIMATELY HERE, IN TOKYO, CORRECT?
SANZENIN
NERIMA
THAT'S RIGHT, SO?
AND AS YOU SEE, KUJUKURI-HAMA IS AROUND HERE, IN THIS AREA?
KUJUKURI-HAMA
ABOUT 100 KM*
NERIMA
ARIAKE
BUT, SHOULDN'T YOU BE ABLE TO GET US THERE IN AN HOUR OR SO?

*Approx. 62 miles

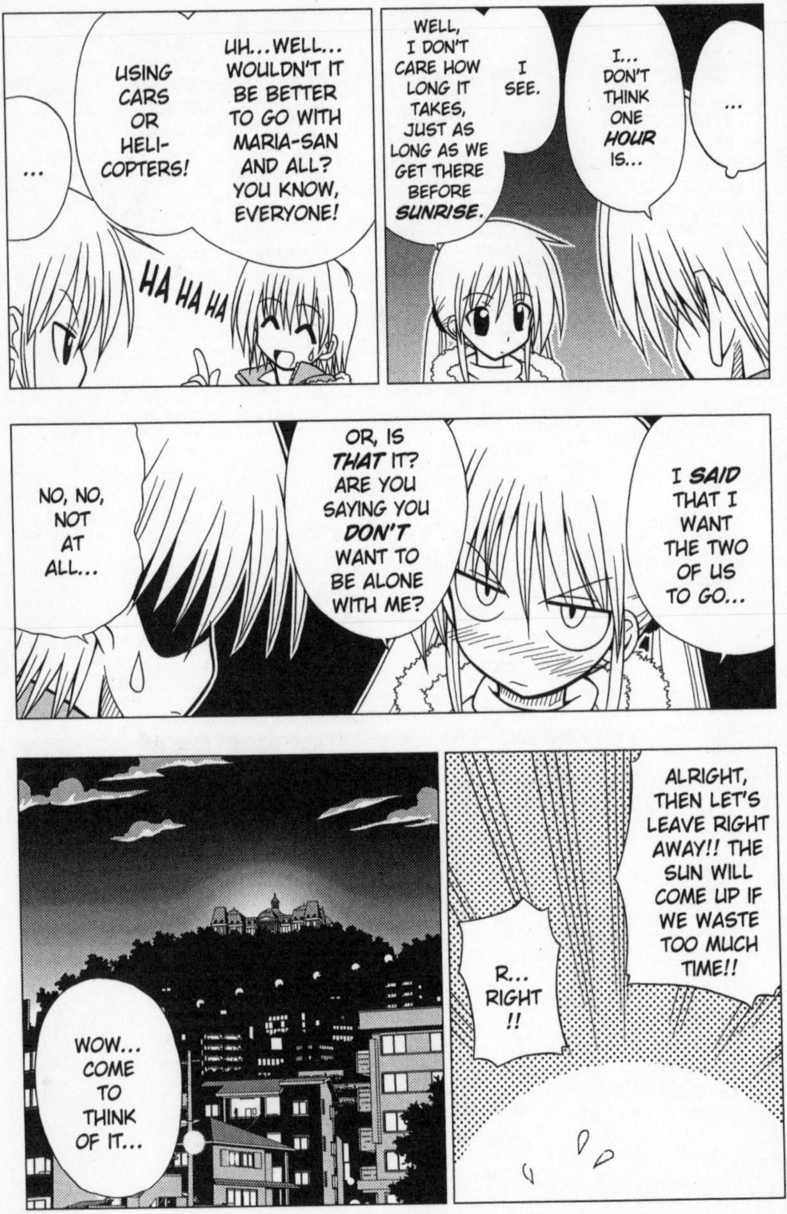
...
I... DON'T THINK ONE HOUR IS...
I SEE.
WELL, I DON'T CARE HOW LONG IT TAKES, JUST AS LONG AS WE GET THERE BEFORE SUNRISE.
UH...WELL... WOULDN'T IT BE BETTER TO GO WITH MARIA-SAN AND ALL? YOU KNOW, EVERYONE!
USING CARS OR HELI-COPTERS!
HA HA HA
...
I SAID THAT I WANT THE TWO OF US TO GO...
OR, IS THAT IT? ARE YOU SAYING YOU DON'T WANT TO BE ALONE WITH ME?
NO, NO, NOT AT ALL...
ALRIGHT, THEN LET'S LEAVE RIGHT AWAY!! THE SUN WILL COME UP IF WE WASTE TOO MUCH TIME!!
R... RIGHT!!
WOW... COME TO THINK OF IT...

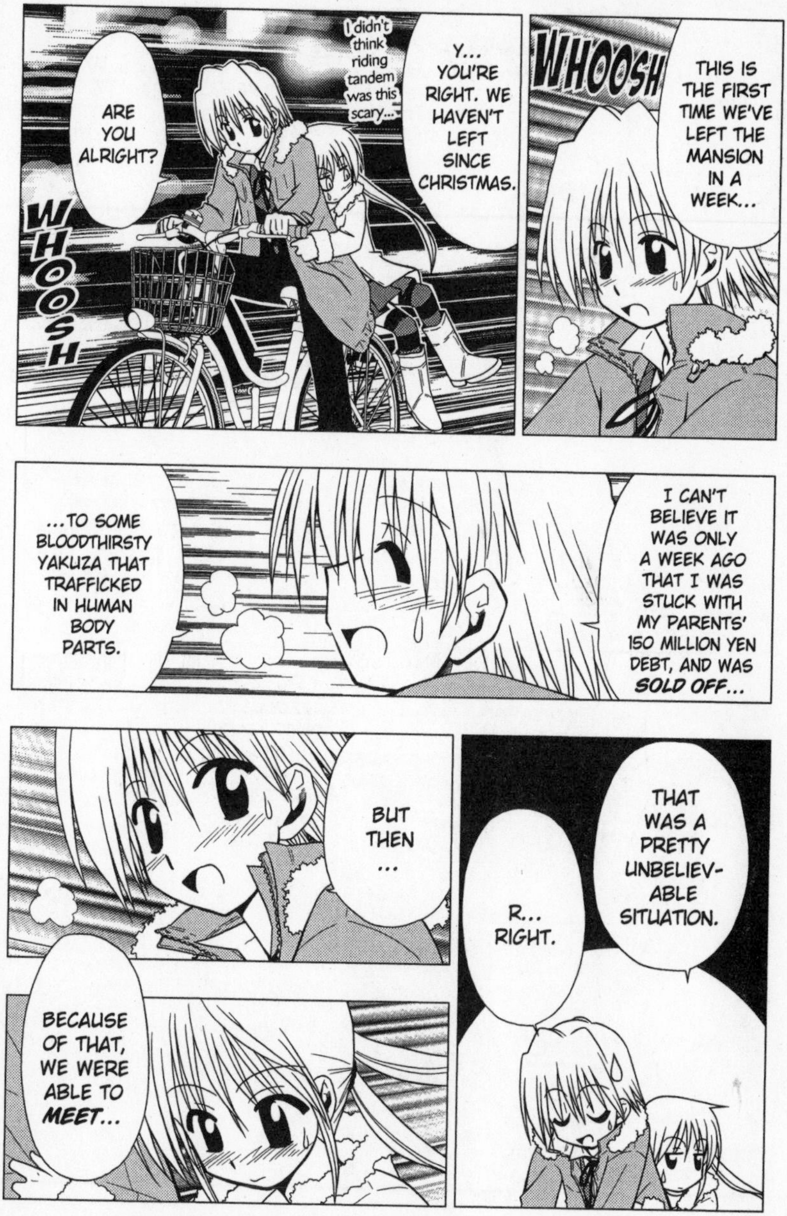
WHOOSH
THIS IS THE FIRST TIME WE'VE LEFT THE MANSION IN A WEEK...
Y... YOU'RE RIGHT. WE HAVEN'T LEFT SINCE CHRISTMAS.
I didn't think riding tandem was this scary...
ARE YOU ALRIGHT?
WHOOSH
I CAN'T BELIEVE IT WAS ONLY A WEEK AGO THAT I WAS STUCK WITH MY PARENTS' 150 MILLION YEN DEBT, AND WAS ***SOLD OFF...***
...TO SOME BLOODTHIRSTY YAKUZA THAT TRAFFICKED IN HUMAN BODY PARTS.
THAT WAS A PRETTY UNBELIEV-ABLE SITUATION.
R... RIGHT.
BUT THEN ...
BECAUSE OF THAT, WE WERE ABLE TO ***MEET...***

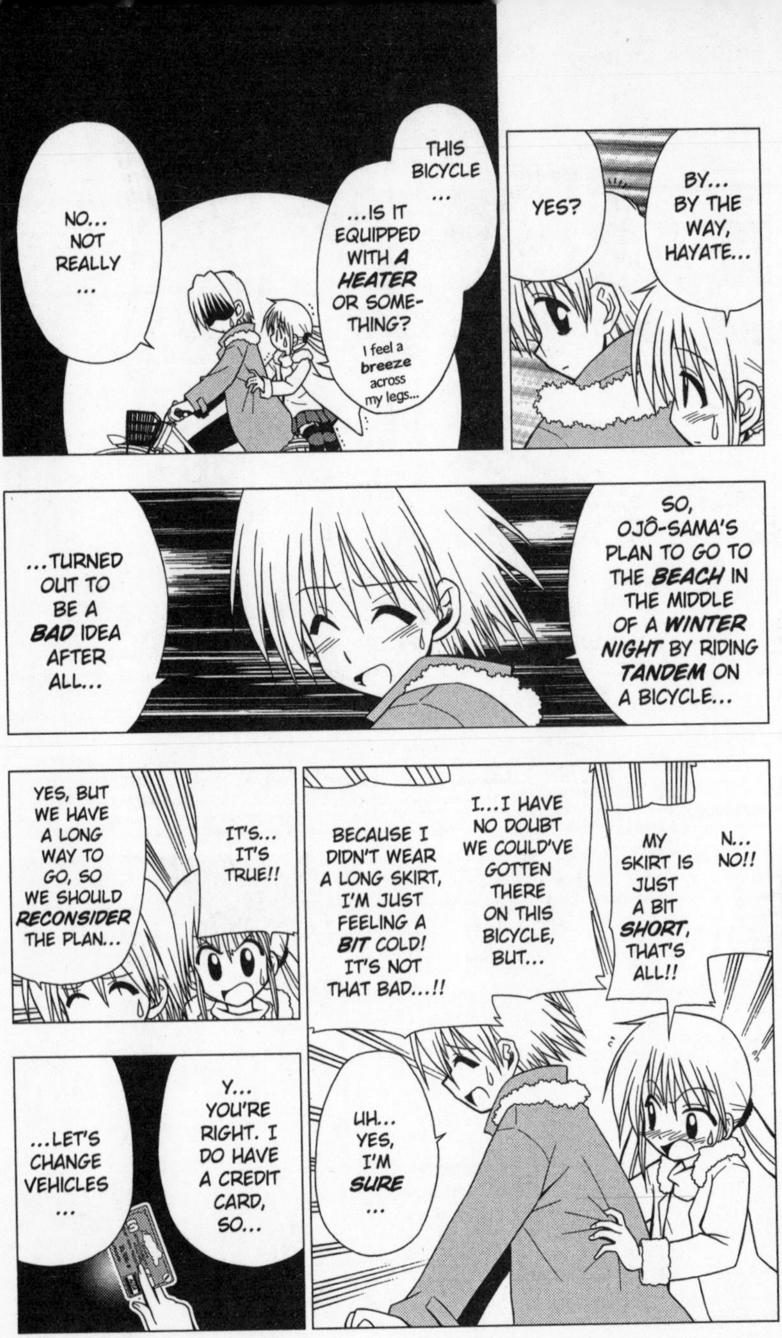
BY... BY THE WAY, HAYATE...
YES?
THIS BICYCLE ...
...IS IT EQUIPPED WITH A ***HEATER*** OR SOMETHING?
I feel a **breeze** across my legs...
NO... NOT REALLY ...
SO, OJÔ-SAMA'S PLAN TO GO TO THE ***BEACH*** IN THE MIDDLE OF A ***WINTER NIGHT*** BY RIDING ***TANDEM*** ON A BICYCLE...
...TURNED OUT TO BE A ***BAD*** IDEA AFTER ALL...
N... NO!!
MY SKIRT IS JUST A BIT ***SHORT***, THAT'S ALL!!
I...I HAVE NO DOUBT WE COULD'VE GOTTEN THERE ON THIS BICYCLE, BUT...
BECAUSE I DIDN'T WEAR A LONG SKIRT, I'M JUST FEELING A ***BIT*** COLD! IT'S NOT THAT BAD...!!
UH... YES, I'M ***SURE*** ...
IT'S... IT'S TRUE!!
YES, BUT WE HAVE A LONG WAY TO GO, SO WE SHOULD ***RECONSIDER*** THE PLAN...
Y... YOU'RE RIGHT. I DO HAVE A CREDIT CARD, SO...
...LET'S CHANGE VEHICLES ...

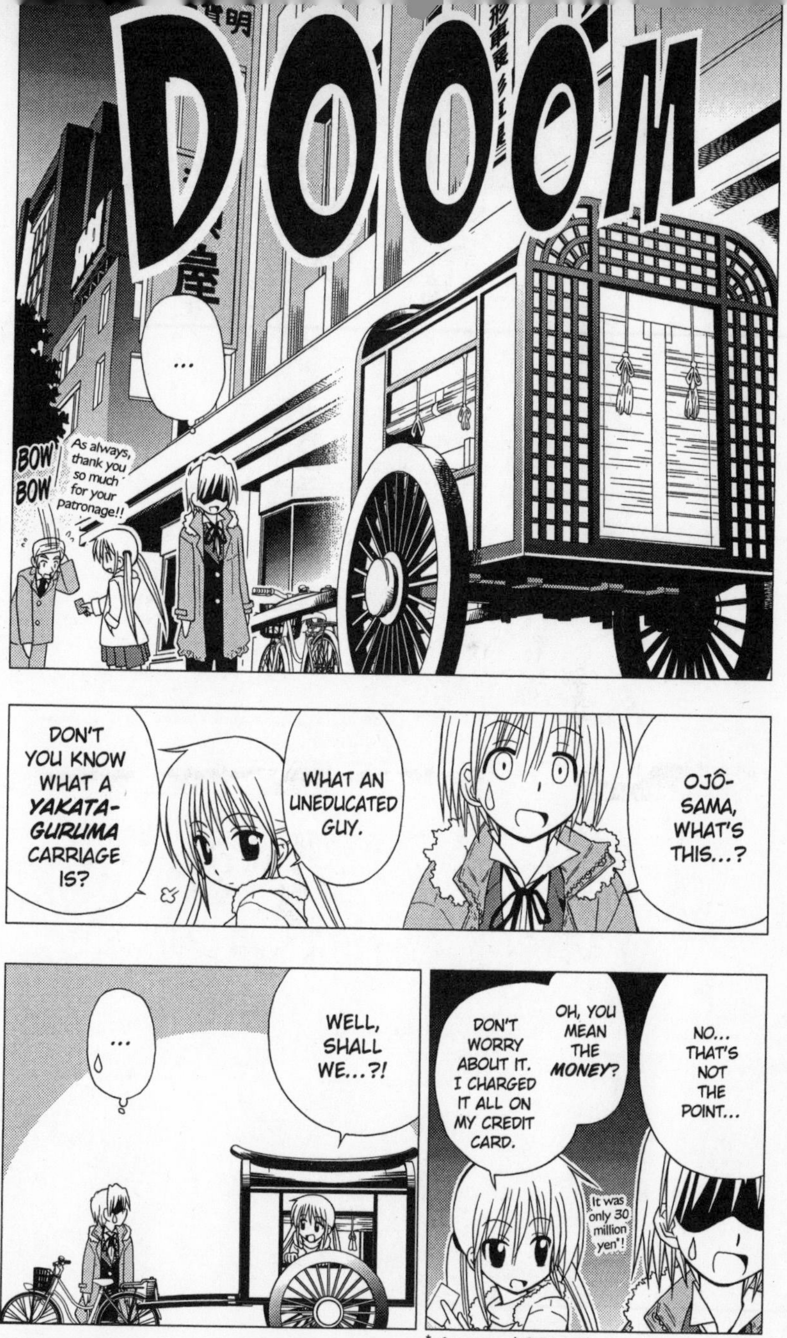
DOOOM
...
As always, thank you so much for your patronage!!
BOW BOW
OJÔ-SAMA, WHAT'S THIS...?
WHAT AN UNEDUCATED GUY.
DON'T YOU KNOW WHAT A *YAKATA-GURUMA* CARRIAGE IS?
NO... THAT'S NOT THE POINT...
OH, YOU MEAN THE *MONEY*?
DON'T WORRY ABOUT IT. I CHARGED IT ALL ON MY CREDIT CARD.
It was only 30 million yen*!
WELL, SHALL WE...?!
...

* Approx. $270,000

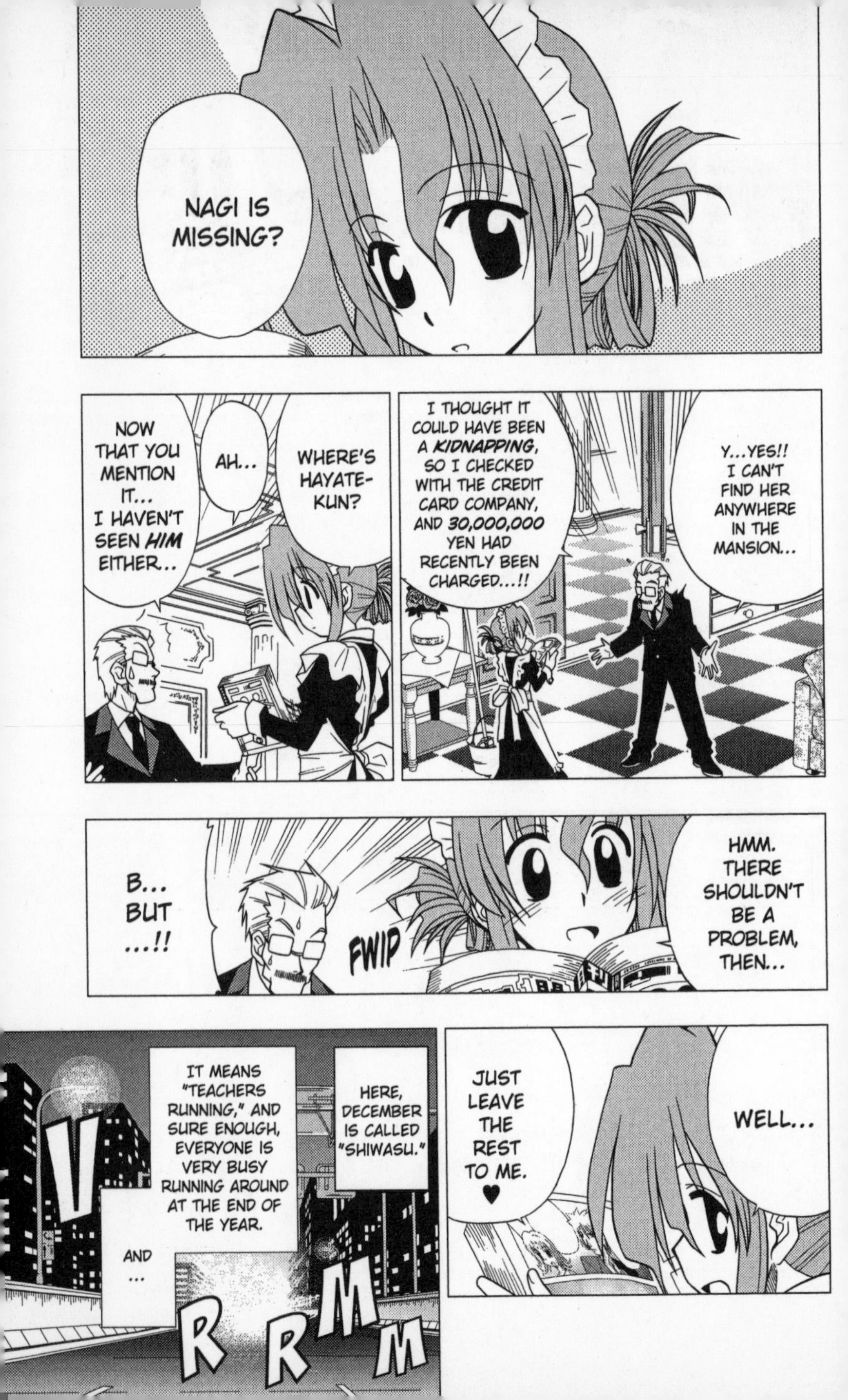
NAGI IS MISSING?
Y...YES!! I CAN'T FIND HER ANYWHERE IN THE MANSION...
I THOUGHT IT COULD HAVE BEEN A *KIDNAPPING*, SO I CHECKED WITH THE CREDIT CARD COMPANY, AND *30,000,000* YEN HAD RECENTLY BEEN CHARGED...!!
WHERE'S HAYATE-KUN?
AH...
NOW THAT YOU MENTION IT... I HAVEN'T SEEN *HIM* EITHER...
HMM. THERE SHOULDN'T BE A PROBLEM, THEN...
FWIP
B... BUT ...!!
WELL...
JUST LEAVE THE REST TO ME. ♥
HERE, DECEMBER IS CALLED "SHIWASU."
IT MEANS "TEACHERS RUNNING," AND SURE ENOUGH, EVERYONE IS VERY BUSY RUNNING AROUND AT THE END OF THE YEAR.
AND ...
VRRMM

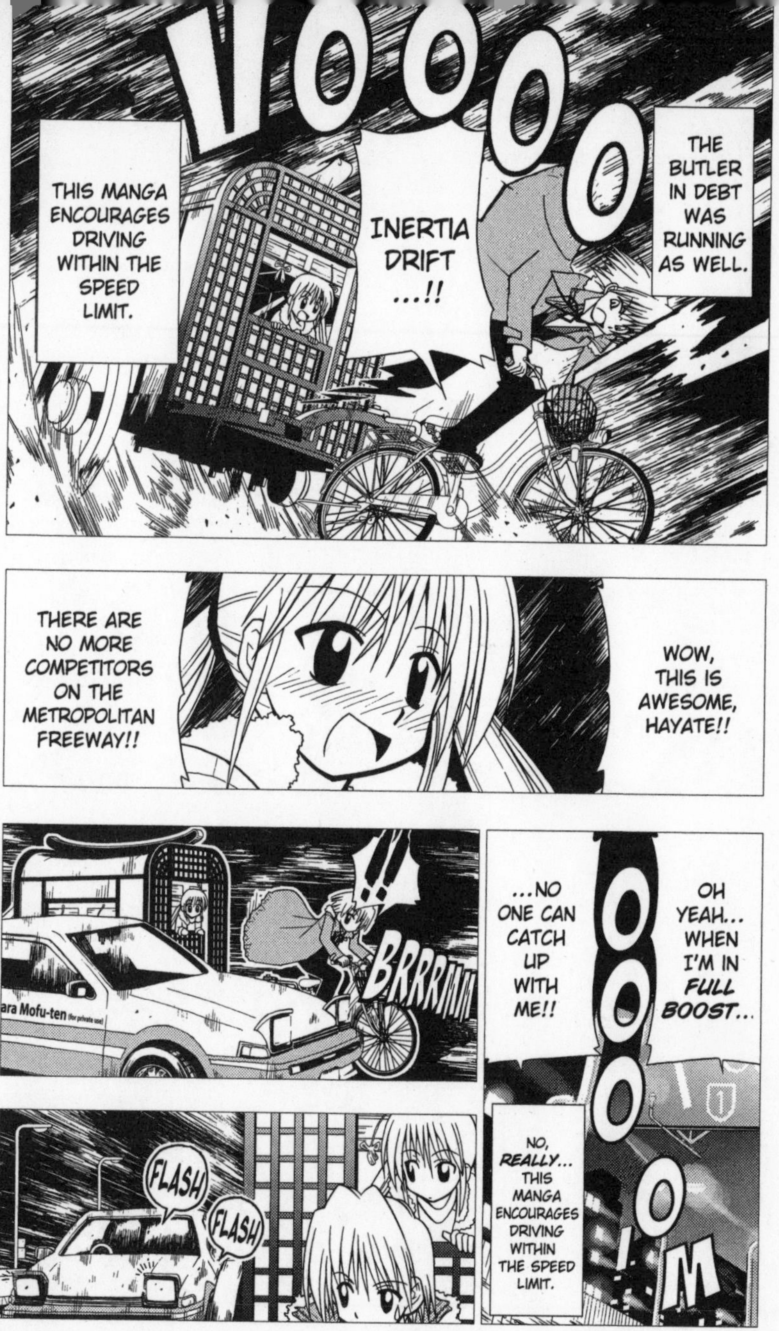
VOOOOO
THE BUTLER IN DEBT WAS RUNNING AS WELL.
INERTIA DRIFT ...!!
THIS MANGA ENCOURAGES DRIVING WITHIN THE SPEED LIMIT.
WOW, THIS IS AWESOME, HAYATE!!
THERE ARE NO MORE COMPETITORS ON THE METROPOLITAN FREEWAY!!
OH YEAH... WHEN I'M IN *FULL BOOST*...
...NO ONE CAN CATCH UP WITH ME!!
OOOOOM
NO, *REALLY*... THIS MANGA ENCOURAGES DRIVING WITHIN THE SPEED LIMIT.
!!
BRRRM
ara Mofu-ten (for private use)
FLASH
FLASH

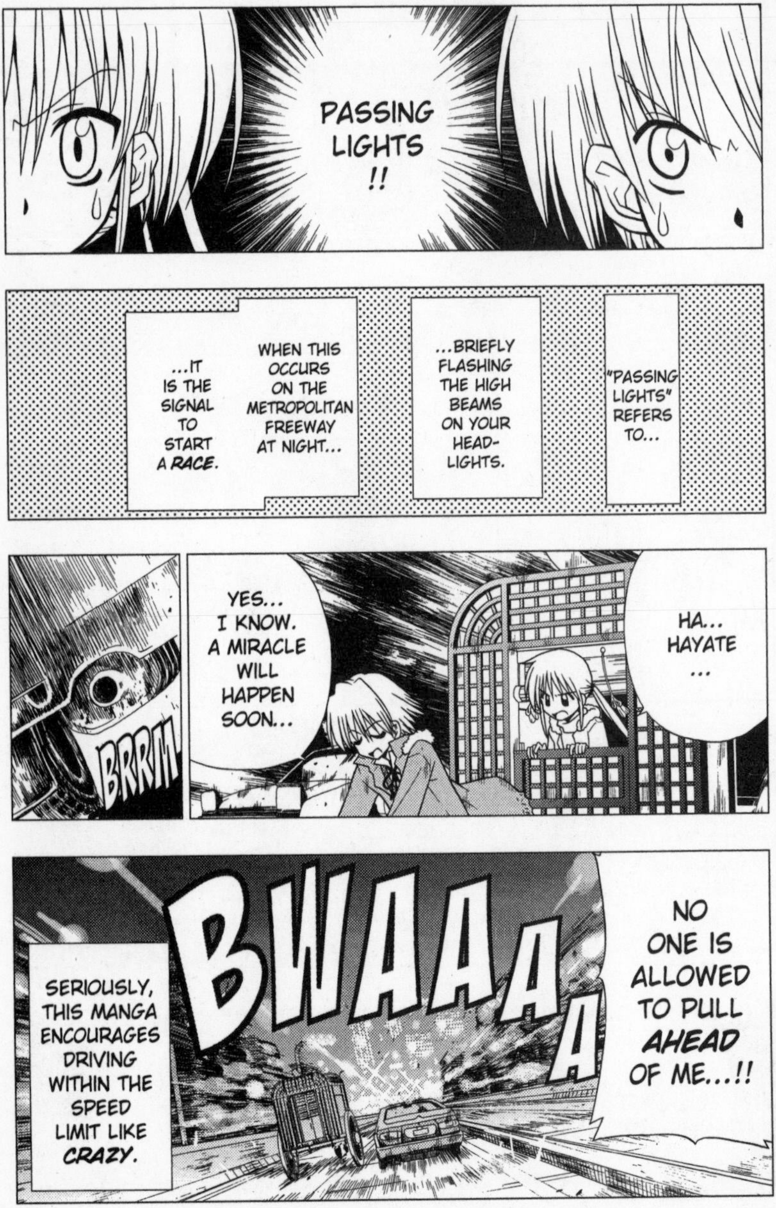
PASSING LIGHTS !!
"PASSING LIGHTS" REFERS TO...
...BRIEFLY FLASHING THE HIGH BEAMS ON YOUR HEAD-LIGHTS.
WHEN THIS OCCURS ON THE METROPOLITAN FREEWAY AT NIGHT...
...IT IS THE SIGNAL TO START A *RACE*.
HA... HAYATE ...
YES... I KNOW. A MIRACLE WILL HAPPEN SOON...
BRRM
NO ONE IS ALLOWED TO PULL *AHEAD* OF ME...!!
BWAAAAA
SERIOUSLY, THIS MANGA ENCOURAGES DRIVING WITHIN THE SPEED LIMIT LIKE *CRAZY*.

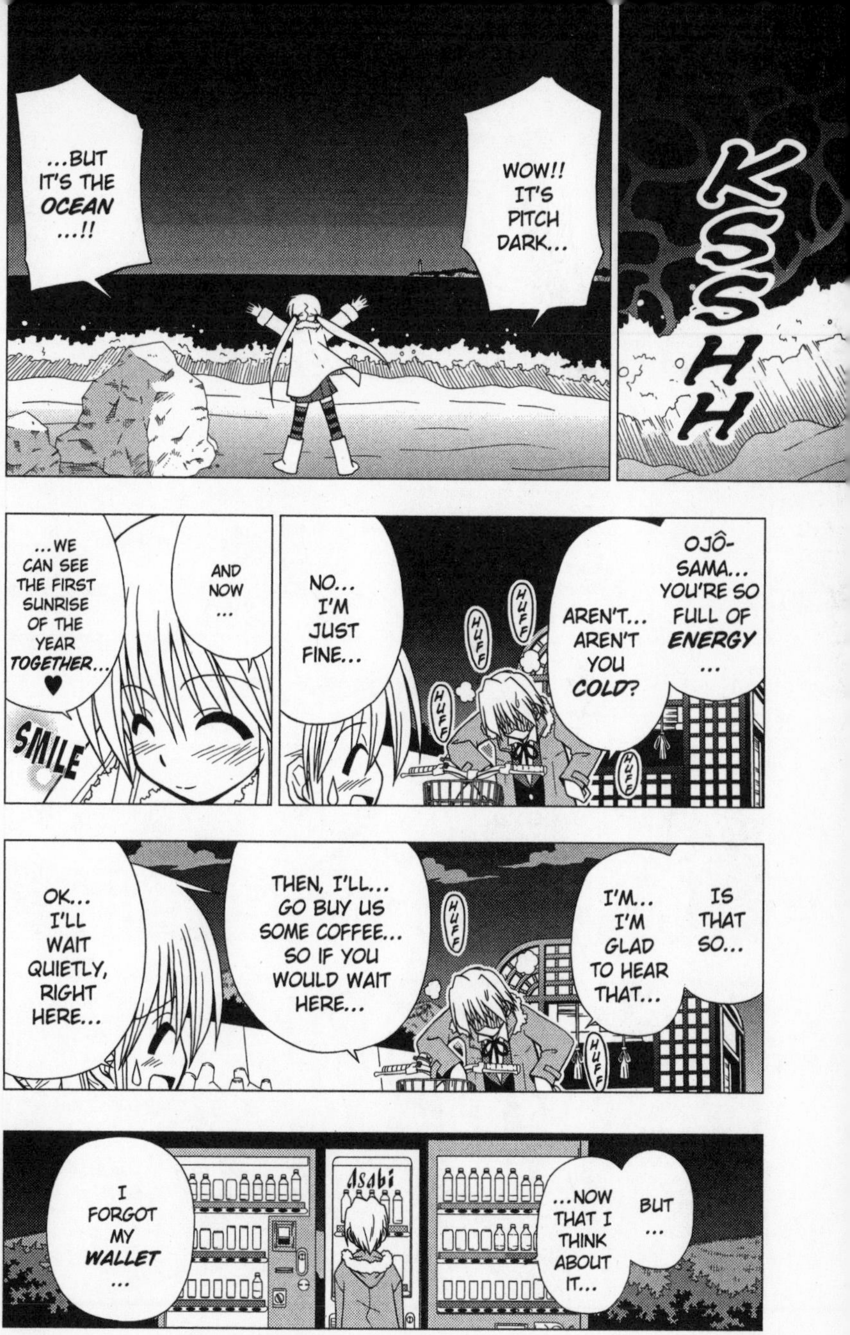
KSSHH
WOW!! IT'S PITCH DARK...
...BUT IT'S THE OCEAN ...!!
OJÔ-SAMA... YOU'RE SO FULL OF ENERGY ...
AREN'T... AREN'T YOU COLD?
HUFF
HUFF
HUFF
HUFF
NO... I'M JUST FINE...
AND NOW ...
...WE CAN SEE THE FIRST SUNRISE OF THE YEAR TOGETHER...♥
SMILE
IS THAT SO...
I'M... I'M GLAD TO HEAR THAT...
HUFF
HUFF
THEN, I'LL... GO BUY US SOME COFFEE... SO IF YOU WOULD WAIT HERE...
OK... I'LL WAIT QUIETLY, RIGHT HERE...
BUT ...
...NOW THAT I THINK ABOUT IT...
Asahi
I FORGOT MY WALLET ...

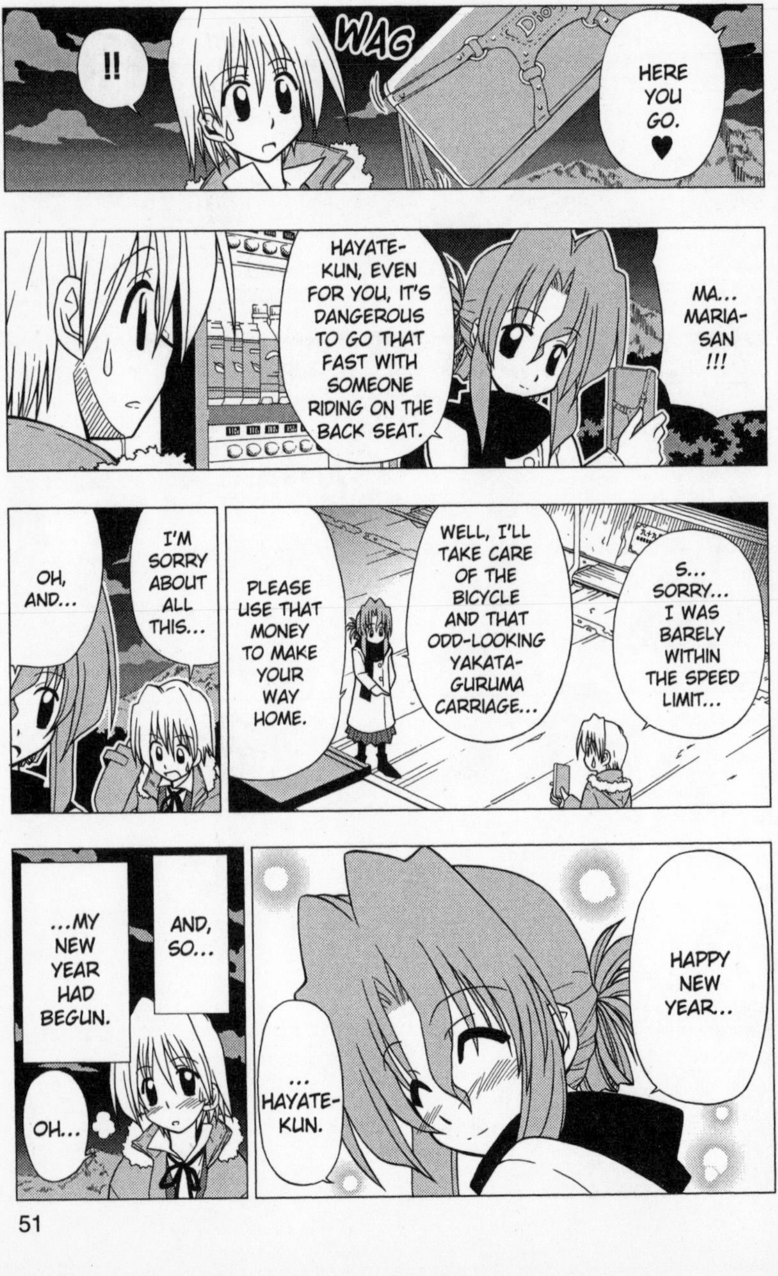
HERE YOU GO. ♥
WAG
!!
MA... MARIA-SAN !!!
HAYATE-KUN, EVEN FOR YOU, IT'S DANGEROUS TO GO THAT FAST WITH SOMEONE RIDING ON THE BACK SEAT.
S... SORRY... I WAS BARELY WITHIN THE SPEED LIMIT...
WELL, I'LL TAKE CARE OF THE BICYCLE AND THAT ODD-LOOKING YAKATA-GURUMA CARRIAGE...
PLEASE USE THAT MONEY TO MAKE YOUR WAY HOME.
I'M SORRY ABOUT ALL THIS...
OH, AND...
HAPPY NEW YEAR...
... HAYATE-KUN.
AND, SO...
...MY NEW YEAR HAD BEGUN.
OH...

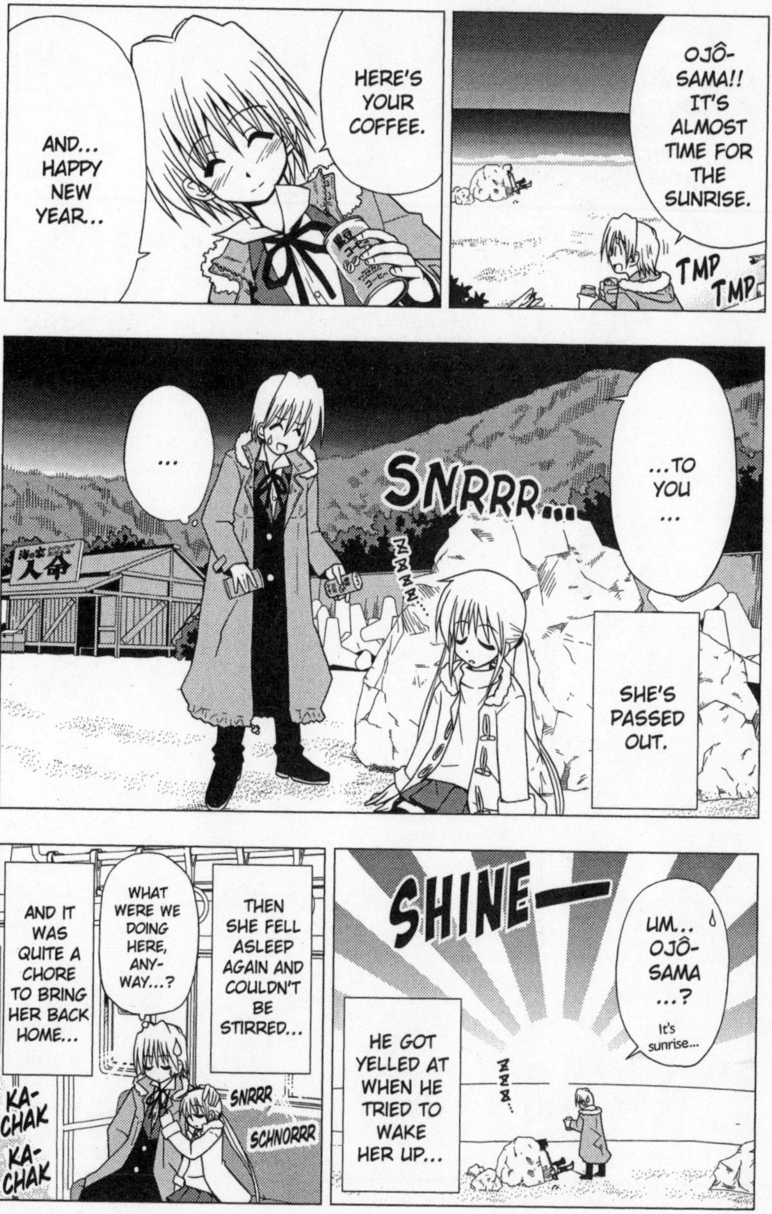
OJÔ-SAMA!! IT'S ALMOST TIME FOR THE SUNRISE.
TMP TMP
HERE'S YOUR COFFEE.
AND... HAPPY NEW YEAR...
...TO YOU ...
SNRRR...
...
SHE'S PASSED OUT.
SHINE—
UM... OJÔ-SAMA ...?
It's sunrise...
HE GOT YELLED AT WHEN HE TRIED TO WAKE HER UP...
THEN SHE FELL ASLEEP AGAIN AND COULDN'T BE STIRRED...
WHAT WERE WE DOING HERE, ANY-WAY...?
AND IT WAS QUITE A CHORE TO BRING HER BACK HOME...
SNRRR
SCHNORRR
KA-CHAK KA-CHAK

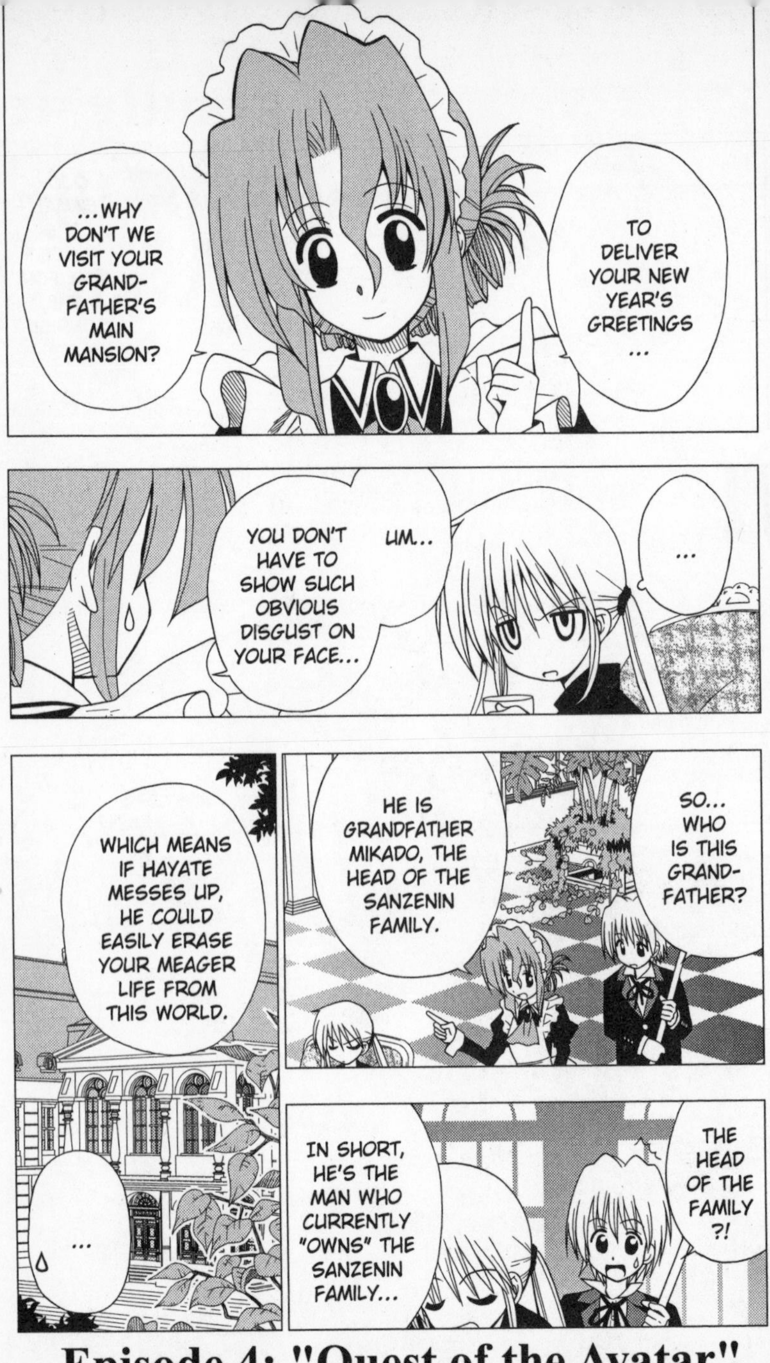
TO DELIVER YOUR NEW YEAR'S GREETINGS...
...WHY DON'T WE VISIT YOUR GRAND-FATHER'S MAIN MANSION?
...
UM...
YOU DON'T HAVE TO SHOW SUCH OBVIOUS DISGUST ON YOUR FACE...
SO... WHO IS THIS GRAND-FATHER?
HE IS GRANDFATHER MIKADO, THE HEAD OF THE SANZENIN FAMILY.
THE HEAD OF THE FAMILY?!
IN SHORT, HE'S THE MAN WHO CURRENTLY "OWNS" THE SANZENIN FAMILY...
WHICH MEANS IF HAYATE MESSES UP, HE COULD EASILY ERASE YOUR MEAGER LIFE FROM THIS WORLD.
...

Episode 4: "Quest of the Avatar"

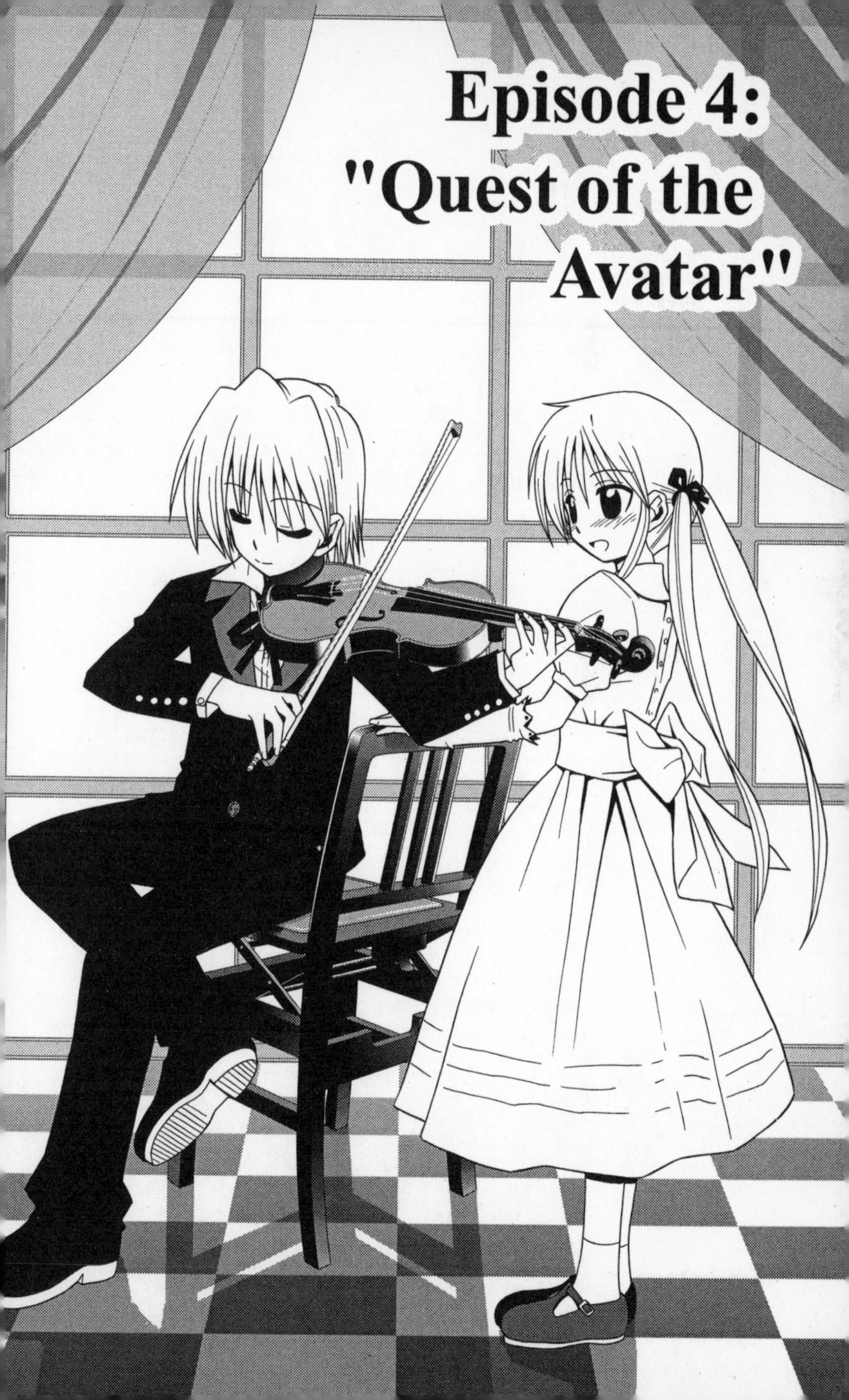
Episode 4:
"Quest of the
Avatar"

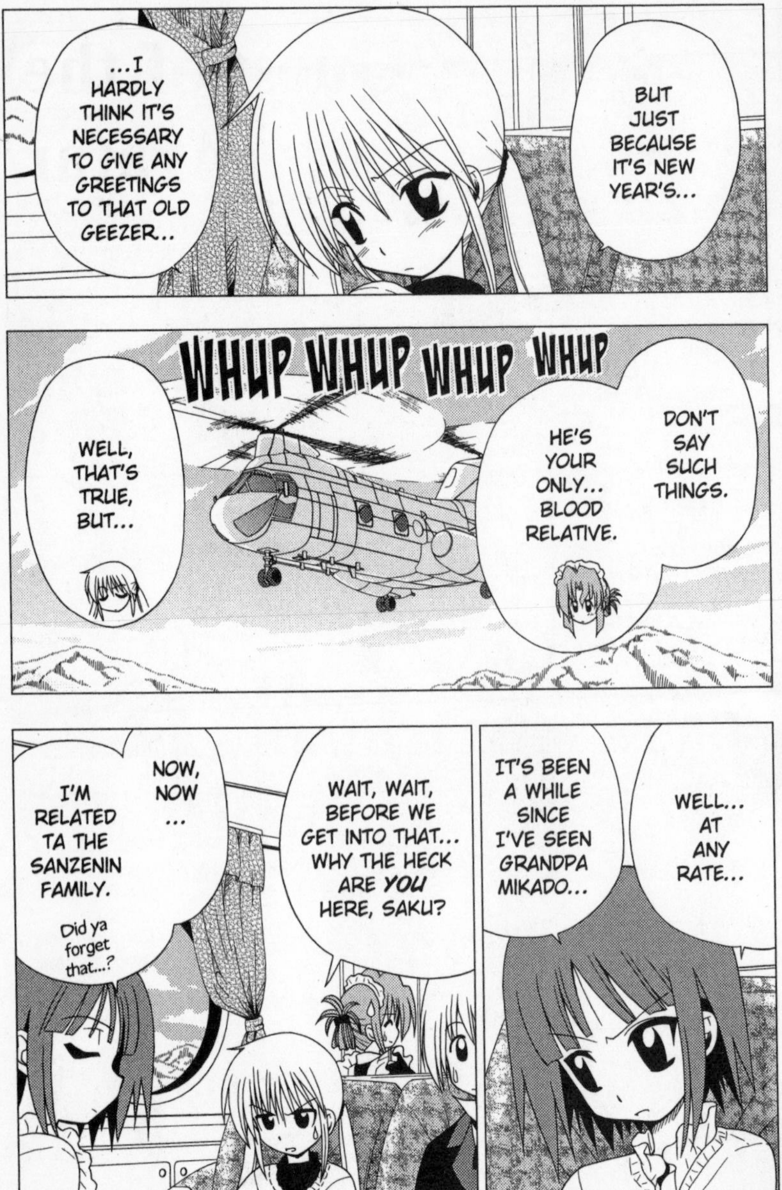
BUT JUST BECAUSE IT'S NEW YEAR'S...
...I HARDLY THINK IT'S NECESSARY TO GIVE ANY GREETINGS TO THAT OLD GEEZER...
WHUP WHUP WHUP WHUP
DON'T SAY SUCH THINGS.
HE'S YOUR ONLY... BLOOD RELATIVE.
WELL, THAT'S TRUE, BUT...
WELL... AT ANY RATE...
IT'S BEEN A WHILE SINCE I'VE SEEN GRANDPA MIKADO...
WAIT, WAIT, BEFORE WE GET INTO THAT... WHY THE HECK ARE *YOU* HERE, SAKU?
NOW, NOW ...
I'M RELATED TA THE SANZENIN FAMILY.
Did ya forget that...?

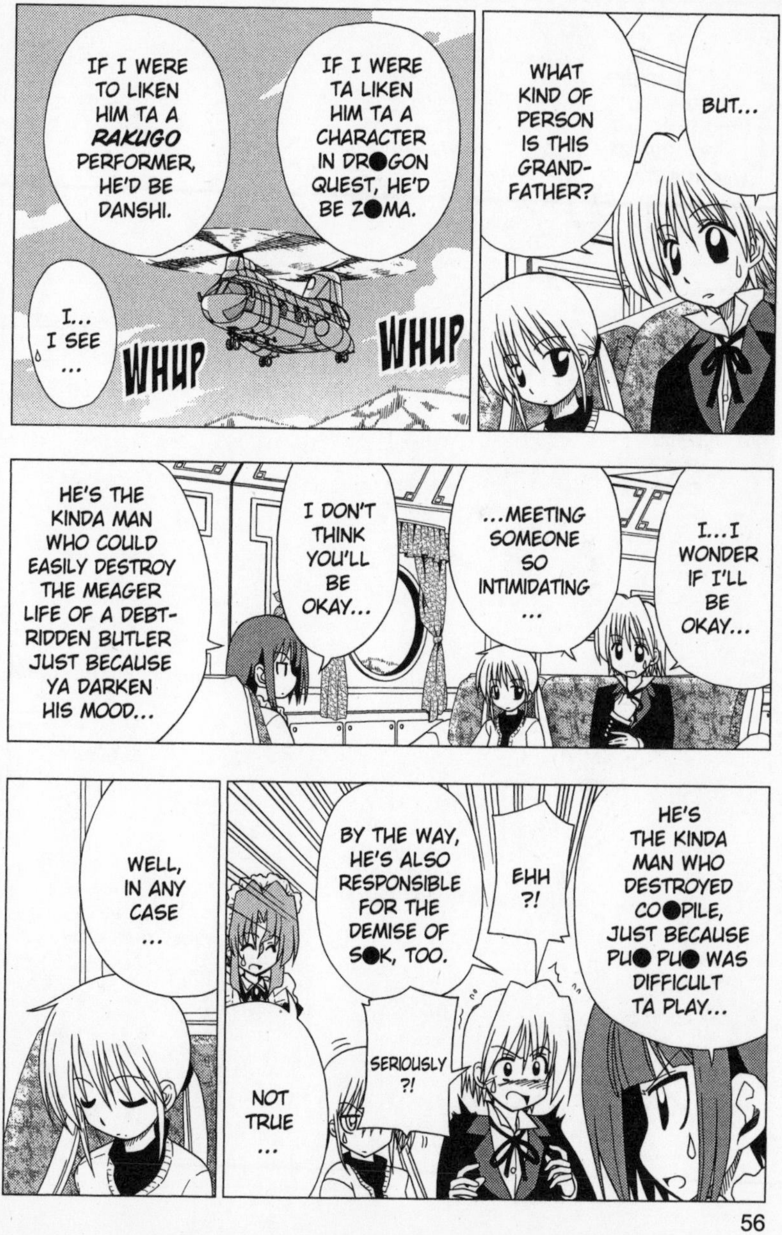
BUT...
WHAT KIND OF PERSON IS THIS GRANDFATHER?
IF I WERE TA LIKEN HIM TA A CHARACTER IN DR●GON QUEST, HE'D BE Z●MA.
IF I WERE TO LIKEN HIM TA A *RAKUGO* PERFORMER, HE'D BE DANSHI.
WHUP
WHUP
I... I SEE ...
I...I WONDER IF I'LL BE OKAY...
...MEETING SOMEONE SO INTIMIDATING ...
I DON'T THINK YOU'LL BE OKAY...
HE'S THE KINDA MAN WHO COULD EASILY DESTROY THE MEAGER LIFE OF A DEBT-RIDDEN BUTLER JUST BECAUSE YA DARKEN HIS MOOD...
HE'S THE KINDA MAN WHO DESTROYED CO●PILE, JUST BECAUSE PU● PU● WAS DIFFICULT TA PLAY...
EHH ?!
BY THE WAY, HE'S ALSO RESPONSIBLE FOR THE DEMISE OF S●K, TOO.
SERIOUSLY ?!
NOT TRUE ...
WELL, IN ANY CASE ...

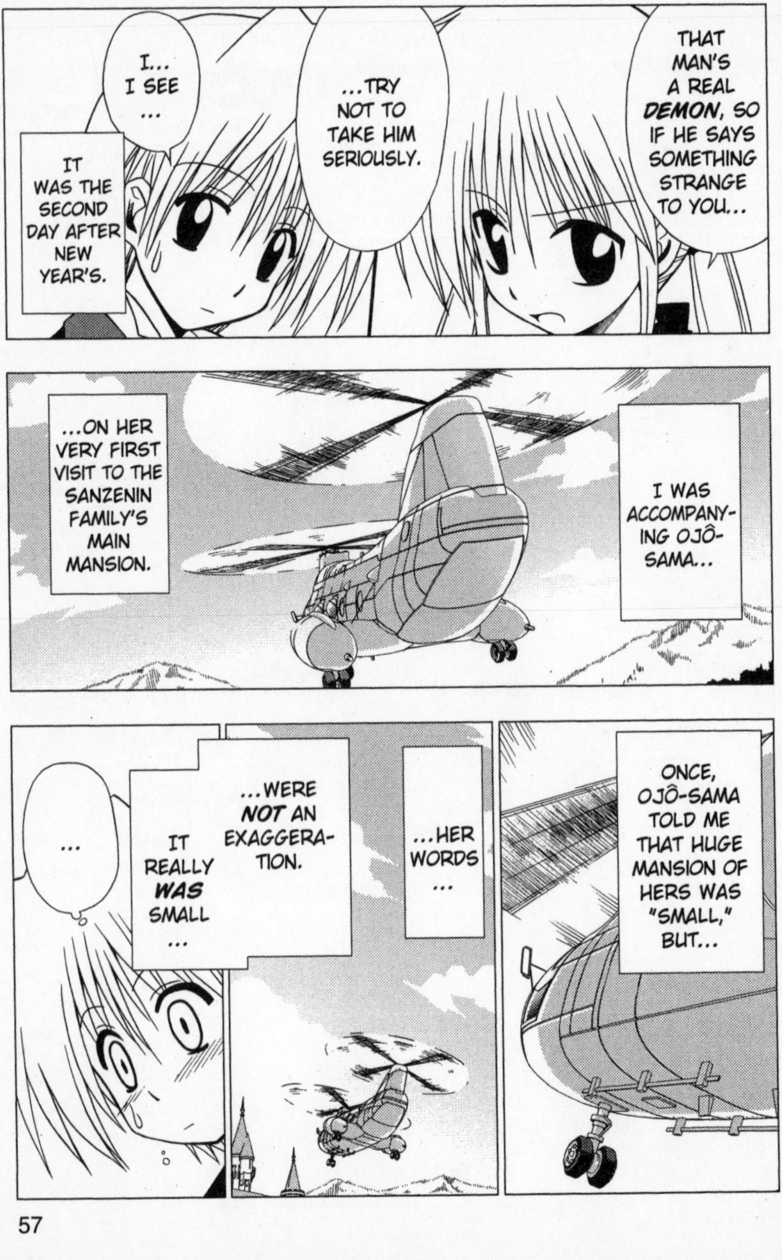
THAT MAN'S A REAL **DEMON**, SO IF HE SAYS SOMETHING STRANGE TO YOU...
...TRY NOT TO TAKE HIM SERIOUSLY.
I... I SEE ...
IT WAS THE SECOND DAY AFTER NEW YEAR'S.
I WAS ACCOMPANYING OJÔ-SAMA...
...ON HER VERY FIRST VISIT TO THE SANZENIN FAMILY'S MAIN MANSION.
ONCE, OJÔ-SAMA TOLD ME THAT HUGE MANSION OF HERS WAS "SMALL," BUT...
...HER WORDS ...
...WERE **NOT** AN EXAGGERA-TION.
IT REALLY **WAS** SMALL ...
...

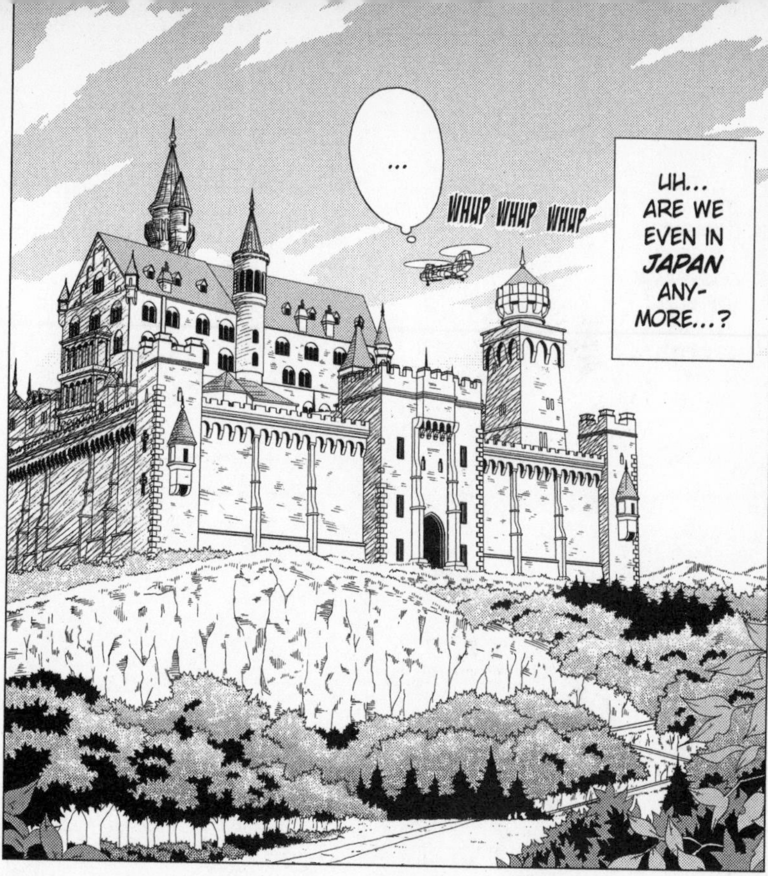
UH... ARE WE EVEN IN JAPAN ANY-MORE...?
...
WHUP WHUP WHUP
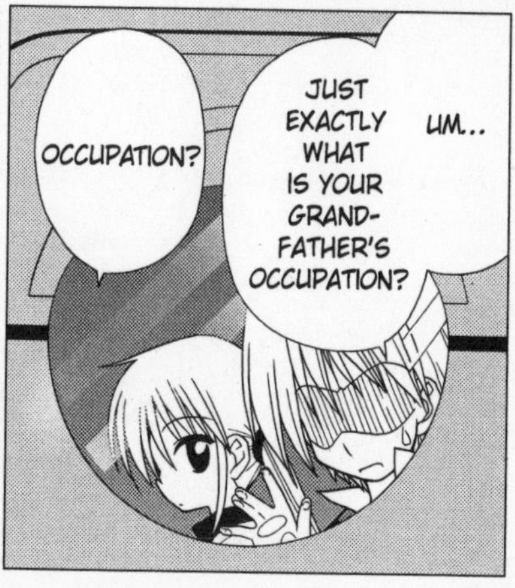
UM...
JUST EXACTLY WHAT IS YOUR GRAND-FATHER'S OCCUPATION?
OCCUPATION?
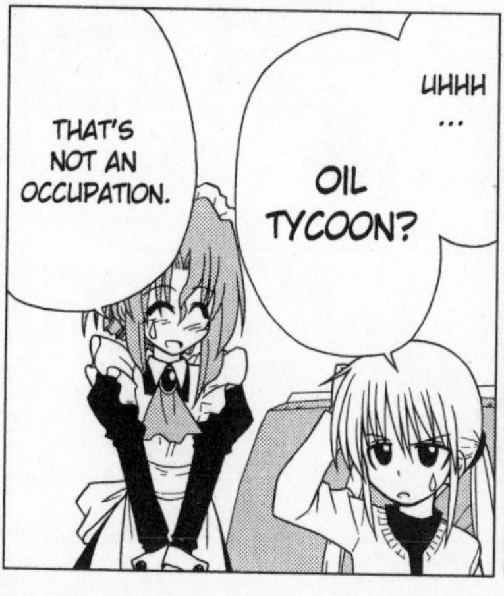
UHHH ...
OIL TYCOON?
THAT'S NOT AN OCCUPATION.

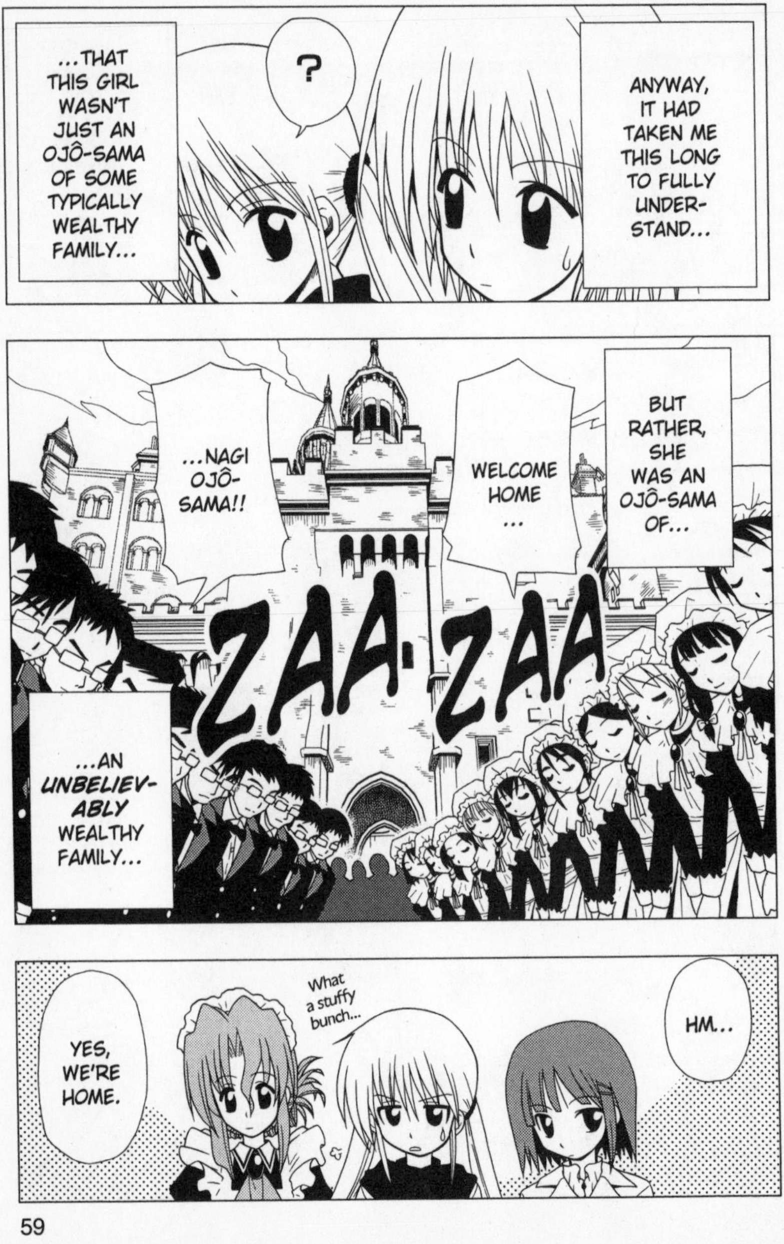
ANYWAY, IT HAD TAKEN ME THIS LONG TO FULLY UNDERSTAND...
?
...THAT THIS GIRL WASN'T JUST AN OJÔ-SAMA OF SOME TYPICALLY WEALTHY FAMILY...
BUT RATHER, SHE WAS AN OJÔ-SAMA OF...
WELCOME HOME ...
...NAGI OJÔ-SAMA!!
ZAA ZAA
...AN *UNBELIEVABLY* WEALTHY FAMILY...
HM...
What a stuffy bunch...
YES, WE'RE HOME.

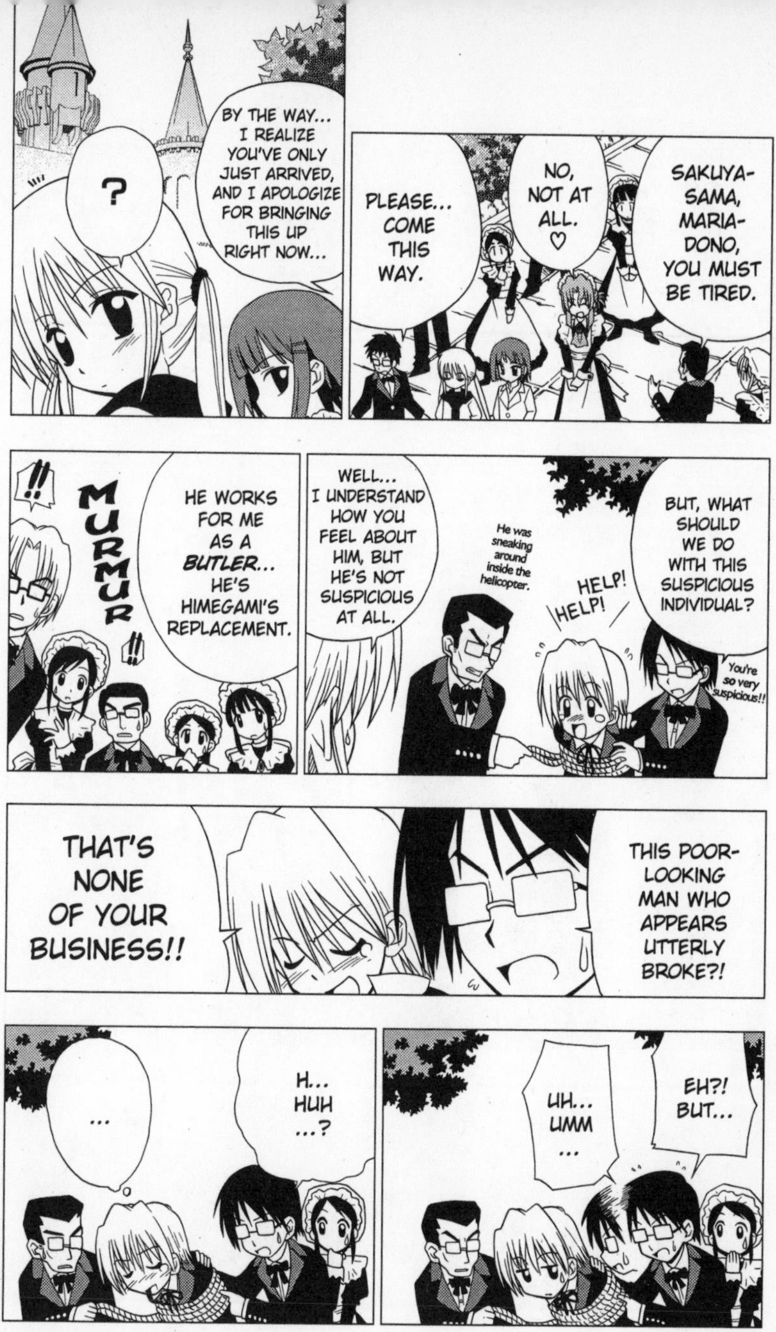
SAKUYA-SAMA, MARIA-DONO, YOU MUST BE TIRED.
NO, NOT AT ALL. ♡
PLEASE... COME THIS WAY.
BY THE WAY... I REALIZE YOU'VE ONLY JUST ARRIVED, AND I APOLOGIZE FOR BRINGING THIS UP RIGHT NOW...
?
BUT, WHAT SHOULD WE DO WITH THIS SUSPICIOUS INDIVIDUAL?
You're so very suspicious!!
HELP! HELP!
He was sneaking around inside the helicopter.
WELL... I UNDERSTAND HOW YOU FEEL ABOUT HIM, BUT HE'S NOT SUSPICIOUS AT ALL.
HE WORKS FOR ME AS A *BUTLER*... HE'S HIMEGAMI'S REPLACEMENT.
MURMUR
!!
!!
THIS POOR-LOOKING MAN WHO APPEARS UTTERLY BROKE?!
THAT'S NONE OF YOUR BUSINESS!!
EH?! BUT...
UH... UMM ...
H... HUH ...?
...

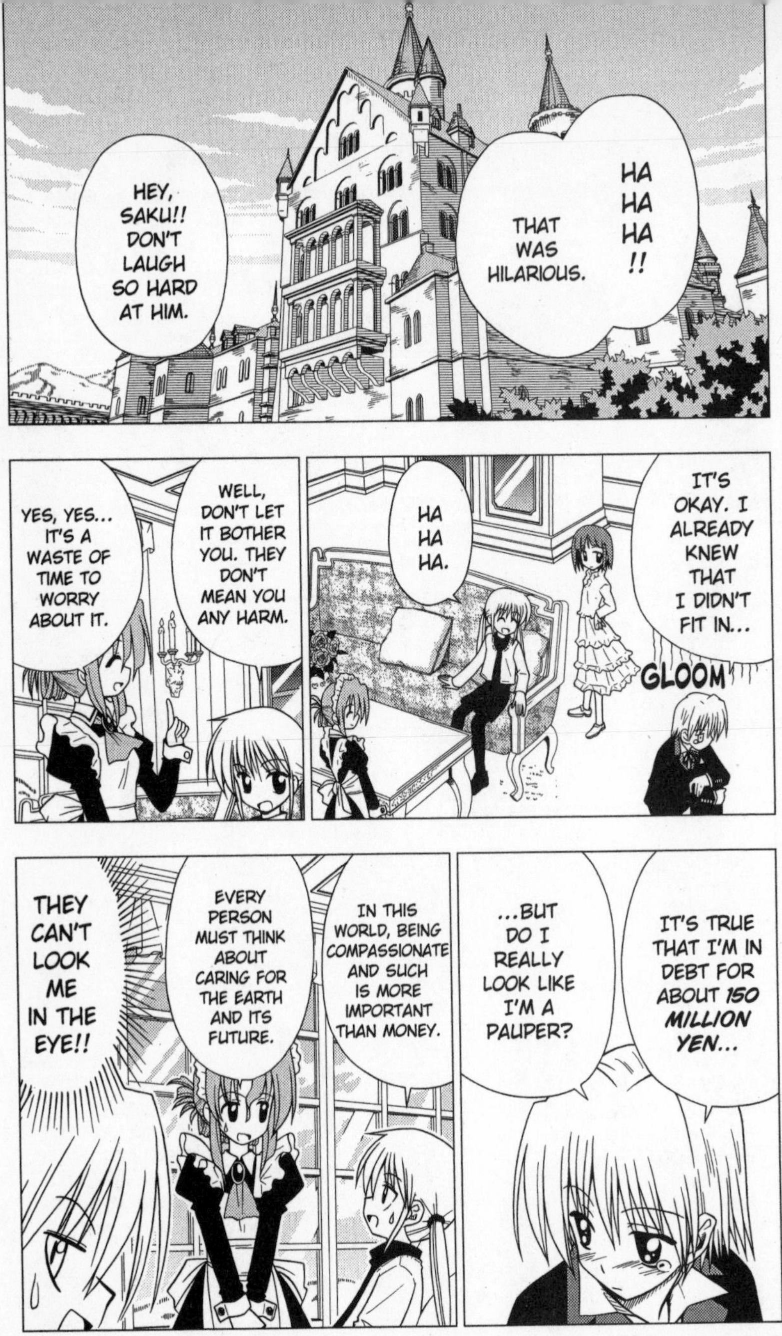
HA HA HA!!
THAT WAS HILARIOUS.
HEY, SAKU!! DON'T LAUGH SO HARD AT HIM.
IT'S OKAY. I ALREADY KNEW THAT I DIDN'T FIT IN...
GLOOM
HA HA HA.
WELL, DON'T LET IT BOTHER YOU. THEY DON'T MEAN YOU ANY HARM.
YES, YES... IT'S A WASTE OF TIME TO WORRY ABOUT IT.
IT'S TRUE THAT I'M IN DEBT FOR ABOUT *150 MILLION YEN*...
...BUT DO I REALLY LOOK LIKE I'M A PAUPER?
IN THIS WORLD, BEING COMPASSIONATE AND SUCH IS MORE IMPORTANT THAN MONEY.
EVERY PERSON MUST THINK ABOUT CARING FOR THE EARTH AND ITS FUTURE.
THEY CAN'T LOOK ME IN THE EYE!!

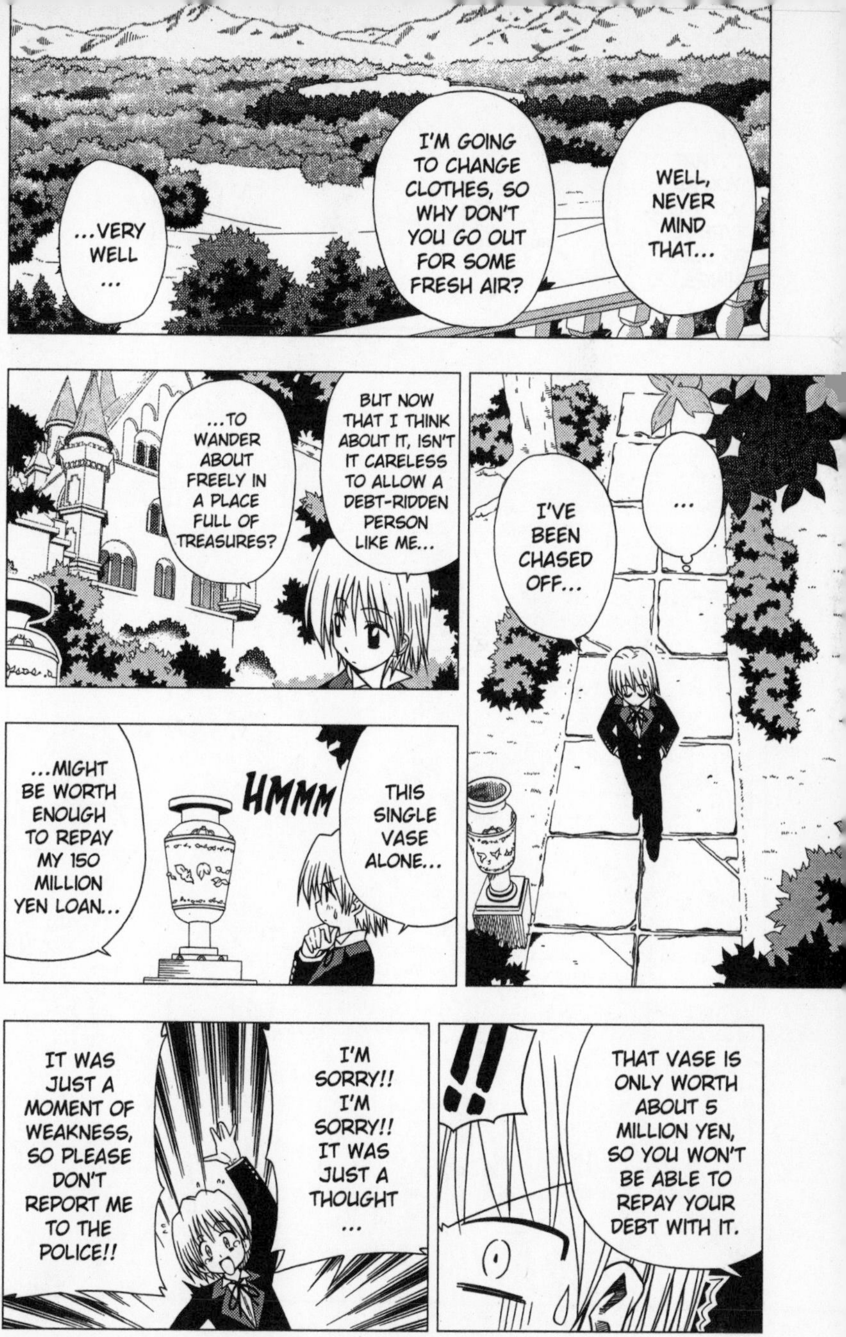
WELL, NEVER MIND THAT...
I'M GOING TO CHANGE CLOTHES, SO WHY DON'T YOU GO OUT FOR SOME FRESH AIR?
...VERY WELL ...
...
I'VE BEEN CHASED OFF...
BUT NOW THAT I THINK ABOUT IT, ISN'T IT CARELESS TO ALLOW A DEBT-RIDDEN PERSON LIKE ME...
...TO WANDER ABOUT FREELY IN A PLACE FULL OF TREASURES?
THIS SINGLE VASE ALONE...
HMMM
...MIGHT BE WORTH ENOUGH TO REPAY MY 150 MILLION YEN LOAN...
THAT VASE IS ONLY WORTH ABOUT 5 MILLION YEN, SO YOU WON'T BE ABLE TO REPAY YOUR DEBT WITH IT.
!!
I'M SORRY!! I'M SORRY!! IT WAS JUST A THOUGHT ...
IT WAS JUST A MOMENT OF WEAKNESS, SO PLEASE DON'T REPORT ME TO THE POLICE!!

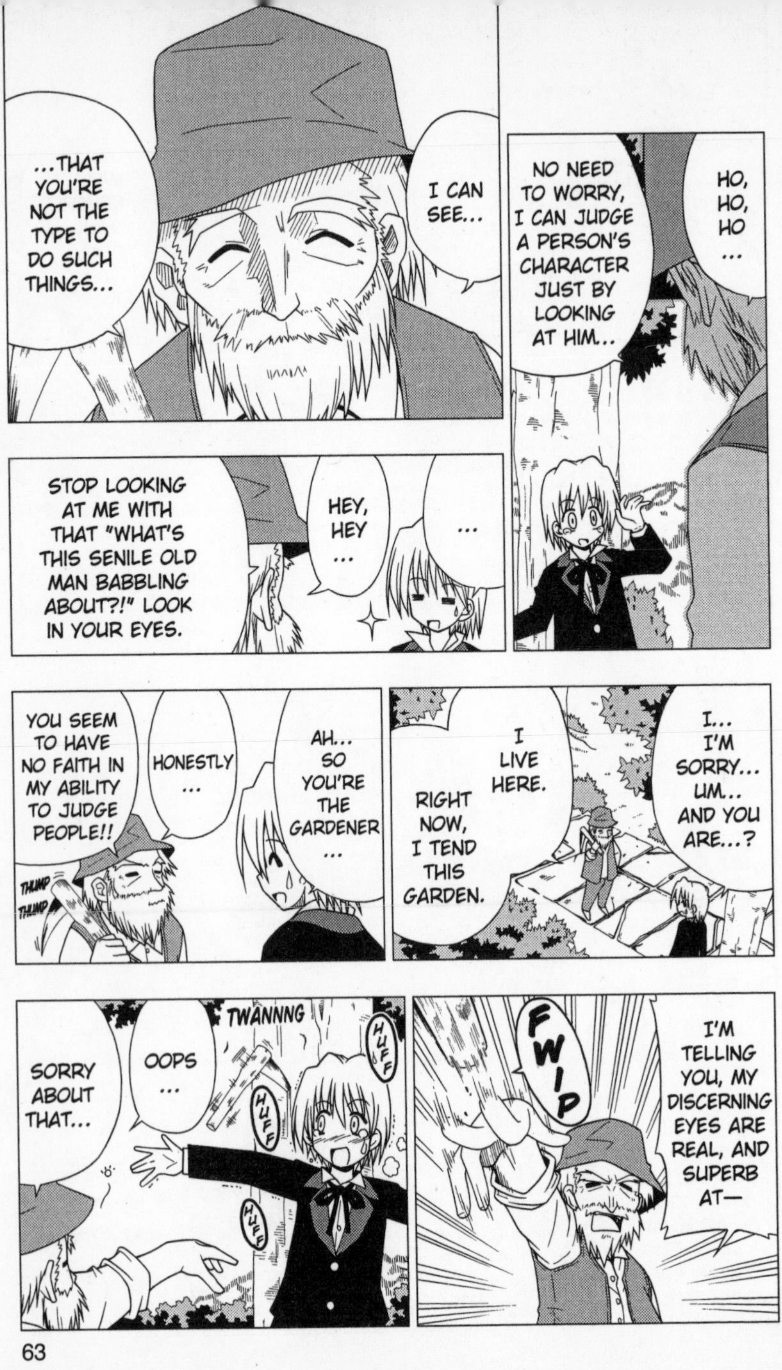
HO, HO, HO...
NO NEED TO WORRY, I CAN JUDGE A PERSON'S CHARACTER JUST BY LOOKING AT HIM...
I CAN SEE...
...THAT YOU'RE NOT THE TYPE TO DO SUCH THINGS...
...
HEY, HEY...
STOP LOOKING AT ME WITH THAT "WHAT'S THIS SENILE OLD MAN BABBLING ABOUT?!" LOOK IN YOUR EYES.
I... I'M SORRY... UM... AND YOU ARE...?
I LIVE HERE.
RIGHT NOW, I TEND THIS GARDEN.
AH... SO YOU'RE THE GARDENER...
HONESTLY...
YOU SEEM TO HAVE NO FAITH IN MY ABILITY TO JUDGE PEOPLE!!
THUMP THUMP
I'M TELLING YOU, MY DISCERNING EYES ARE REAL, AND SUPERB AT—
FWIP
HUFF
HUFF
HUFF
TWANNNG
OOPS...
SORRY ABOUT THAT...

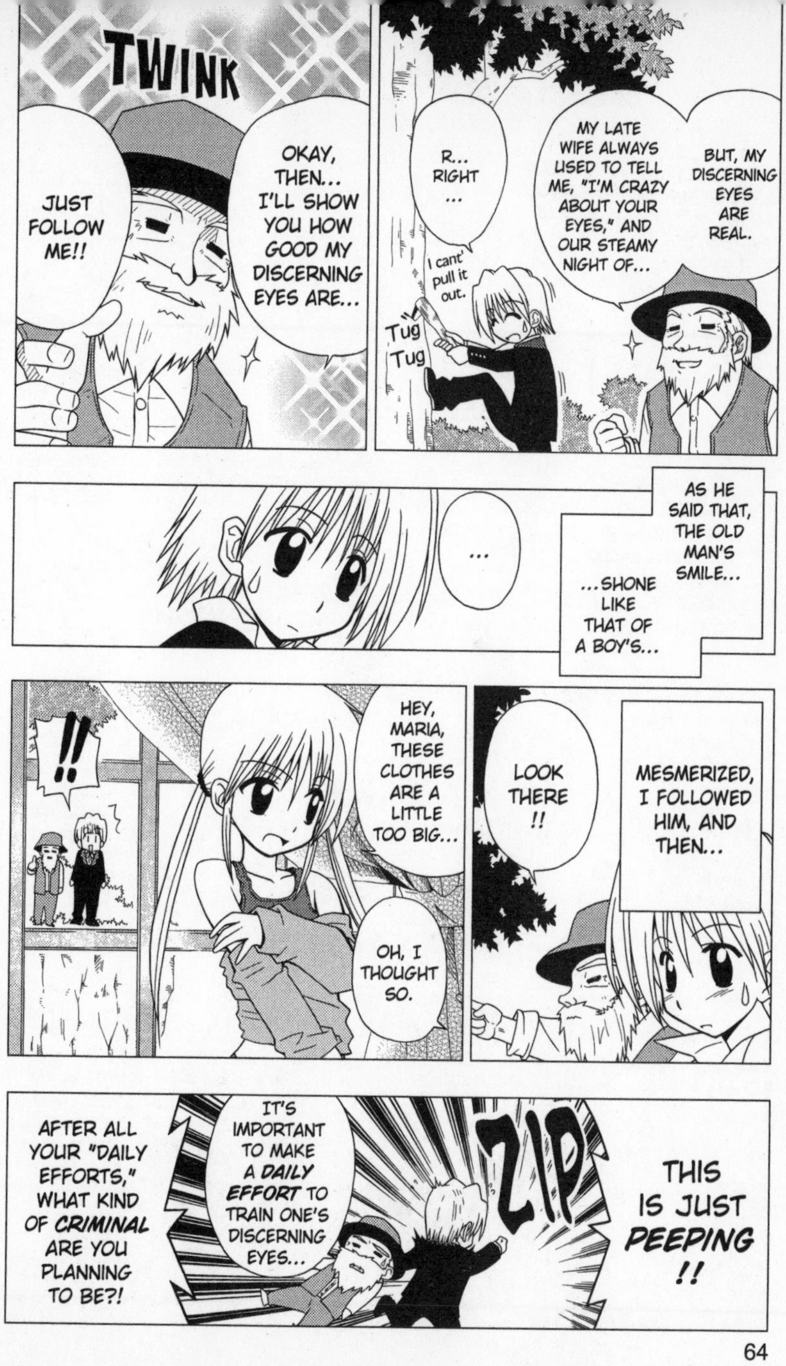
BUT, MY DISCERNING EYES ARE REAL.
MY LATE WIFE ALWAYS USED TO TELL ME, "I'M CRAZY ABOUT YOUR EYES," AND OUR STEAMY NIGHT OF...
I cant' pull it out.
Tug Tug
R... RIGHT ...
TWINK
OKAY, THEN... I'LL SHOW YOU HOW GOOD MY DISCERNING EYES ARE...
JUST FOLLOW ME!!
AS HE SAID THAT, THE OLD MAN'S SMILE...
...SHONE LIKE THAT OF A BOY'S...
...
MESMERIZED, I FOLLOWED HIM, AND THEN...
LOOK THERE !!
HEY, MARIA, THESE CLOTHES ARE A LITTLE TOO BIG...
OH, I THOUGHT SO.
!!
THIS IS JUST *PEEPING* !!
ZIP
IT'S IMPORTANT TO MAKE A *DAILY EFFORT* TO TRAIN ONE'S DISCERNING EYES...
AFTER ALL YOUR "DAILY EFFORTS," WHAT KIND OF *CRIMINAL* ARE YOU PLANNING TO BE?!

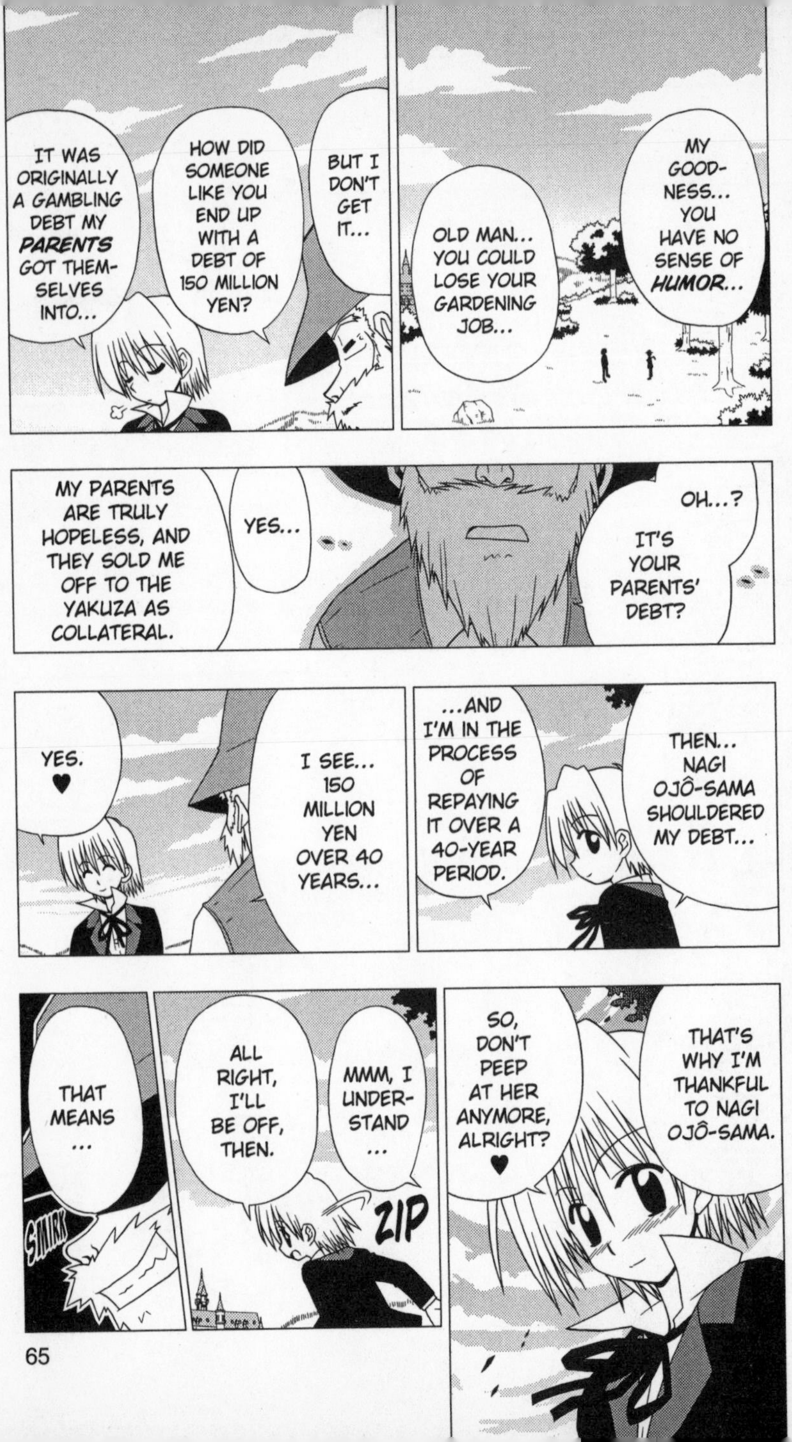
MY GOODNESS... YOU HAVE NO SENSE OF *HUMOR*...
OLD MAN... YOU COULD LOSE YOUR GARDENING JOB...
BUT I DON'T GET IT...
HOW DID SOMEONE LIKE YOU END UP WITH A DEBT OF 150 MILLION YEN?
IT WAS ORIGINALLY A GAMBLING DEBT MY *PARENTS* GOT THEMSELVES INTO...
OH...? IT'S YOUR PARENTS' DEBT?
YES...
MY PARENTS ARE TRULY HOPELESS, AND THEY SOLD ME OFF TO THE YAKUZA AS COLLATERAL.
THEN... NAGI OJÔ-SAMA SHOULDERED MY DEBT...
...AND I'M IN THE PROCESS OF REPAYING IT OVER A 40-YEAR PERIOD.
I SEE... 150 MILLION YEN OVER 40 YEARS...
YES. ♥
THAT'S WHY I'M THANKFUL TO NAGI OJÔ-SAMA.
SO, DON'T PEEP AT HER ANYMORE, ALRIGHT? ♥
MMM, I UNDERSTAND...
ALL RIGHT, I'LL BE OFF, THEN.
ZIP
THAT MEANS...
SMIRK

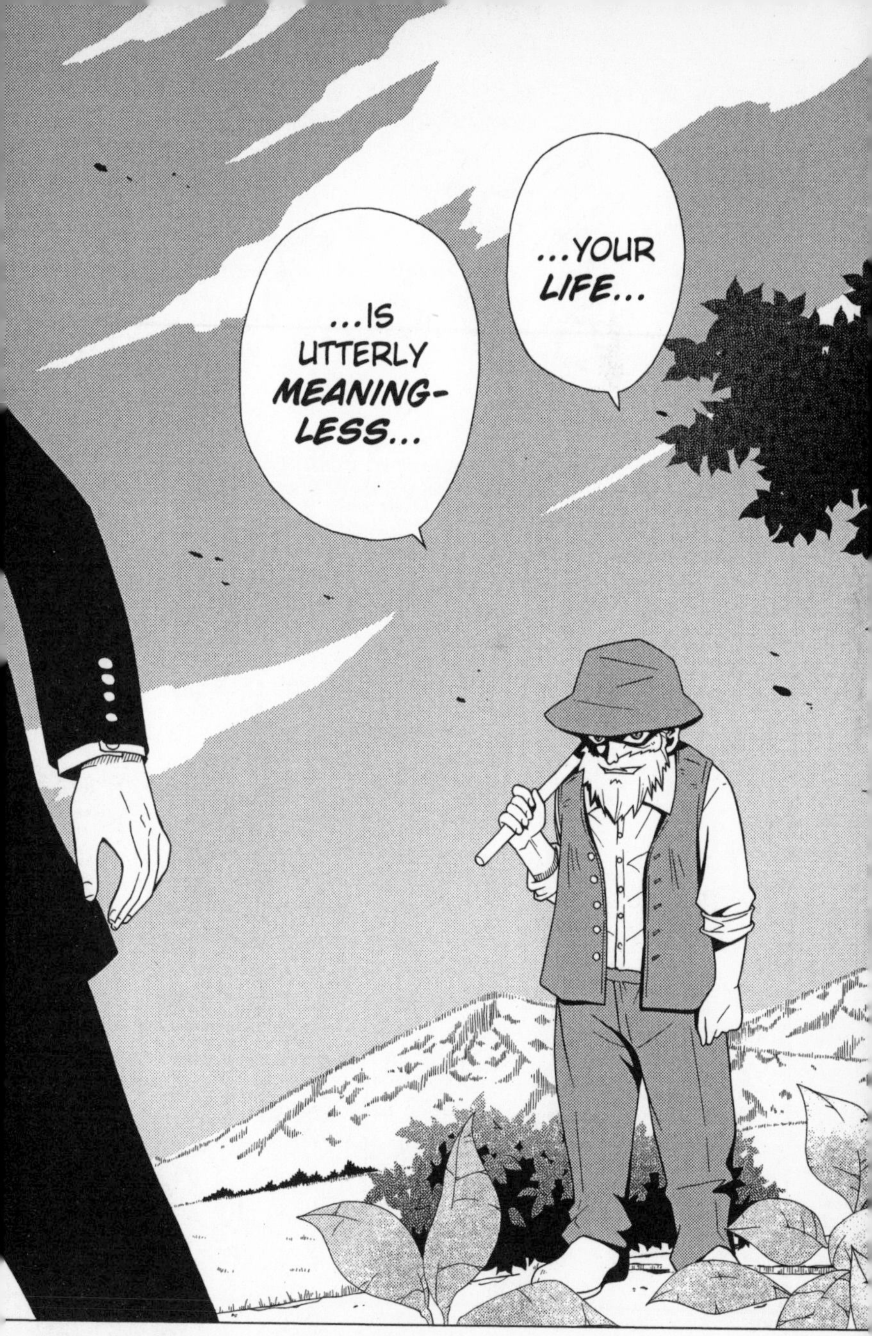
...YOUR LIFE...
...IS UTTERLY MEANING-LESS...

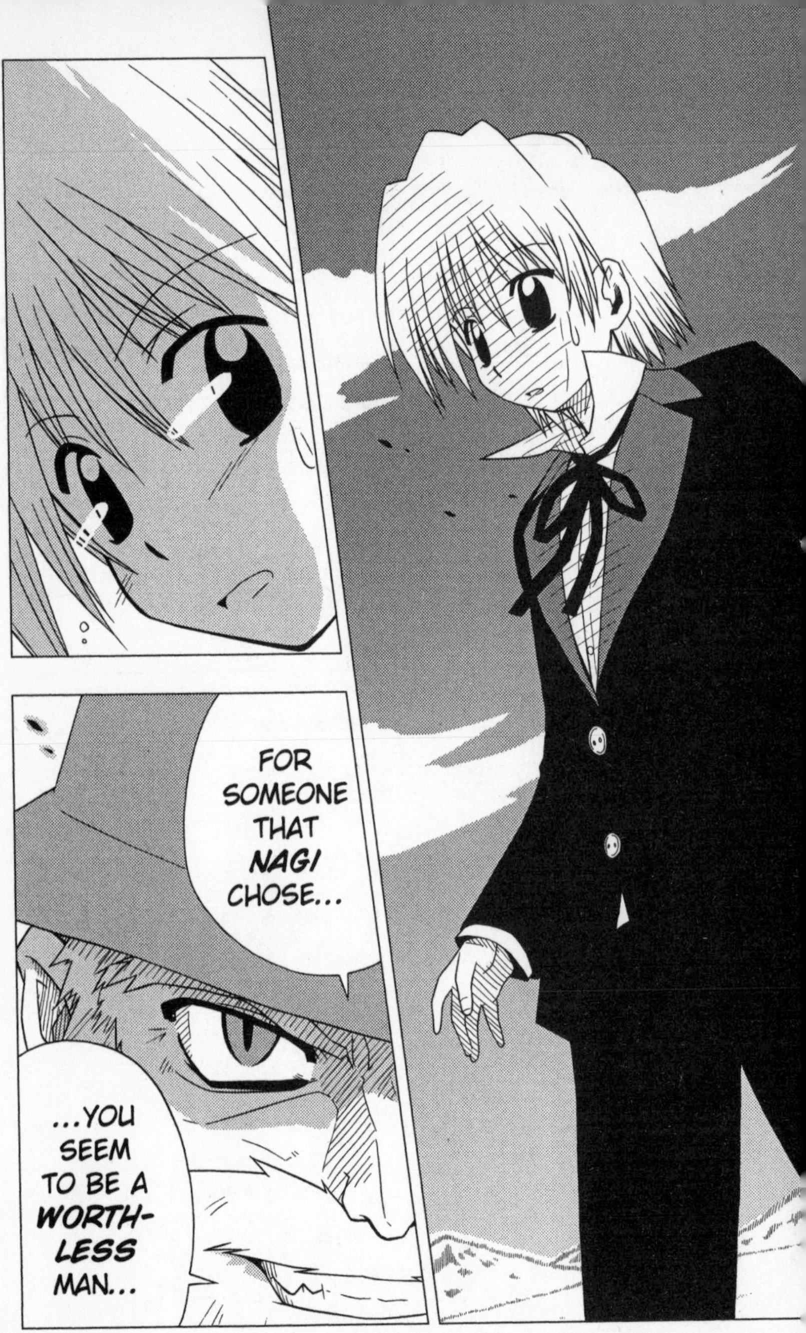
FOR SOMEONE THAT NAGI CHOSE...
...YOU SEEM TO BE A WORTH-LESS MAN...

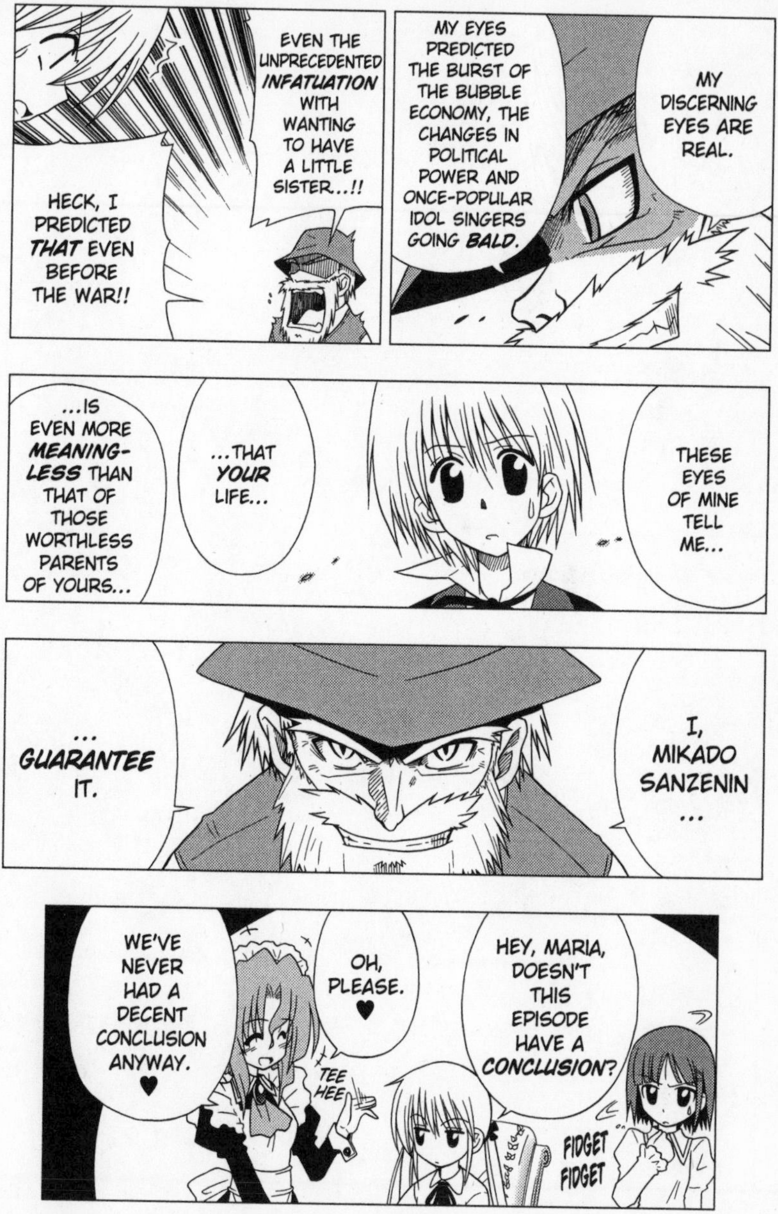
MY DISCERNING EYES ARE REAL.
MY EYES PREDICTED THE BURST OF THE BUBBLE ECONOMY, THE CHANGES IN POLITICAL POWER AND ONCE-POPULAR IDOL SINGERS GOING *BALD*.
EVEN THE UNPRECEDENTED *INFATUATION* WITH WANTING TO HAVE A LITTLE SISTER...!!
HECK, I PREDICTED *THAT* EVEN BEFORE THE WAR!!
THESE EYES OF MINE TELL ME...
...THAT *YOUR* LIFE...
...IS EVEN MORE *MEANINGLESS* THAN THAT OF THOSE WORTHLESS PARENTS OF YOURS...
I, MIKADO SANZENIN ...
... **GUARANTEE** IT.
HEY, MARIA, DOESN'T THIS EPISODE HAVE A *CONCLUSION*?
FIDGET FIDGET
OH, PLEASE. ♥
TEE HEE
WE'VE NEVER HAD A DECENT CONCLUSION ANYWAY. ♥

Episode 5: "How Much Is Your Life?"

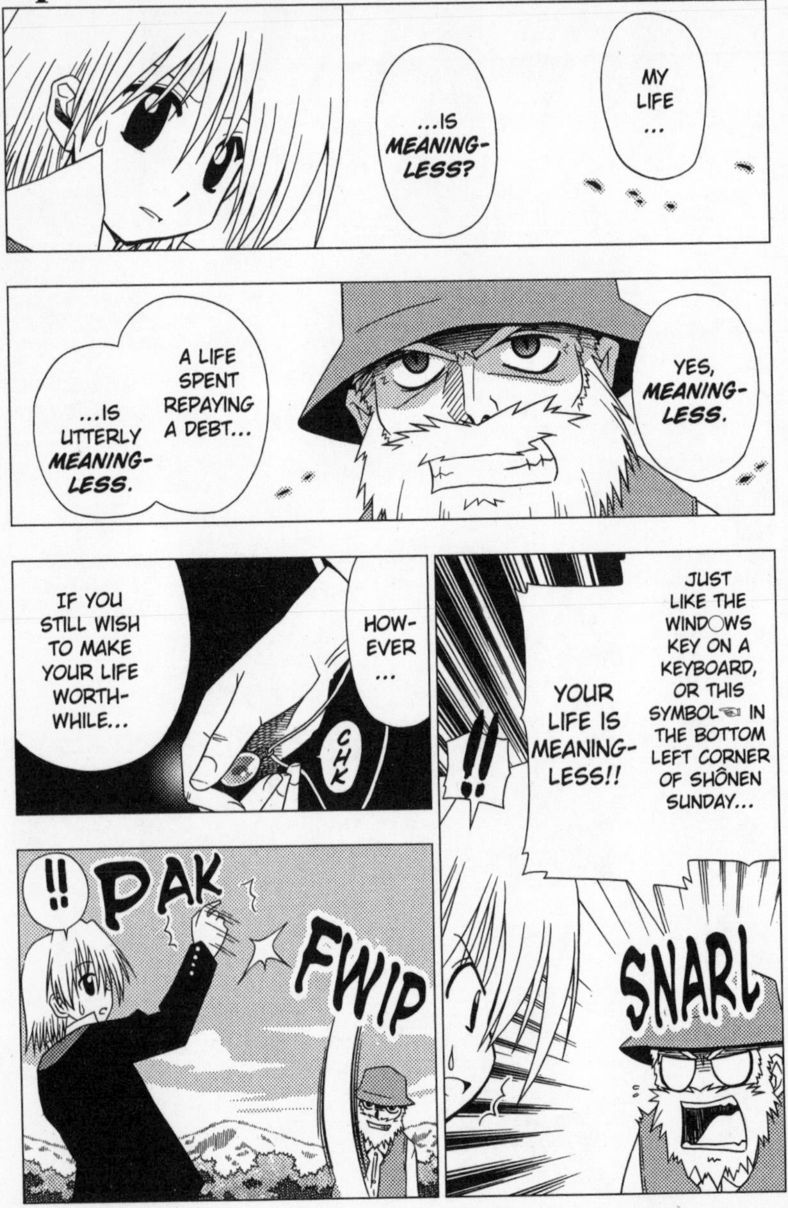

MY LIFE ...
...IS *MEANING-LESS?*
YES, *MEANING-LESS.*
A LIFE SPENT REPAYING A DEBT...
...IS UTTERLY *MEANING-LESS.*
JUST LIKE THE WINDOWS KEY ON A KEYBOARD, OR THIS SYMBOL☜ IN THE BOTTOM LEFT CORNER OF SHÔNEN SUNDAY...
YOUR LIFE IS MEANING-LESS!!
!!
SNARL
HOW-EVER ...
CHK
IF YOU STILL WISH TO MAKE YOUR LIFE WORTH-WHILE...
!!
PAK
FWIP

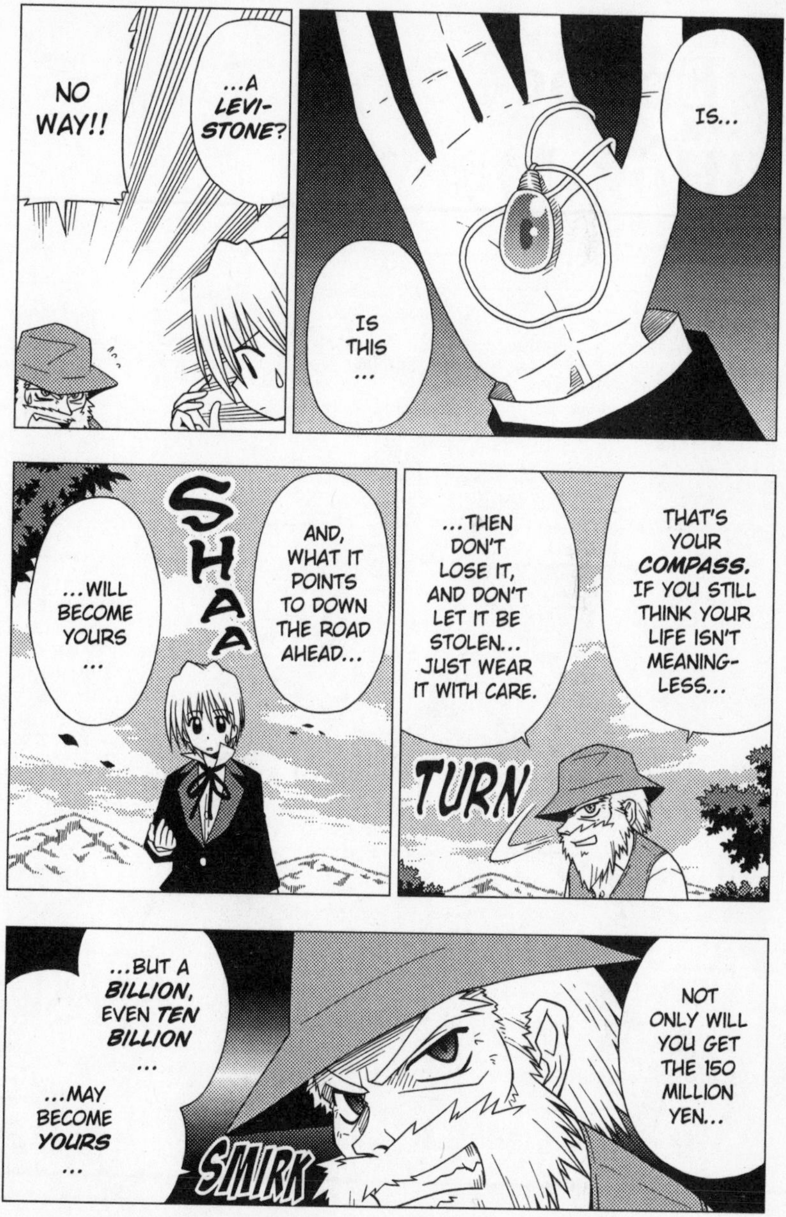
IS...
IS THIS ...
...A LEVI-STONE?
NO WAY!!
THAT'S YOUR COMPASS. IF YOU STILL THINK YOUR LIFE ISN'T MEANING-LESS...
...THEN DON'T LOSE IT, AND DON'T LET IT BE STOLEN... JUST WEAR IT WITH CARE.
TURN
AND, WHAT IT POINTS TO DOWN THE ROAD AHEAD...
SHAA
...WILL BECOME YOURS ...
NOT ONLY WILL YOU GET THE 150 MILLION YEN...
...BUT A BILLION, EVEN TEN BILLION ...
...MAY BECOME YOURS ...
SMIRK

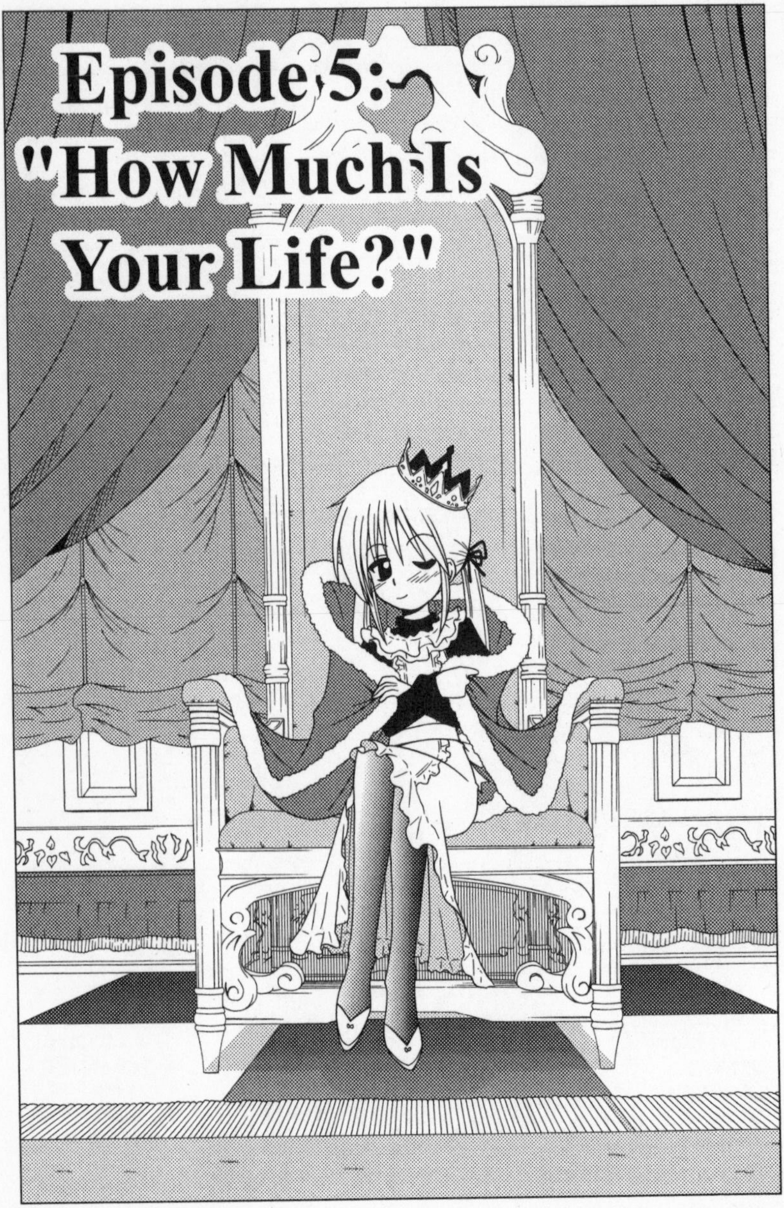
Episode 5:
"How Much Is
Your Life?"

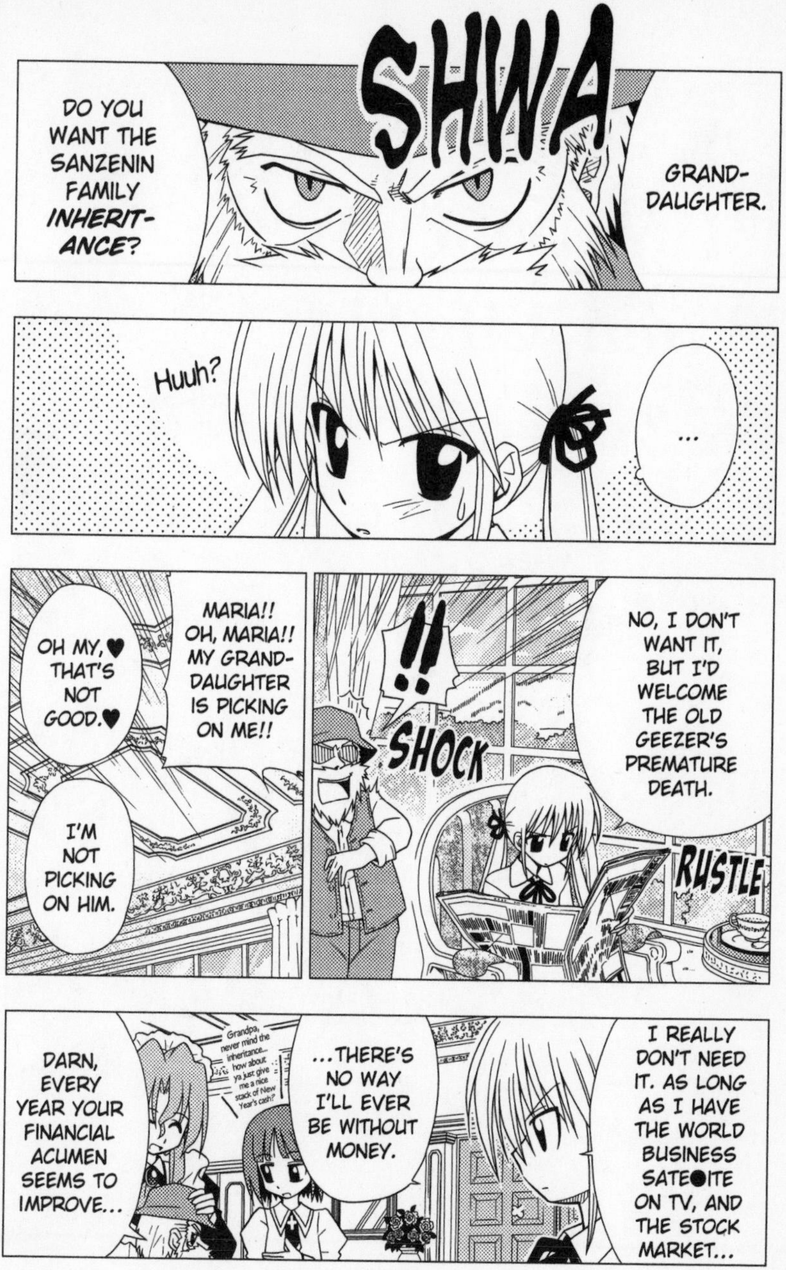
SHWA
DO YOU WANT THE SANZENIN FAMILY *INHERITANCE?*
GRAND-DAUGHTER.
...
Huuh?
NO, I DON'T WANT IT, BUT I'D WELCOME THE OLD GEEZER'S PREMATURE DEATH.
!!
SHOCK
RUSTLE
MARIA!! OH, MARIA!! MY GRAND-DAUGHTER IS PICKING ON ME!!
OH MY,♥ THAT'S NOT GOOD.♥
I'M NOT PICKING ON HIM.
I REALLY DON'T NEED IT. AS LONG AS I HAVE THE WORLD BUSINESS SATE●ITE ON TV, AND THE STOCK MARKET...
...THERE'S NO WAY I'LL EVER BE WITHOUT MONEY.
Grandpa, never mind the inheritance... how about ya just give me a nice stack of New Year's cash?
DARN, EVERY YEAR YOUR FINANCIAL ACUMEN SEEMS TO IMPROVE...

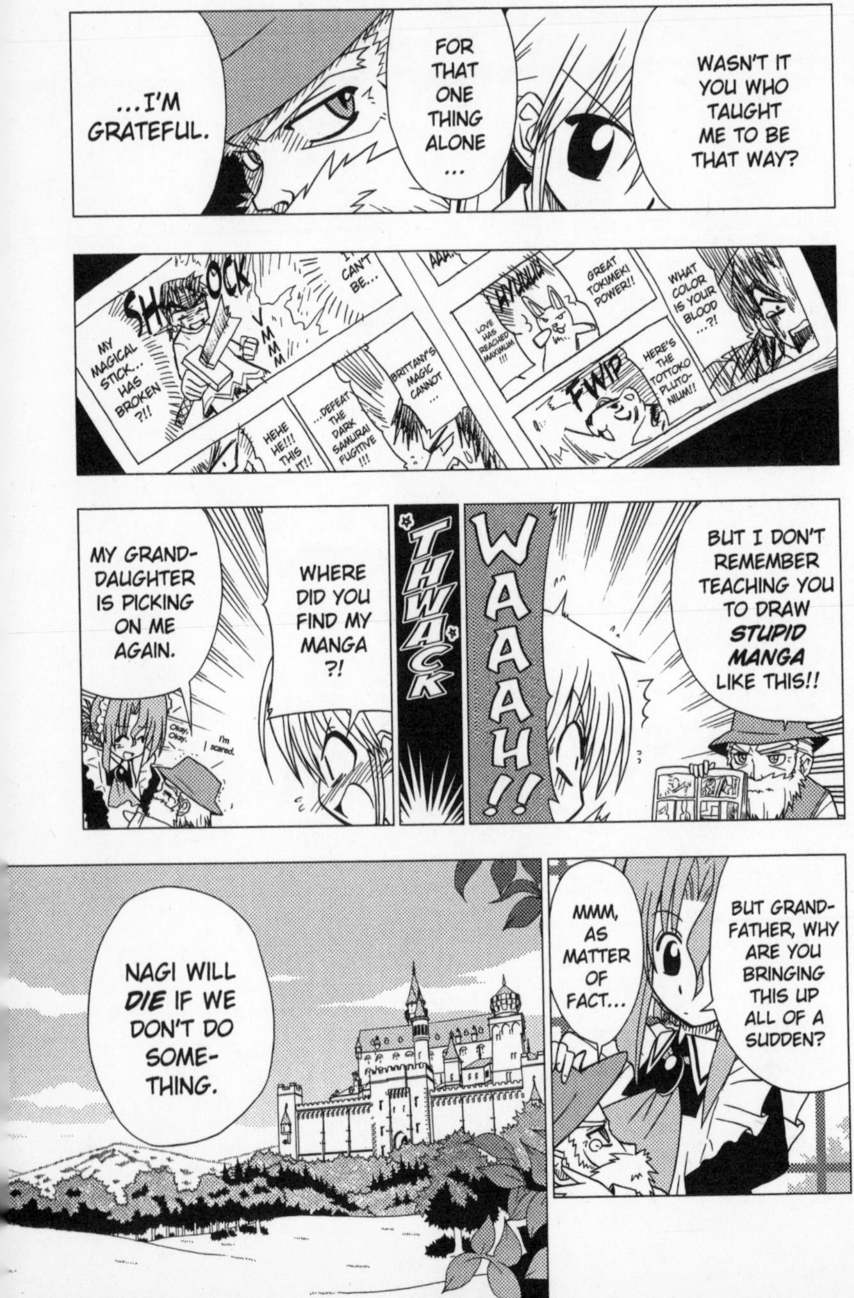
WASN'T IT YOU WHO TAUGHT ME TO BE THAT WAY?
FOR THAT ONE THING ALONE ...
...I'M GRATEFUL.
WHAT COLOR IS YOUR BLOOD ...?!
GREAT TOKIMEKI POWER!!
LOVE HAS REACHED MAXIMUM !!!
HERE'S THE TOTTOKO PLUTO-NIUM!!
FWIP
I CAN'T BE...
SHOCK
VMMM
MY MAGICAL STICK... HAS BROKEN ?!!
BRITTANY'S MAGIC CANNOT ...
...DEFEAT THE DARK SAMURAI FUGITIVE !!!
BUT I DON'T REMEMBER TEACHING YOU TO DRAW ***STUPID MANGA*** LIKE THIS!!
WAAAAH!!
THWACK
WHERE DID YOU FIND MY MANGA ?!
MY GRAND-DAUGHTER IS PICKING ON ME AGAIN.
I'm scared.
Okay. Okay.
BUT GRAND-FATHER, WHY ARE YOU BRINGING THIS UP ALL OF A SUDDEN?
MMM, AS MATTER OF FACT...
NAGI WILL ***DIE*** IF WE DON'T DO SOME-THING.

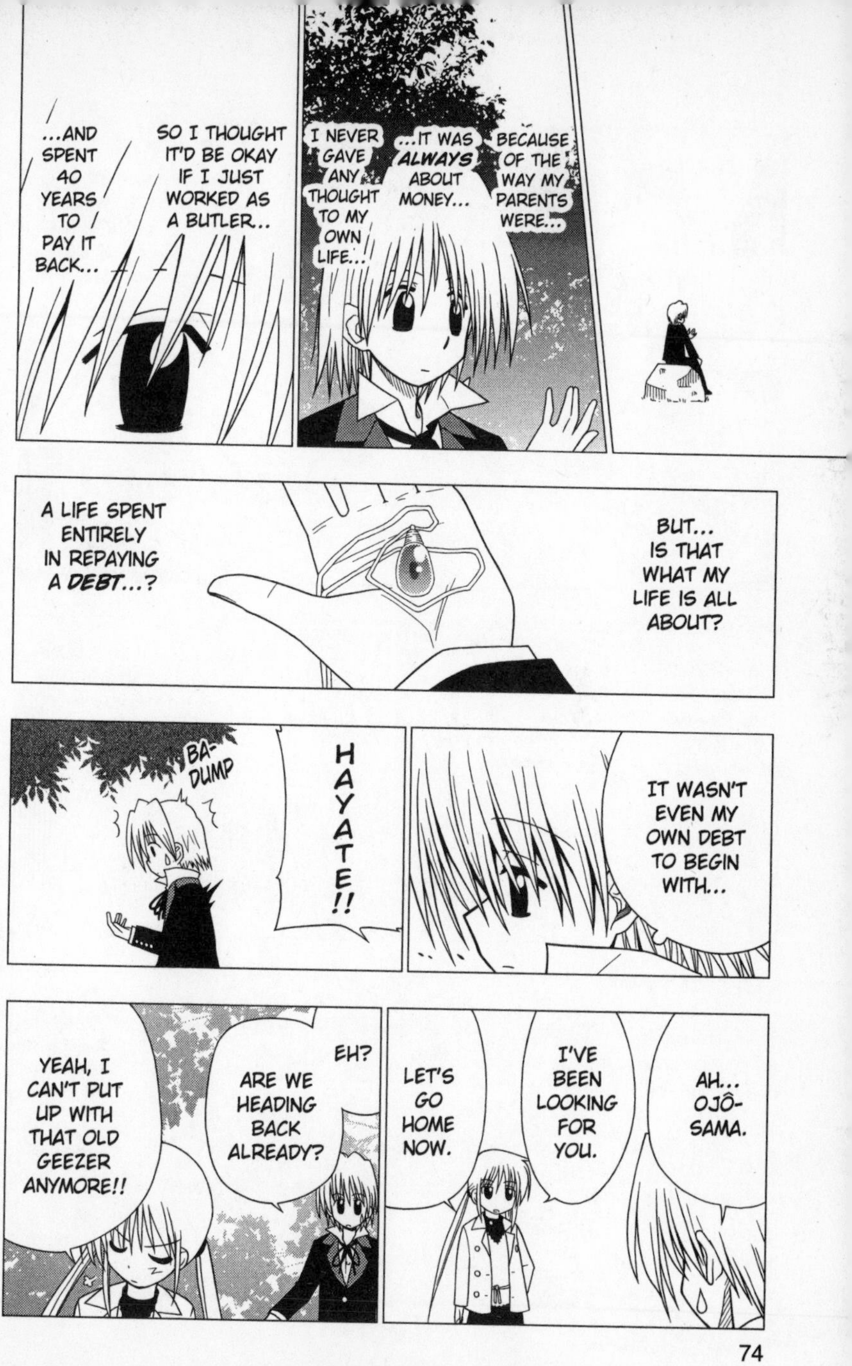
BECAUSE OF THE WAY MY PARENTS WERE...
...IT WAS *ALWAYS* ABOUT MONEY...
I NEVER GAVE ANY THOUGHT TO MY OWN LIFE...
SO I THOUGHT IT'D BE OKAY IF I JUST WORKED AS A BUTLER...
...AND SPENT 40 YEARS TO PAY IT BACK...
BUT... IS THAT WHAT MY LIFE IS ALL ABOUT?
A LIFE SPENT ENTIRELY IN REPAYING A *DEBT*...?
IT WASN'T EVEN MY OWN DEBT TO BEGIN WITH...
HAYATE!!
BA-DUMP
AH... OJÔ-SAMA.
I'VE BEEN LOOKING FOR YOU.
LET'S GO HOME NOW.
EH?
ARE WE HEADING BACK ALREADY?
YEAH, I CAN'T PUT UP WITH THAT OLD GEEZER ANYMORE!!

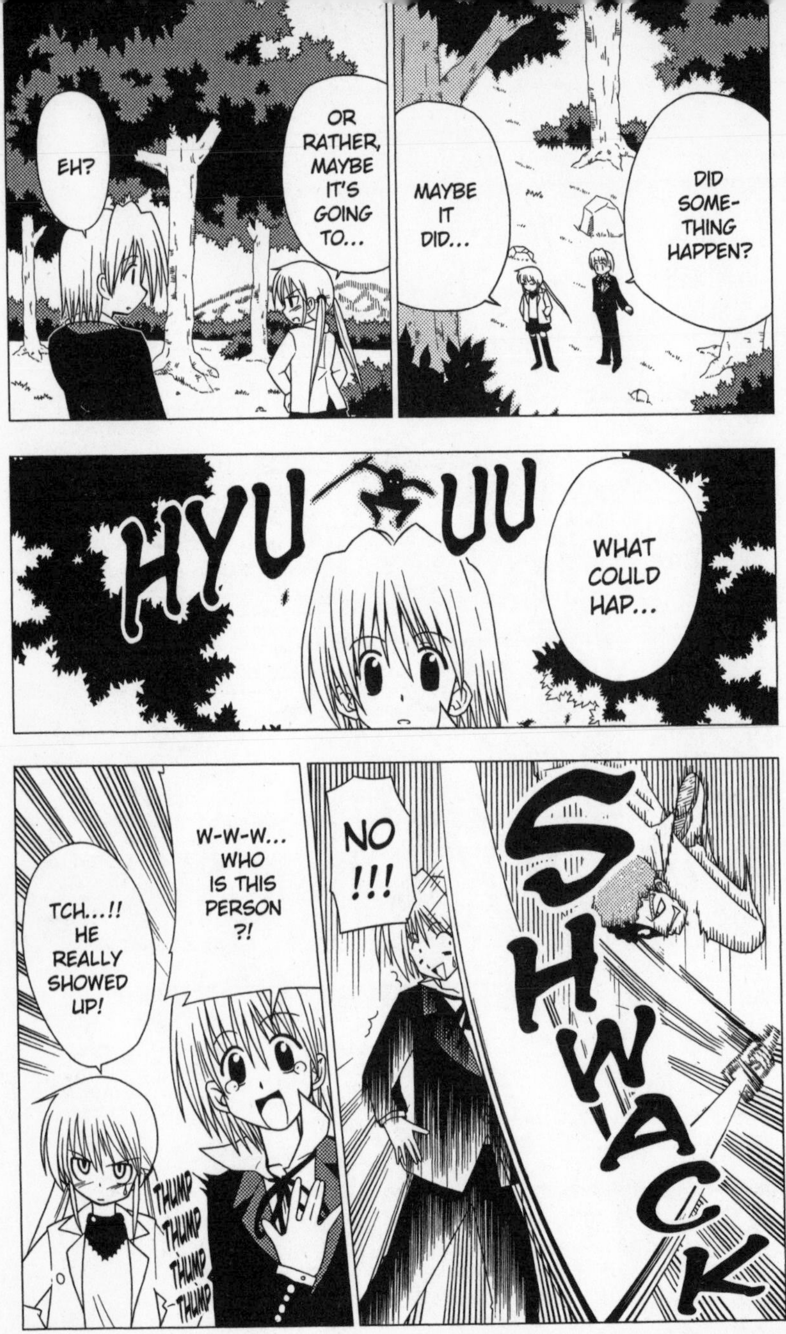
DID SOMETHING HAPPEN?
MAYBE IT DID...
OR RATHER, MAYBE IT'S GOING TO...
EH?
WHAT COULD HAP...
HYU UU
SHWACK
NO !!!
W-W-W... WHO IS THIS PERSON ?!
TCH...!! HE REALLY SHOWED UP!
THUMP THUMP THUMP THUMP

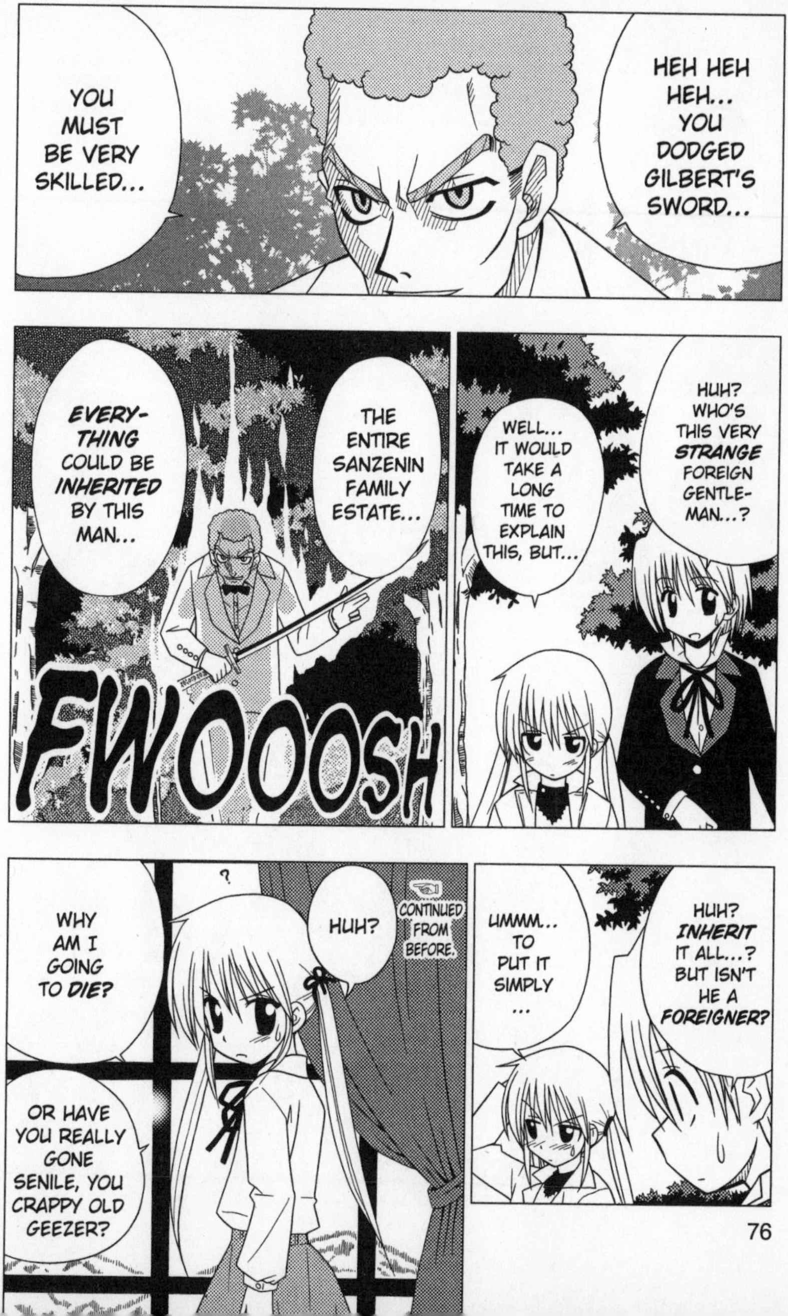
HEH HEH HEH... YOU DODGED GILBERT'S SWORD...
YOU MUST BE VERY SKILLED...
HUH? WHO'S THIS VERY *STRANGE* FOREIGN GENTLE-MAN...?
WELL... IT WOULD TAKE A LONG TIME TO EXPLAIN THIS, BUT...
THE ENTIRE SANZENIN FAMILY ESTATE...
EVERY-THING COULD BE *INHERITED* BY THIS MAN...
FWOOOSH
HUH? *INHERIT* IT ALL...? BUT ISN'T HE A *FOREIGNER?*
UMMM... TO PUT IT SIMPLY ...
CONTINUED FROM BEFORE.
HUH?
?
WHY AM I GOING TO *DIE?*
OR HAVE YOU REALLY GONE SENILE, YOU CRAPPY OLD GEEZER?

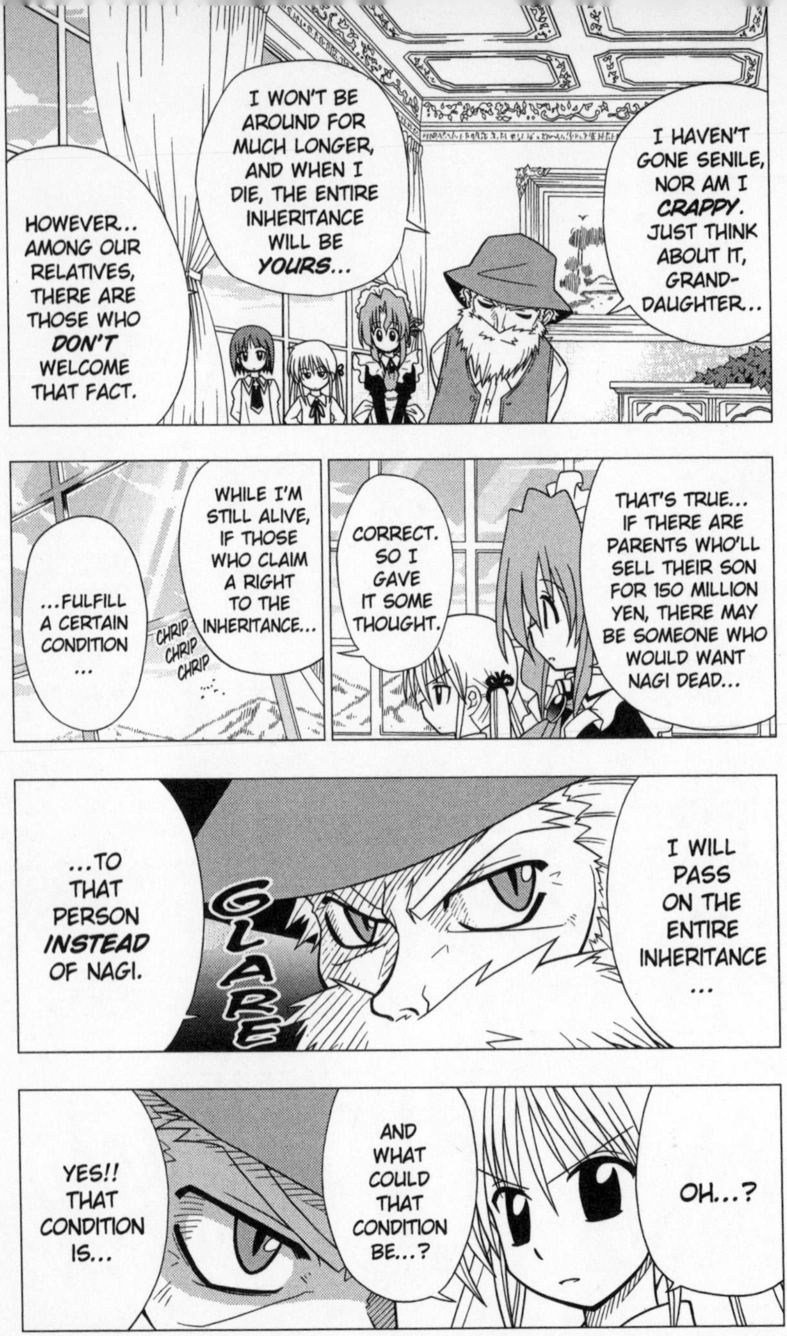
I HAVEN'T GONE SENILE, NOR AM I CRAPPY. JUST THINK ABOUT IT, GRAND-DAUGHTER...
I WON'T BE AROUND FOR MUCH LONGER, AND WHEN I DIE, THE ENTIRE INHERITANCE WILL BE YOURS...
HOWEVER... AMONG OUR RELATIVES, THERE ARE THOSE WHO DON'T WELCOME THAT FACT.
THAT'S TRUE... IF THERE ARE PARENTS WHO'LL SELL THEIR SON FOR 150 MILLION YEN, THERE MAY BE SOMEONE WHO WOULD WANT NAGI DEAD...
CORRECT. SO I GAVE IT SOME THOUGHT.
WHILE I'M STILL ALIVE, IF THOSE WHO CLAIM A RIGHT TO THE INHERITANCE...
CHRIP CHRIP CHRIP
...FULFILL A CERTAIN CONDITION ...
I WILL PASS ON THE ENTIRE INHERITANCE ...
GLARE
...TO THAT PERSON INSTEAD OF NAGI.
OH...?
AND WHAT COULD THAT CONDITION BE...?
YES!! THAT CONDITION IS...

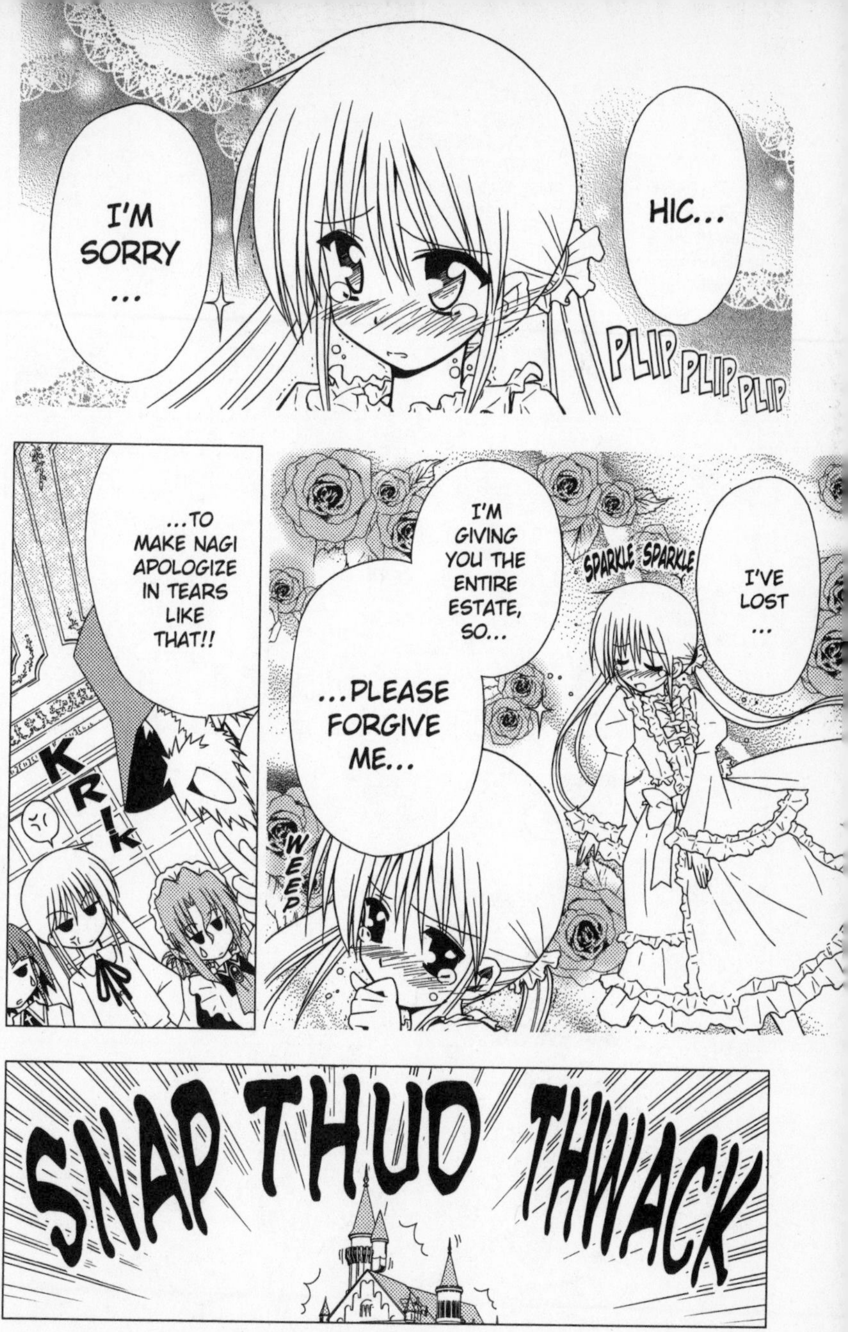
HIC...
I'M SORRY ...
PLIP PLIP PLIP
SPARKLE SPARKLE
I'VE LOST ...
I'M GIVING YOU THE ENTIRE ESTATE, SO...
...PLEASE FORGIVE ME...
WEEP
...TO MAKE NAGI APOLOGIZE IN TEARS LIKE THAT!!
KRIK
SNAP THUD THWACK

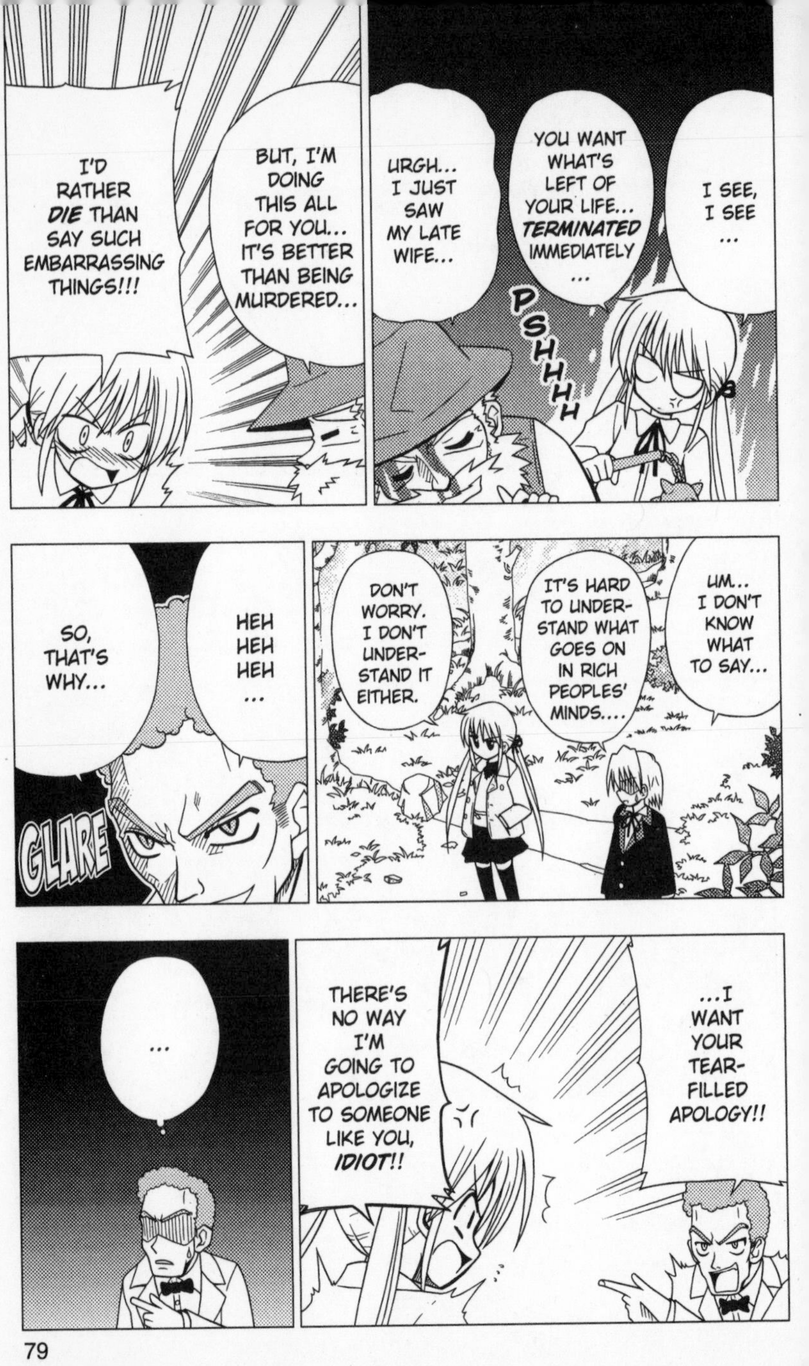
I SEE, I SEE ...
YOU WANT WHAT'S LEFT OF YOUR LIFE... TERMINATED IMMEDIATELY ...
PSHHHH
URGH... I JUST SAW MY LATE WIFE...
BUT, I'M DOING THIS ALL FOR YOU... IT'S BETTER THAN BEING MURDERED...
I'D RATHER DIE THAN SAY SUCH EMBARRASSING THINGS!!!
UM... I DON'T KNOW WHAT TO SAY...
IT'S HARD TO UNDER-STAND WHAT GOES ON IN RICH PEOPLES' MINDS....
DON'T WORRY. I DON'T UNDER-STAND IT EITHER.
HEH HEH HEH ...
SO, THAT'S WHY...
GLARE
...I WANT YOUR TEAR-FILLED APOLOGY!!
THERE'S NO WAY I'M GOING TO APOLOGIZE TO SOMEONE LIKE YOU, IDIOT!!
...

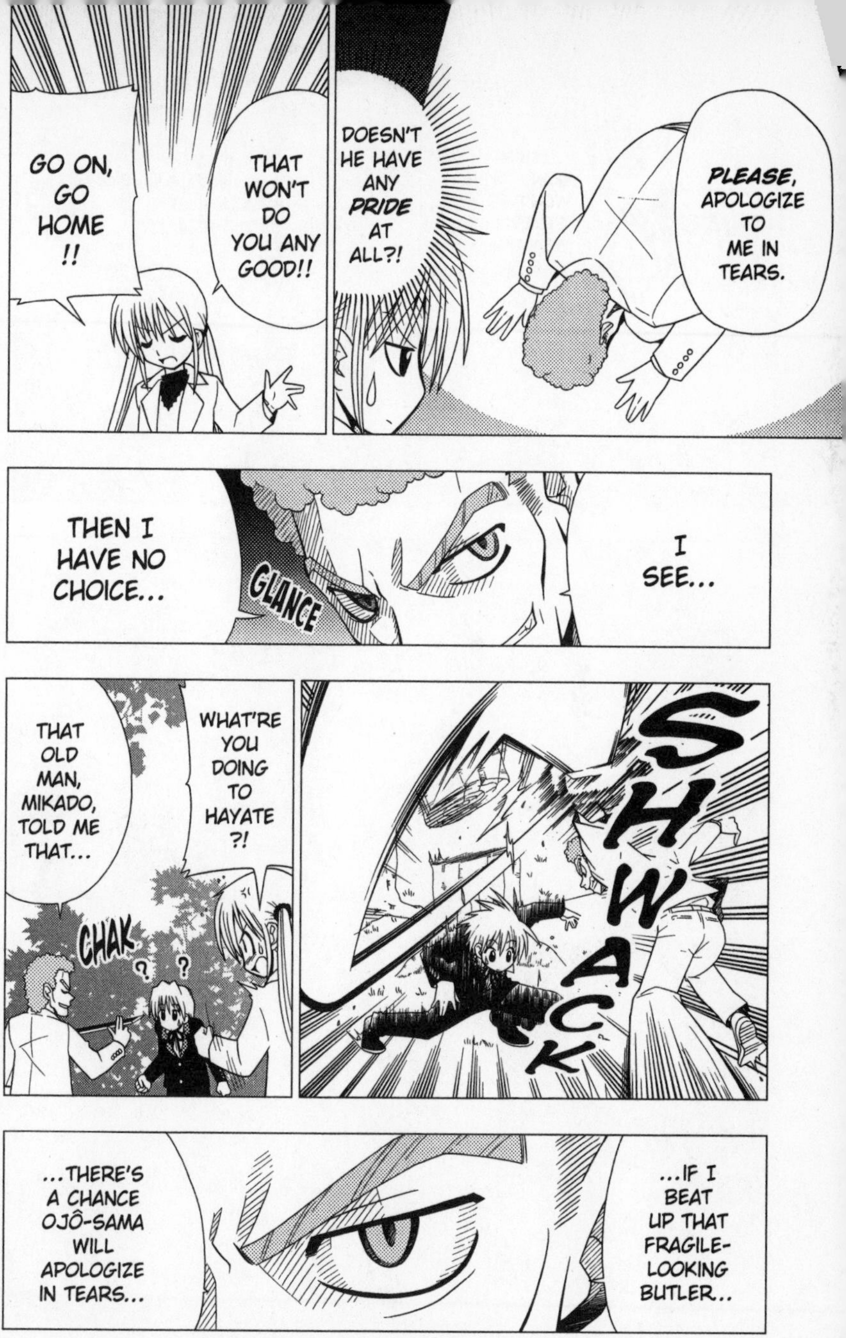
PLEASE, APOLOGIZE TO ME IN TEARS.
DOESN'T HE HAVE ANY PRIDE AT ALL?!
THAT WON'T DO YOU ANY GOOD!!
GO ON, GO HOME!!
I SEE...
GLANCE
THEN I HAVE NO CHOICE...
SHWACK
WHAT'RE YOU DOING TO HAYATE?!
THAT OLD MAN, MIKADO, TOLD ME THAT...
CHAK
? ?
...IF I BEAT UP THAT FRAGILE-LOOKING BUTLER...
...THERE'S A CHANCE OJÔ-SAMA WILL APOLOGIZE IN TEARS...

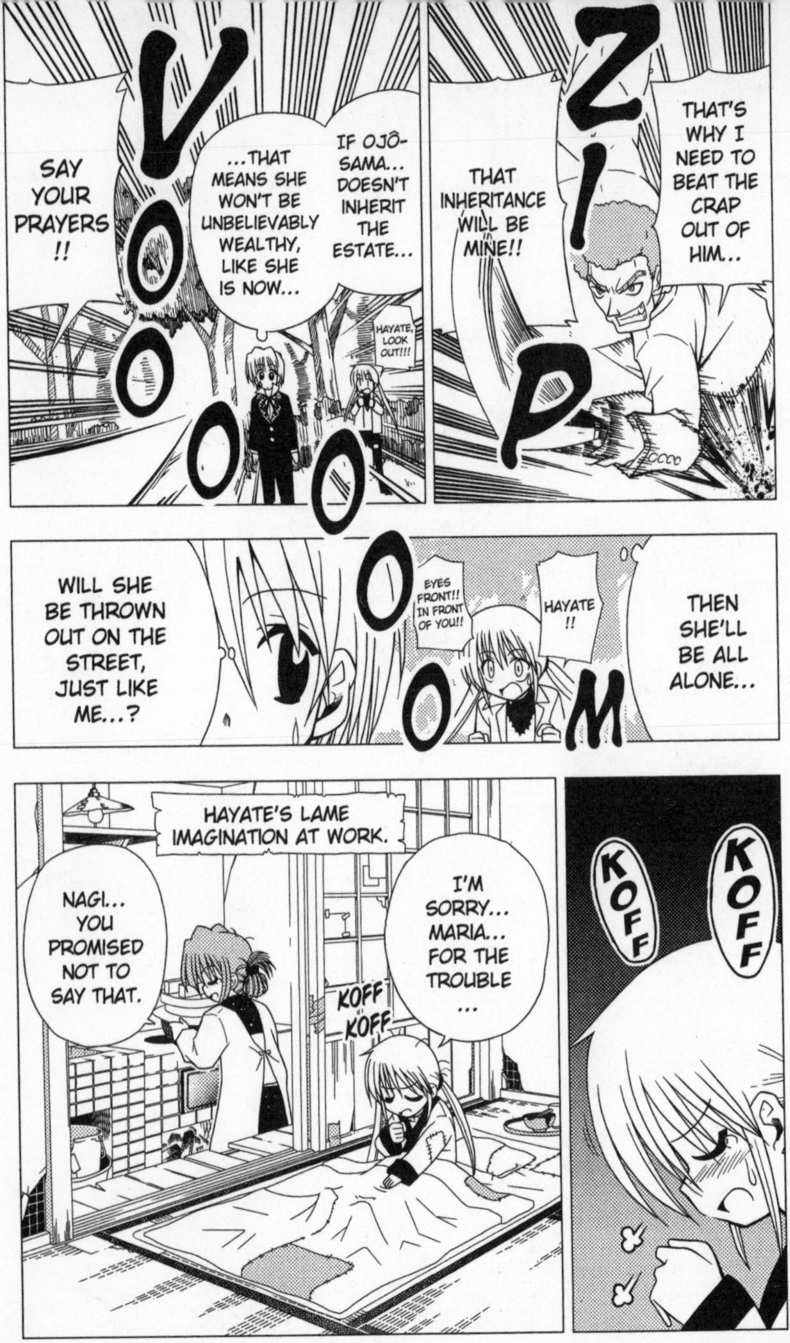
ZIP
THAT'S WHY I NEED TO BEAT THE CRAP OUT OF HIM...
THAT INHERITANCE WILL BE MINE!!
IF OJÔ-SAMA... DOESN'T INHERIT THE ESTATE...
...THAT MEANS SHE WON'T BE UNBELIEVABLY WEALTHY, LIKE SHE IS NOW...
HAYATE, LOOK OUT!!!
SAY YOUR PRAYERS !!
VOOOOOOOM
THEN SHE'LL BE ALL ALONE...
HAYATE !!
EYES FRONT!! IN FRONT OF YOU!!
WILL SHE BE THROWN OUT ON THE STREET, JUST LIKE ME...?
KOFF KOFF
KOFF KOFF
HAYATE'S LAME IMAGINATION AT WORK.
I'M SORRY... MARIA... FOR THE TROUBLE ...
KOFF KOFF
NAGI... YOU PROMISED NOT TO SAY THAT.

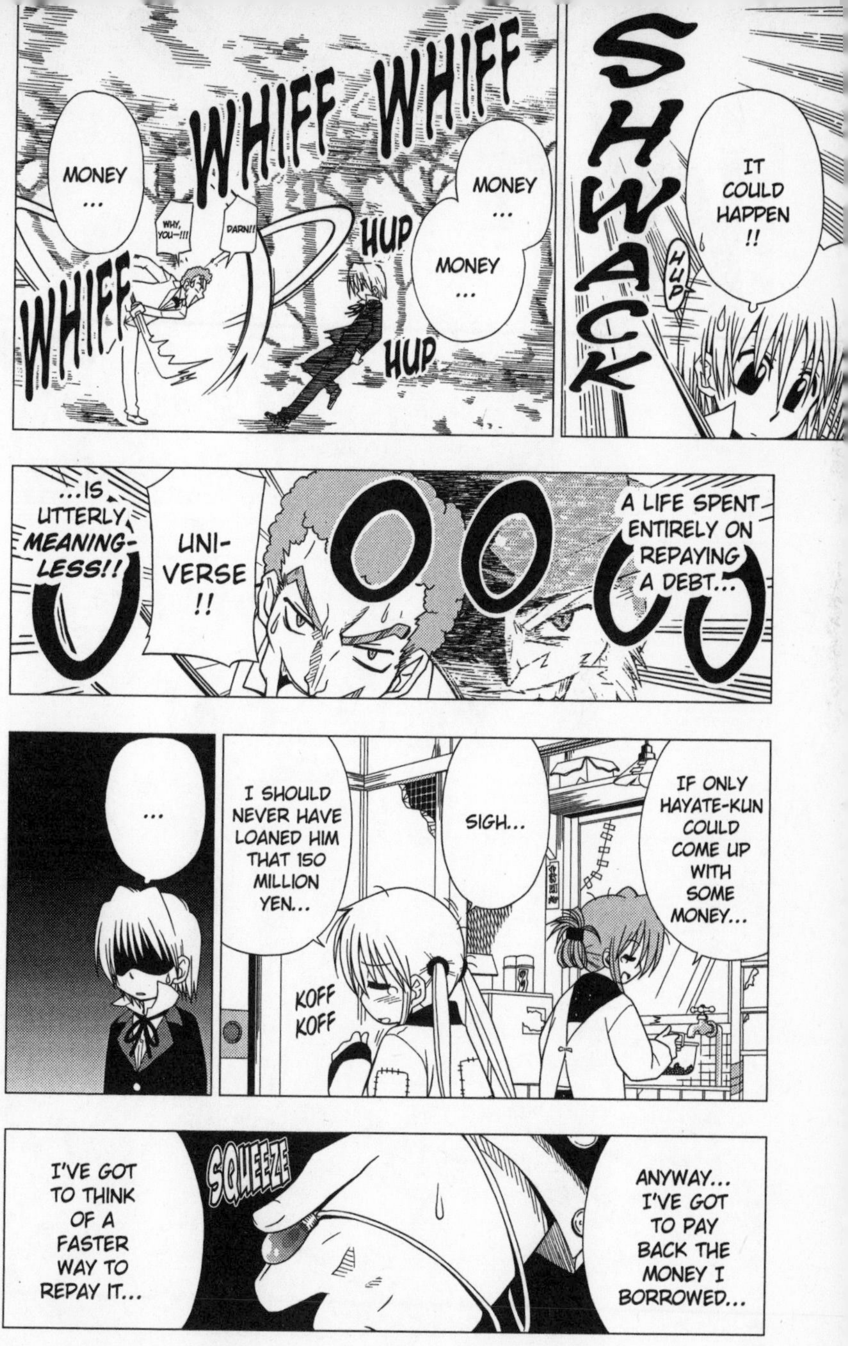
SHWACK
IT COULD HAPPEN!!
HUP
WHIFF WHIFF
MONEY...
MONEY...
HUP
HUP
DARN!!
WHY, YOU—!!!
MONEY...
WHIFF
A LIFE SPENT ENTIRELY ON REPAYING A DEBT...
UNI-VERSE!!
...IS UTTERLY MEANING-LESS!!
IF ONLY HAYATE-KUN COULD COME UP WITH SOME MONEY...
SIGH...
I SHOULD NEVER HAVE LOANED HIM THAT 150 MILLION YEN...
KOFF KOFF
...
ANYWAY... I'VE GOT TO PAY BACK THE MONEY I BORROWED...
SQUEEZE
I'VE GOT TO THINK OF A FASTER WAY TO REPAY IT...

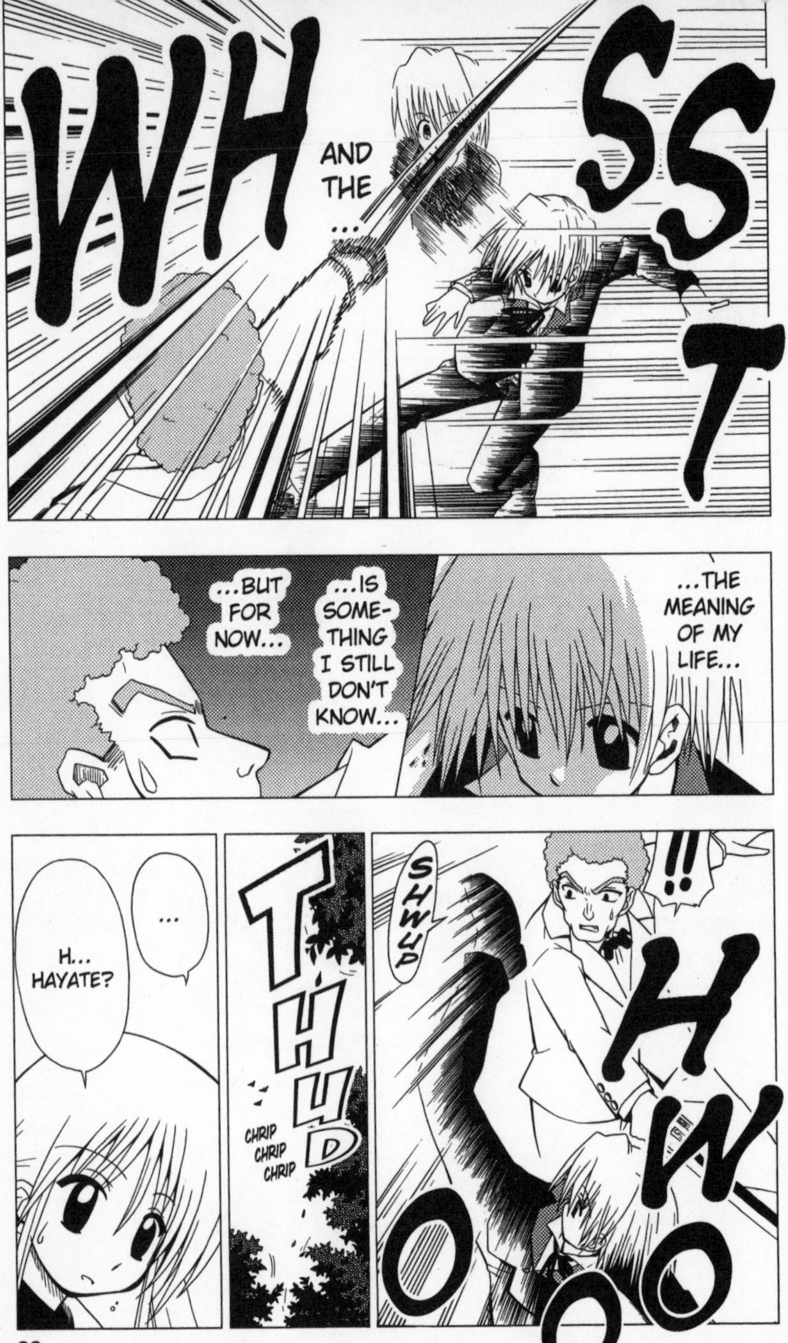
WH SS T
AND THE ...
...THE MEANING OF MY LIFE...
...IS SOMETHING I STILL DON'T KNOW...
...BUT FOR NOW...
!!
SHWUP
HWOOOO
THUD
CHRIP CHRIP CHRIP
...
H... HAYATE?

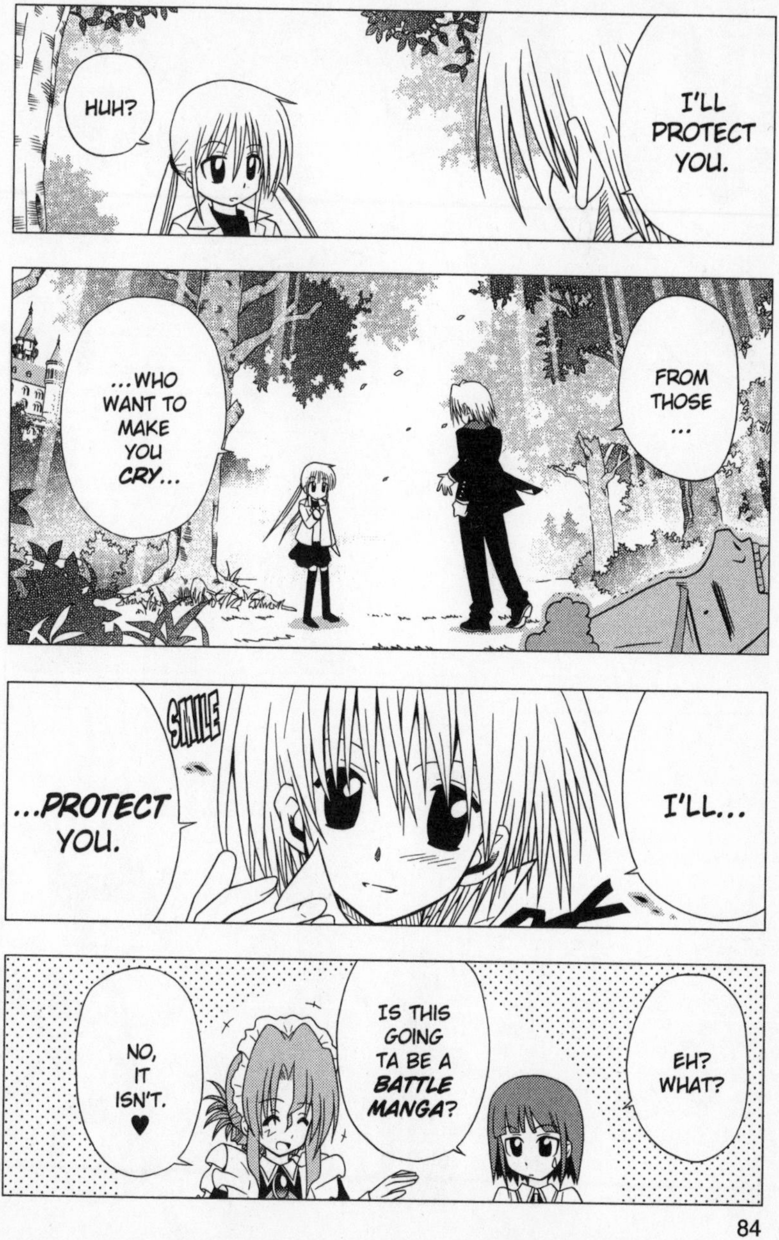
I'LL PROTECT YOU.
HUH?
FROM THOSE...
...WHO WANT TO MAKE YOU CRY...
I'LL...
SMILE
...PROTECT YOU.
EH? WHAT?
IS THIS GOING TA BE A BATTLE MANGA?
NO, IT ISN'T. ♥

Episode 6: "A Way to Lose the Golden Feather"

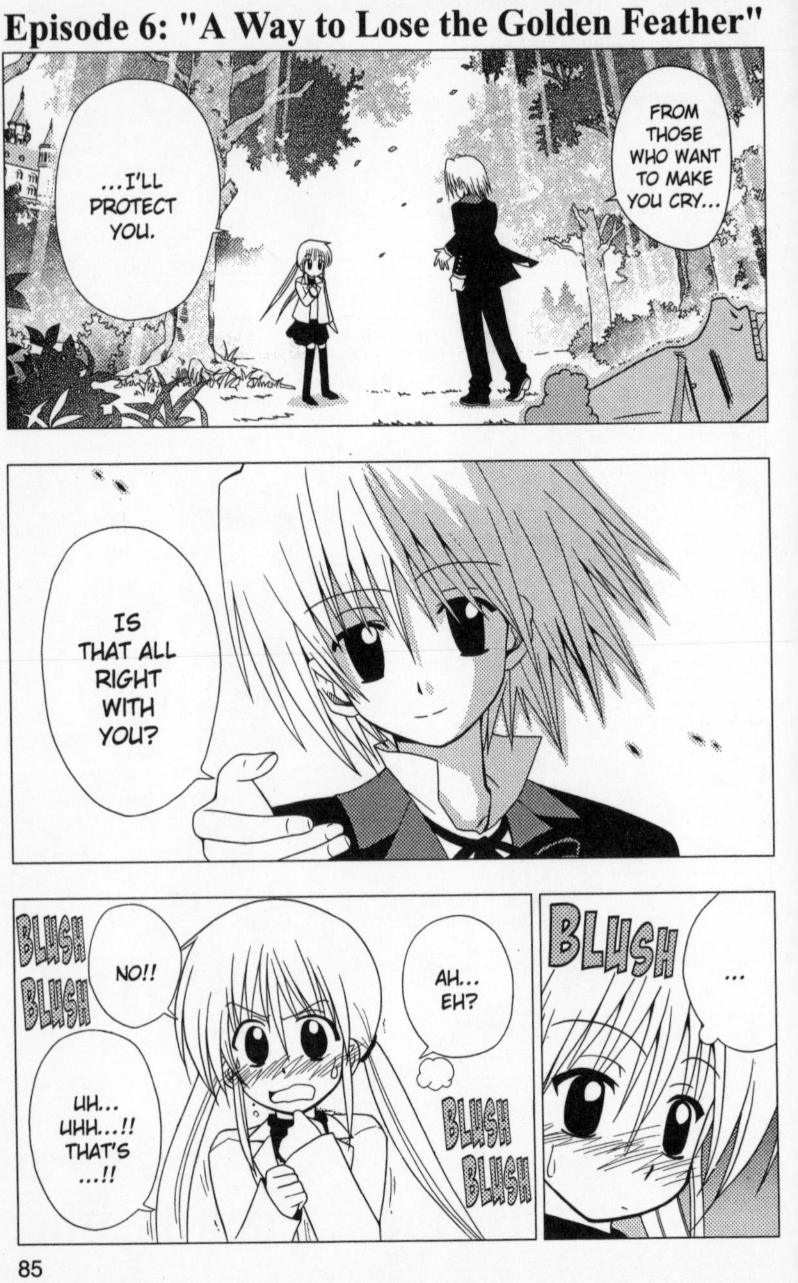
FROM THOSE WHO WANT TO MAKE YOU CRY...
...I'LL PROTECT YOU.
IS THAT ALL RIGHT WITH YOU?
BLUSH
...
AH... EH?
NO!!
BLUSH BLUSH
BLUSH BLUSH
UH... UHH...!! THAT'S ...!!

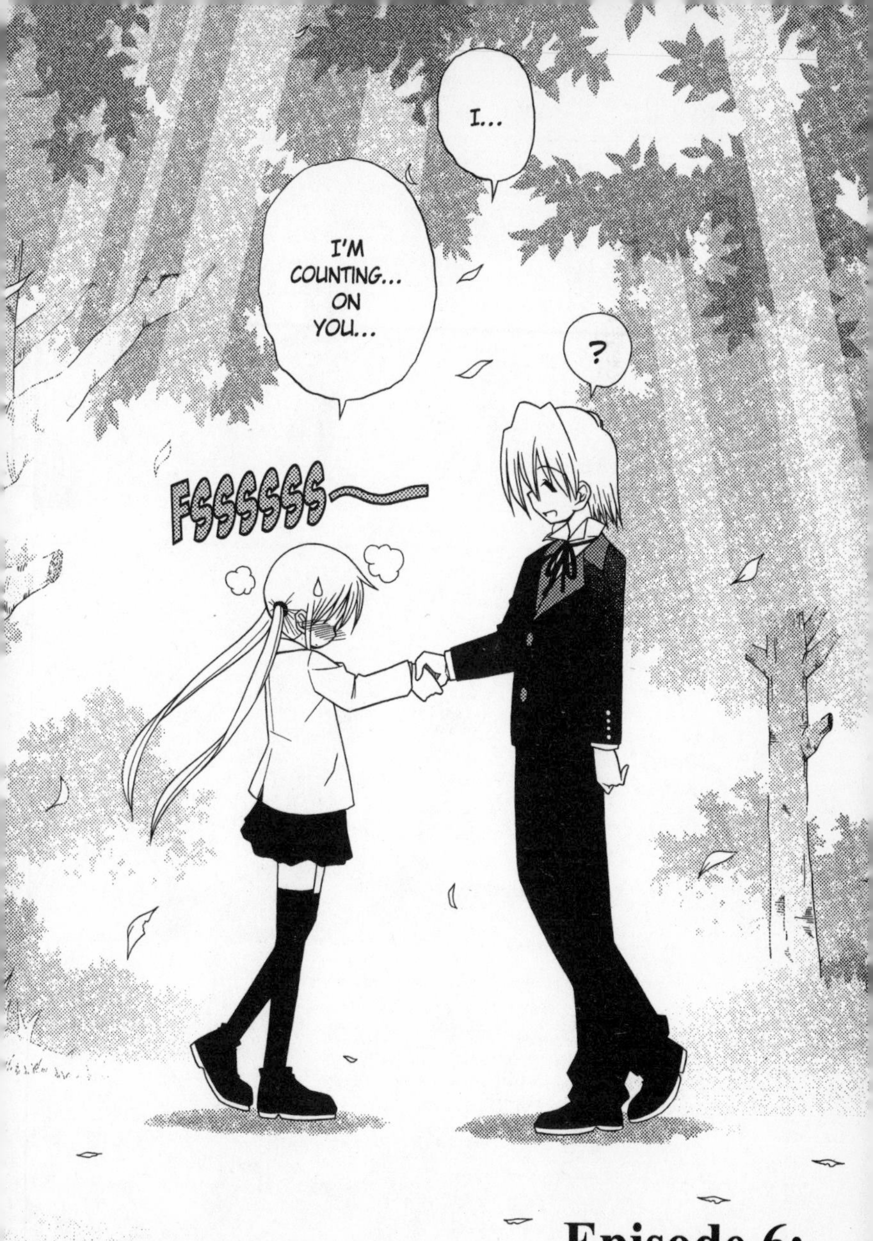
I...
I'M COUNTING... ON YOU...
?
FSSSSSS

Episode 6: A Way to Lose the Golden Feather"

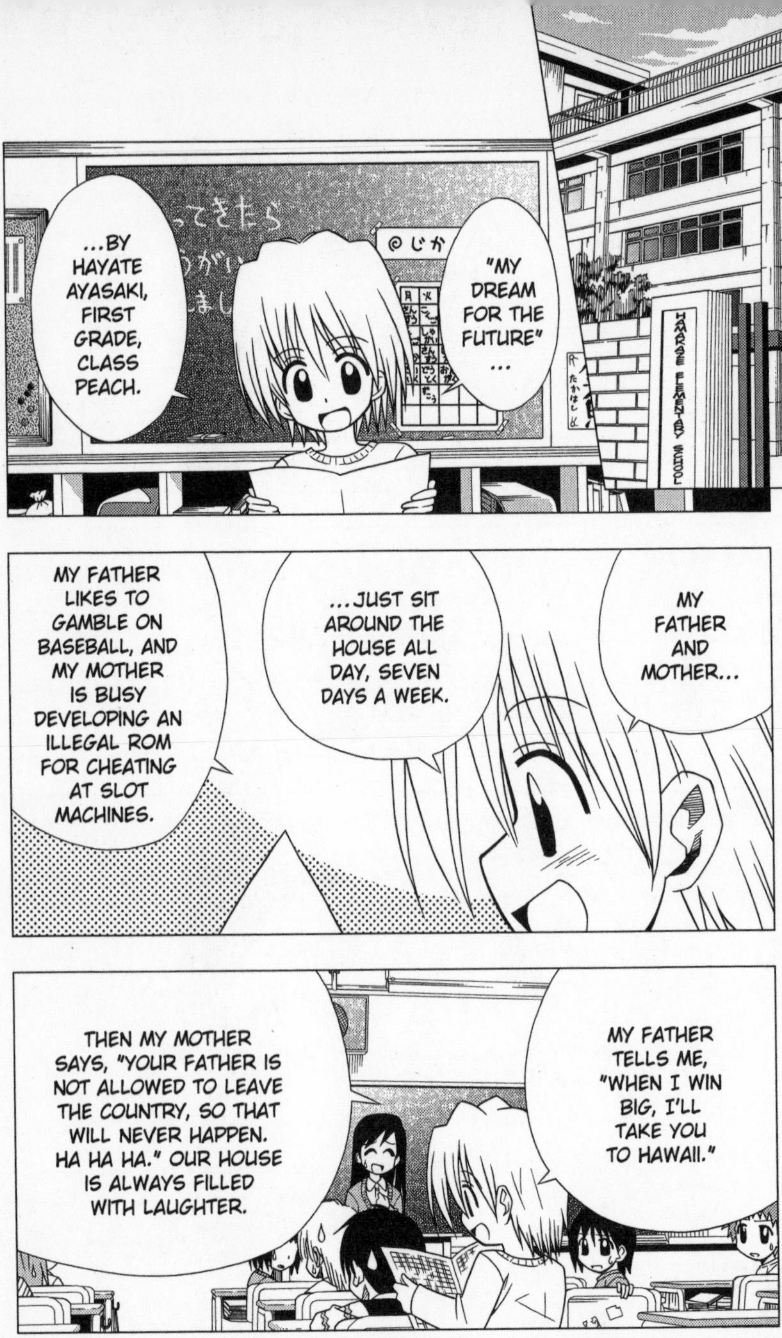
HAMAKAZE ELEMENTARY SCHOOL
"MY DREAM FOR THE FUTURE"...
...BY HAYATE AYASAKI, FIRST GRADE, CLASS PEACH.
MY FATHER AND MOTHER...
...JUST SIT AROUND THE HOUSE ALL DAY, SEVEN DAYS A WEEK.
MY FATHER LIKES TO GAMBLE ON BASEBALL, AND MY MOTHER IS BUSY DEVELOPING AN ILLEGAL ROM FOR CHEATING AT SLOT MACHINES.
MY FATHER TELLS ME, "WHEN I WIN BIG, I'LL TAKE YOU TO HAWAII."
THEN MY MOTHER SAYS, "YOUR FATHER IS NOT ALLOWED TO LEAVE THE COUNTRY, SO THAT WILL NEVER HAPPEN. HA HA HA." OUR HOUSE IS ALWAYS FILLED WITH LAUGHTER.

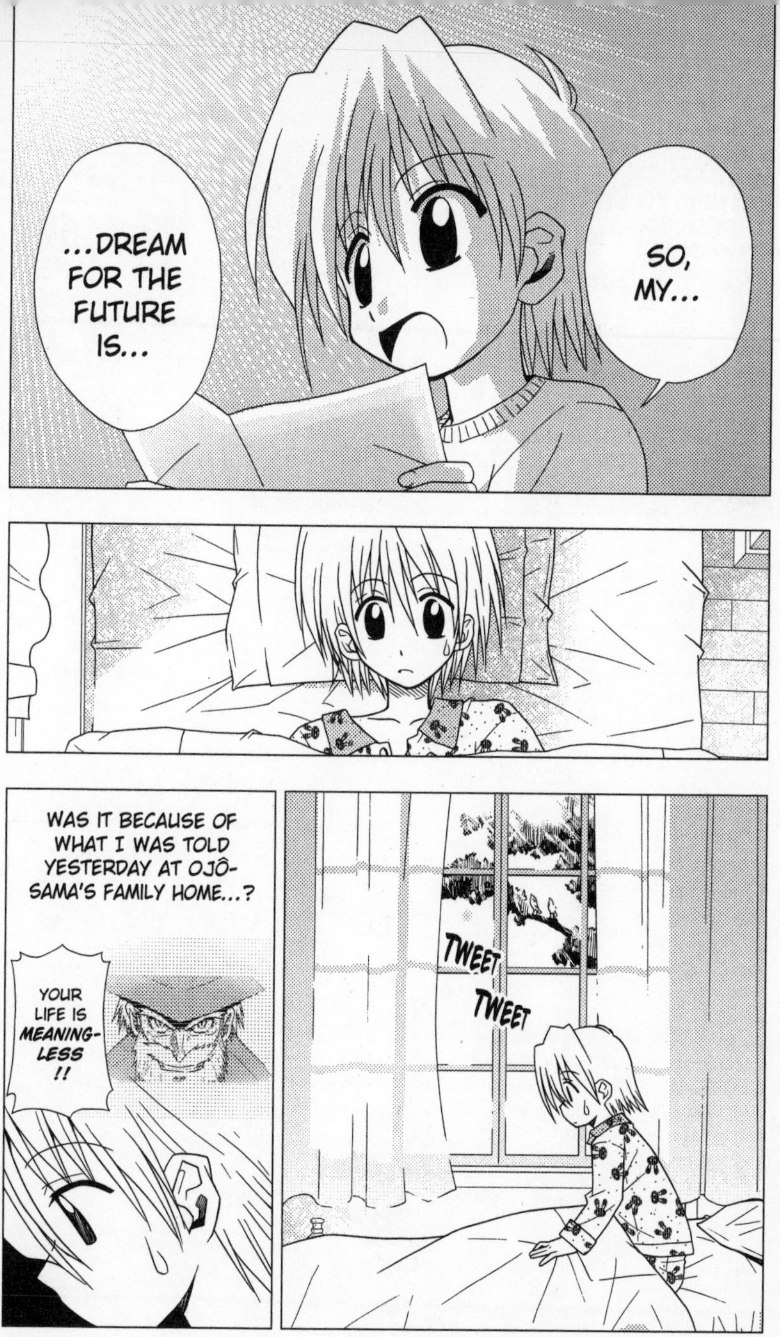
SO, MY...
...DREAM FOR THE FUTURE IS...
TWEET
TWEET
WAS IT BECAUSE OF WHAT I WAS TOLD YESTERDAY AT OJÔ-SAMA'S FAMILY HOME...?
YOUR LIFE IS MEANING-LESS !!

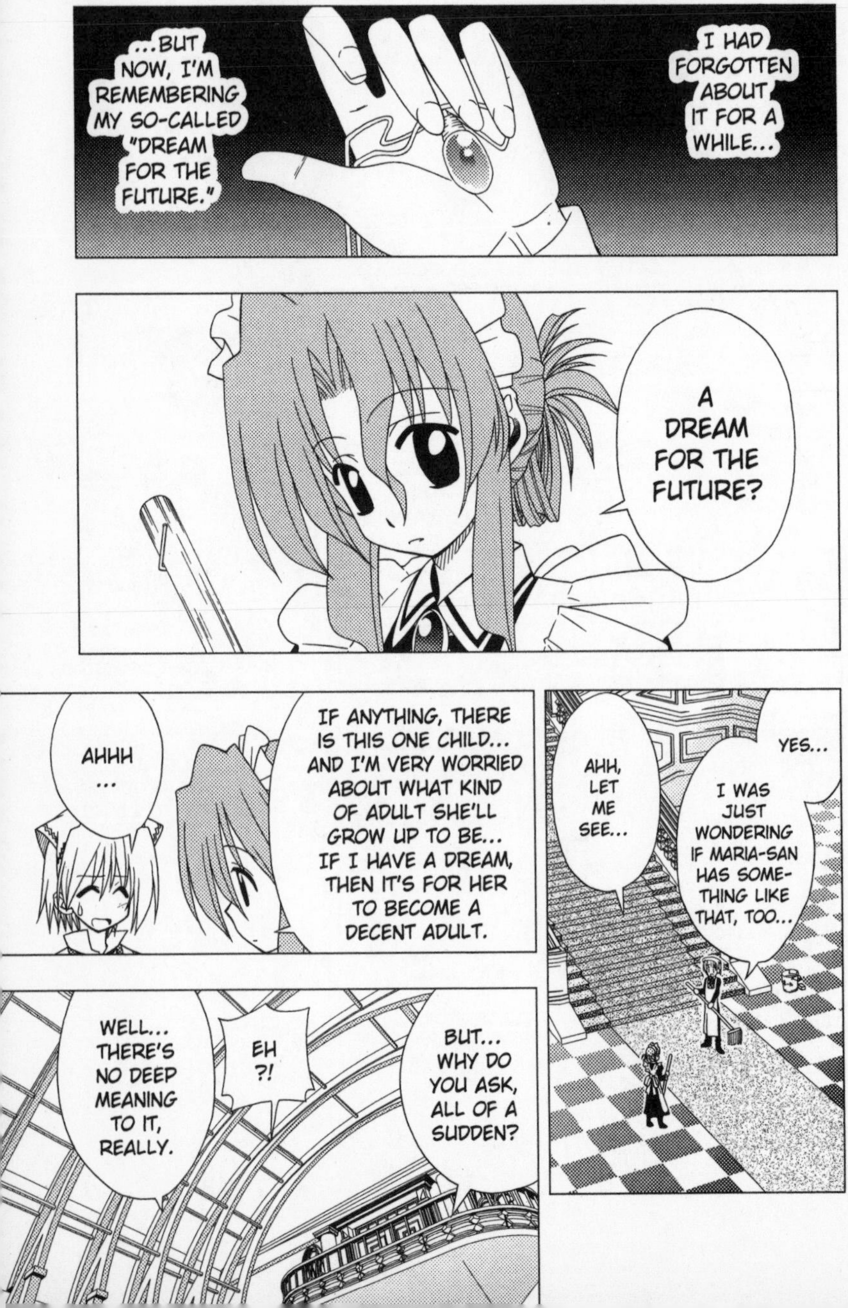
I HAD FORGOTTEN ABOUT IT FOR A WHILE...
...BUT NOW, I'M REMEMBERING MY SO-CALLED "DREAM FOR THE FUTURE."
A DREAM FOR THE FUTURE?
YES... I WAS JUST WONDERING IF MARIA-SAN HAS SOME-THING LIKE THAT, TOO...
AHH, LET ME SEE...
IF ANYTHING, THERE IS THIS ONE CHILD... AND I'M VERY WORRIED ABOUT WHAT KIND OF ADULT SHE'LL GROW UP TO BE... IF I HAVE A DREAM, THEN IT'S FOR HER TO BECOME A DECENT ADULT.
AHHH ...
BUT... WHY DO YOU ASK, ALL OF A SUDDEN?
EH ?!
WELL... THERE'S NO DEEP MEANING TO IT, REALLY.

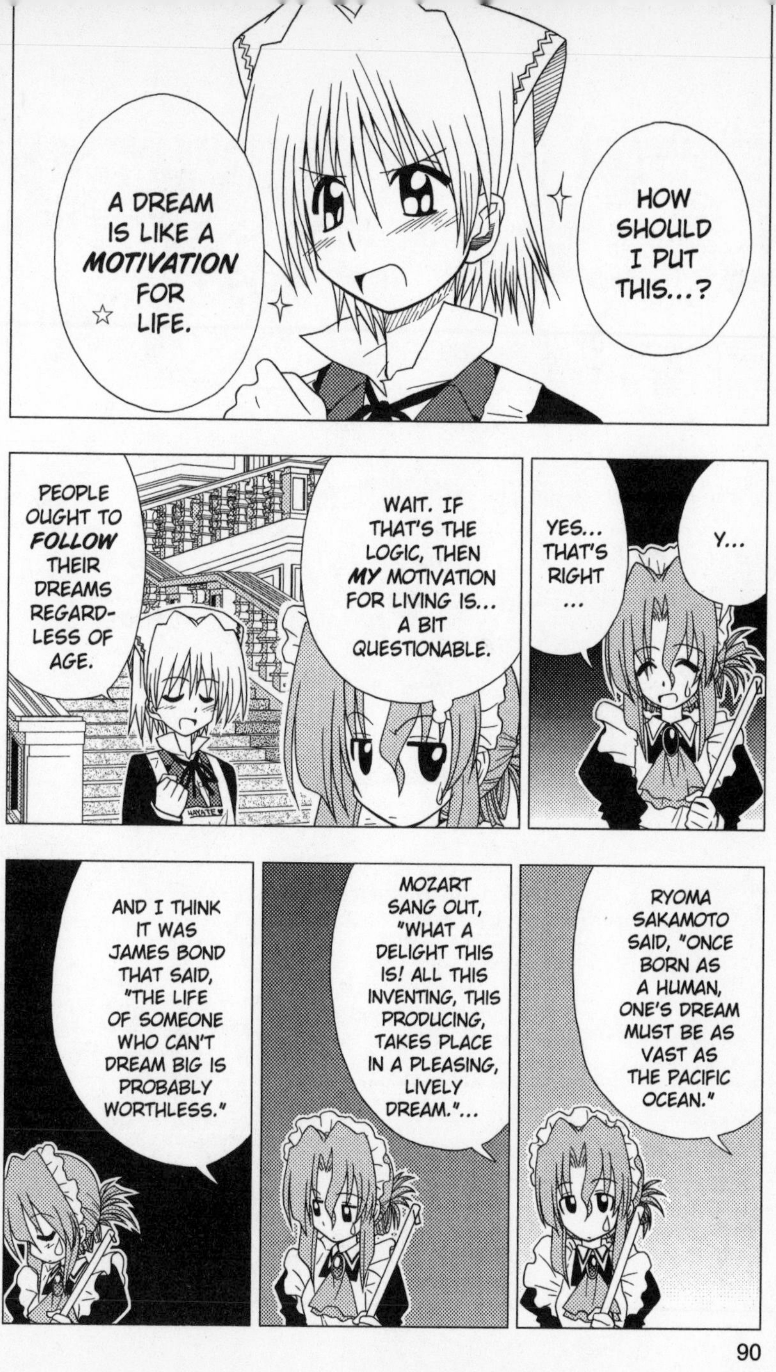
HOW SHOULD I PUT THIS...?
A DREAM IS LIKE A *MOTIVATION* FOR LIFE. ☆
Y...
YES... THAT'S RIGHT ...
WAIT. IF THAT'S THE LOGIC, THEN *MY* MOTIVATION FOR LIVING IS... A BIT QUESTIONABLE.
PEOPLE OUGHT TO *FOLLOW* THEIR DREAMS REGARDLESS OF AGE.
HAYATE
RYOMA SAKAMOTO SAID, "ONCE BORN AS A HUMAN, ONE'S DREAM MUST BE AS VAST AS THE PACIFIC OCEAN."
MOZART SANG OUT, "WHAT A DELIGHT THIS IS! ALL THIS INVENTING, THIS PRODUCING, TAKES PLACE IN A PLEASING, LIVELY DREAM."...
AND I THINK IT WAS JAMES BOND THAT SAID, "THE LIFE OF SOMEONE WHO CAN'T DREAM BIG IS PROBABLY WORTHLESS."

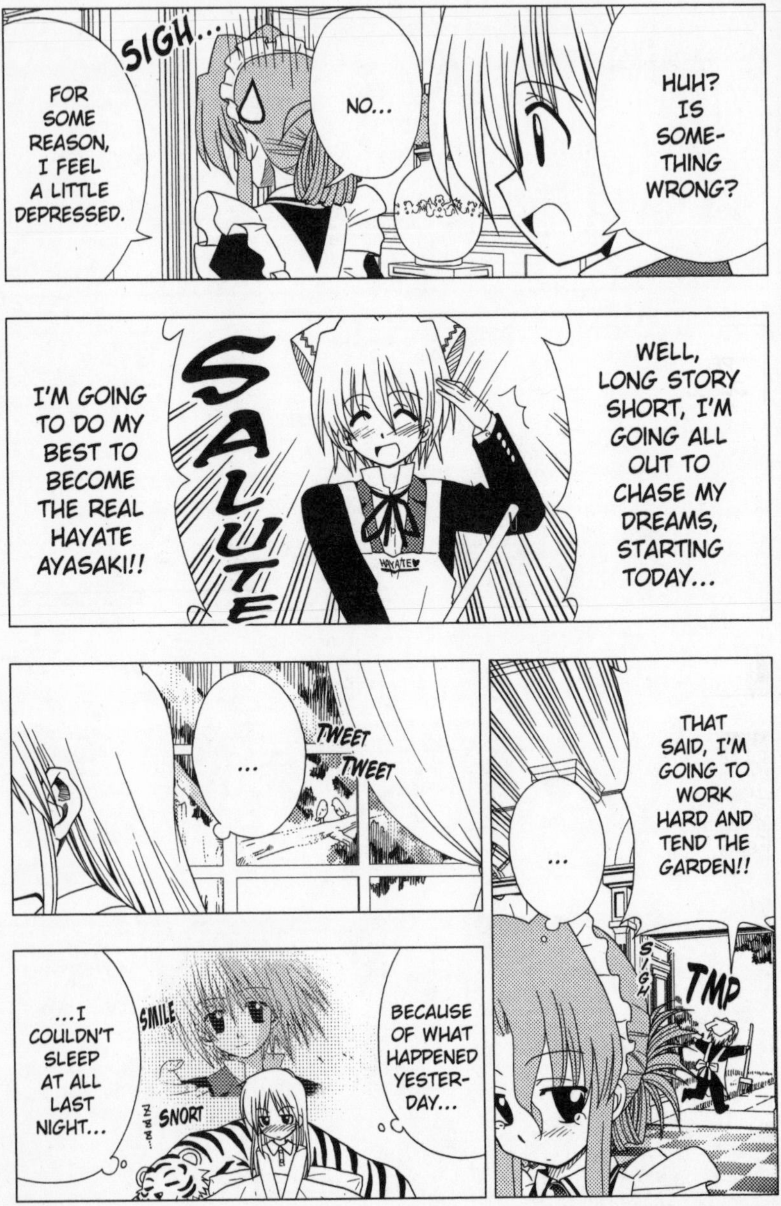
HUH? IS SOMETHING WRONG?
NO...
SIGH...
FOR SOME REASON, I FEEL A LITTLE DEPRESSED.
WELL, LONG STORY SHORT, I'M GOING ALL OUT TO CHASE MY DREAMS, STARTING TODAY...
HAYATE
SALUTE
I'M GOING TO DO MY BEST TO BECOME THE REAL HAYATE AYASAKI!!
THAT SAID, I'M GOING TO WORK HARD AND TEND THE GARDEN!!
...
SIGH
TMP
TWEET
TWEET
...
BECAUSE OF WHAT HAPPENED YESTERDAY...
SMILE
SNORT
...I COULDN'T SLEEP AT ALL LAST NIGHT...

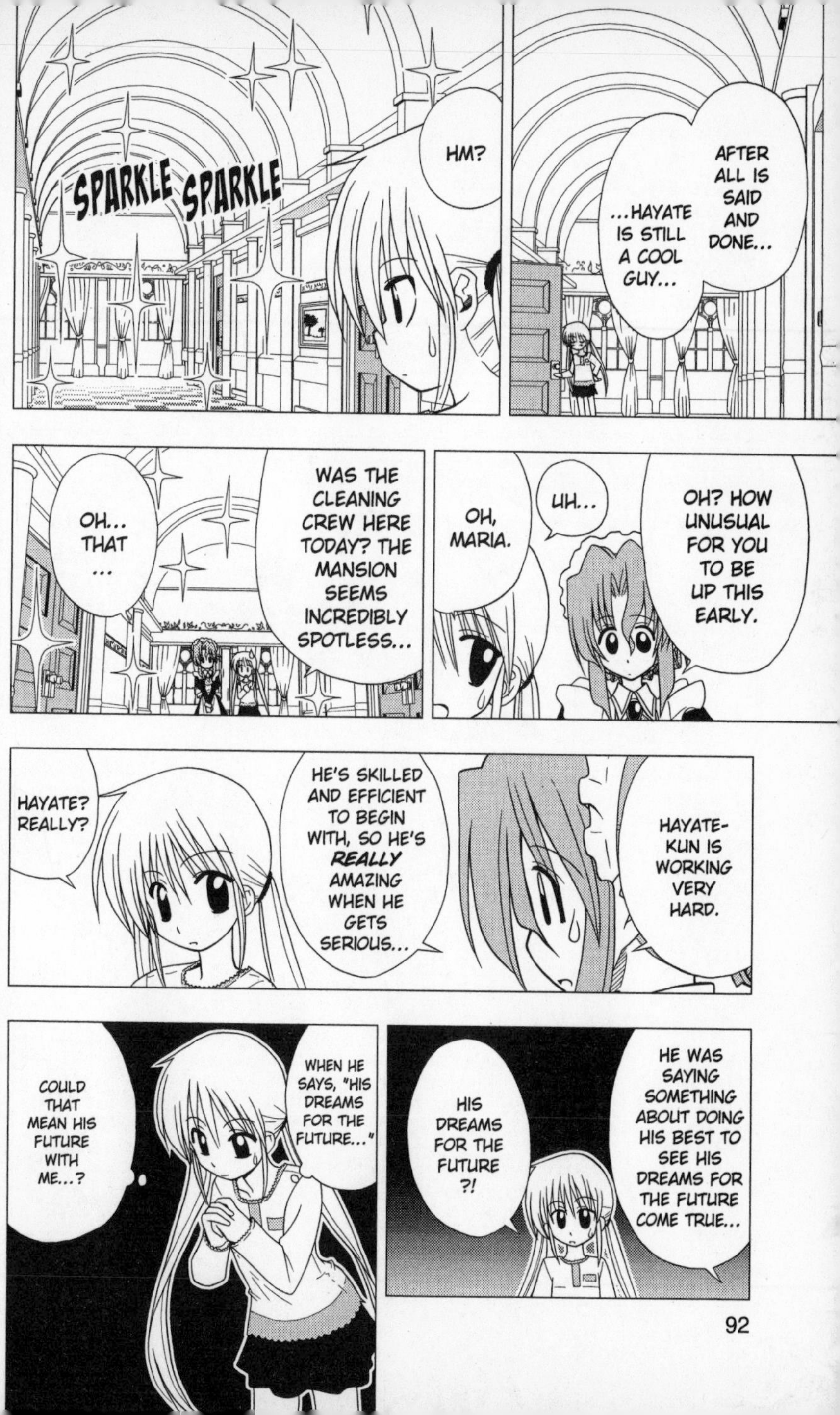

AFTER ALL IS SAID AND DONE...
...HAYATE IS STILL A COOL GUY...
HM?
SPARKLE SPARKLE
OH? HOW UNUSUAL FOR YOU TO BE UP THIS EARLY.
UH...
OH, MARIA.
WAS THE CLEANING CREW HERE TODAY? THE MANSION SEEMS INCREDIBLY SPOTLESS...
OH... THAT ...
HAYATE-KUN IS WORKING VERY HARD.
HE'S SKILLED AND EFFICIENT TO BEGIN WITH, SO HE'S ***REALLY*** AMAZING WHEN HE GETS SERIOUS...
HAYATE? REALLY?
HE WAS SAYING SOMETHING ABOUT DOING HIS BEST TO SEE HIS DREAMS FOR THE FUTURE COME TRUE...
HIS DREAMS FOR THE FUTURE ?!
WHEN HE SAYS, "HIS DREAMS FOR THE FUTURE..."
COULD THAT MEAN HIS FUTURE WITH ME...?

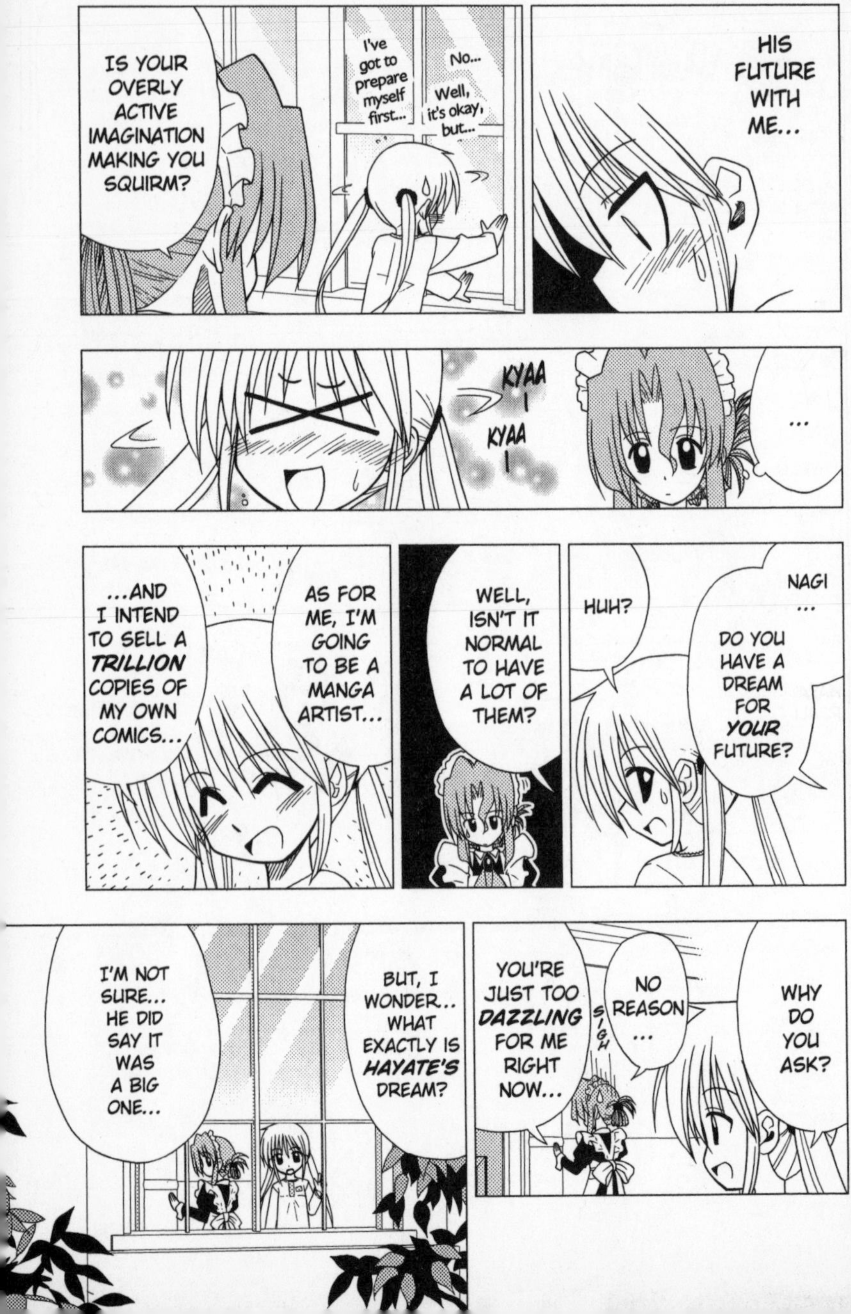
HIS FUTURE WITH ME...
No... Well, it's okay, but...
I've got to prepare myself first...
IS YOUR OVERLY ACTIVE IMAGINATION MAKING YOU SQUIRM?
...
KYAA KYAA
NAGI... DO YOU HAVE A DREAM FOR *YOUR* FUTURE?
HUH?
WELL, ISN'T IT NORMAL TO HAVE A LOT OF THEM?
AS FOR ME, I'M GOING TO BE A MANGA ARTIST...
...AND I INTEND TO SELL A *TRILLION* COPIES OF MY OWN COMICS...
WHY DO YOU ASK?
NO REASON...
SIGH
YOU'RE JUST TOO *DAZZLING* FOR ME RIGHT NOW...
BUT, I WONDER... WHAT EXACTLY IS *HAYATE'S* DREAM?
I'M NOT SURE... HE DID SAY IT WAS A BIG ONE...

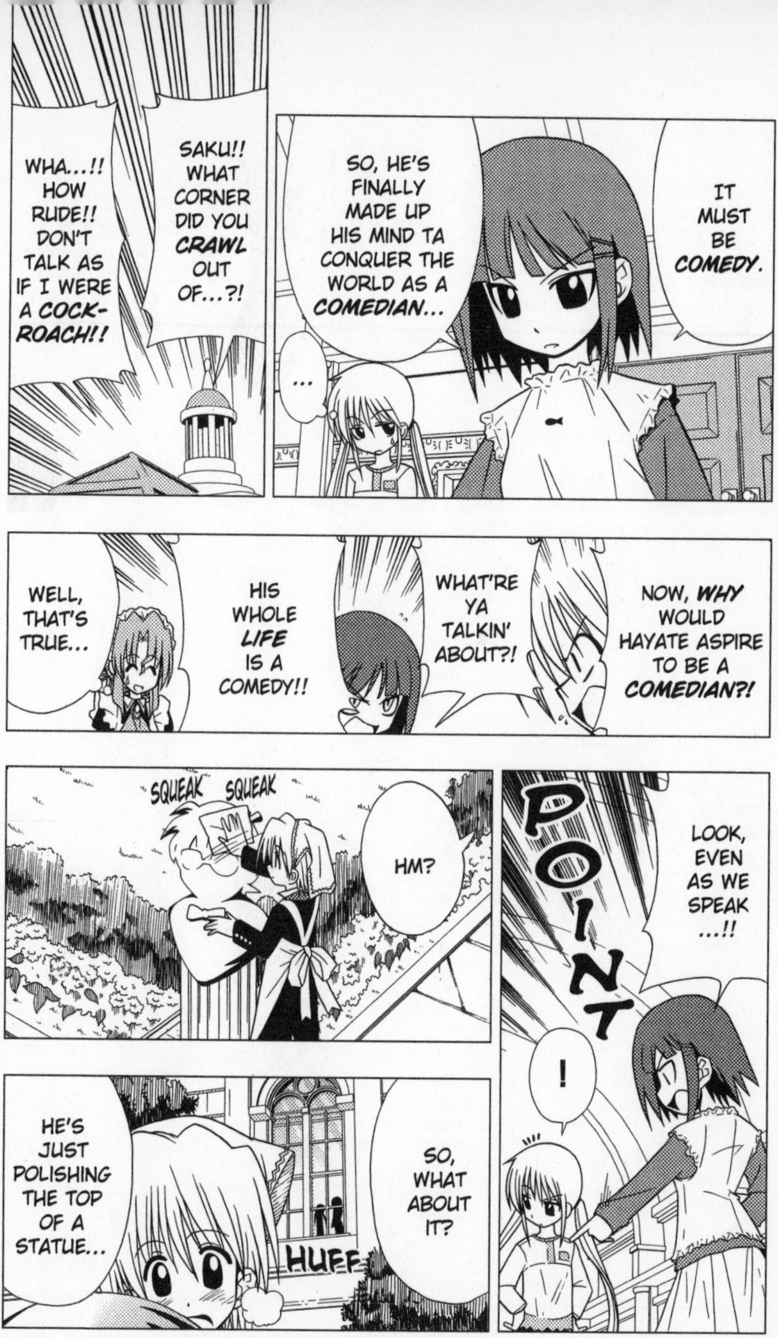
IT MUST BE COMEDY.
SO, HE'S FINALLY MADE UP HIS MIND TA CONQUER THE WORLD AS A COMEDIAN...
...
SAKU!! WHAT CORNER DID YOU CRAWL OUT OF...?!
WHA...!! HOW RUDE!! DON'T TALK AS IF I WERE A COCK-ROACH!!
NOW, WHY WOULD HAYATE ASPIRE TO BE A COMEDIAN?!
WHAT'RE YA TALKIN' ABOUT?!
HIS WHOLE LIFE IS A COMEDY!!
WELL, THAT'S TRUE...
POINT
LOOK, EVEN AS WE SPEAK ...!!
!
HM?
SQUEAK SQUEAK
SO, WHAT ABOUT IT?
HE'S JUST POLISHING THE TOP OF A STATUE...
HUFF

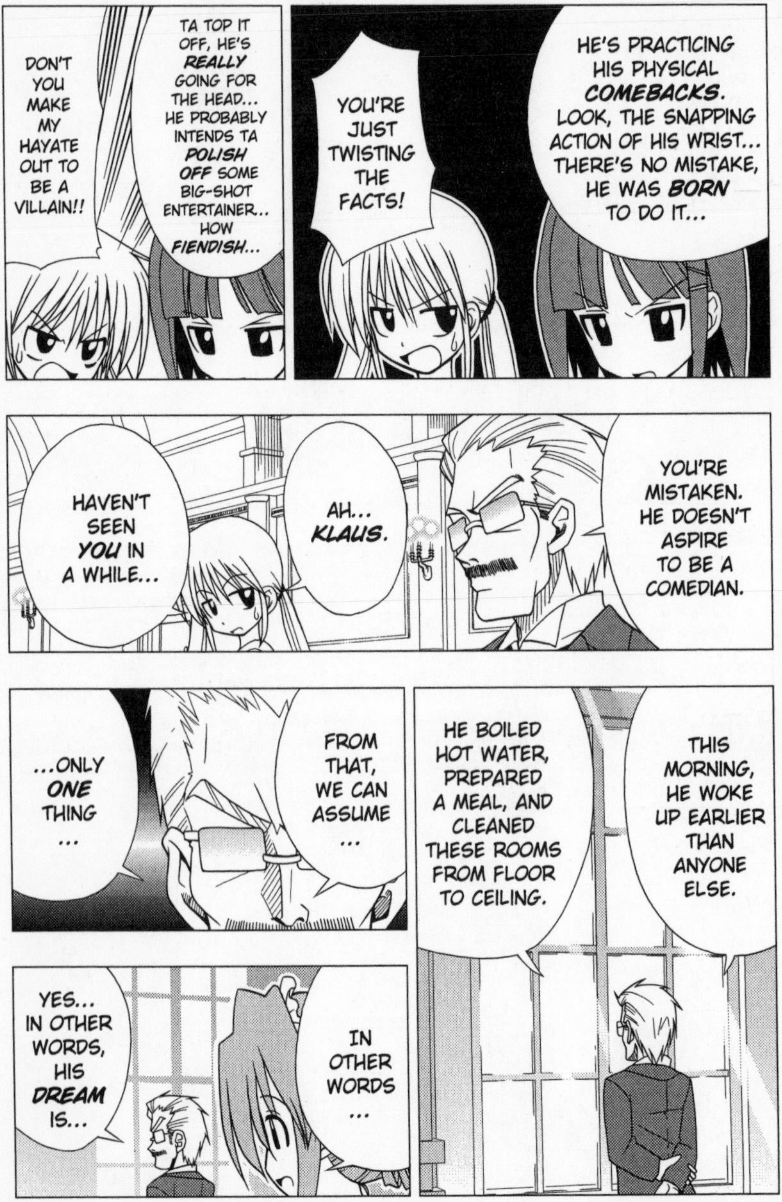
HE'S PRACTICING HIS PHYSICAL COMEBACKS. LOOK, THE SNAPPING ACTION OF HIS WRIST... THERE'S NO MISTAKE, HE WAS BORN TO DO IT...
YOU'RE JUST TWISTING THE FACTS!
TA TOP IT OFF, HE'S REALLY GOING FOR THE HEAD... HE PROBABLY INTENDS TA POLISH OFF SOME BIG-SHOT ENTERTAINER... HOW FIENDISH...
DON'T YOU MAKE MY HAYATE OUT TO BE A VILLAIN!!
YOU'RE MISTAKEN. HE DOESN'T ASPIRE TO BE A COMEDIAN.
AH... KLAUS.
HAVEN'T SEEN YOU IN A WHILE...
THIS MORNING, HE WOKE UP EARLIER THAN ANYONE ELSE.
HE BOILED HOT WATER, PREPARED A MEAL, AND CLEANED THESE ROOMS FROM FLOOR TO CEILING.
FROM THAT, WE CAN ASSUME...
...ONLY ONE THING...
IN OTHER WORDS...
YES... IN OTHER WORDS, HIS DREAM IS...

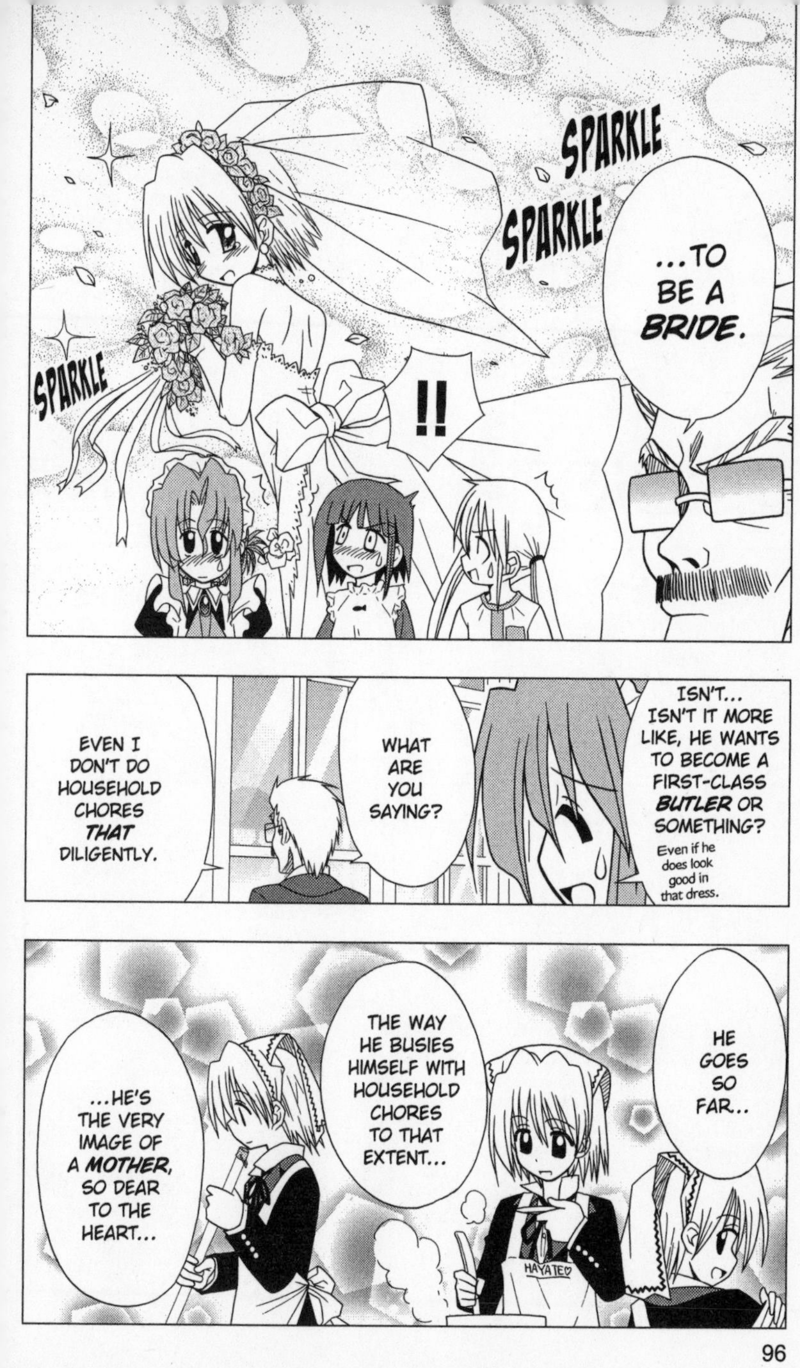
...TO BE A BRIDE.
SPARKLE
SPARKLE
!!
SPARKLE
ISN'T... ISN'T IT MORE LIKE, HE WANTS TO BECOME A FIRST-CLASS BUTLER OR SOMETHING?
Even if he does look good in that dress.
WHAT ARE YOU SAYING?
EVEN I DON'T DO HOUSEHOLD CHORES THAT DILIGENTLY.
HE GOES SO FAR...
THE WAY HE BUSIES HIMSELF WITH HOUSEHOLD CHORES TO THAT EXTENT...
HAYATE♥
...HE'S THE VERY IMAGE OF A MOTHER, SO DEAR TO THE HEART...

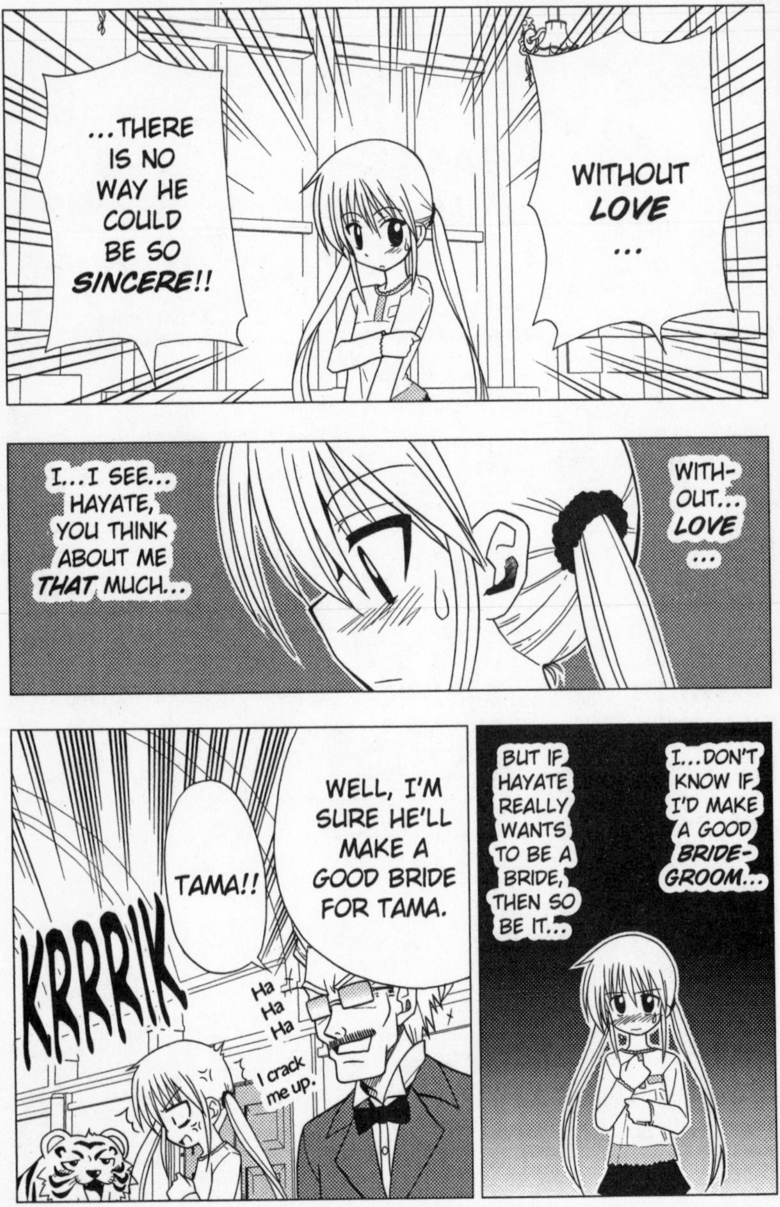
WITHOUT LOVE ...
...THERE IS NO WAY HE COULD BE SO SINCERE!!
WITH-OUT... LOVE ...
I...I SEE... HAYATE, YOU THINK ABOUT ME THAT MUCH...
I...DON'T KNOW IF I'D MAKE A GOOD BRIDE-GROOM...
BUT IF HAYATE REALLY WANTS TO BE A BRIDE, THEN SO BE IT...
WELL, I'M SURE HE'LL MAKE A GOOD BRIDE FOR TAMA.
TAMA!!
Ha Ha Ha
I crack me up.
KRRRIK

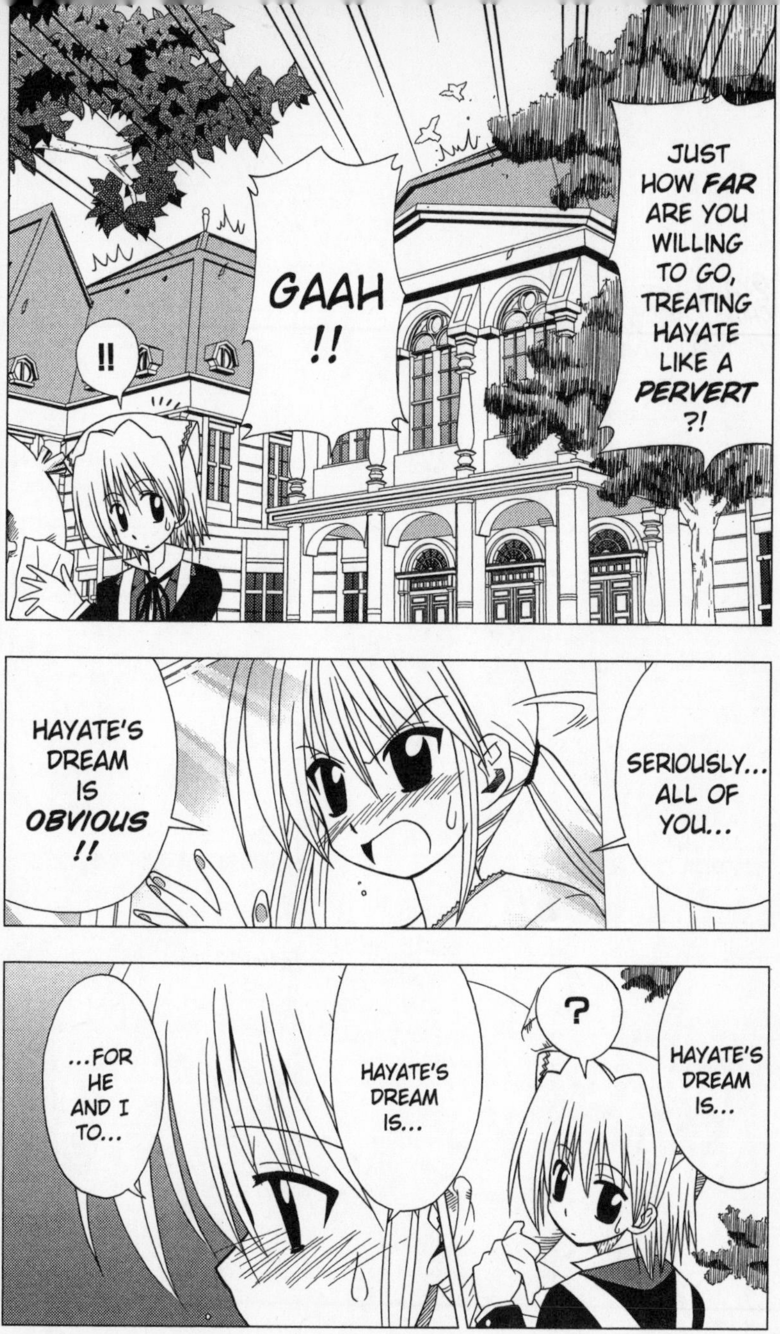
JUST HOW FAR ARE YOU WILLING TO GO, TREATING HAYATE LIKE A PERVERT ?!
GAAH !!
!!
SERIOUSLY... ALL OF YOU...
HAYATE'S DREAM IS OBVIOUS !!
HAYATE'S DREAM IS...
?
HAYATE'S DREAM IS...
...FOR HE AND I TO...

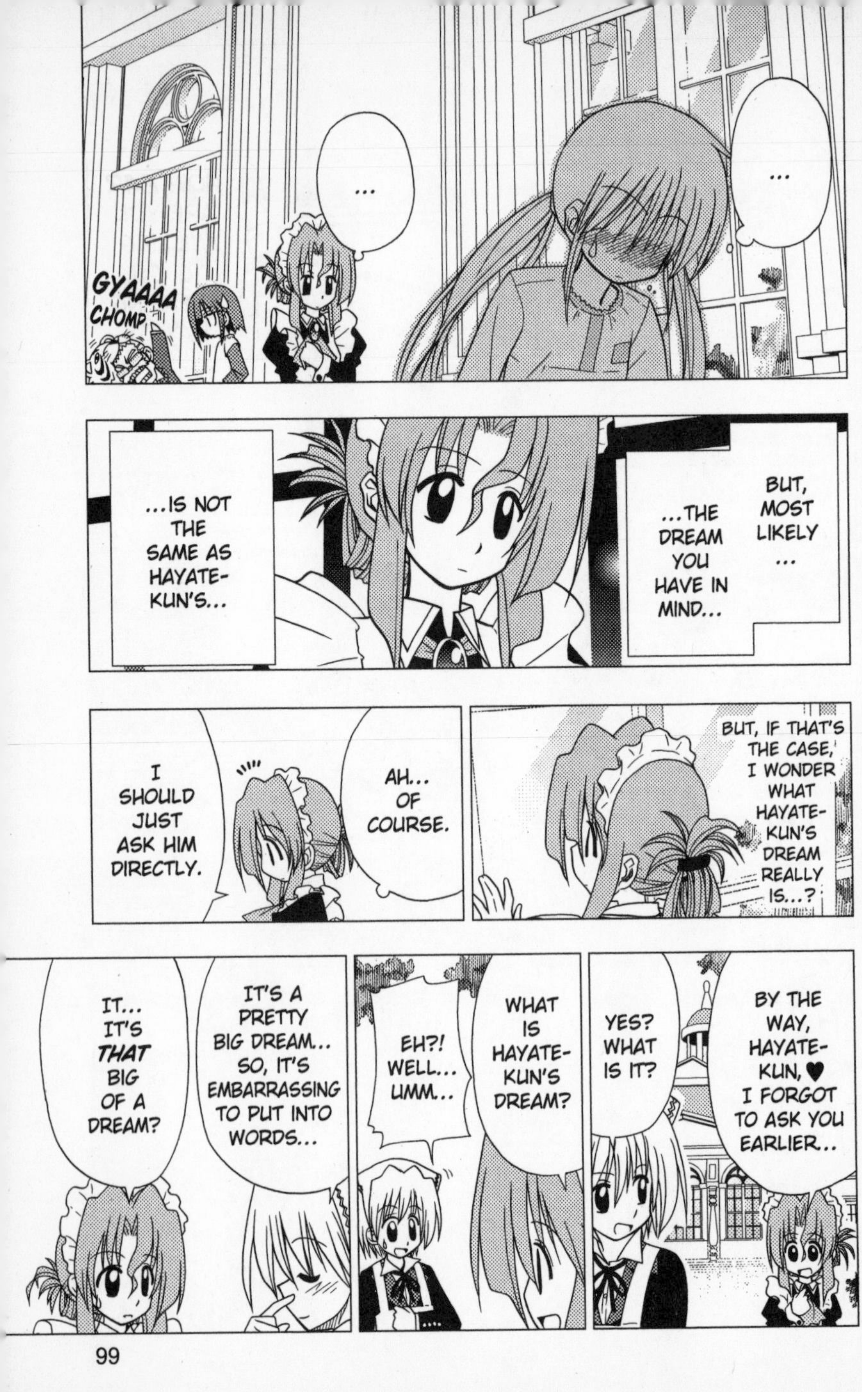
...
...
GYAAAA
CHOMP
BUT, MOST LIKELY...
...THE DREAM YOU HAVE IN MIND...
...IS NOT THE SAME AS HAYATE-KUN'S...
BUT, IF THAT'S THE CASE, I WONDER WHAT HAYATE-KUN'S DREAM REALLY IS...?
AH... OF COURSE.
I SHOULD JUST ASK HIM DIRECTLY.
BY THE WAY, HAYATE-KUN, ♥ I FORGOT TO ASK YOU EARLIER...
YES? WHAT IS IT?
WHAT IS HAYATE-KUN'S DREAM?
EH?! WELL... UMM...
IT'S A PRETTY BIG DREAM... SO, IT'S EMBARRASSING TO PUT INTO WORDS...
IT... IT'S *THAT* BIG OF A DREAM?

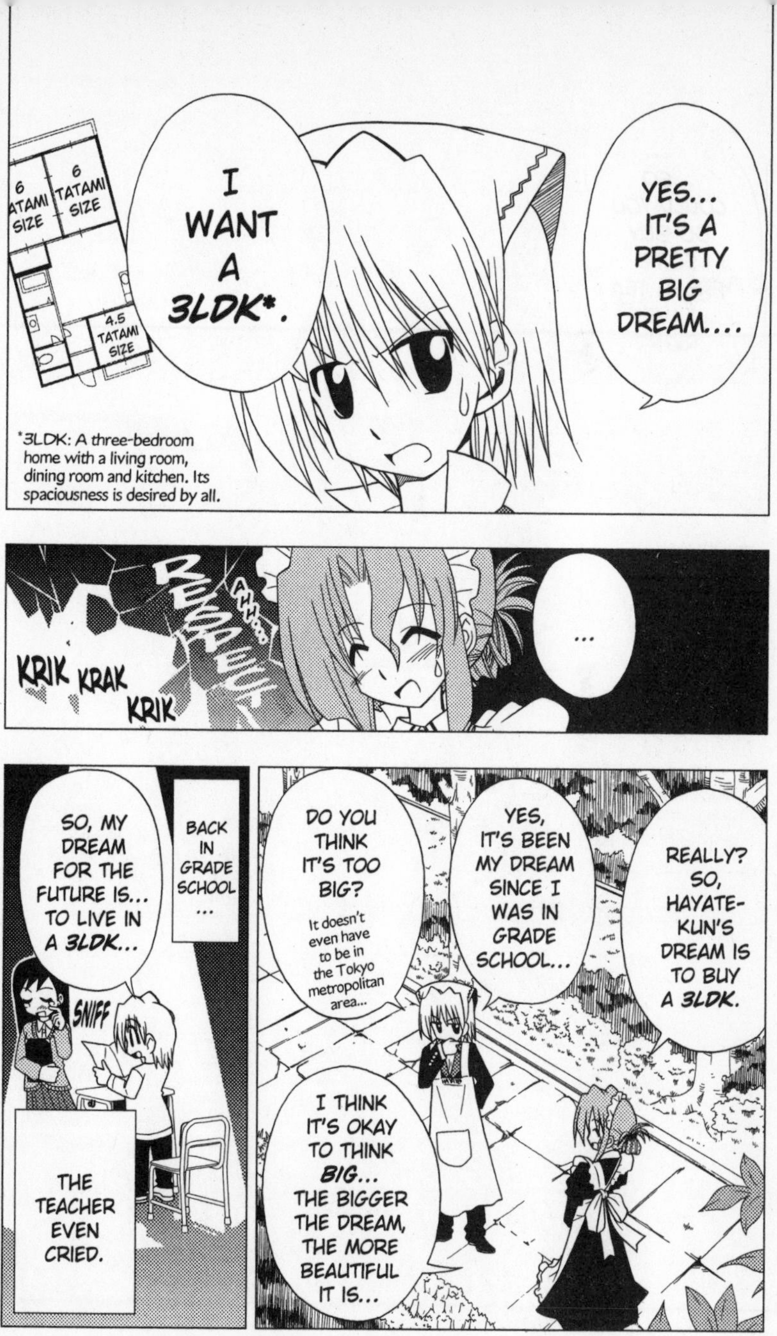
YES... IT'S A PRETTY BIG DREAM....
I WANT A 3LDK*.
6 TATAMI SIZE
6 TATAMI SIZE
4.5 TATAMI SIZE
*3LDK: A three-bedroom home with a living room, dining room and kitchen. Its spaciousness is desired by all.
...
RESPECT
AHH...
KRIK KRAK KRIK
REALLY? SO, HAYATE-KUN'S DREAM IS TO BUY A 3LDK.
YES, IT'S BEEN MY DREAM SINCE I WAS IN GRADE SCHOOL...
DO YOU THINK IT'S TOO BIG?
It doesn't even have to be in the Tokyo metropolitan area...
I THINK IT'S OKAY TO THINK BIG... THE BIGGER THE DREAM, THE MORE BEAUTIFUL IT IS...
BACK IN GRADE SCHOOL ...
SO, MY DREAM FOR THE FUTURE IS... TO LIVE IN A 3LDK...
SNIFF
THE TEACHER EVEN CRIED.

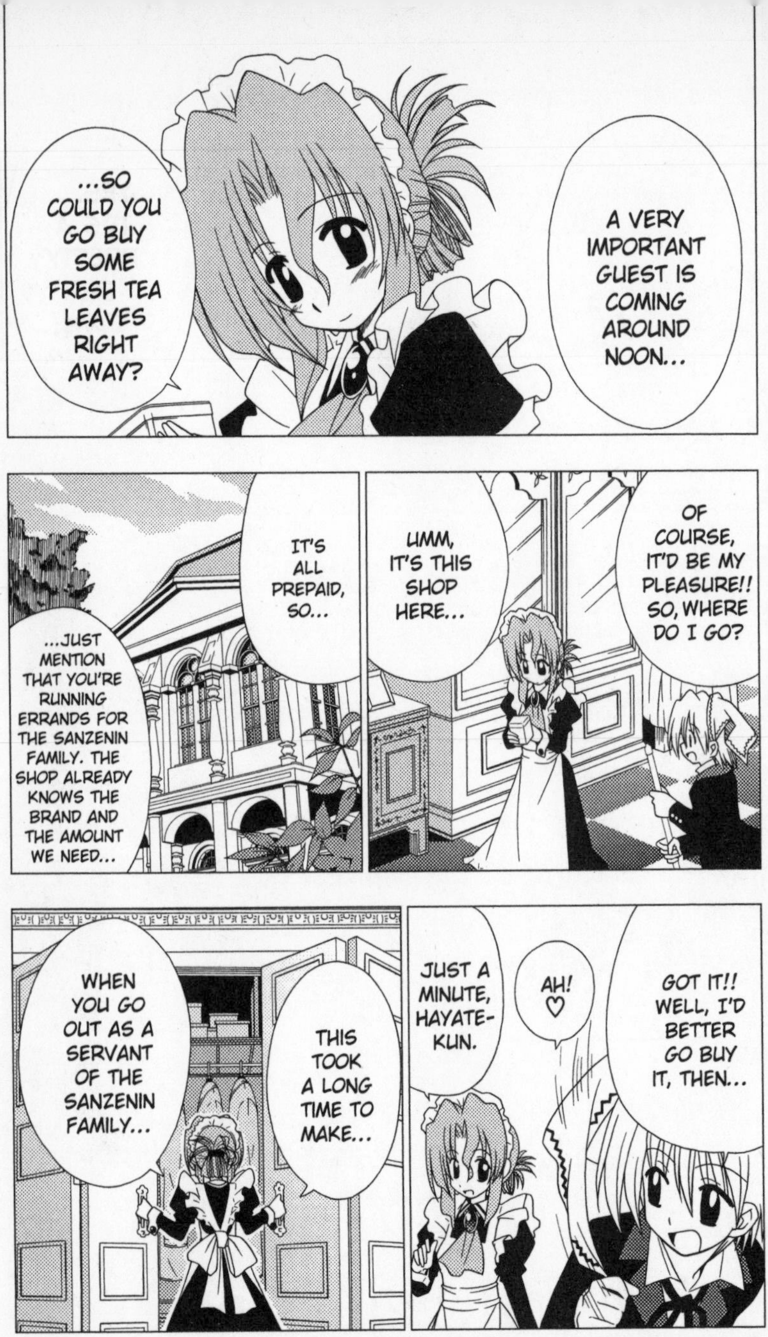
A VERY IMPORTANT GUEST IS COMING AROUND NOON...
...SO COULD YOU GO BUY SOME FRESH TEA LEAVES RIGHT AWAY?
OF COURSE, IT'D BE MY PLEASURE!! SO, WHERE DO I GO?
UMM, IT'S THIS SHOP HERE...
IT'S ALL PREPAID, SO...
...JUST MENTION THAT YOU'RE RUNNING ERRANDS FOR THE SANZENIN FAMILY. THE SHOP ALREADY KNOWS THE BRAND AND THE AMOUNT WE NEED...
GOT IT!! WELL, I'D BETTER GO BUY IT, THEN...
AH! ♡
JUST A MINUTE, HAYATE-KUN.
THIS TOOK A LONG TIME TO MAKE...
WHEN YOU GO OUT AS A SERVANT OF THE SANZENIN FAMILY...

Episode 7: "Careless Kindness Brings Unhappiness"

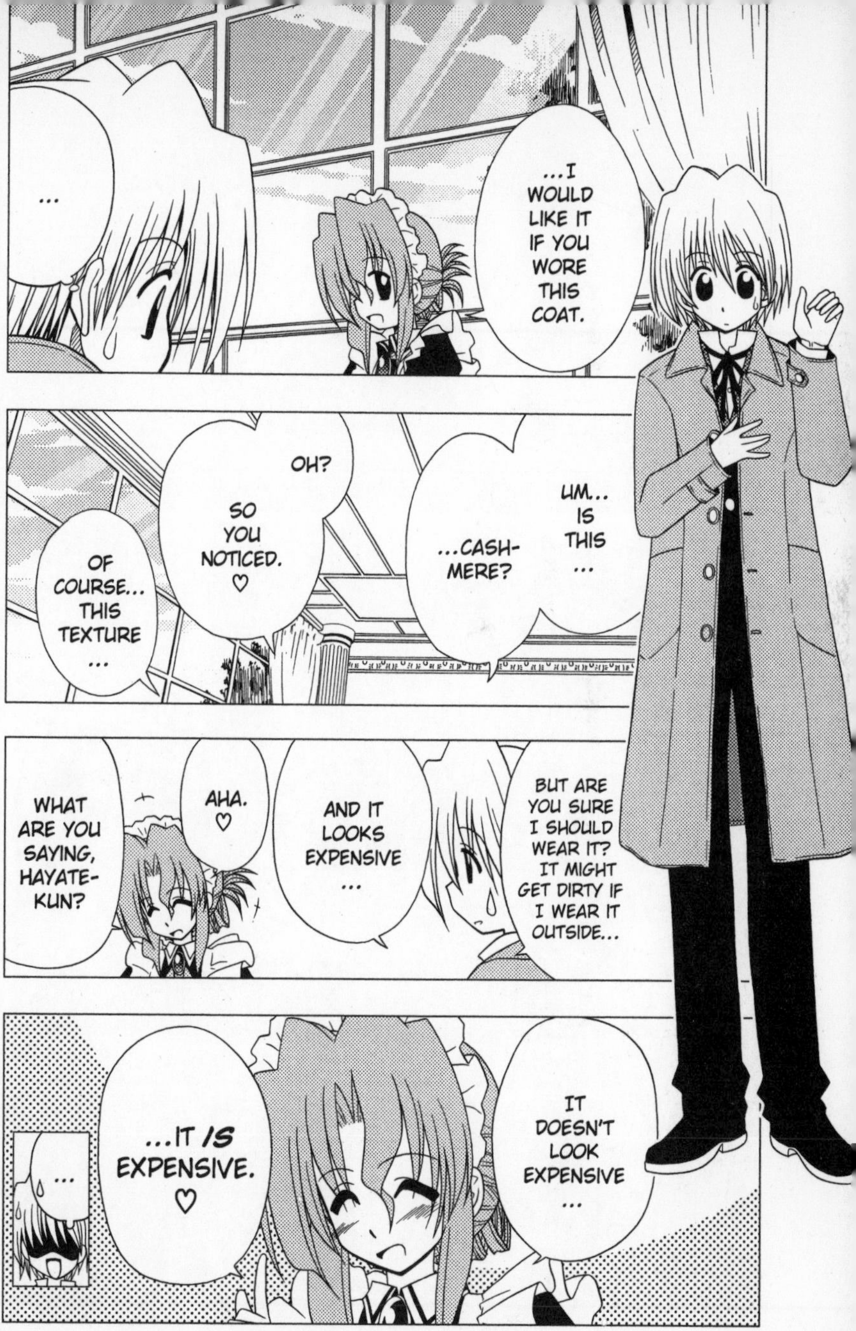
...I WOULD LIKE IT IF YOU WORE THIS COAT.
...
UM... IS THIS ...
...CASH-MERE?
OH?
SO YOU NOTICED. ♡
OF COURSE... THIS TEXTURE ...
BUT ARE YOU SURE I SHOULD WEAR IT? IT MIGHT GET DIRTY IF I WEAR IT OUTSIDE...
AND IT LOOKS EXPENSIVE ...
AHA. ♡
WHAT ARE YOU SAYING, HAYATE-KUN?
IT DOESN'T LOOK EXPENSIVE ...
...IT *IS* EXPENSIVE. ♡
...

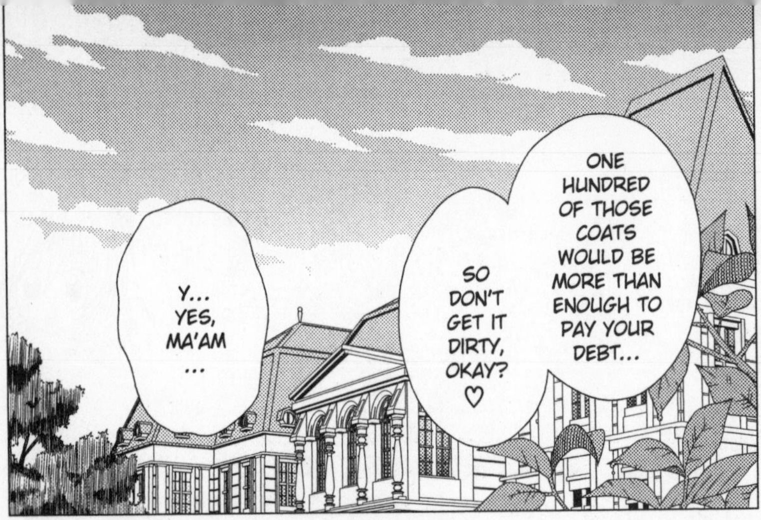
ONE HUNDRED OF THOSE COATS WOULD BE MORE THAN ENOUGH TO PAY YOUR DEBT...
SO DON'T GET IT DIRTY, OKAY? ♡
Y... YES, MA'AM ...

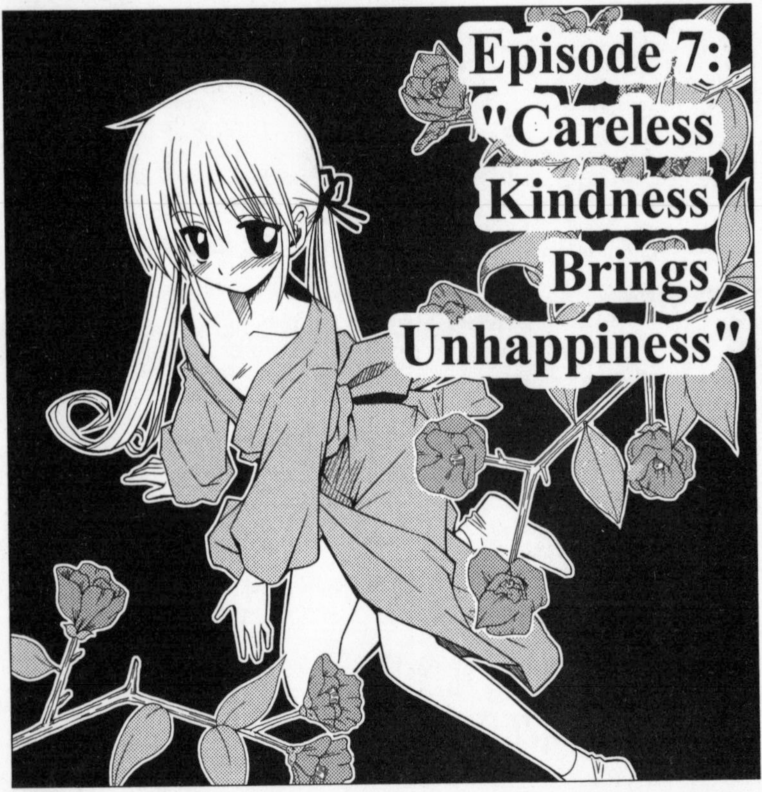
Episode 7: "Careless Kindness Brings Unhappiness"

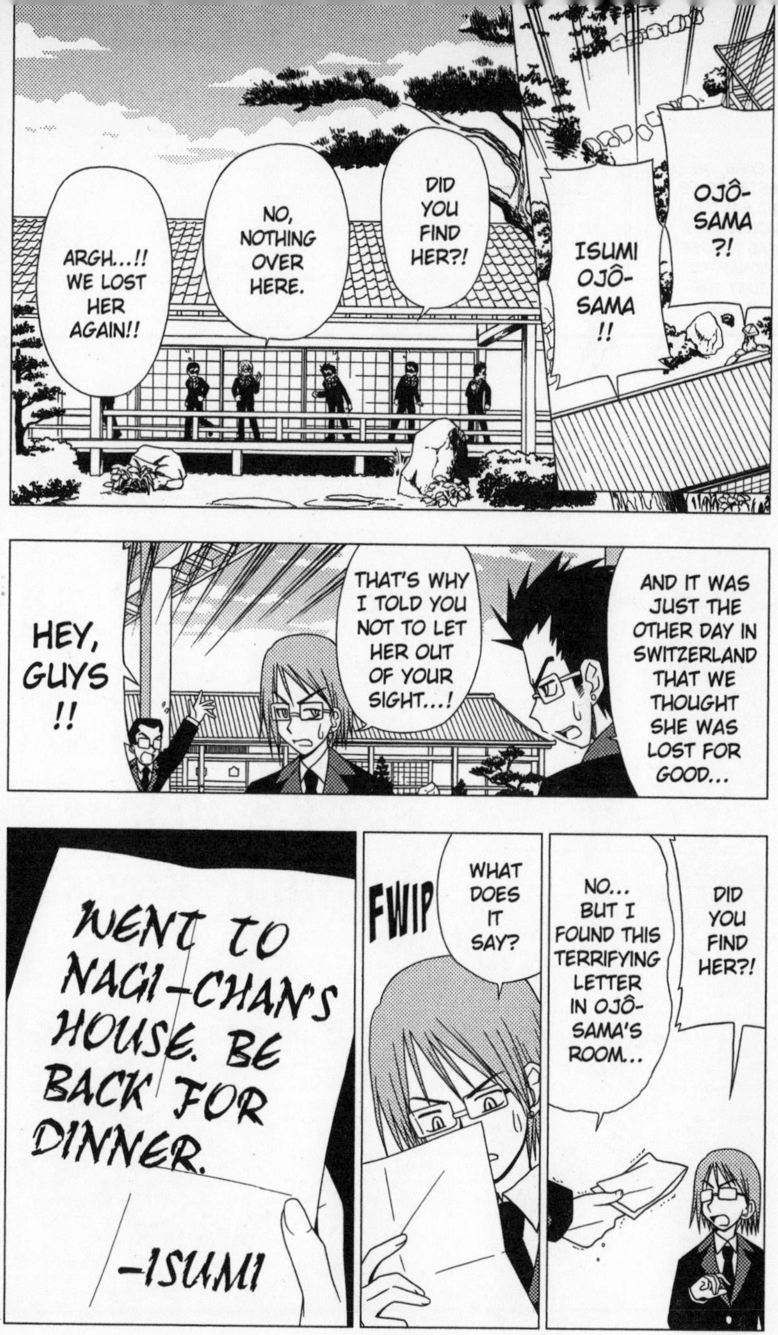
OJÔ-SAMA?!
ISUMI OJÔ-SAMA!!
DID YOU FIND HER?!
NO, NOTHING OVER HERE.
ARGH...!! WE LOST HER AGAIN!!
AND IT WAS JUST THE OTHER DAY IN SWITZERLAND THAT WE THOUGHT SHE WAS LOST FOR GOOD...
THAT'S WHY I TOLD YOU NOT TO LET HER OUT OF YOUR SIGHT...!
HEY, GUYS!!
DID YOU FIND HER?!
NO... BUT I FOUND THIS TERRIFYING LETTER IN OJÔ-SAMA'S ROOM...
WHAT DOES IT SAY?
FWIP
WENT TO NAGI-CHAN'S HOUSE. BE BACK FOR DINNER.
-ISUMI

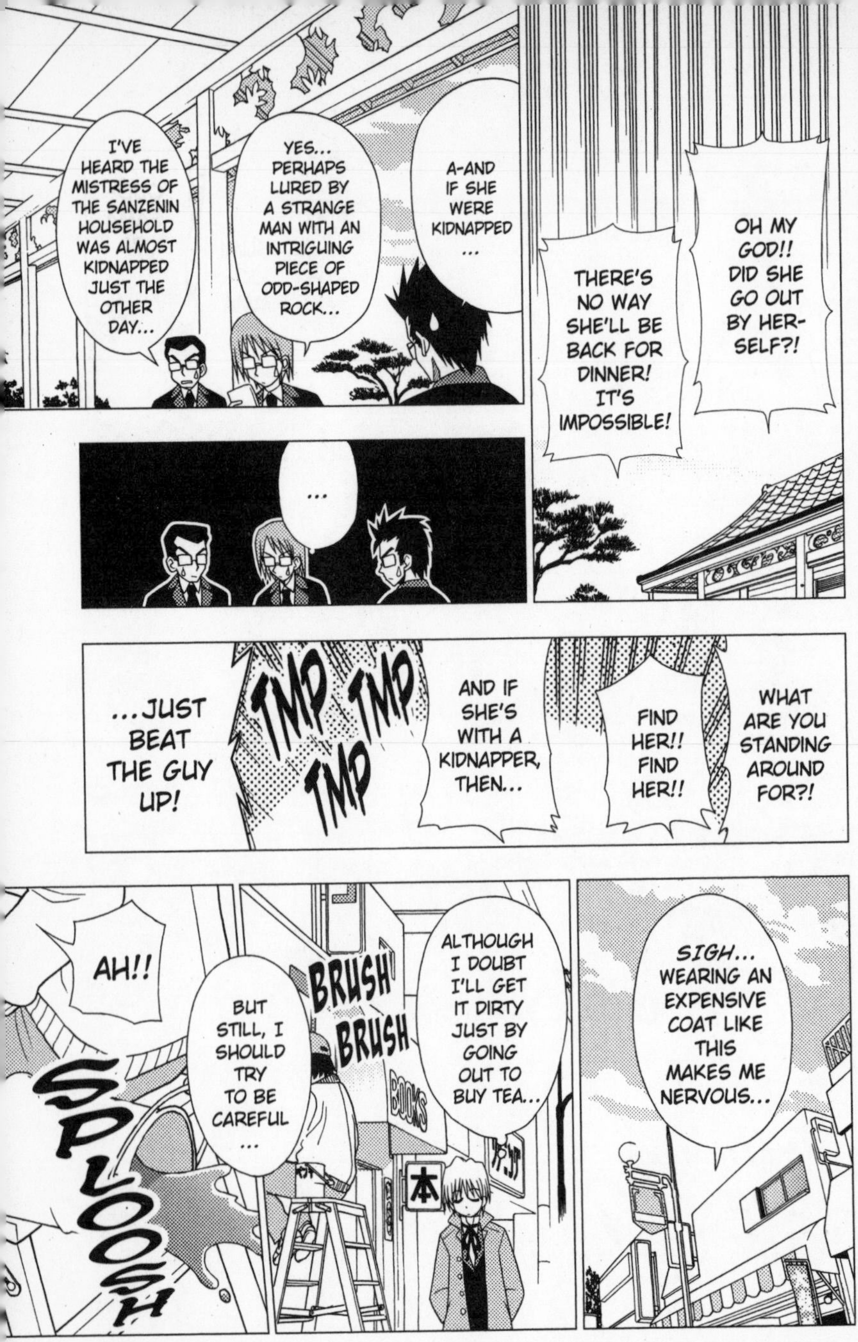
OH MY GOD!! DID SHE GO OUT BY HER-SELF?!
THERE'S NO WAY SHE'LL BE BACK FOR DINNER! IT'S IMPOSSIBLE!
A-AND IF SHE WERE KIDNAPPED ...
YES... PERHAPS LURED BY A STRANGE MAN WITH AN INTRIGUING PIECE OF ODD-SHAPED ROCK...
I'VE HEARD THE MISTRESS OF THE SANZENIN HOUSEHOLD WAS ALMOST KIDNAPPED JUST THE OTHER DAY...
...
WHAT ARE YOU STANDING AROUND FOR?!
FIND HER!! FIND HER!!
AND IF SHE'S WITH A KIDNAPPER, THEN...
TMP TMP TMP
...JUST BEAT THE GUY UP!
SIGH... WEARING AN EXPENSIVE COAT LIKE THIS MAKES ME NERVOUS...
ALTHOUGH I DOUBT I'LL GET IT DIRTY JUST BY GOING OUT TO BUY TEA...
BRUSH BRUSH
BOOKS
本
BUT STILL, I SHOULD TRY TO BE CAREFUL ...
AH!!
SPLOOSH

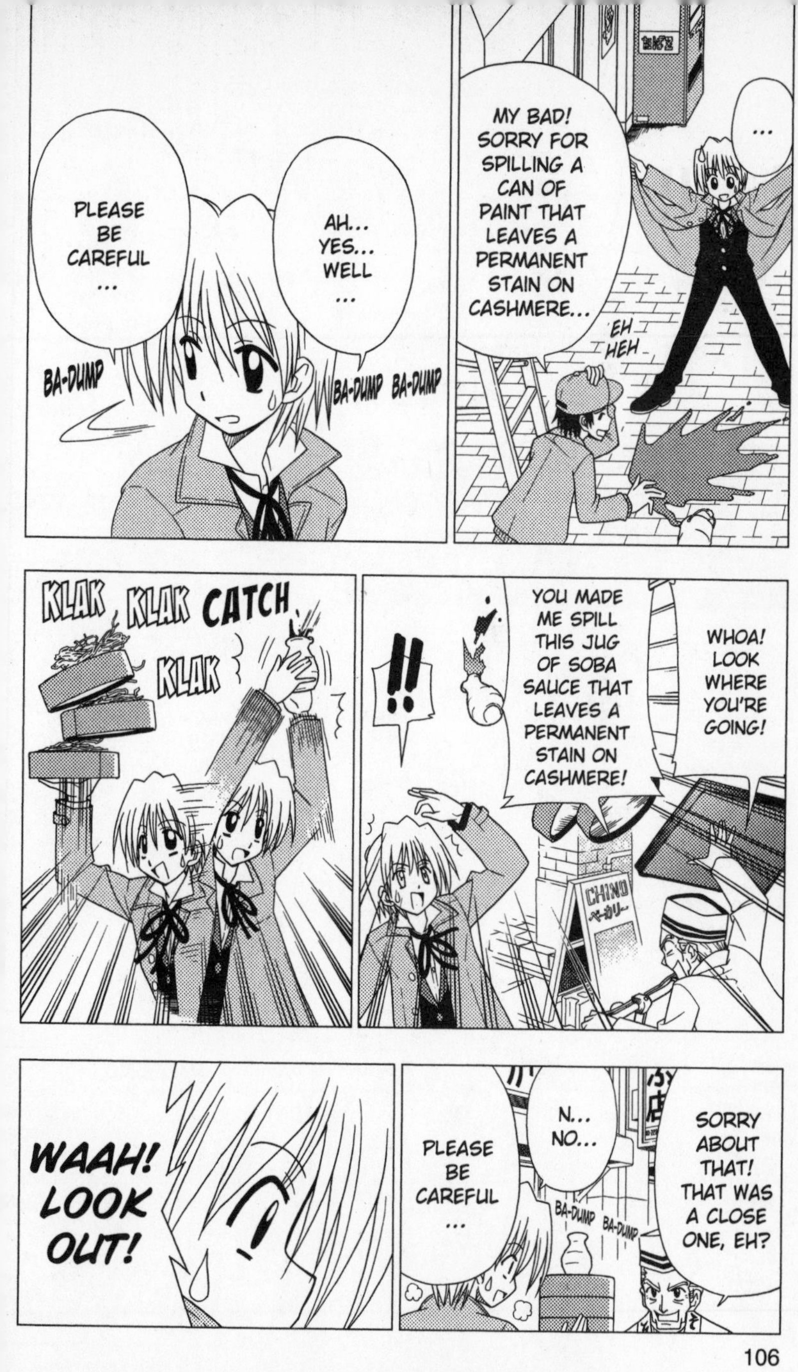
...
MY BAD! SORRY FOR SPILLING A CAN OF PAINT THAT LEAVES A PERMANENT STAIN ON CASHMERE...
EH HEH
AH... YES... WELL...
PLEASE BE CAREFUL...
BA-DUMP
BA-DUMP BA-DUMP
WHOA! LOOK WHERE YOU'RE GOING!
YOU MADE ME SPILL THIS JUG OF SOBA SAUCE THAT LEAVES A PERMANENT STAIN ON CASHMERE!
!!
CHINO
ベーカリー
CATCH
KLAK
KLAK
KLAK
SORRY ABOUT THAT! THAT WAS A CLOSE ONE, EH?
N... NO...
PLEASE BE CAREFUL...
BA-DUMP BA-DUMP
WAAH! LOOK OUT!

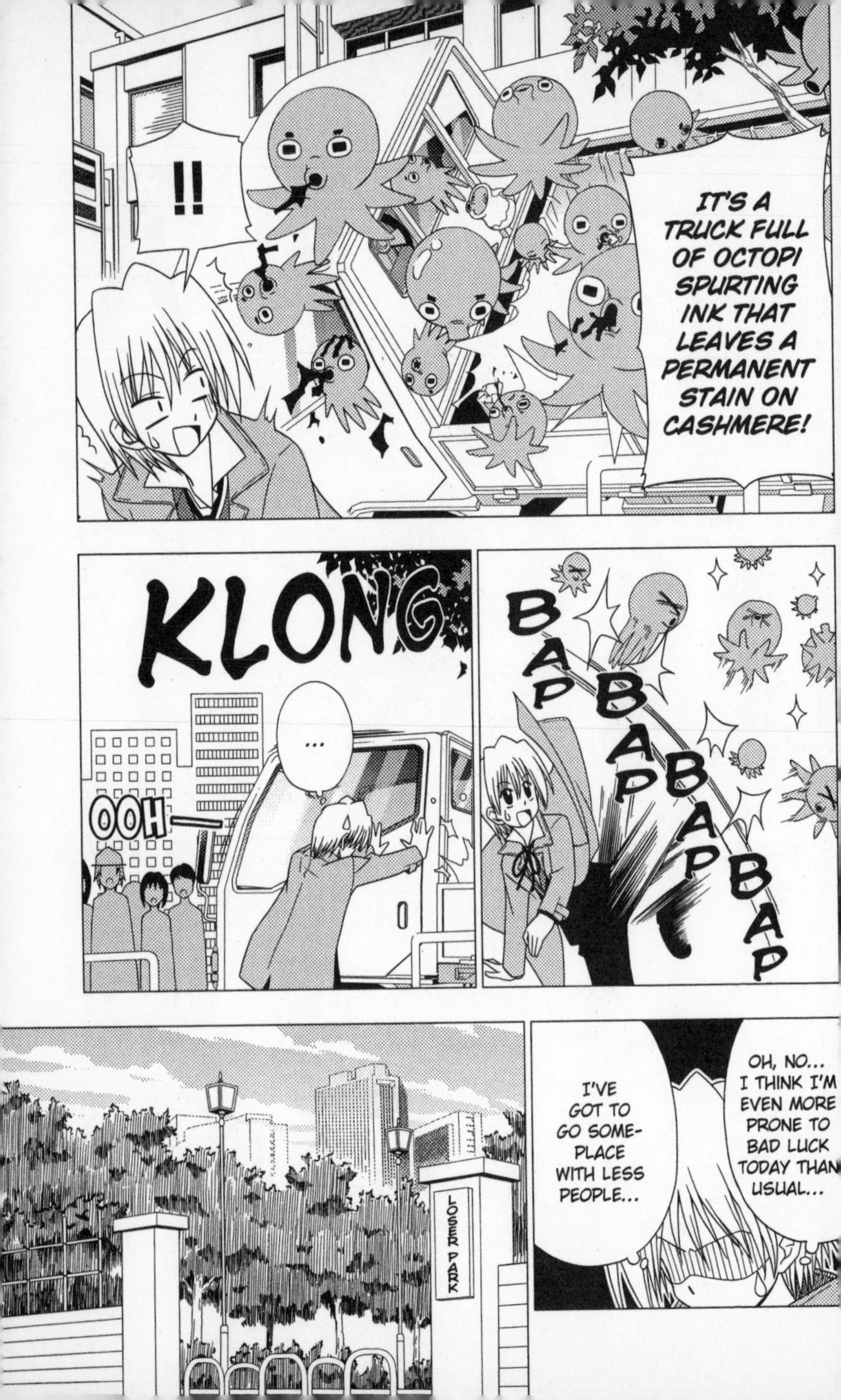

IT'S A TRUCK FULL OF OCTOPI SPURTING INK THAT LEAVES A PERMANENT STAIN ON CASHMERE!
!!
BAP BAP BAP BAP BAP BAP
KLONG
...
OOH—
OH, NO... I THINK I'M EVEN MORE PRONE TO BAD LUCK TODAY THAN USUAL...
I'VE GOT TO GO SOME-PLACE WITH LESS PEOPLE...
LOSER PARK

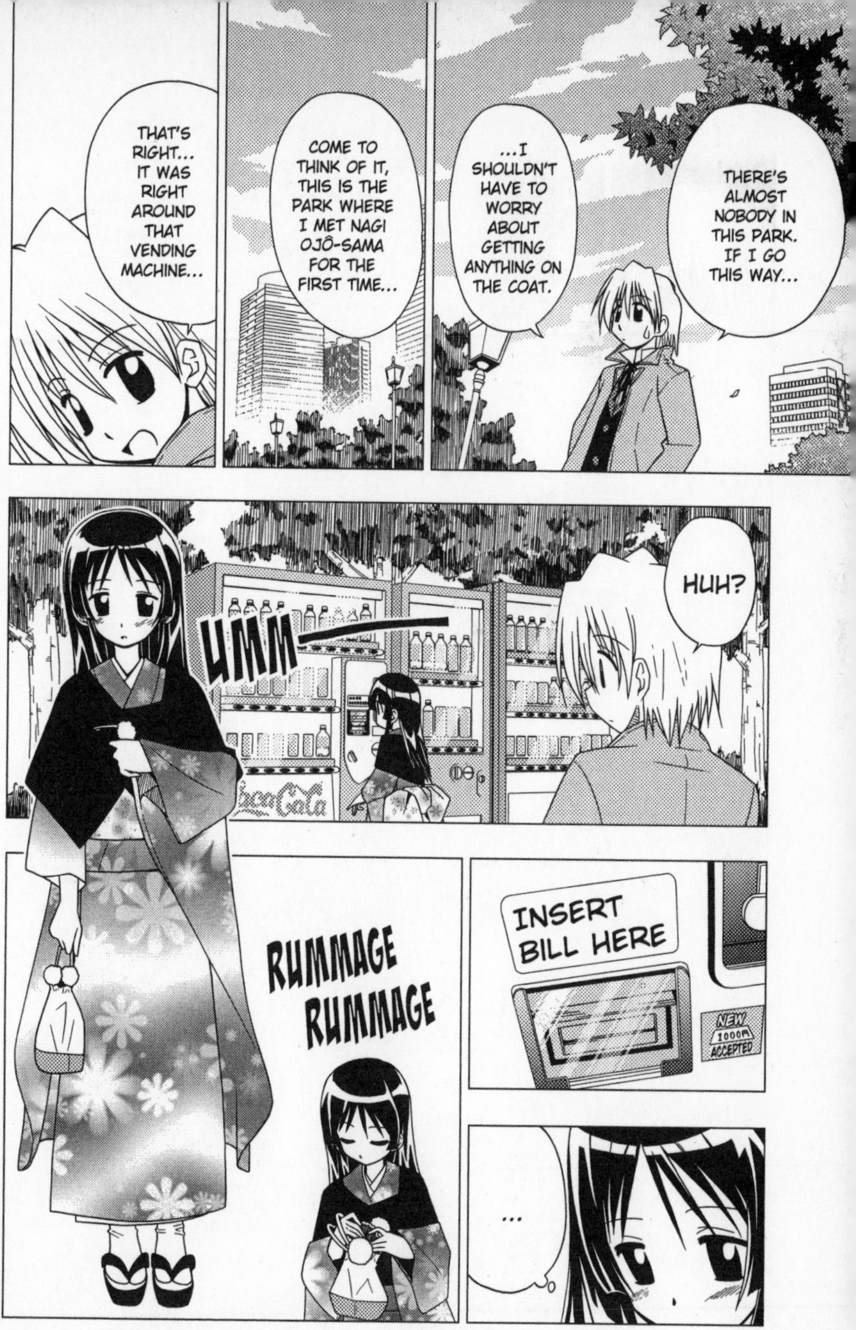
THERE'S ALMOST NOBODY IN THIS PARK. IF I GO THIS WAY...
...I SHOULDN'T HAVE TO WORRY ABOUT GETTING ANYTHING ON THE COAT.
COME TO THINK OF IT, THIS IS THE PARK WHERE I MET NAGI OJÔ-SAMA FOR THE FIRST TIME...
THAT'S RIGHT... IT WAS RIGHT AROUND THAT VENDING MACHINE...
HUH?
UMM—
INSERT BILL HERE
NEW 1000円 ACCEPTED
...
RUMMAGE RUMMAGE

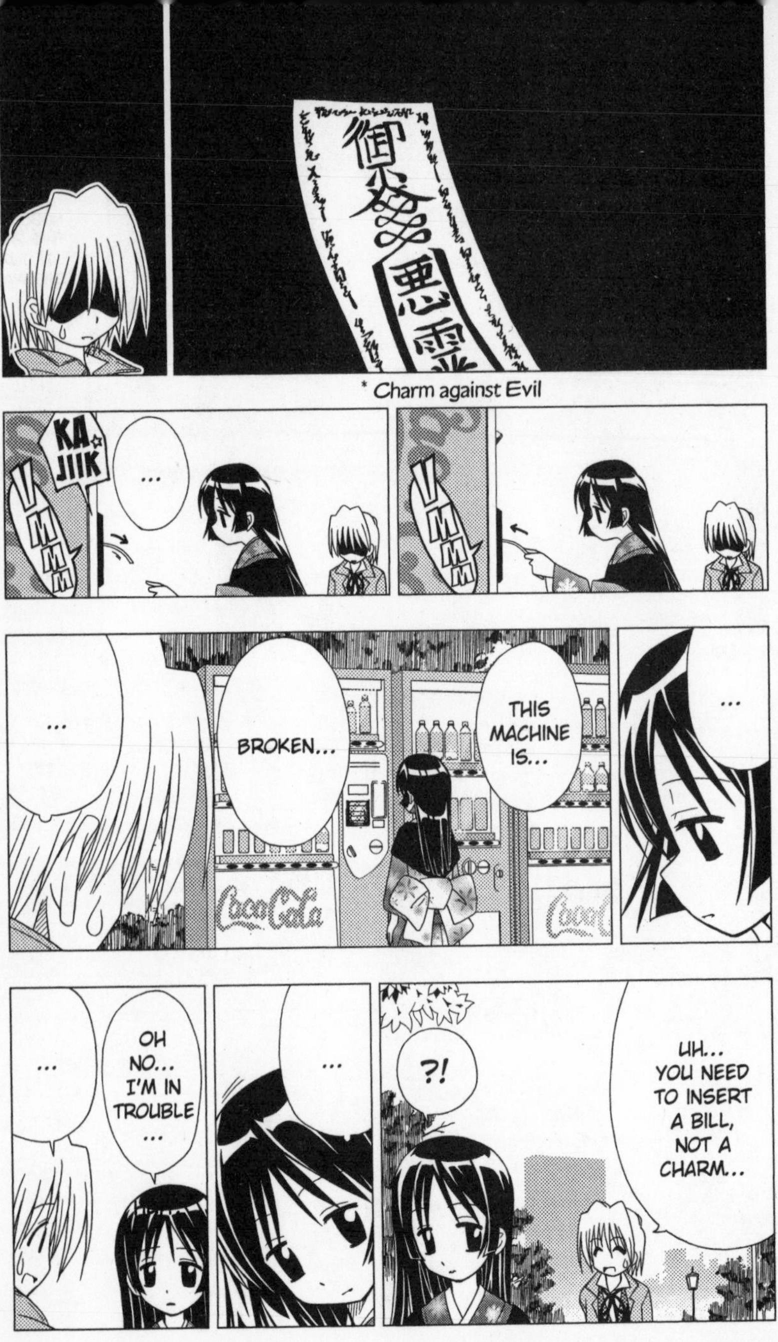
VMMMM
KA☆JIIK
VMMMM
...
...
THIS MACHINE IS...
BROKEN...
...
UH... YOU NEED TO INSERT A BILL, NOT A CHARM...
?!
...
OH NO... I'M IN TROUBLE ...
...
* Charm against Evil

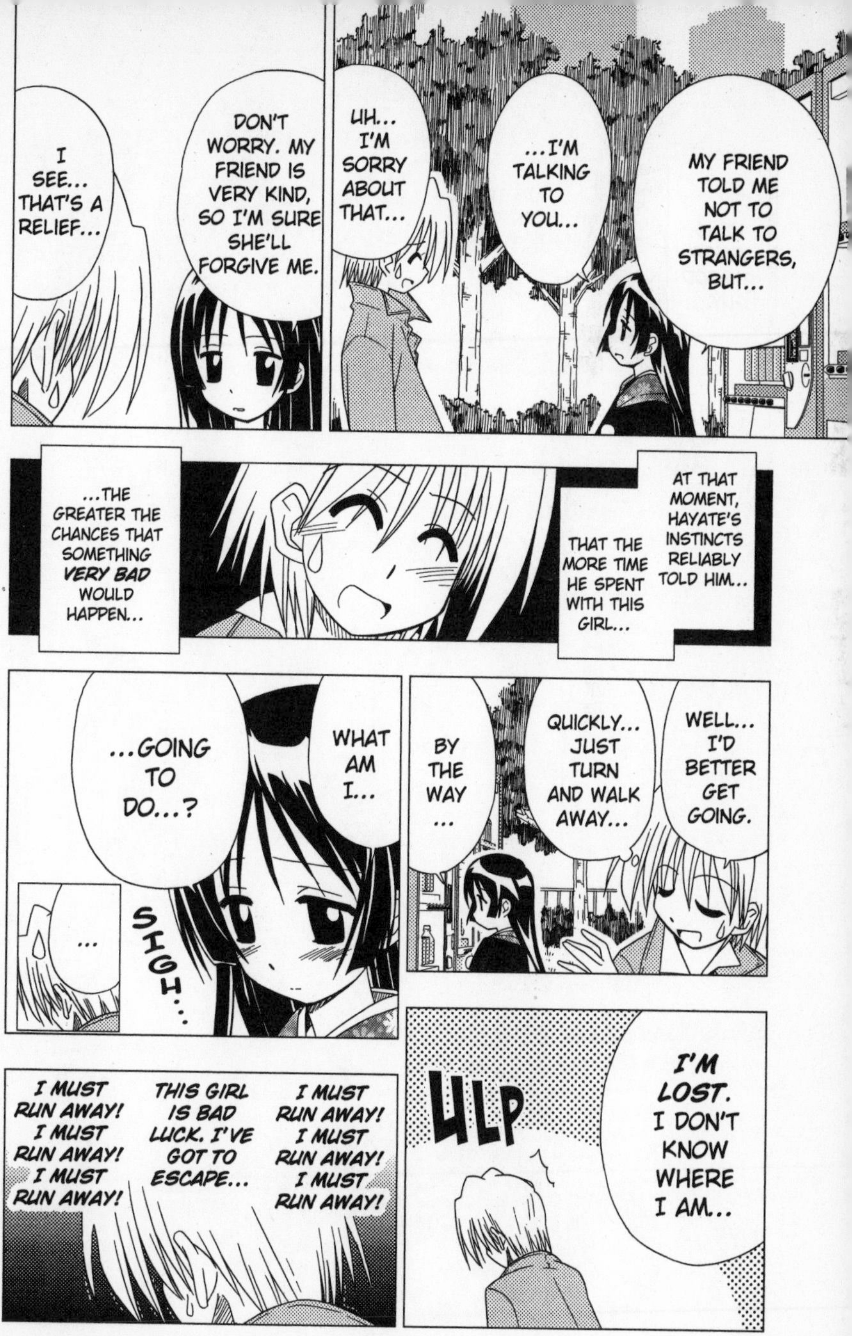
MY FRIEND TOLD ME NOT TO TALK TO STRANGERS, BUT...
...I'M TALKING TO YOU...
UH... I'M SORRY ABOUT THAT...
DON'T WORRY. MY FRIEND IS VERY KIND, SO I'M SURE SHE'LL FORGIVE ME.
I SEE... THAT'S A RELIEF...
AT THAT MOMENT, HAYATE'S INSTINCTS RELIABLY TOLD HIM...
THAT THE MORE TIME HE SPENT WITH THIS GIRL...
...THE GREATER THE CHANCES THAT SOMETHING *VERY BAD* WOULD HAPPEN...
WELL... I'D BETTER GET GOING.
QUICKLY... JUST TURN AND WALK AWAY...
BY THE WAY...
WHAT AM I...
...GOING TO DO...?
SIGH...
...
I'M LOST. I DON'T KNOW WHERE I AM...
ULP
I MUST RUN AWAY! I MUST RUN AWAY! I MUST RUN AWAY!
THIS GIRL IS BAD LUCK. I'VE GOT TO ESCAPE...
I MUST RUN AWAY! I MUST RUN AWAY! I MUST RUN AWAY!

I MUST RUN AWAY!
TMP
UM...
IS THERE ANYTHING I CAN DO TO HELP?
?!
HE IS SUCH A GOOD GUY...
DO YOU KNOW YOUR WAY AROUND HERE?
NO... NOT REALLY, BUT...
IF I LEAVE A GIRL LIKE YOU HERE ALONE...
...I'M WORRIED THAT YOU MIGHT BE KIDNAPPED ...
...
MY FRIEND TELLS ME...
...THE SAME THING ALL THE TIME.
SMILE
...

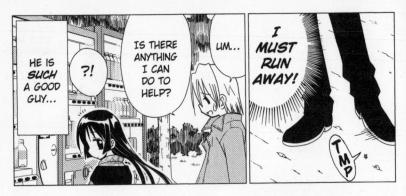

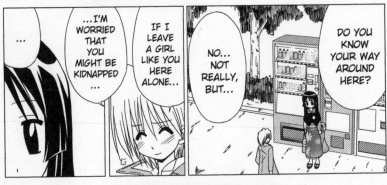

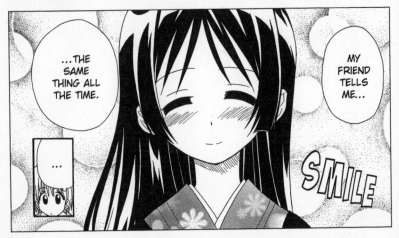

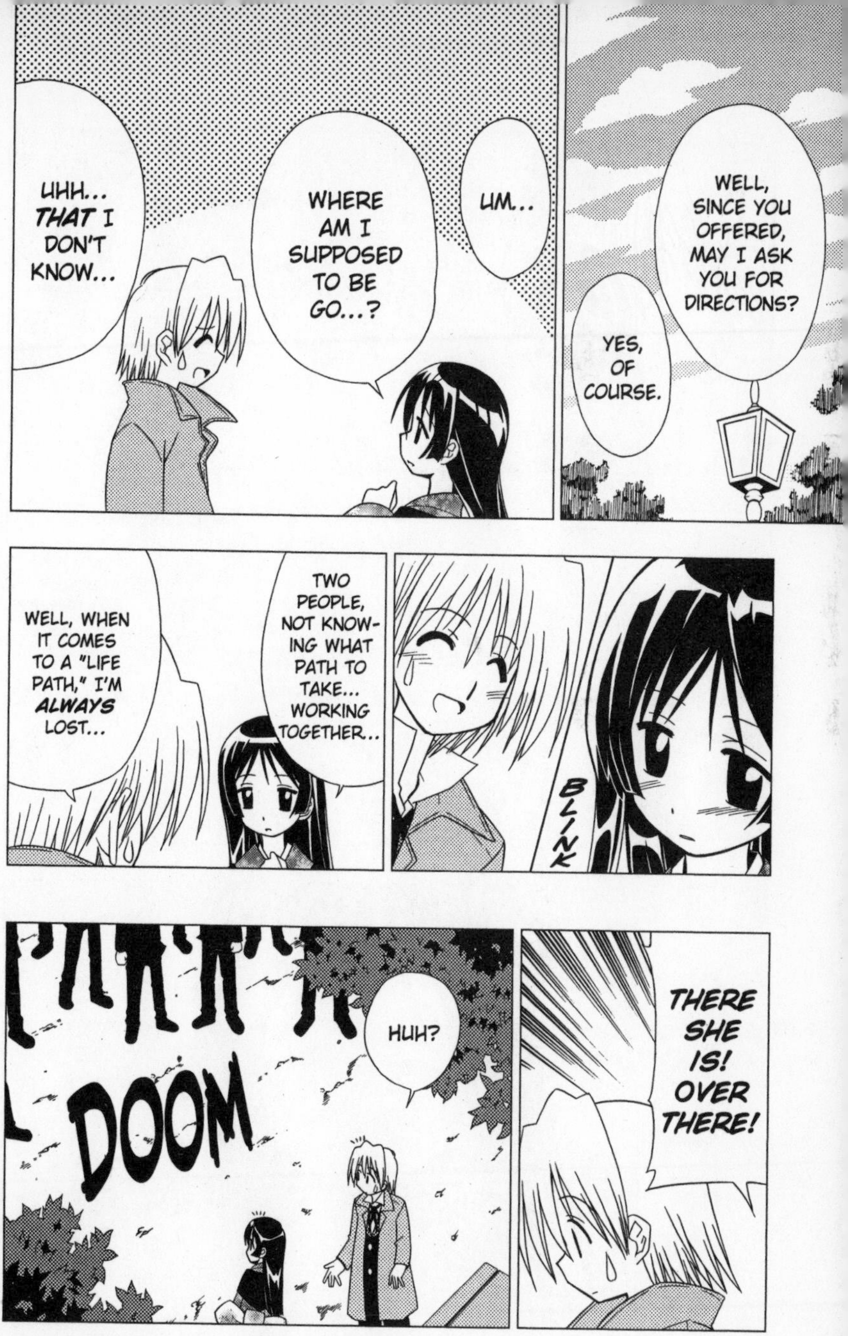
WELL, SINCE YOU OFFERED, MAY I ASK YOU FOR DIRECTIONS?
YES, OF COURSE.
UM...
WHERE AM I SUPPOSED TO BE GO...?
UHH... *THAT* I DON'T KNOW...
BLINK
TWO PEOPLE, NOT KNOWING WHAT PATH TO TAKE... WORKING TOGETHER...
WELL, WHEN IT COMES TO A "LIFE PATH," I'M *ALWAYS* LOST...
THERE SHE IS! OVER THERE!
HUH?
DOOM

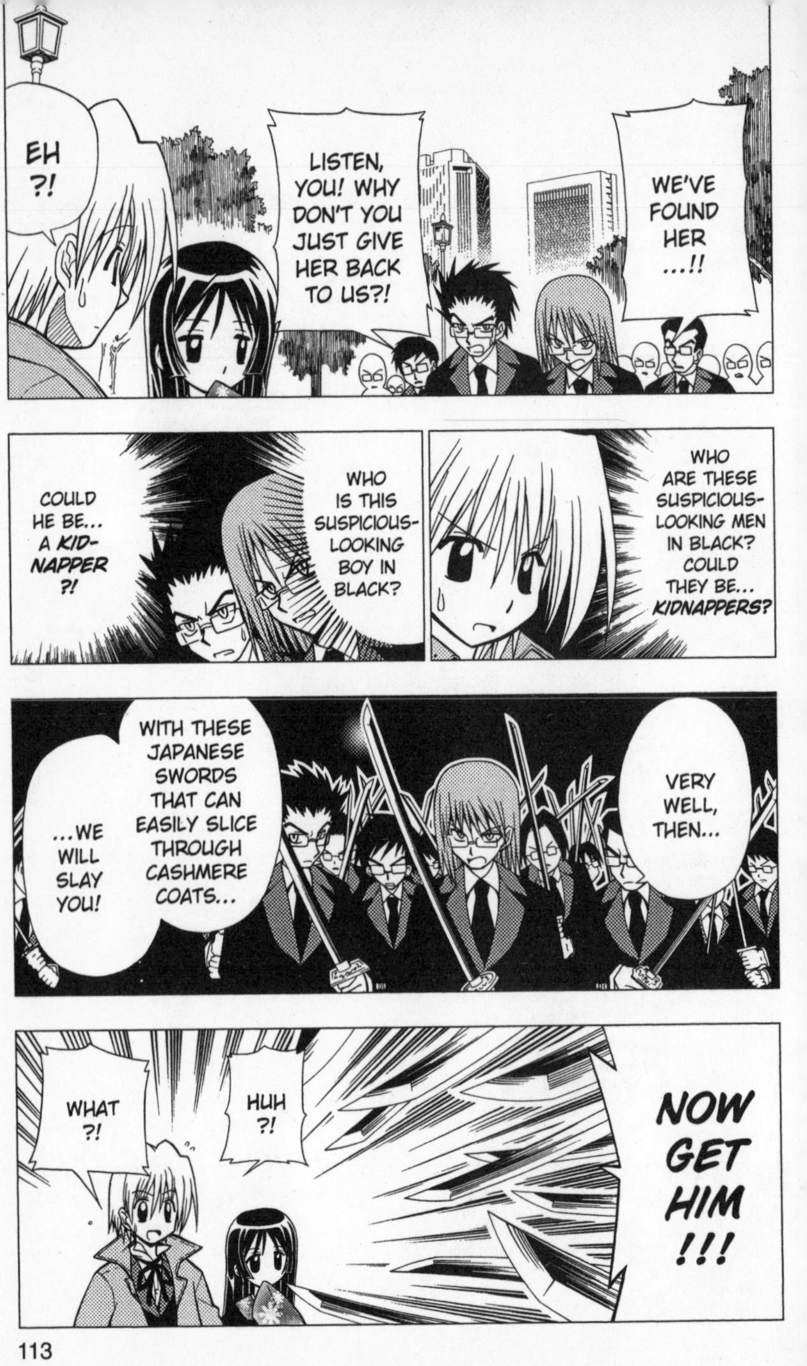
WE'VE FOUND HER ...!!
LISTEN, YOU! WHY DON'T YOU JUST GIVE HER BACK TO US?!
EH ?!
WHO ARE THESE SUSPICIOUS-LOOKING MEN IN BLACK? COULD THEY BE... *KIDNAPPERS?*
WHO IS THIS SUSPICIOUS-LOOKING BOY IN BLACK?
COULD HE BE... A *KID-NAPPER ?!*
VERY WELL, THEN...
WITH THESE JAPANESE SWORDS THAT CAN EASILY SLICE THROUGH CASHMERE COATS...
...WE WILL SLAY YOU!
NOW GET HIM !!!
HUH ?!
WHAT ?!

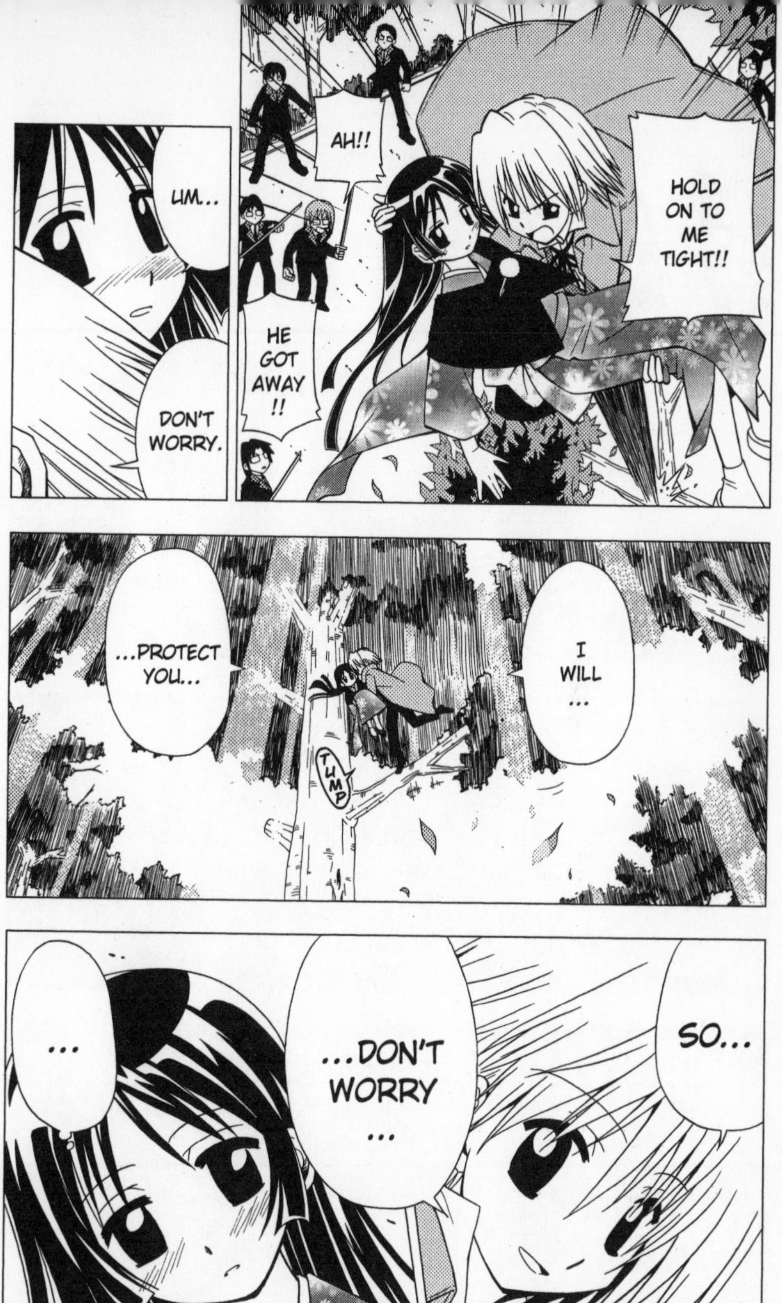
HOLD ON TO ME TIGHT!!
AH!!
HE GOT AWAY!!
UM...
DON'T WORRY.
I WILL...
...PROTECT YOU...
THUMP
SO...
...DON'T WORRY...
...

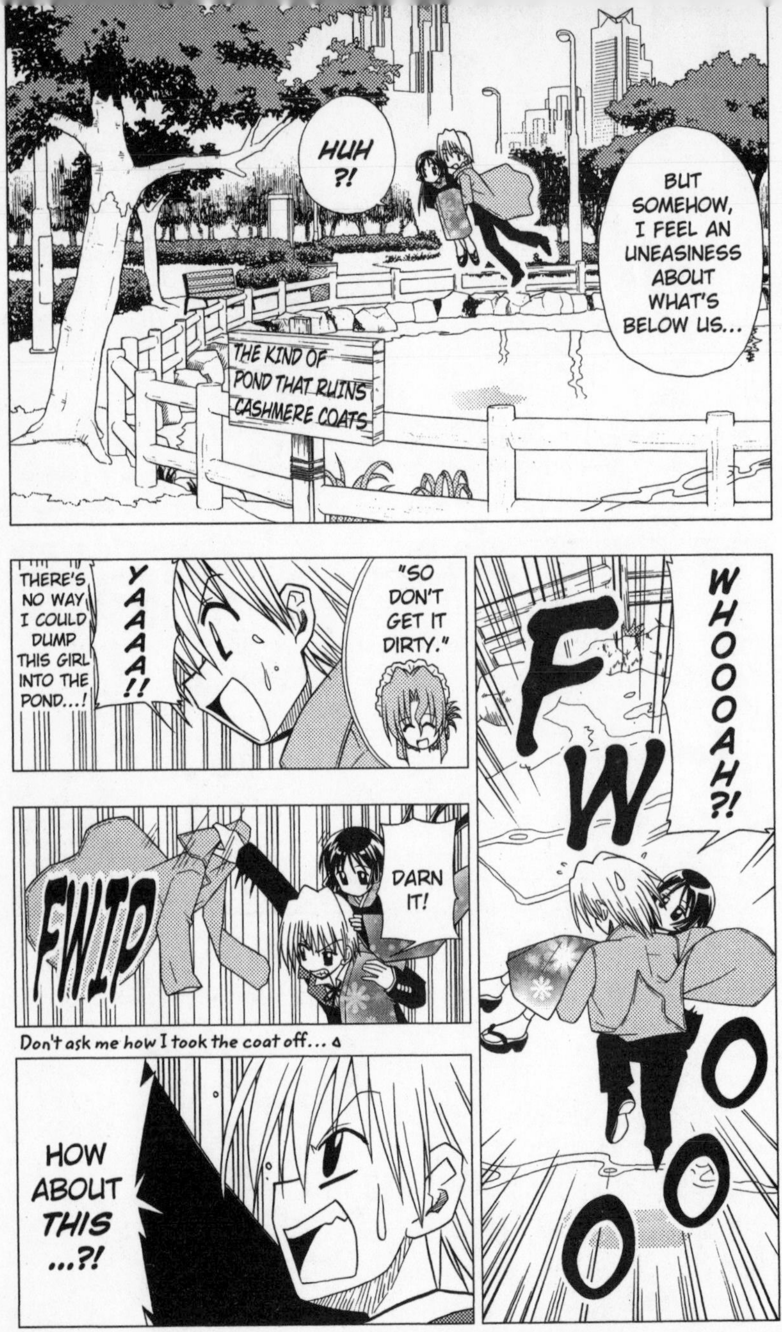
BUT SOMEHOW, I FEEL AN UNEASINESS ABOUT WHAT'S BELOW US...
HUH?!
THE KIND OF POND THAT RUINS CASHMERE COATS
WHOOOOAH?!
FW
OOOO
"SO DON'T GET IT DIRTY."
YAAAAA!!
THERE'S NO WAY I COULD DUMP THIS GIRL INTO THE POND...!
DARN IT!
FWIP
Don't ask me how I took the coat off...
HOW ABOUT THIS ...?!

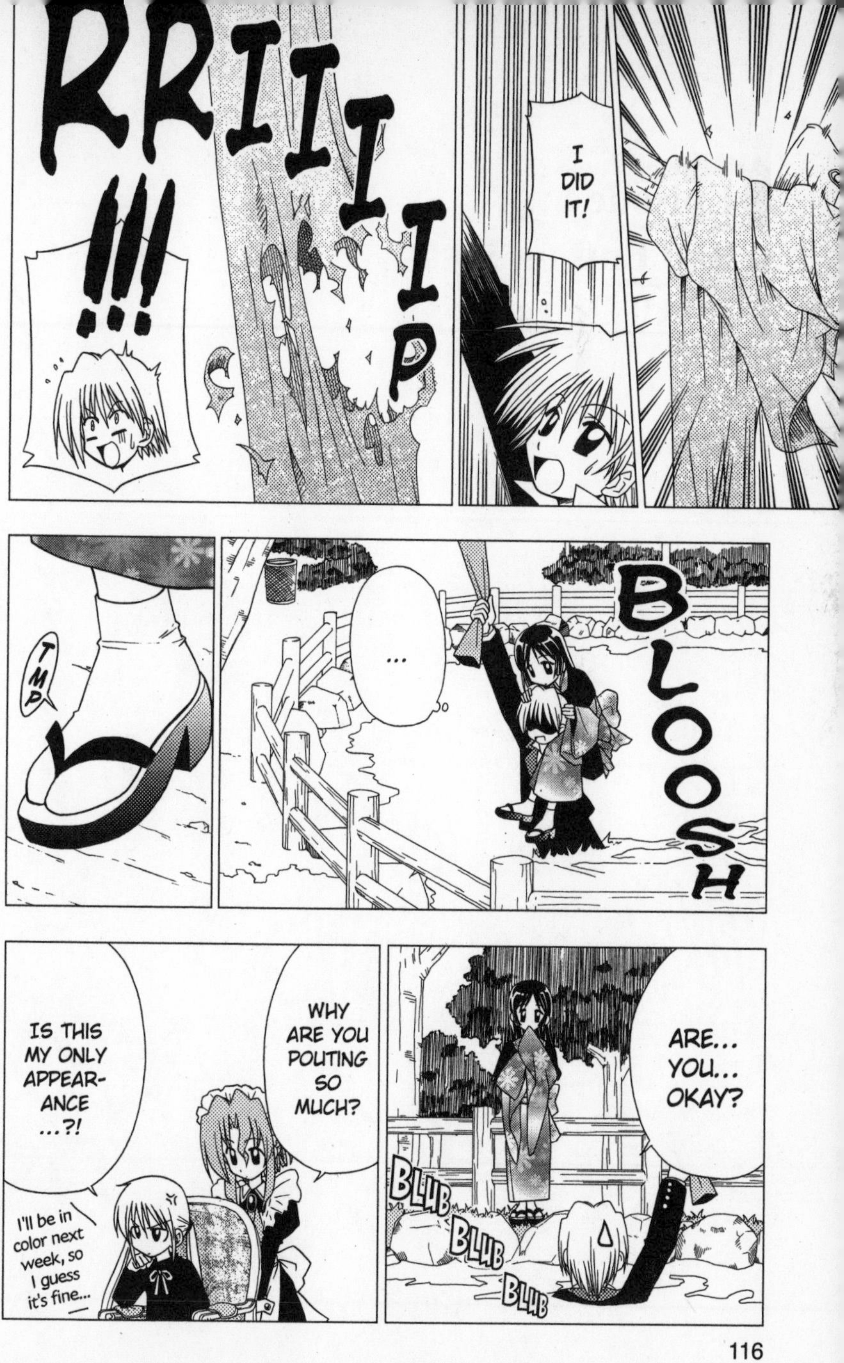
I DID IT!
RRIIIIIP!!!!
...
BLOOSH
TMP
ARE... YOU... OKAY?
BLUB
BLUB
BLUB
WHY ARE YOU POUTING SO MUCH?
IS THIS MY ONLY APPEARANCE...?!
I'll be in color next week, so I guess it's fine...

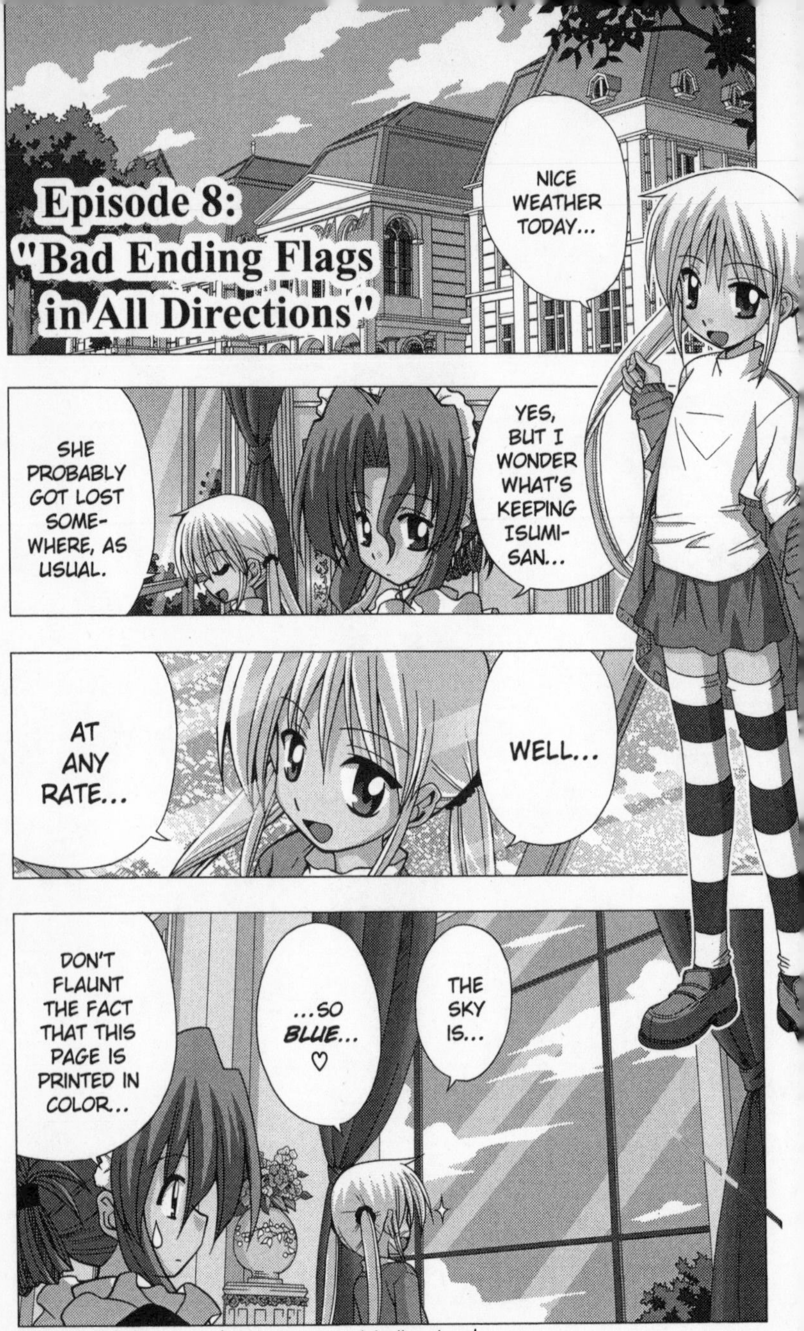
Episode 8: "Bad Ending Flags in All Directions"
NICE WEATHER TODAY...
YES, BUT I WONDER WHAT'S KEEPING ISUMI-SAN...
SHE PROBABLY GOT LOST SOME-WHERE, AS USUAL.
WELL...
AT ANY RATE...
THE SKY IS...
...SO *BLUE*... ♡
DON'T FLAUNT THE FACT THAT THIS PAGE IS PRINTED IN COLOR...

* As you probably guessed, this page was originally printed in color in Shônen Sunday. Yes, I knew this would happen...

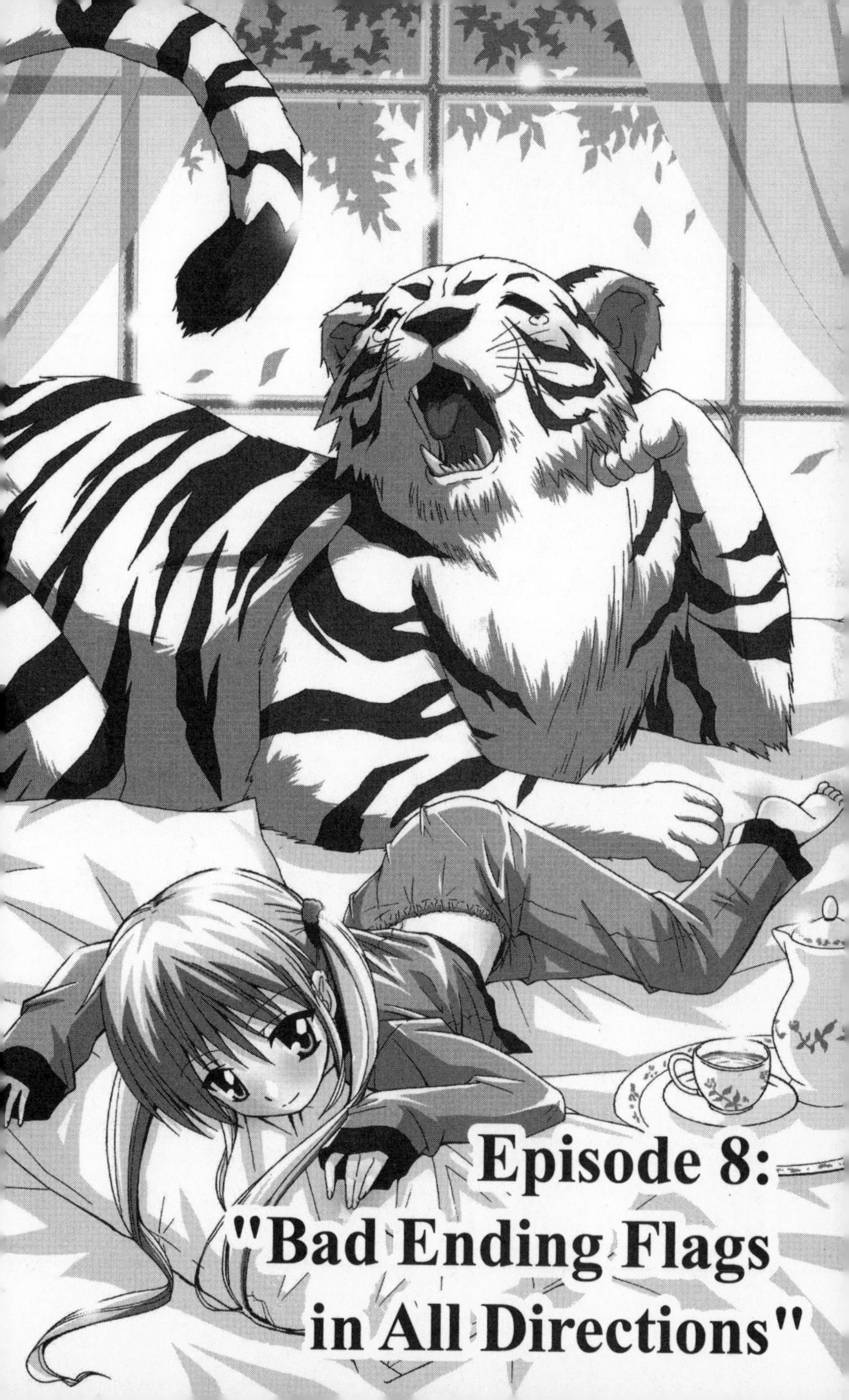
Episode 8:
"Bad Ending Flags
in All Directions"

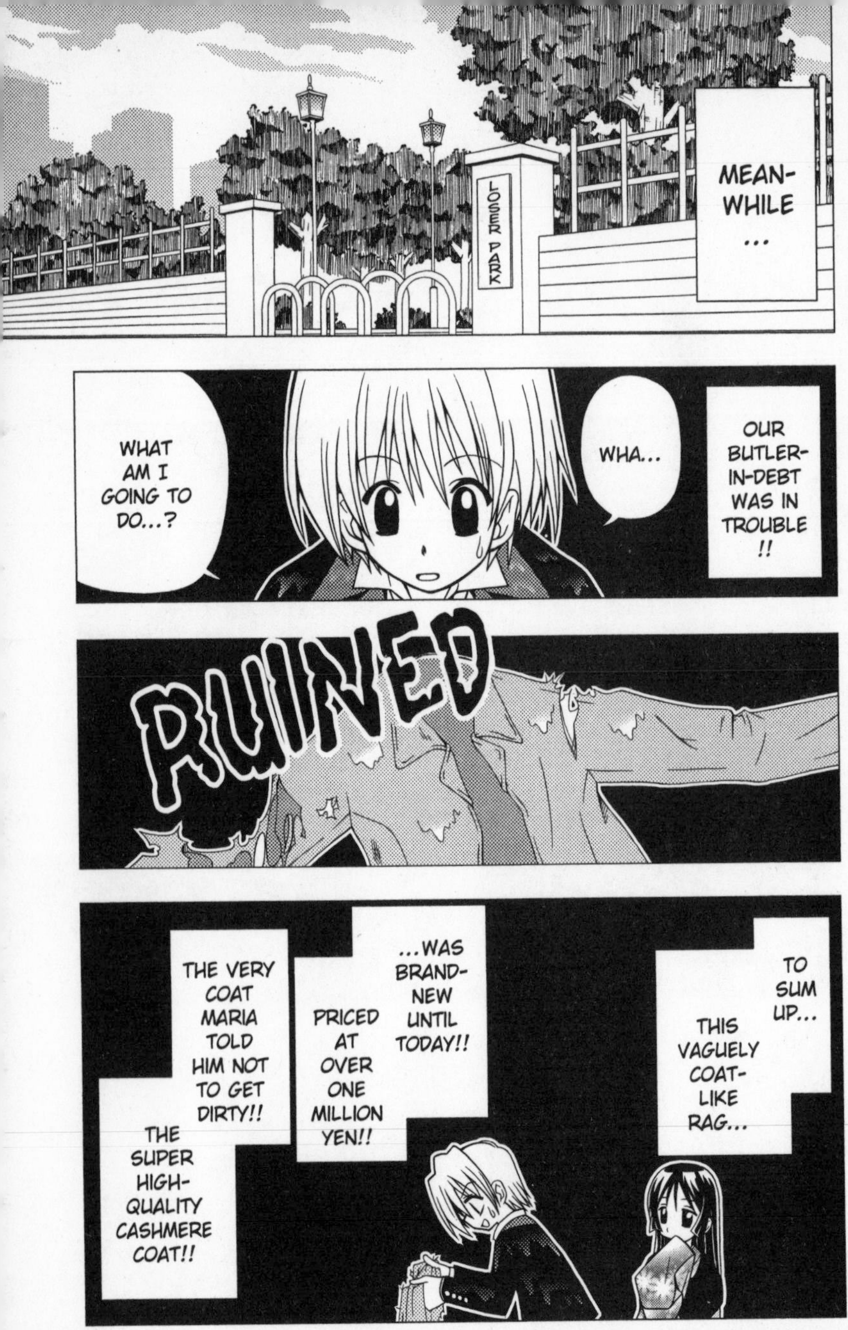
MEAN-WHILE ...
LOSER PARK
OUR BUTLER-IN-DEBT WAS IN TROUBLE !!
WHA...
WHAT AM I GOING TO DO...?
RUINED
TO SUM UP...
THIS VAGUELY COAT-LIKE RAG...
...WAS BRAND-NEW UNTIL TODAY!!
PRICED AT OVER ONE MILLION YEN!!
THE VERY COAT MARIA TOLD HIM NOT TO GET DIRTY!!
THE SUPER HIGH-QUALITY CASHMERE COAT!!

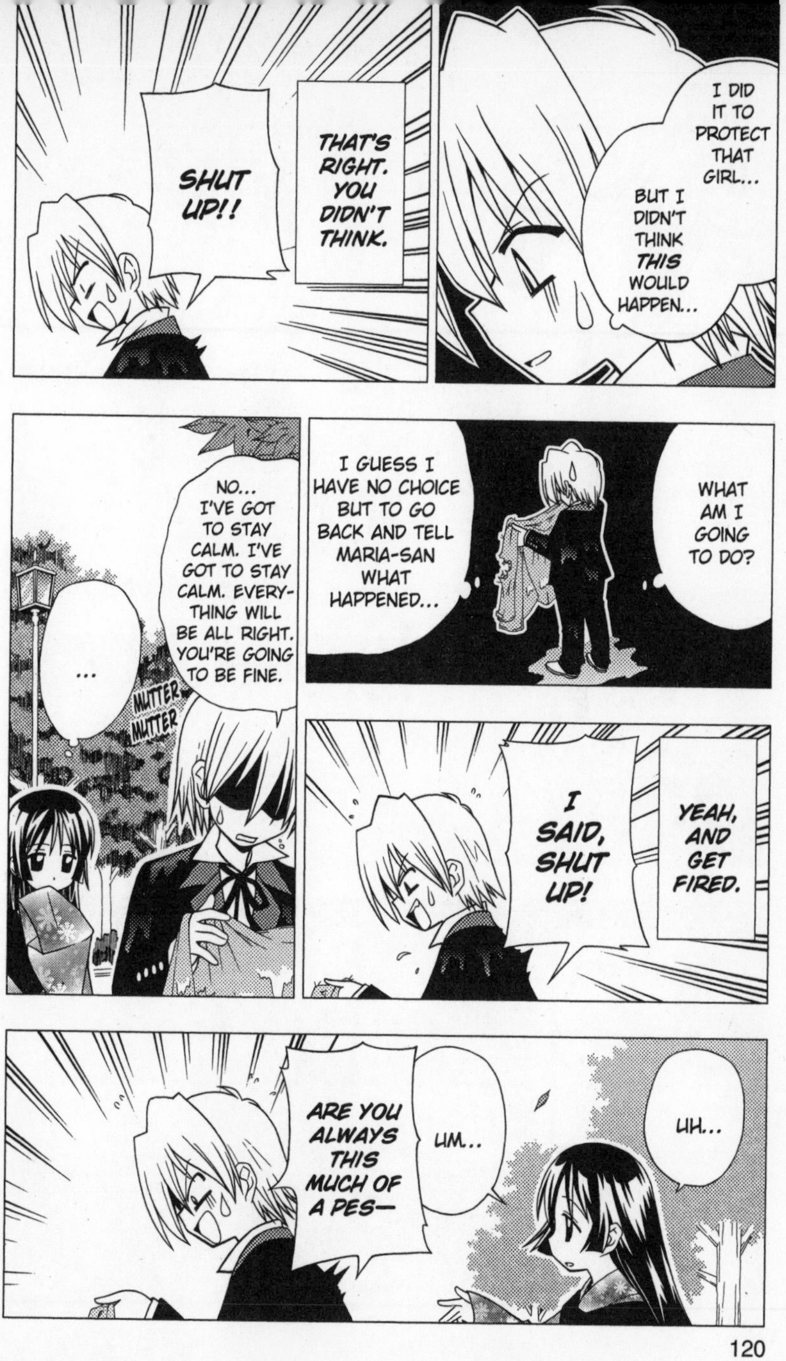
I DID IT TO PROTECT THAT GIRL...
BUT I DIDN'T THINK THIS WOULD HAPPEN...
THAT'S RIGHT. YOU DIDN'T THINK.
SHUT UP!!
WHAT AM I GOING TO DO?
I GUESS I HAVE NO CHOICE BUT TO GO BACK AND TELL MARIA-SAN WHAT HAPPENED...
YEAH, AND GET FIRED.
I SAID, SHUT UP!
NO... I'VE GOT TO STAY CALM. I'VE GOT TO STAY CALM. EVERYTHING WILL BE ALL RIGHT. YOU'RE GOING TO BE FINE.
MUTTER MUTTER
...
UH...
UM...
ARE YOU ALWAYS THIS MUCH OF A PES—

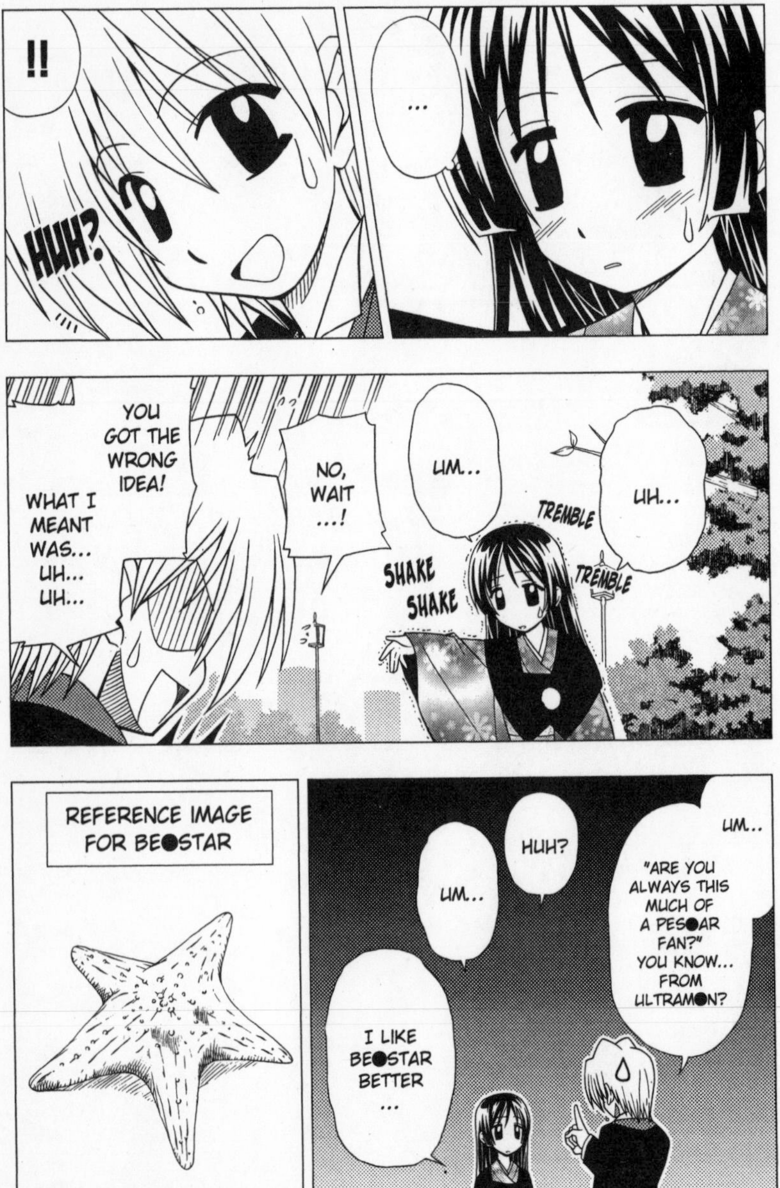
...
!!
HUH?
UH...
TREMBLE
TREMBLE
UM...
SHAKE SHAKE
NO, WAIT ...!
YOU GOT THE WRONG IDEA!
WHAT I MEANT WAS... UH... UH...
UM... "ARE YOU ALWAYS THIS MUCH OF A PES●AR FAN?" YOU KNOW... FROM ULTRAM●N?
HUH?
UM...
I LIKE BE●STAR BETTER ...
REFERENCE IMAGE FOR BE●STAR

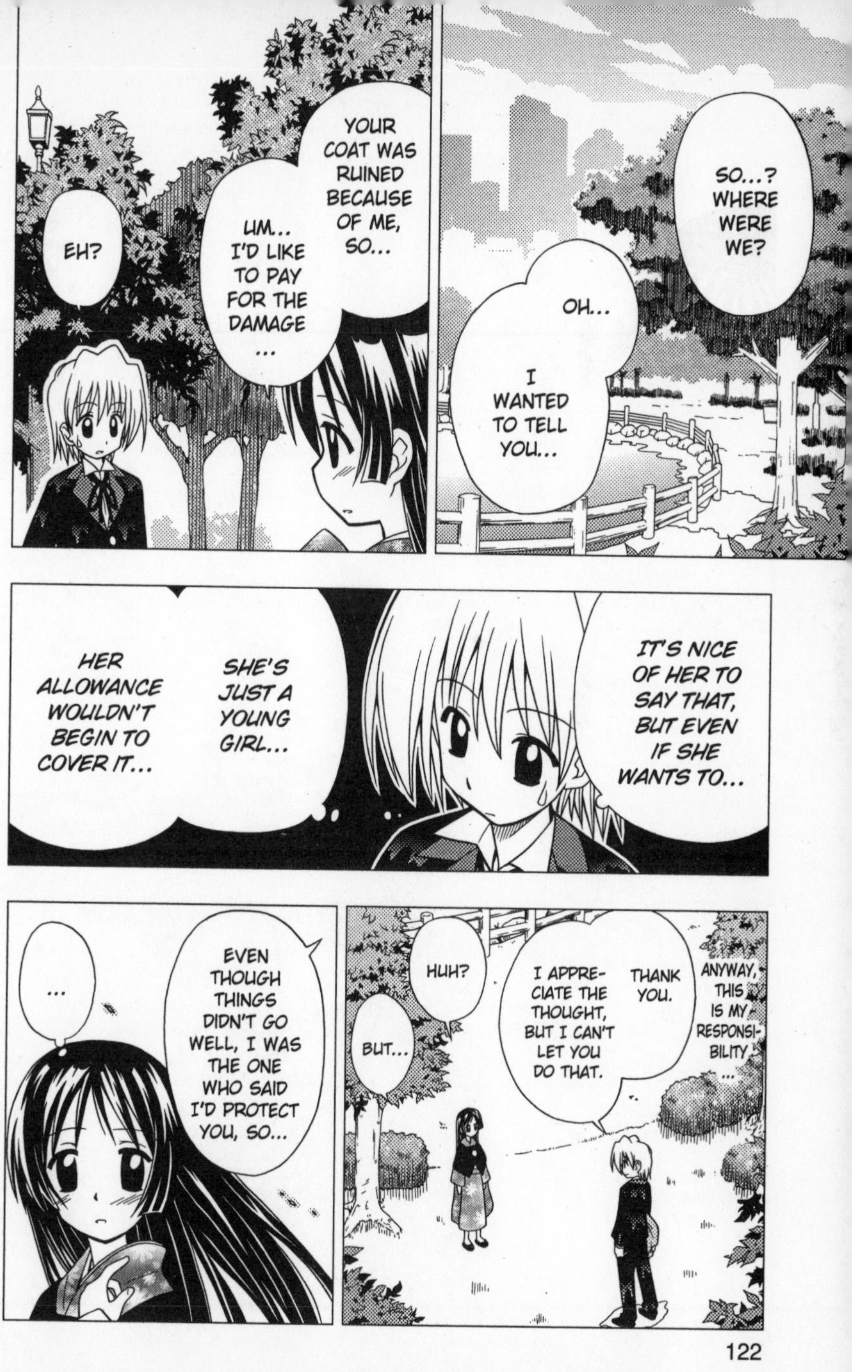
SO...? WHERE WERE WE?
OH...
I WANTED TO TELL YOU...
YOUR COAT WAS RUINED BECAUSE OF ME, SO...
UM... I'D LIKE TO PAY FOR THE DAMAGE...
EH?
IT'S NICE OF HER TO SAY THAT, BUT EVEN IF SHE WANTS TO...
SHE'S JUST A YOUNG GIRL...
HER ALLOWANCE WOULDN'T BEGIN TO COVER IT...
ANYWAY, THIS IS MY RESPONSIBILITY...
THANK YOU.
I APPRECIATE THE THOUGHT, BUT I CAN'T LET YOU DO THAT.
HUH?
BUT...
EVEN THOUGH THINGS DIDN'T GO WELL, I WAS THE ONE WHO SAID I'D PROTECT YOU, SO...
...

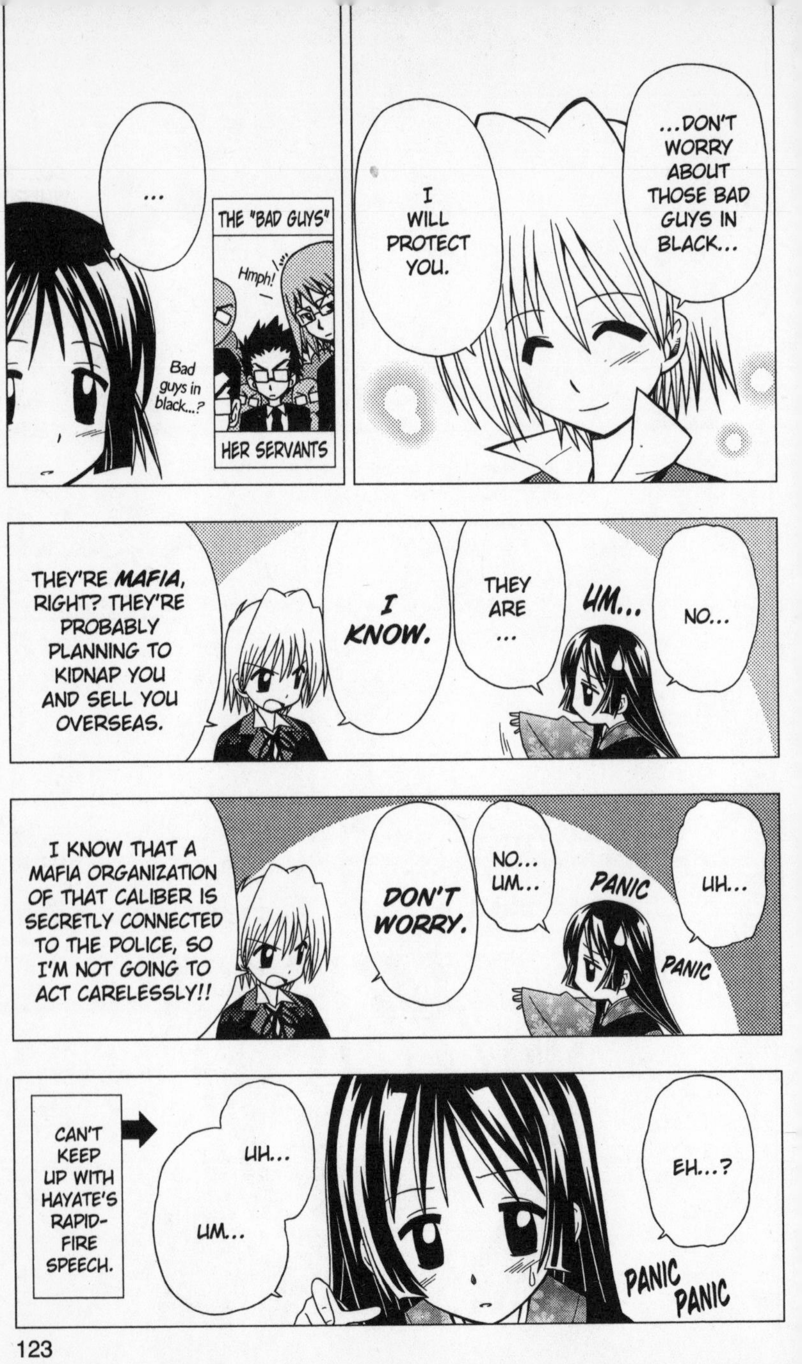
...DON'T WORRY ABOUT THOSE BAD GUYS IN BLACK...
I WILL PROTECT YOU.
...
THE "BAD GUYS"
Hmph!
HER SERVANTS
Bad guys in black...?
NO...
UM...
THEY ARE ...
I KNOW.
THEY'RE *MAFIA*, RIGHT? THEY'RE PROBABLY PLANNING TO KIDNAP YOU AND SELL YOU OVERSEAS.
UH...
PANIC
PANIC
NO... UM...
DON'T WORRY.
I KNOW THAT A MAFIA ORGANIZATION OF THAT CALIBER IS SECRETLY CONNECTED TO THE POLICE, SO I'M NOT GOING TO ACT CARELESSLY!!
EH...?
PANIC PANIC
UH...
UM...
CAN'T KEEP UP WITH HAYATE'S RAPID-FIRE SPEECH.

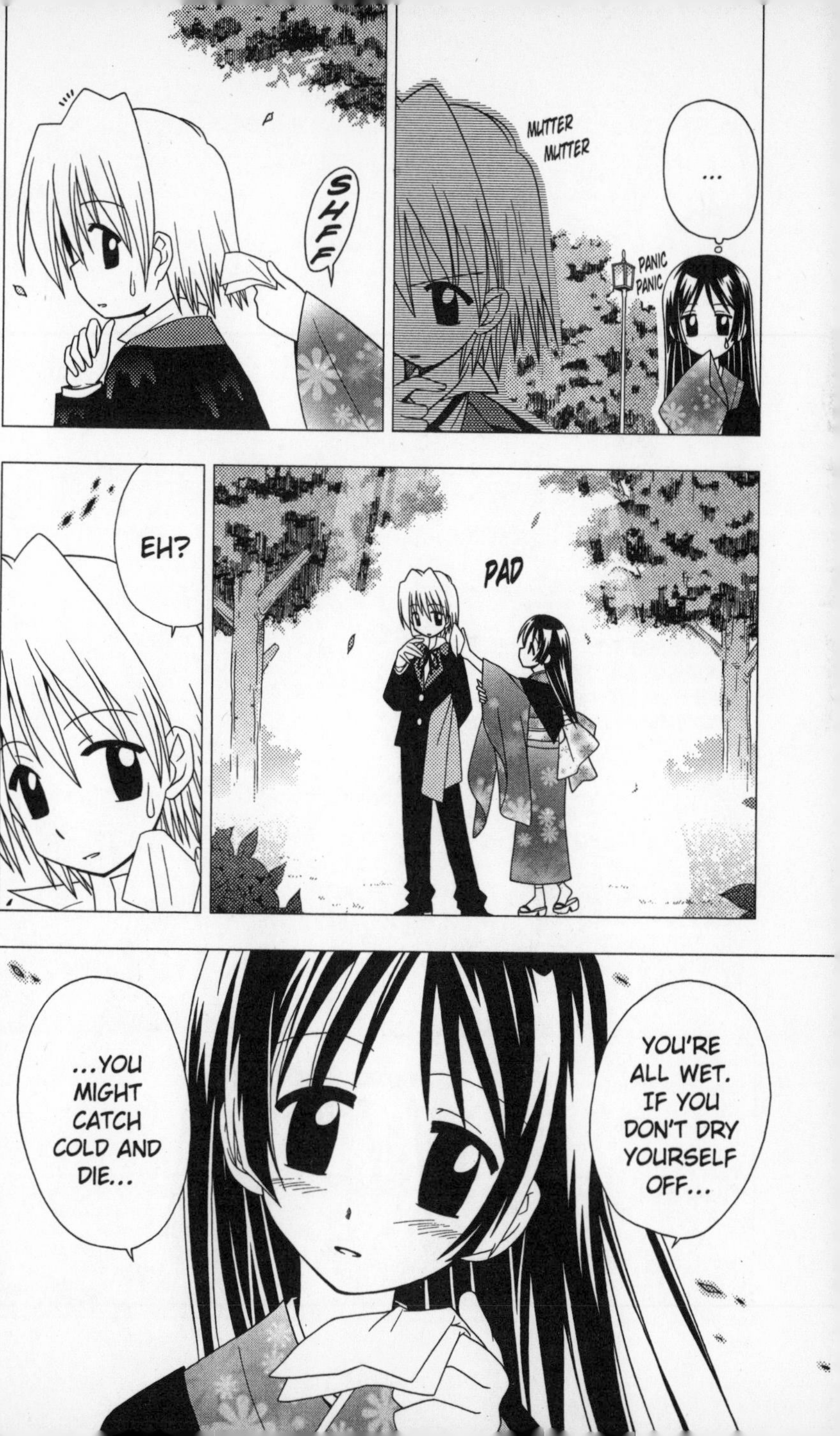
...
MUTTER MUTTER
PANIC PANIC
SHFF
PAD
EH?
YOU'RE ALL WET. IF YOU DON'T DRY YOURSELF OFF...
...YOU MIGHT CATCH COLD AND DIE...

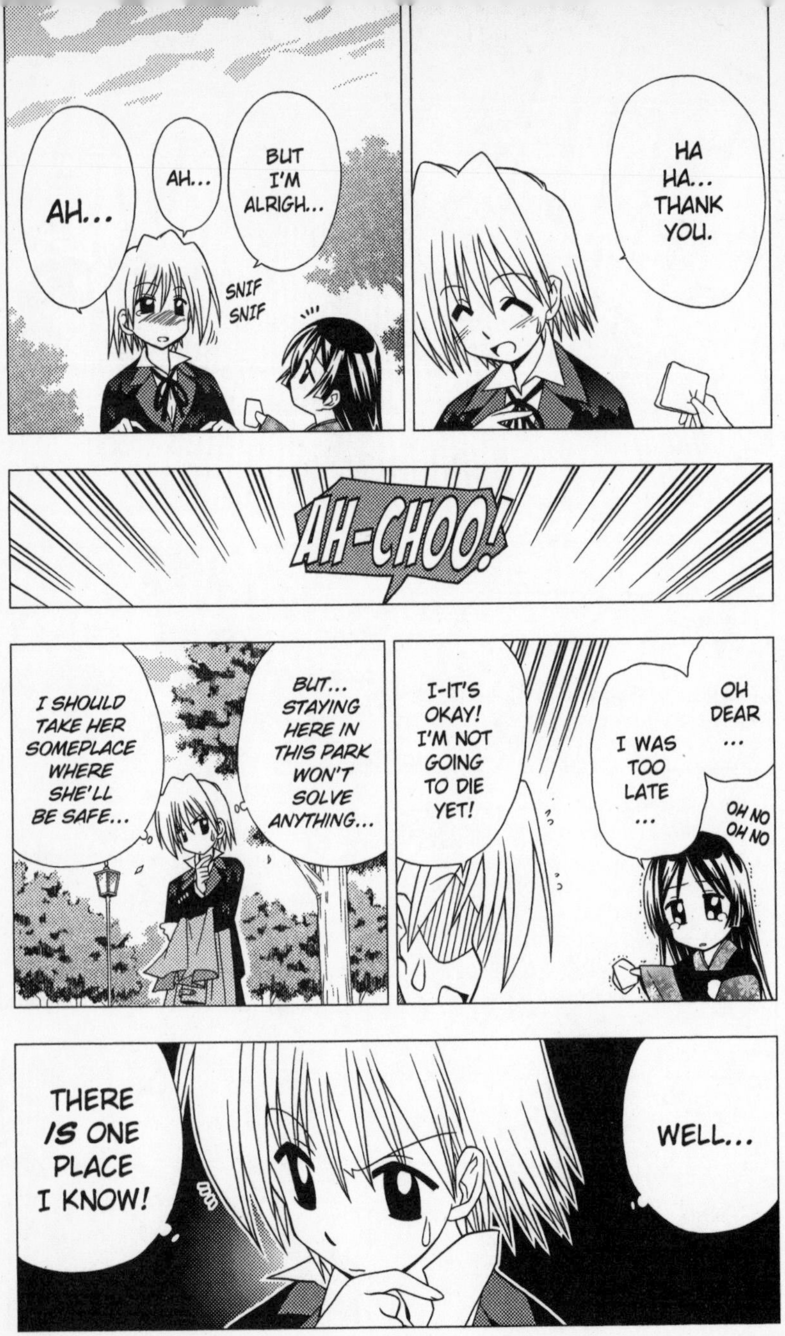
HA HA... THANK YOU.
BUT I'M ALRIGH...
AH...
AH...
SNIF SNIF
AH-CHOO!
OH DEAR ...
I WAS TOO LATE ...
OH NO OH NO
I-IT'S OKAY! I'M NOT GOING TO DIE YET!
BUT... STAYING HERE IN THIS PARK WON'T SOLVE ANYTHING...
I SHOULD TAKE HER SOMEPLACE WHERE SHE'LL BE SAFE...
WELL...
THERE *IS* ONE PLACE I KNOW!

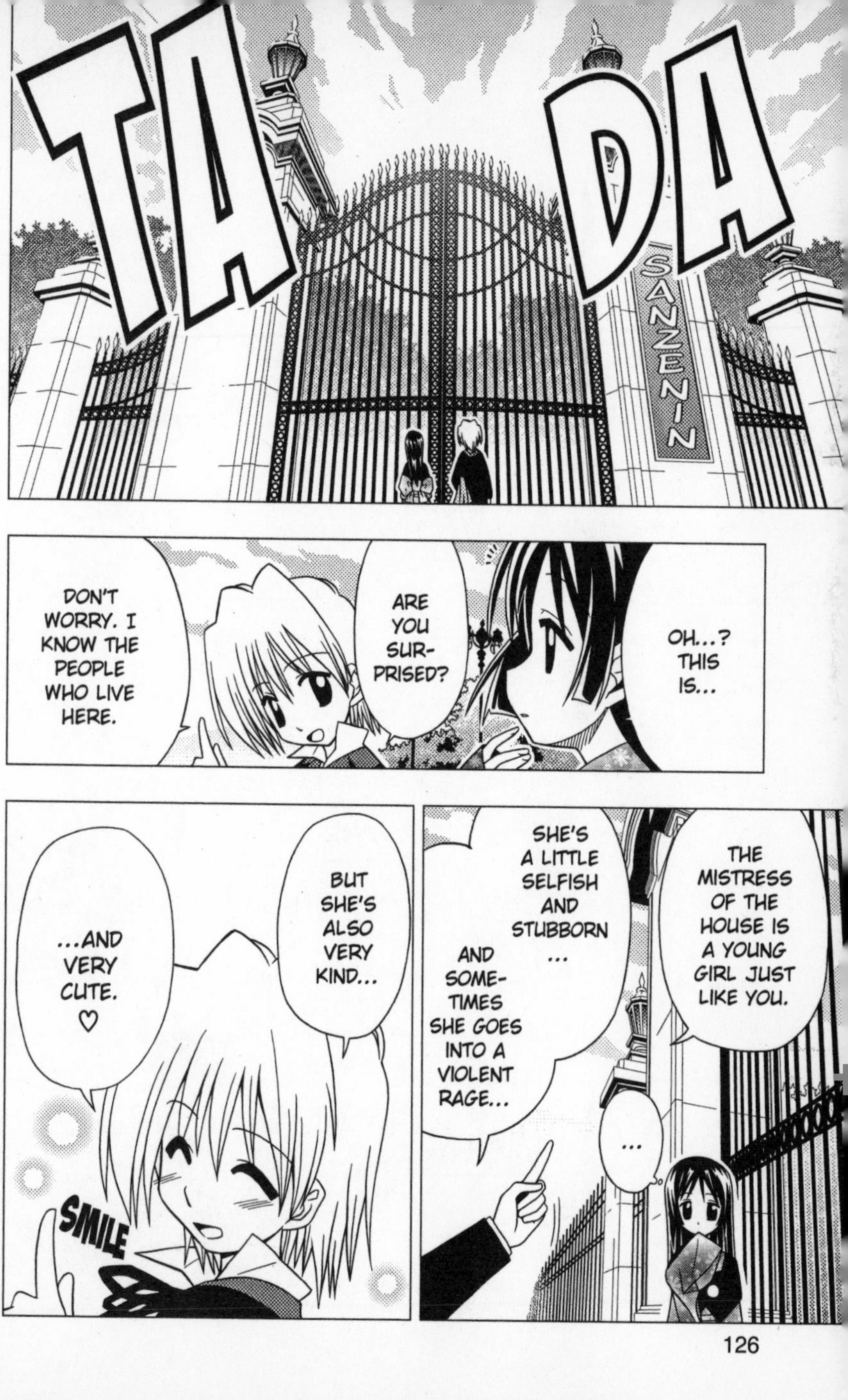
TA DA
SANZENIN
OH...? THIS IS...
ARE YOU SUR-PRISED?
DON'T WORRY. I KNOW THE PEOPLE WHO LIVE HERE.
THE MISTRESS OF THE HOUSE IS A YOUNG GIRL JUST LIKE YOU.
SHE'S A LITTLE SELFISH AND STUBBORN...
AND SOME-TIMES SHE GOES INTO A VIOLENT RAGE...
...
BUT SHE'S ALSO VERY KIND...
...AND VERY CUTE. ♡
SMILE

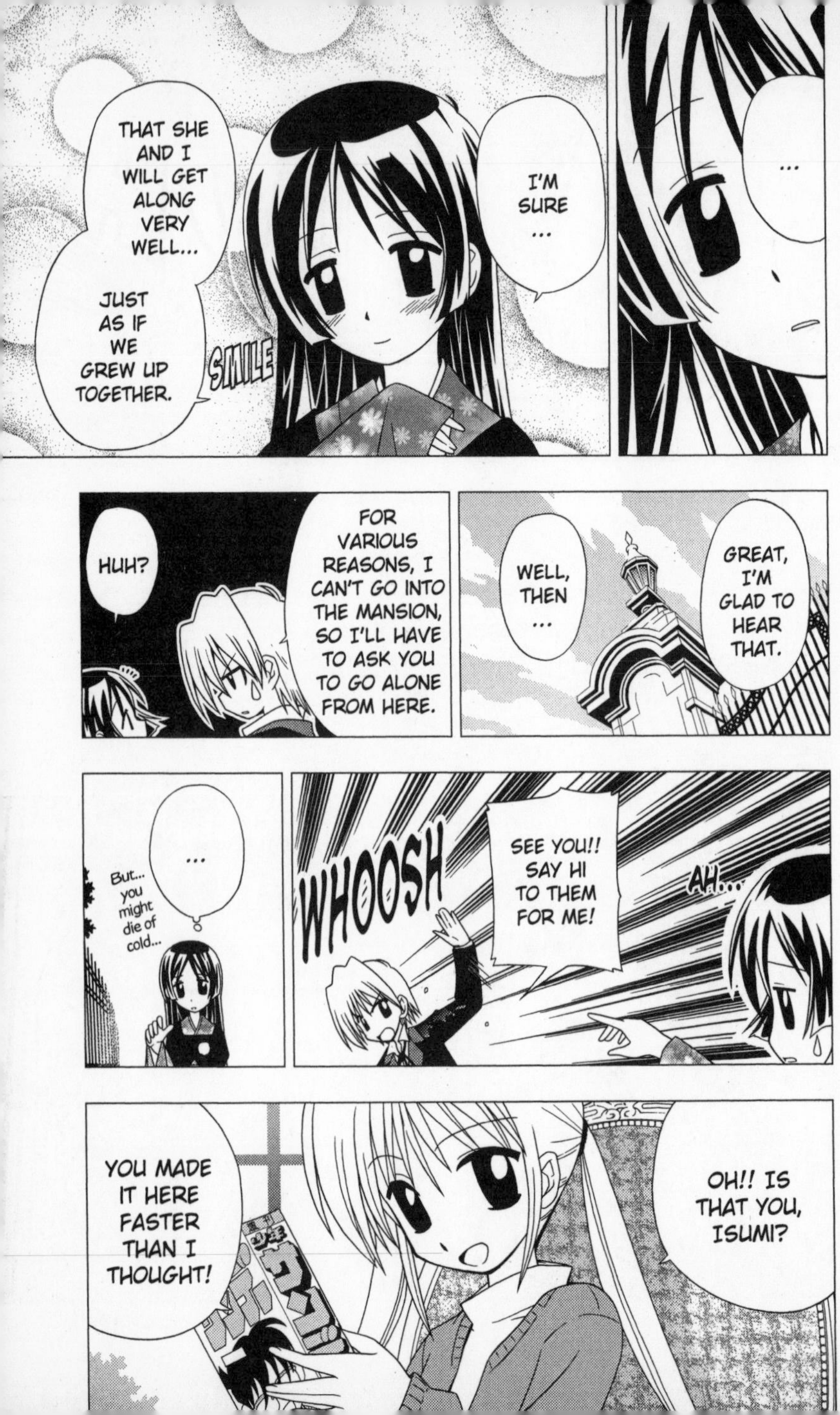
...
I'M SURE ...
THAT SHE AND I WILL GET ALONG VERY WELL...
JUST AS IF WE GREW UP TOGETHER.
SMILE
GREAT, I'M GLAD TO HEAR THAT.
WELL, THEN ...
FOR VARIOUS REASONS, I CAN'T GO INTO THE MANSION, SO I'LL HAVE TO ASK YOU TO GO ALONE FROM HERE.
HUH?
AH...
SEE YOU!! SAY HI TO THEM FOR ME!
WHOOSH
...
But... you might die of cold...
OH!! IS THAT YOU, ISUMI?
YOU MADE IT HERE FASTER THAN I THOUGHT!

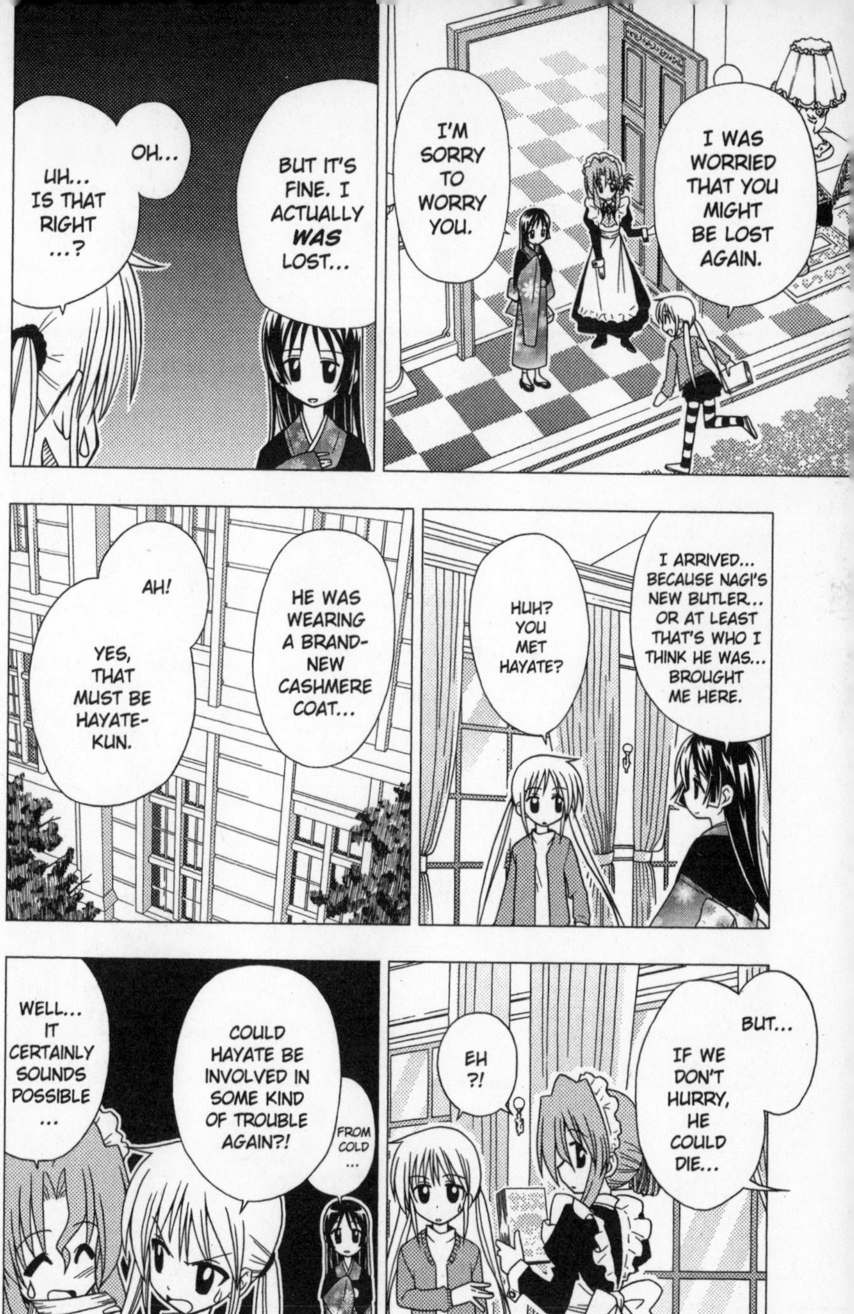
I WAS WORRIED THAT YOU MIGHT BE LOST AGAIN.
I'M SORRY TO WORRY YOU.
BUT IT'S FINE. I ACTUALLY **WAS** LOST...
OH...
UH... IS THAT RIGHT ...?
I ARRIVED... BECAUSE NAGI'S NEW BUTLER... OR AT LEAST THAT'S WHO I THINK HE WAS... BROUGHT ME HERE.
HUH? YOU MET HAYATE?
HE WAS WEARING A BRAND-NEW CASHMERE COAT...
AH!
YES, THAT MUST BE HAYATE-KUN.
BUT...
IF WE DON'T HURRY, HE COULD DIE...
EH ?!
COULD HAYATE BE INVOLVED IN SOME KIND OF TROUBLE AGAIN?!
FROM COLD ...
WELL... IT CERTAINLY SOUNDS POSSIBLE ...

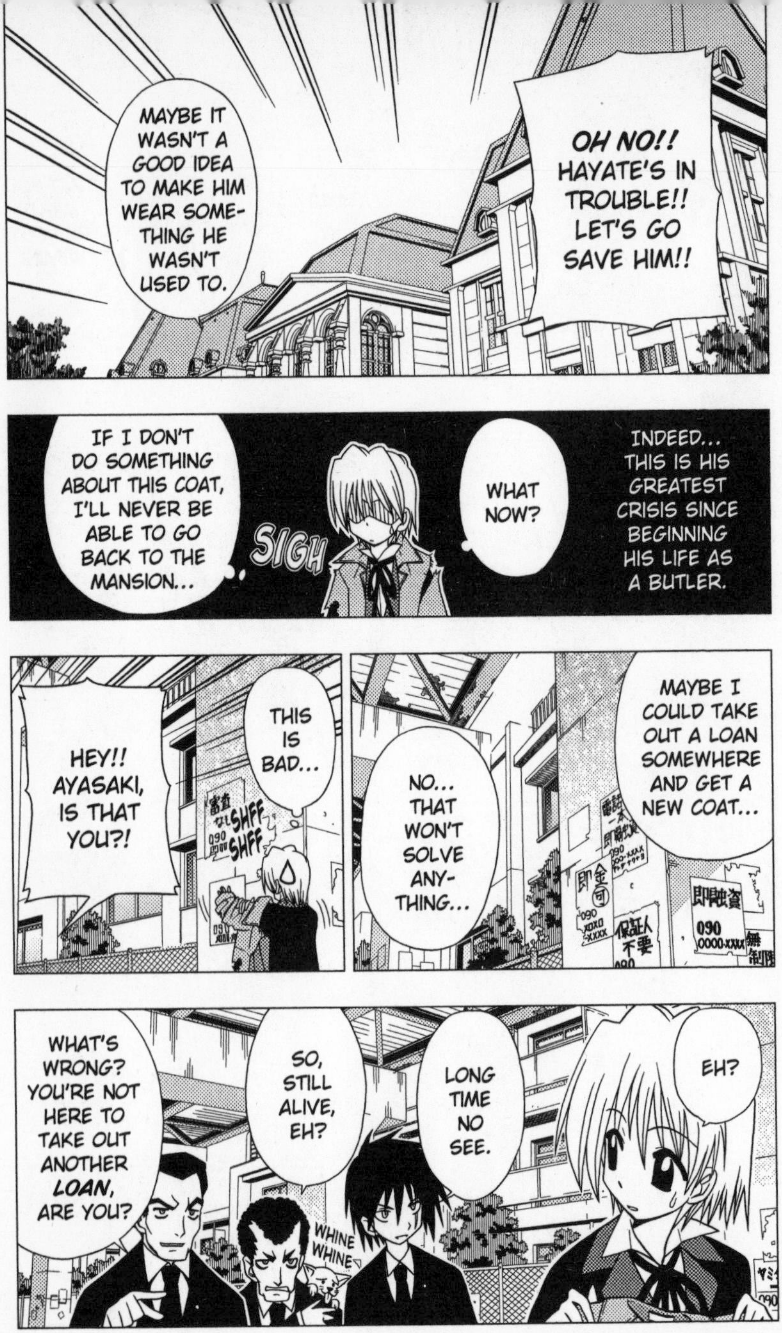
OH NO!! HAYATE'S IN TROUBLE!! LET'S GO SAVE HIM!!
MAYBE IT WASN'T A GOOD IDEA TO MAKE HIM WEAR SOME-THING HE WASN'T USED TO.
INDEED... THIS IS HIS GREATEST CRISIS SINCE BEGINNING HIS LIFE AS A BUTLER.
WHAT NOW?
SIGH
IF I DON'T DO SOMETHING ABOUT THIS COAT, I'LL NEVER BE ABLE TO GO BACK TO THE MANSION...
MAYBE I COULD TAKE OUT A LOAN SOMEWHERE AND GET A NEW COAT...
NO... THAT WON'T SOLVE ANY-THING...
THIS IS BAD...
SHFF SHFF
HEY!! AYASAKI, IS THAT YOU?!
EH?
LONG TIME NO SEE.
SO, STILL ALIVE, EH?
WHINE WHINE
WHAT'S WRONG? YOU'RE NOT HERE TO TAKE OUT ANOTHER LOAN, ARE YOU?

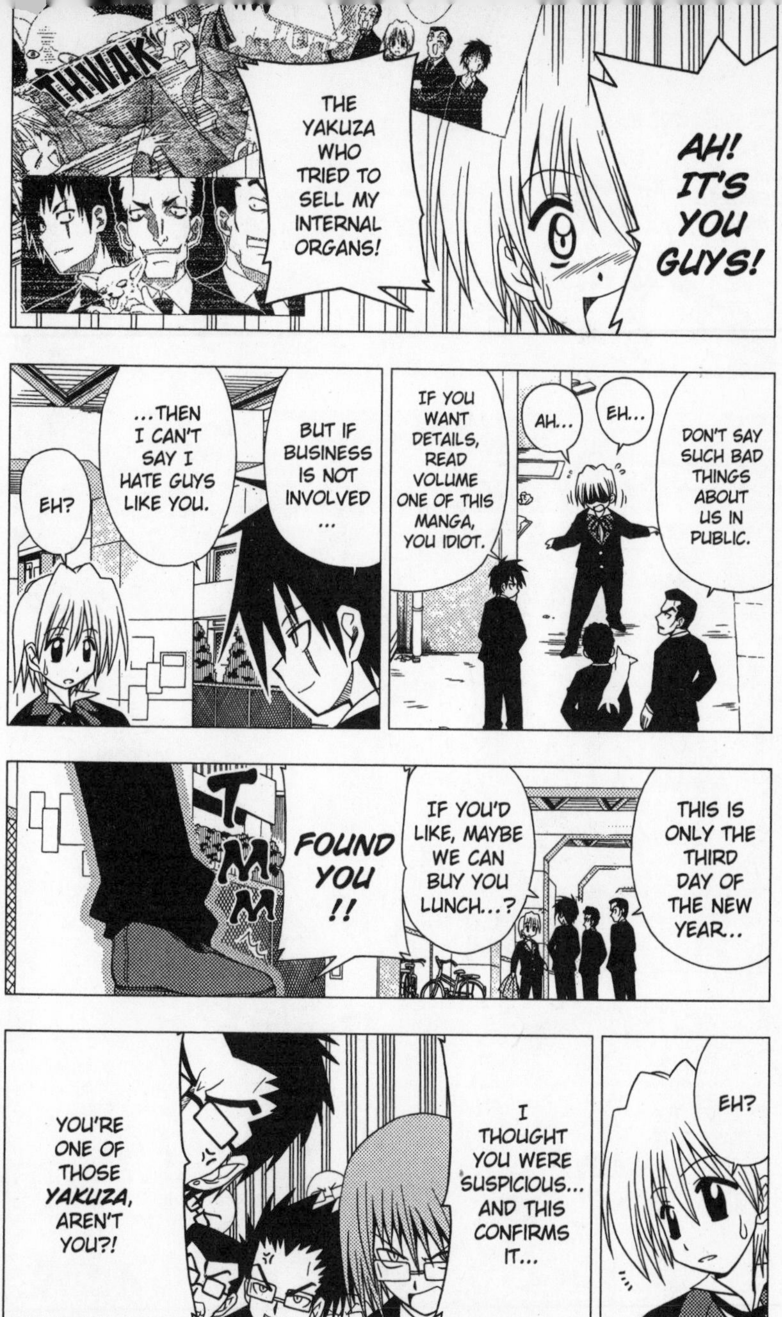
AH! IT'S YOU GUYS!
THE YAKUZA WHO TRIED TO SELL MY INTERNAL ORGANS!
THWAK
DON'T SAY SUCH BAD THINGS ABOUT US IN PUBLIC.
EH...
AH...
IF YOU WANT DETAILS, READ VOLUME ONE OF THIS MANGA, YOU IDIOT.
BUT IF BUSINESS IS NOT INVOLVED ...
...THEN I CAN'T SAY I HATE GUYS LIKE YOU.
EH?
THIS IS ONLY THE THIRD DAY OF THE NEW YEAR...
IF YOU'D LIKE, MAYBE WE CAN BUY YOU LUNCH...?
FOUND YOU !!
T M M
EH?
...
I THOUGHT YOU WERE SUSPICIOUS... AND THIS CONFIRMS IT...
YOU'RE ONE OF THOSE *YAKUZA*, AREN'T YOU?!

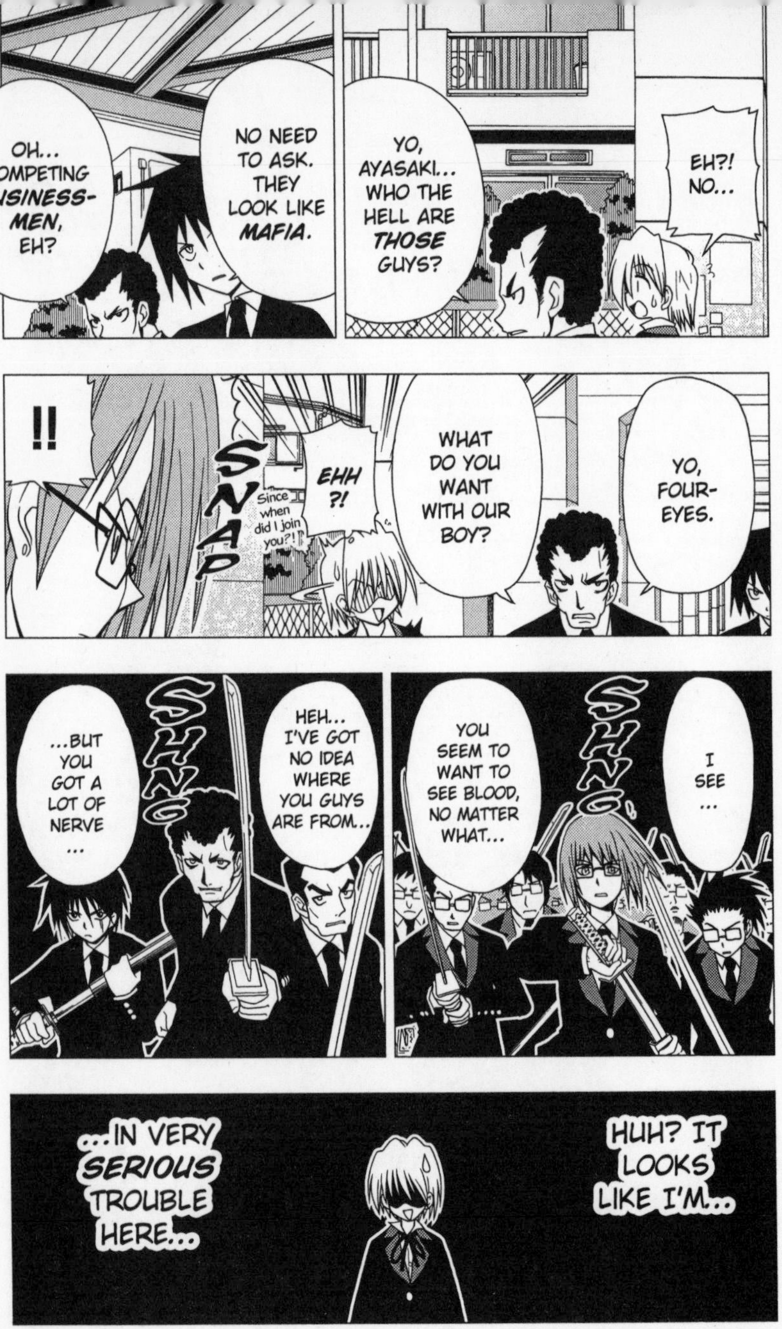
YO, AYASAKI... WHO THE HELL ARE THOSE GUYS?
EH?! NO...
NO NEED TO ASK. THEY LOOK LIKE MAFIA.
OH... COMPETING BUSINESS-MEN, EH?
YO, FOUR-EYES.
WHAT DO YOU WANT WITH OUR BOY?
EHH ?!
Since when did I join you?!
SNAP
!!
I SEE ...
SHNG
YOU SEEM TO WANT TO SEE BLOOD, NO MATTER WHAT...
HEH... I'VE GOT NO IDEA WHERE YOU GUYS ARE FROM...
SHNG
...BUT YOU GOT A LOT OF NERVE ...
HUH? IT LOOKS LIKE I'M...
...IN VERY SERIOUS TROUBLE HERE...

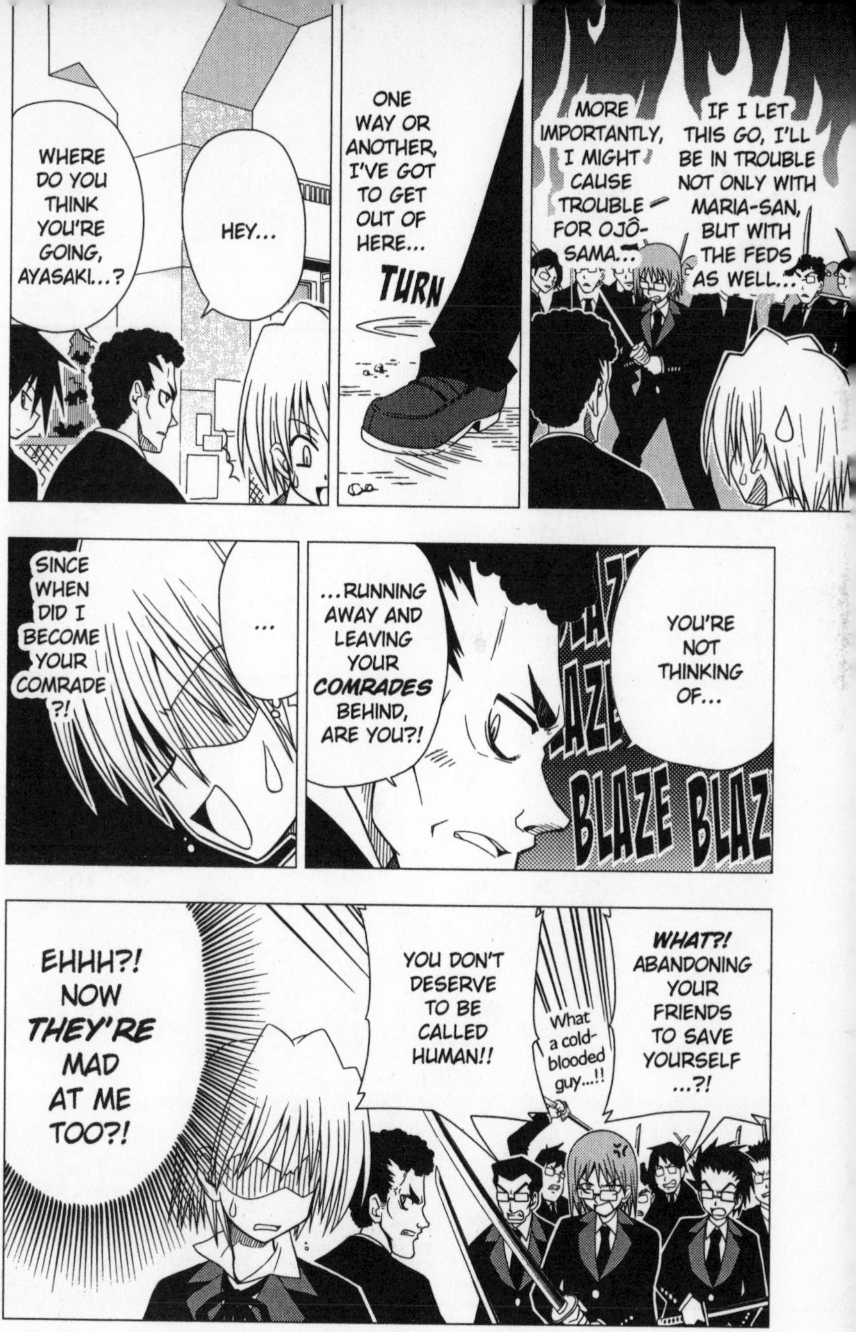
IF I LET THIS GO, I'LL BE IN TROUBLE NOT ONLY WITH MARIA-SAN, BUT WITH THE FEDS AS WELL...
MORE IMPORTANTLY, I MIGHT CAUSE TROUBLE FOR OJÔ-SAMA...
ONE WAY OR ANOTHER, I'VE GOT TO GET OUT OF HERE...
TURN
HEY...
WHERE DO YOU THINK YOU'RE GOING, AYASAKI...?
YOU'RE NOT THINKING OF...
...RUNNING AWAY AND LEAVING YOUR *COMRADES* BEHIND, ARE YOU?!
BLAZE BLAZE BLAZ
...
SINCE WHEN DID I BECOME YOUR COMRADE?!
WHAT?! ABANDONING YOUR FRIENDS TO SAVE YOURSELF ...?!
What a cold-blooded guy...!!
YOU DON'T DESERVE TO BE CALLED HUMAN!!
EHHH?! NOW *THEY'RE* MAD AT ME TOO?!

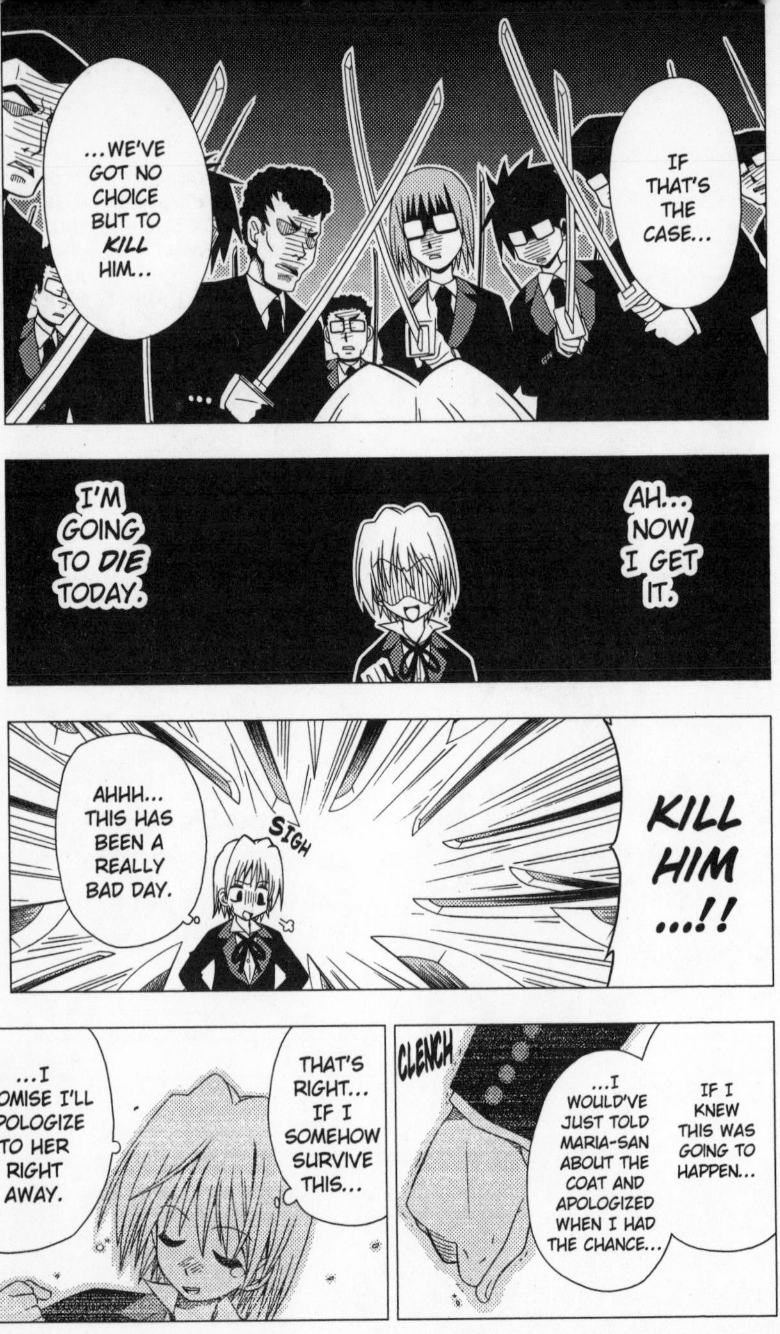
IF THAT'S THE CASE...
...WE'VE GOT NO CHOICE BUT TO KILL HIM...
...
AH... NOW I GET IT.
I'M GOING TO DIE TODAY.
KILL HIM...!!
SIGH
AHHH... THIS HAS BEEN A REALLY BAD DAY.
IF I KNEW THIS WAS GOING TO HAPPEN...
...I WOULD'VE JUST TOLD MARIA-SAN ABOUT THE COAT AND APOLOGIZED WHEN I HAD THE CHANCE...
CLENCH
THAT'S RIGHT... IF I SOMEHOW SURVIVE THIS...
...I PROMISE I'LL APOLOGIZE TO HER RIGHT AWAY.

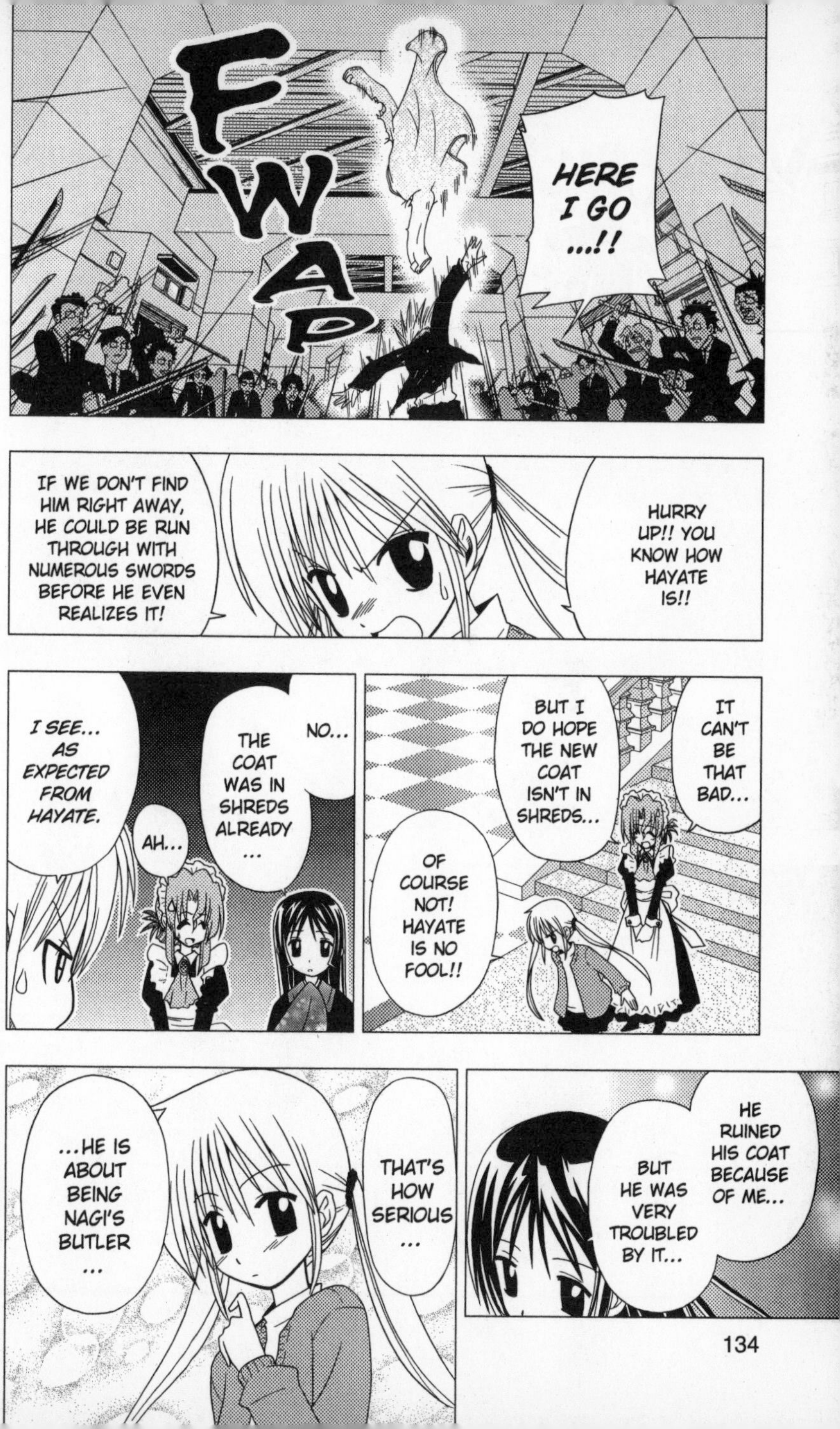
HERE I GO ...!!
FWAP
HURRY UP!! YOU KNOW HOW HAYATE IS!!
IF WE DON'T FIND HIM RIGHT AWAY, HE COULD BE RUN THROUGH WITH NUMEROUS SWORDS BEFORE HE EVEN REALIZES IT!
IT CAN'T BE THAT BAD...
BUT I DO HOPE THE NEW COAT ISN'T IN SHREDS...
OF COURSE NOT! HAYATE IS NO FOOL!!
NO...
THE COAT WAS IN SHREDS ALREADY ...
I SEE... AS EXPECTED FROM HAYATE.
AH...
HE RUINED HIS COAT BECAUSE OF ME...
BUT HE WAS VERY TROUBLED BY IT...
THAT'S HOW SERIOUS ...
...HE IS ABOUT BEING NAGI'S BUTLER ...

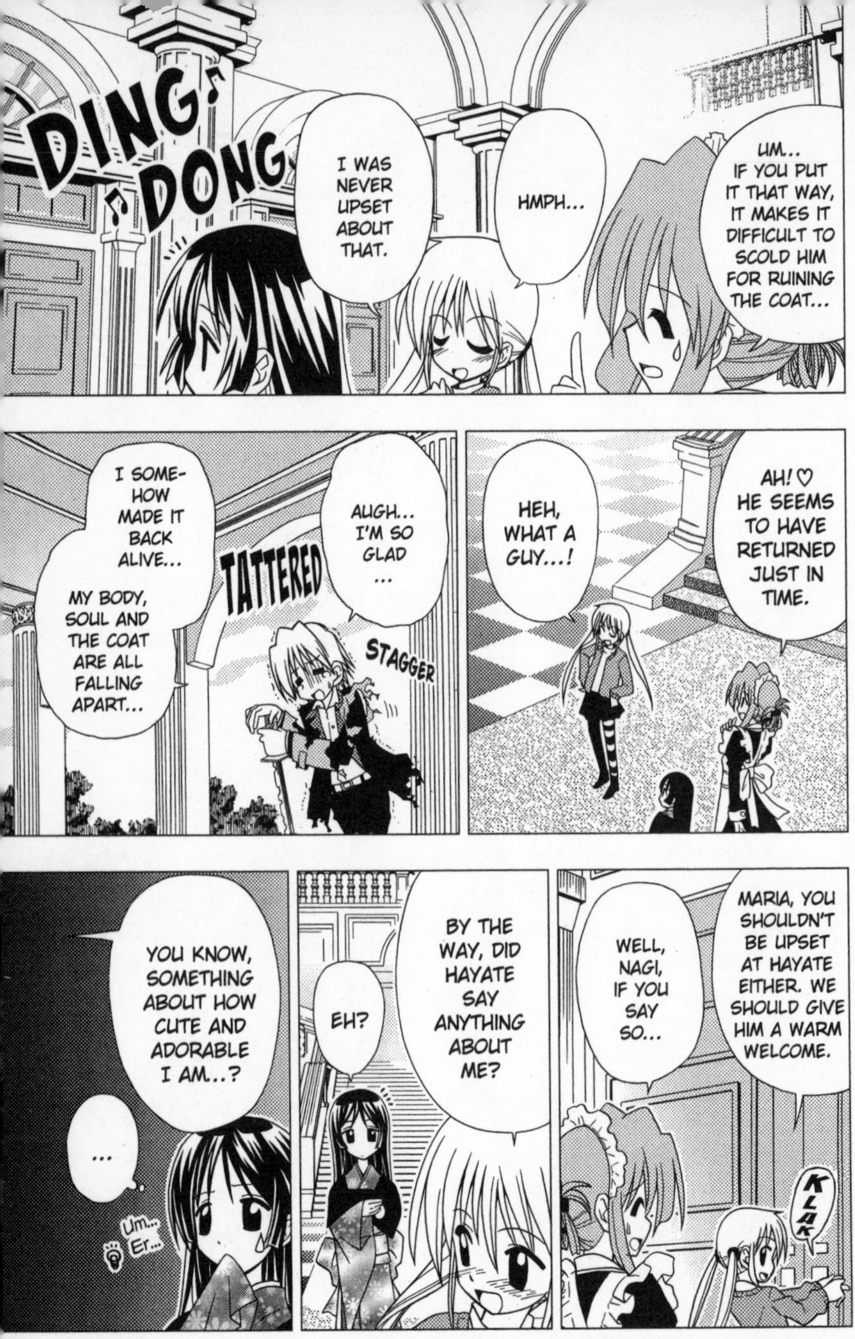
UM... IF YOU PUT IT THAT WAY, IT MAKES IT DIFFICULT TO SCOLD HIM FOR RUINING THE COAT...
HMPH...
I WAS NEVER UPSET ABOUT THAT.
DING DONG
AH! ♡ HE SEEMS TO HAVE RETURNED JUST IN TIME.
HEH, WHAT A GUY...!
AUGH... I'M SO GLAD...
STAGGER
TATTERED
I SOMEHOW MADE IT BACK ALIVE...
MY BODY, SOUL AND THE COAT ARE ALL FALLING APART...
MARIA, YOU SHOULDN'T BE UPSET AT HAYATE EITHER. WE SHOULD GIVE HIM A WARM WELCOME.
KLAK
WELL, NAGI, IF YOU SAY SO...
BY THE WAY, DID HAYATE SAY ANYTHING ABOUT ME?
EH?
YOU KNOW, SOMETHING ABOUT HOW CUTE AND ADORABLE I AM...?
...
Um... Er...

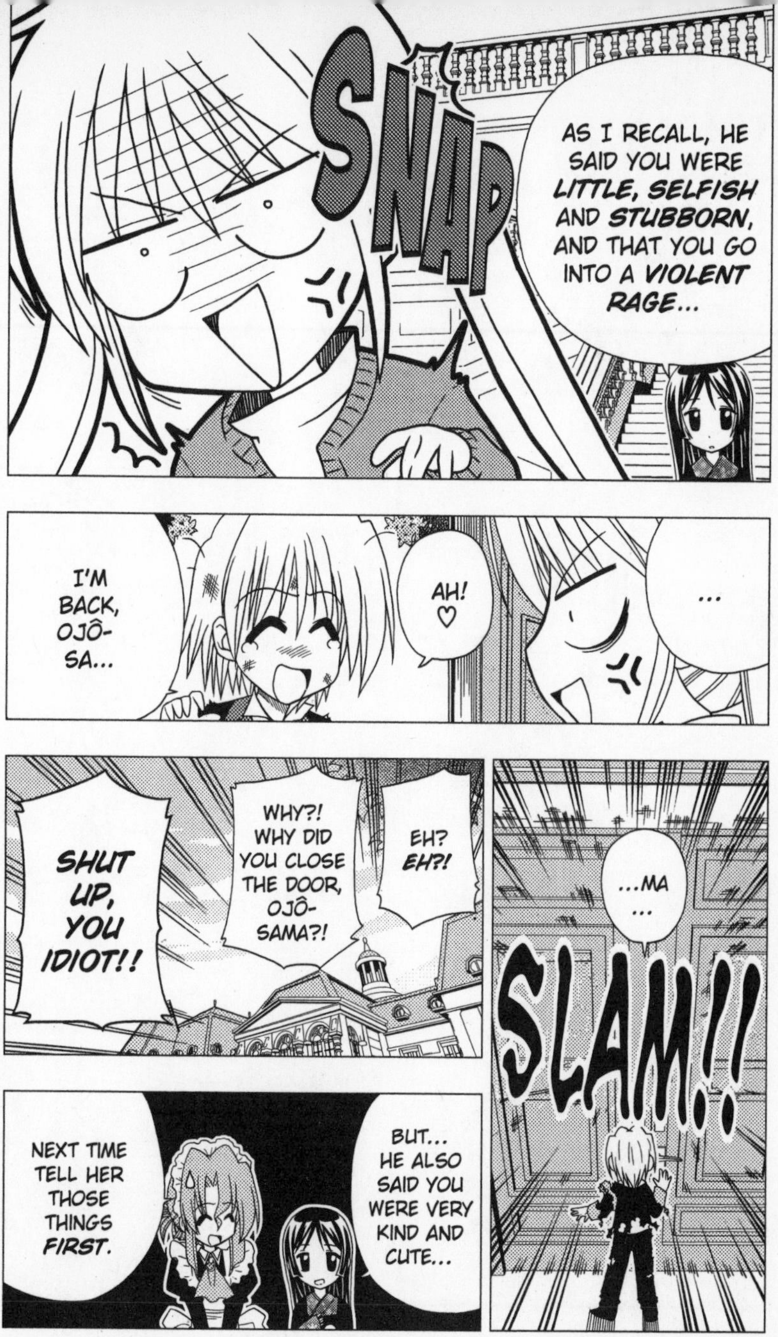
SNAP
AS I RECALL, HE SAID YOU WERE *LITTLE, SELFISH* AND *STUBBORN*, AND THAT YOU GO INTO A *VIOLENT RAGE*...
...
AH! ♡
I'M BACK, OJÔ-SA...
...MA ...
SLAM!!
EH? *EH?!*
WHY?! WHY DID YOU CLOSE THE DOOR, OJÔ-SAMA?!
SHUT UP, YOU IDIOT!!
BUT... HE ALSO SAID YOU WERE VERY KIND AND CUTE...
NEXT TIME TELL HER THOSE THINGS *FIRST*.

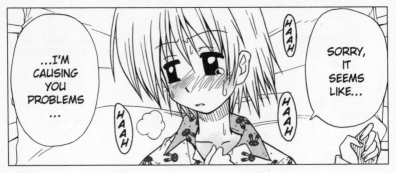

HAAH
SORRY, IT SEEMS LIKE...
HAAH
HAAH
...I'M CAUSING YOU PROBLEMS ...
102.2 DEGREES FAHRENHEIT.
NO DOUBT ABOUT IT. HE HAS A *COLD.*
SERIOUSLY!! JUST BECAUSE IT'S WINTER, HE CAUGHT A COLD SO EASILY...
WHAT A WIMP!!
WELL...
I'M NOT SURE ABOUT HIM BEING A WIMP, BUT...

Episode 9: "Even a Fool Catches Cold, So Please Help Me, Nurse Angel. I'm Not Finished Yet!!"

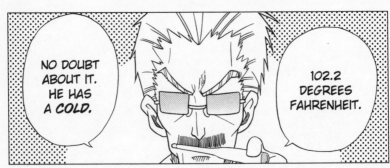

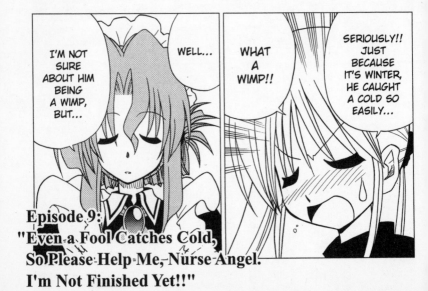

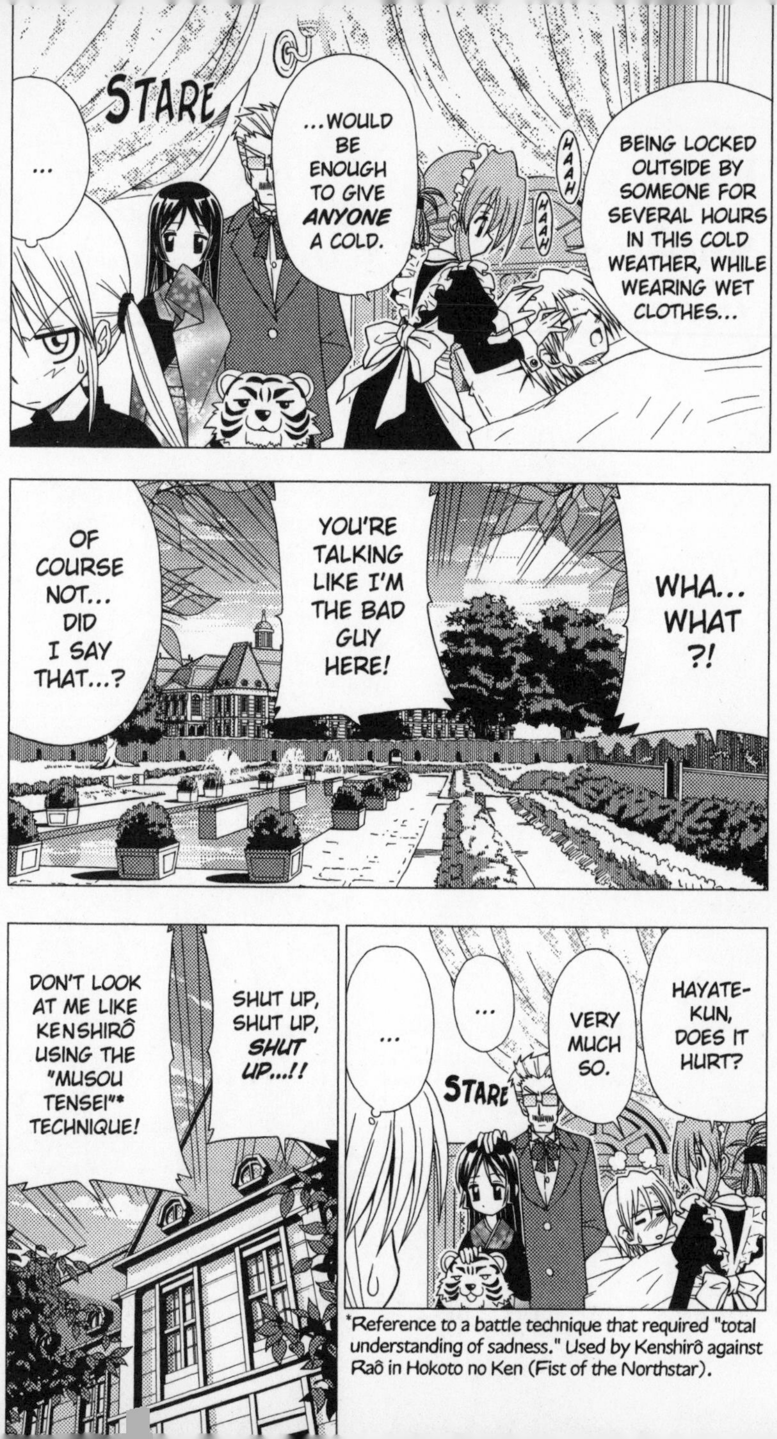
BEING LOCKED OUTSIDE BY SOMEONE FOR SEVERAL HOURS IN THIS COLD WEATHER, WHILE WEARING WET CLOTHES...
HAAH
HAAH
...WOULD BE ENOUGH TO GIVE *ANYONE* A COLD.
STARE
...
WHA... WHAT?!
YOU'RE TALKING LIKE I'M THE BAD GUY HERE!
OF COURSE NOT... DID I SAY THAT...?
HAYATE-KUN, DOES IT HURT?
VERY MUCH SO.
...
STARE
...
SHUT UP, SHUT UP, *SHUT UP...!!*
DON'T LOOK AT ME LIKE KENSHIRÔ USING THE "MUSOU TENSEI"* TECHNIQUE!

*Reference to a battle technique that required "total understanding of sadness." Used by Kenshirô against Raô in Hokoto no Ken (Fist of the Northstar).

Episode 9:
"Even a Fool Catches Cold, So Please Help Me, Nurse Ange I'm Not Finished Yet!!"

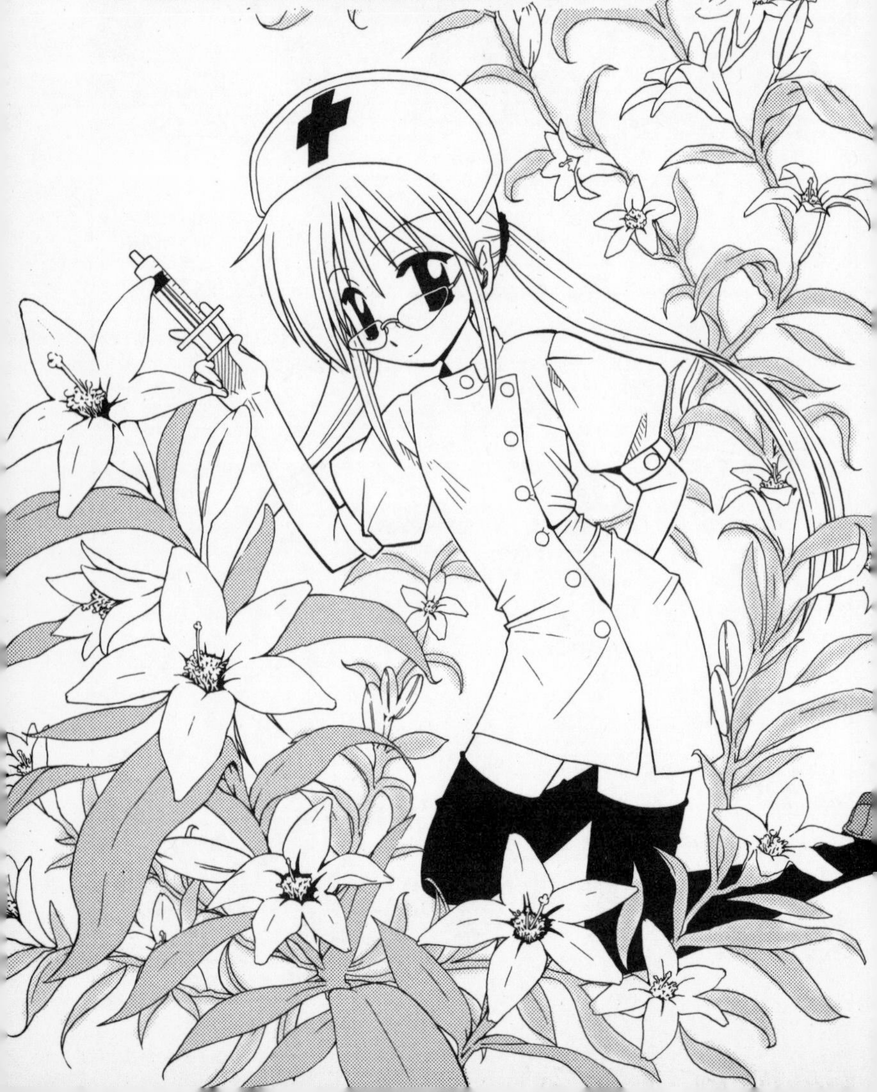

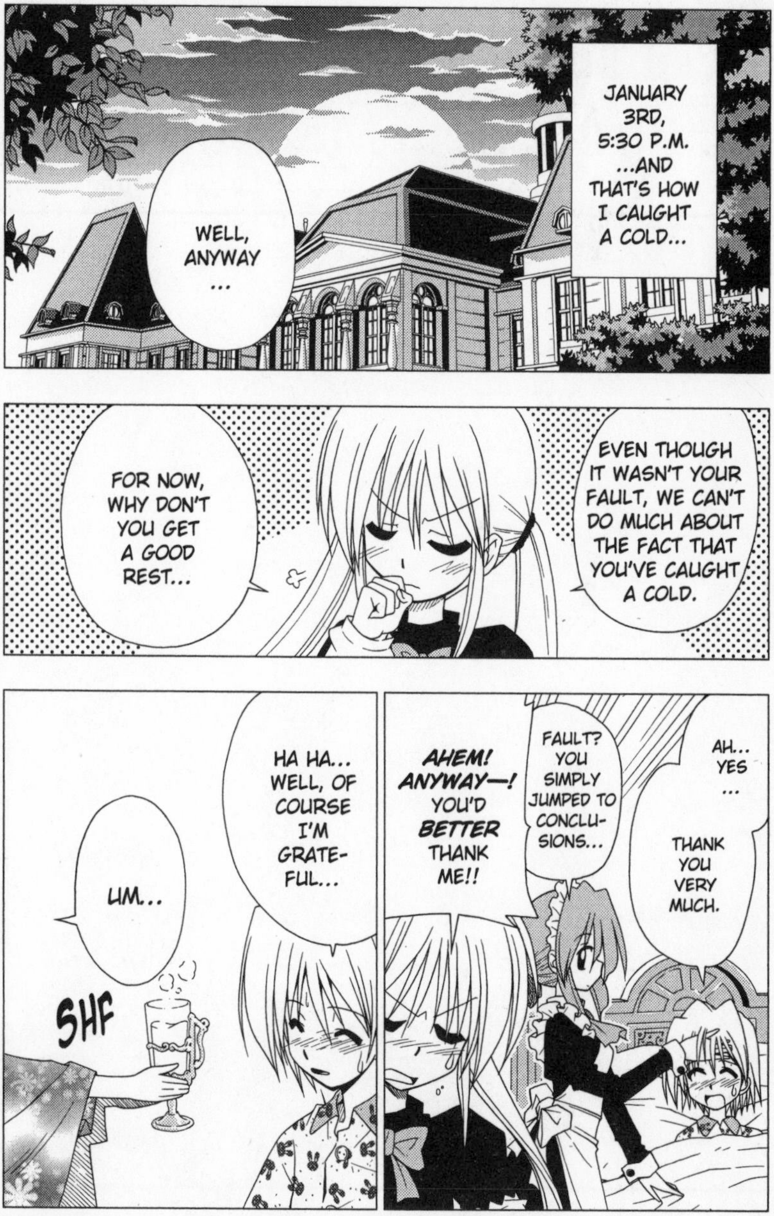
JANUARY 3RD, 5:30 P.M. ...AND THAT'S HOW I CAUGHT A COLD...
WELL, ANYWAY ...
EVEN THOUGH IT WASN'T YOUR FAULT, WE CAN'T DO MUCH ABOUT THE FACT THAT YOU'VE CAUGHT A COLD.
FOR NOW, WHY DON'T YOU GET A GOOD REST...
AH... YES ... THANK YOU VERY MUCH.
FAULT? YOU SIMPLY JUMPED TO CONCLU-SIONS...
AHEM! ANYWAY—! YOU'D BETTER THANK ME!!
HA HA... WELL, OF COURSE I'M GRATE-FUL...
UM...
SHF

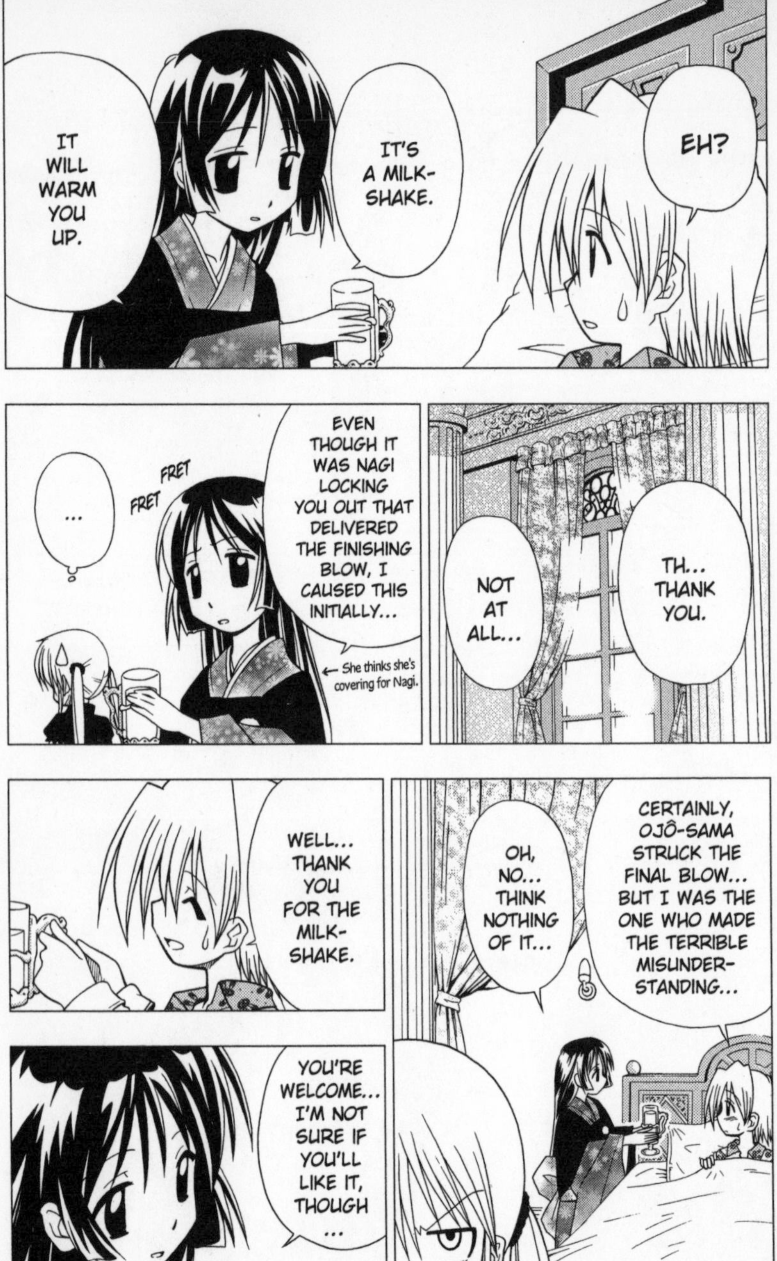
EH?
IT'S A MILK-SHAKE.
IT WILL WARM YOU UP.
TH... THANK YOU.
NOT AT ALL...
EVEN THOUGH IT WAS NAGI LOCKING YOU OUT THAT DELIVERED THE FINISHING BLOW, I CAUSED THIS INITIALLY...
← She thinks she's covering for Nagi.
FRET FRET
...
CERTAINLY, OJÔ-SAMA STRUCK THE FINAL BLOW... BUT I WAS THE ONE WHO MADE THE TERRIBLE MISUNDER-STANDING...
OH, NO... THINK NOTHING OF IT...
WELL... THANK YOU FOR THE MILK-SHAKE.
YOU'RE WELCOME... I'M NOT SURE IF YOU'LL LIKE IT, THOUGH ...

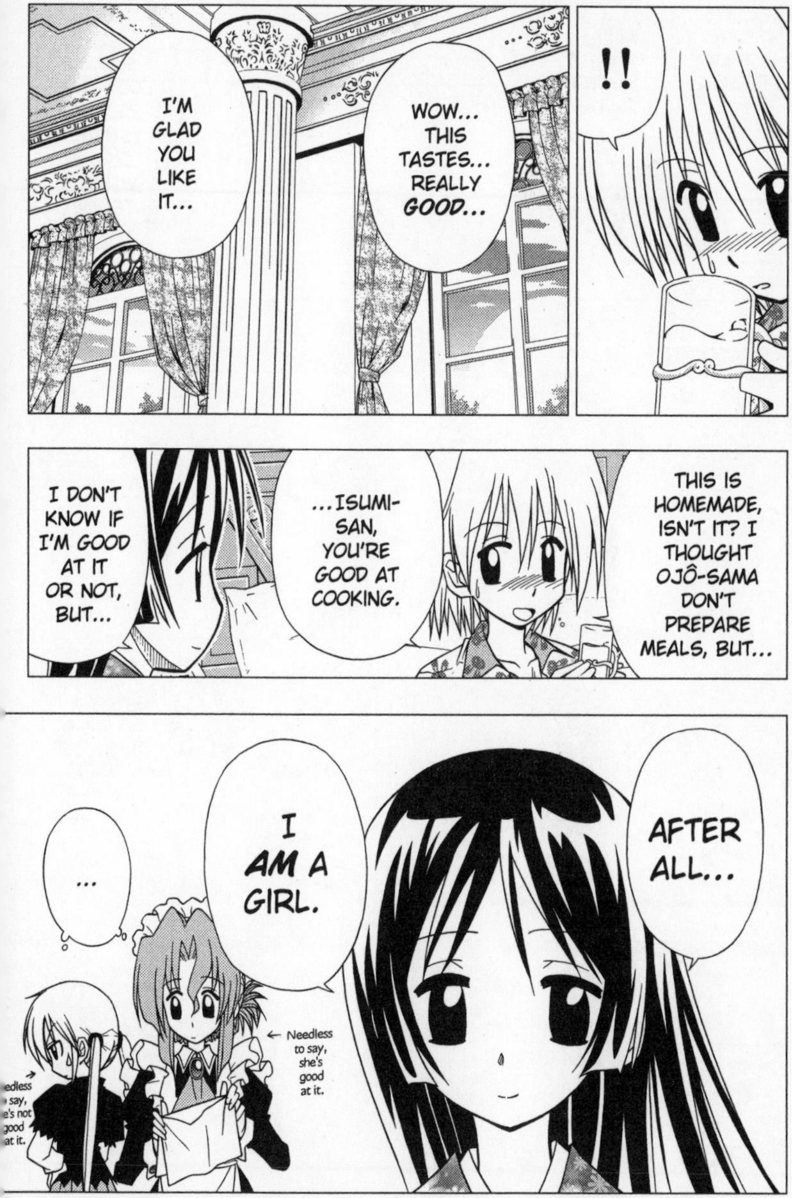
!!
...
WOW... THIS TASTES... REALLY GOOD...
I'M GLAD YOU LIKE IT...
THIS IS HOMEMADE, ISN'T IT? I THOUGHT OJÔ-SAMA DON'T PREPARE MEALS, BUT...
...ISUMI-SAN, YOU'RE GOOD AT COOKING.
I DON'T KNOW IF I'M GOOD AT IT OR NOT, BUT...
AFTER ALL...
I AM A GIRL.
...
Needless to say, she's good at it.
edless say, e's not good at it.

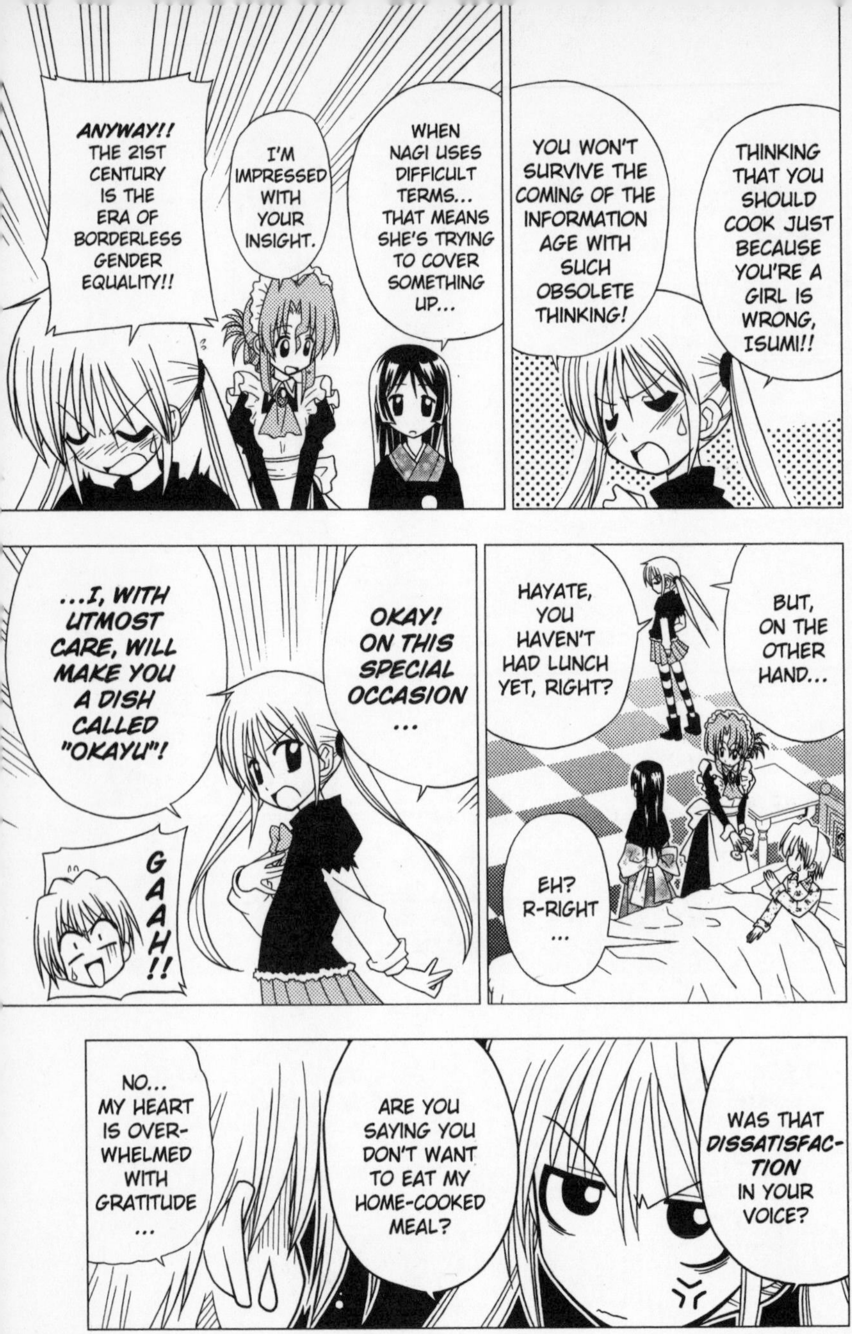
THINKING THAT YOU SHOULD COOK JUST BECAUSE YOU'RE A GIRL IS WRONG, ISUMI!!
YOU WON'T SURVIVE THE COMING OF THE INFORMATION AGE WITH SUCH OBSOLETE THINKING!
WHEN NAGI USES DIFFICULT TERMS... THAT MEANS SHE'S TRYING TO COVER SOMETHING UP...
I'M IMPRESSED WITH YOUR INSIGHT.
ANYWAY!! THE 21ST CENTURY IS THE ERA OF BORDERLESS GENDER EQUALITY!!
BUT, ON THE OTHER HAND...
HAYATE, YOU HAVEN'T HAD LUNCH YET, RIGHT?
EH? R-RIGHT...
OKAY! ON THIS SPECIAL OCCASION...
...I, WITH UTMOST CARE, WILL MAKE YOU A DISH CALLED "OKAYU"!
GAAAH!!
WAS THAT DISSATISFACTION IN YOUR VOICE?
ARE YOU SAYING YOU DON'T WANT TO EAT MY HOME-COOKED MEAL?
NO... MY HEART IS OVER-WHELMED WITH GRATITUDE...

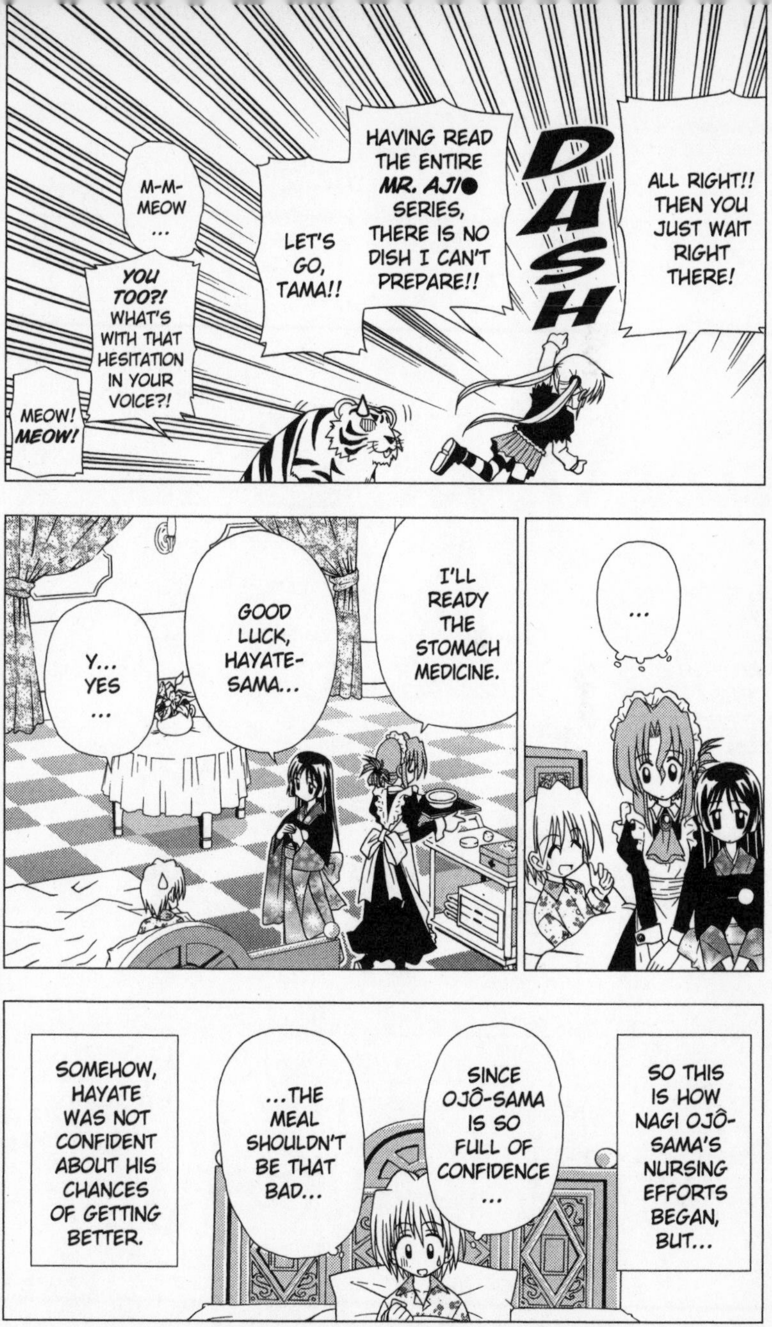
ALL RIGHT!! THEN YOU JUST WAIT RIGHT THERE!
DASH
HAVING READ THE ENTIRE MR. AJI● SERIES, THERE IS NO DISH I CAN'T PREPARE!!
LET'S GO, TAMA!!
M-M-MEOW ...
YOU TOO?! WHAT'S WITH THAT HESITATION IN YOUR VOICE?!
MEOW! MEOW!
...
I'LL READY THE STOMACH MEDICINE.
GOOD LUCK, HAYATE-SAMA...
Y... YES ...
SO THIS IS HOW NAGI OJÔ-SAMA'S NURSING EFFORTS BEGAN, BUT...
SINCE OJÔ-SAMA IS SO FULL OF CONFIDENCE ...
...THE MEAL SHOULDN'T BE THAT BAD...
SOMEHOW, HAYATE WAS NOT CONFIDENT ABOUT HIS CHANCES OF GETTING BETTER.

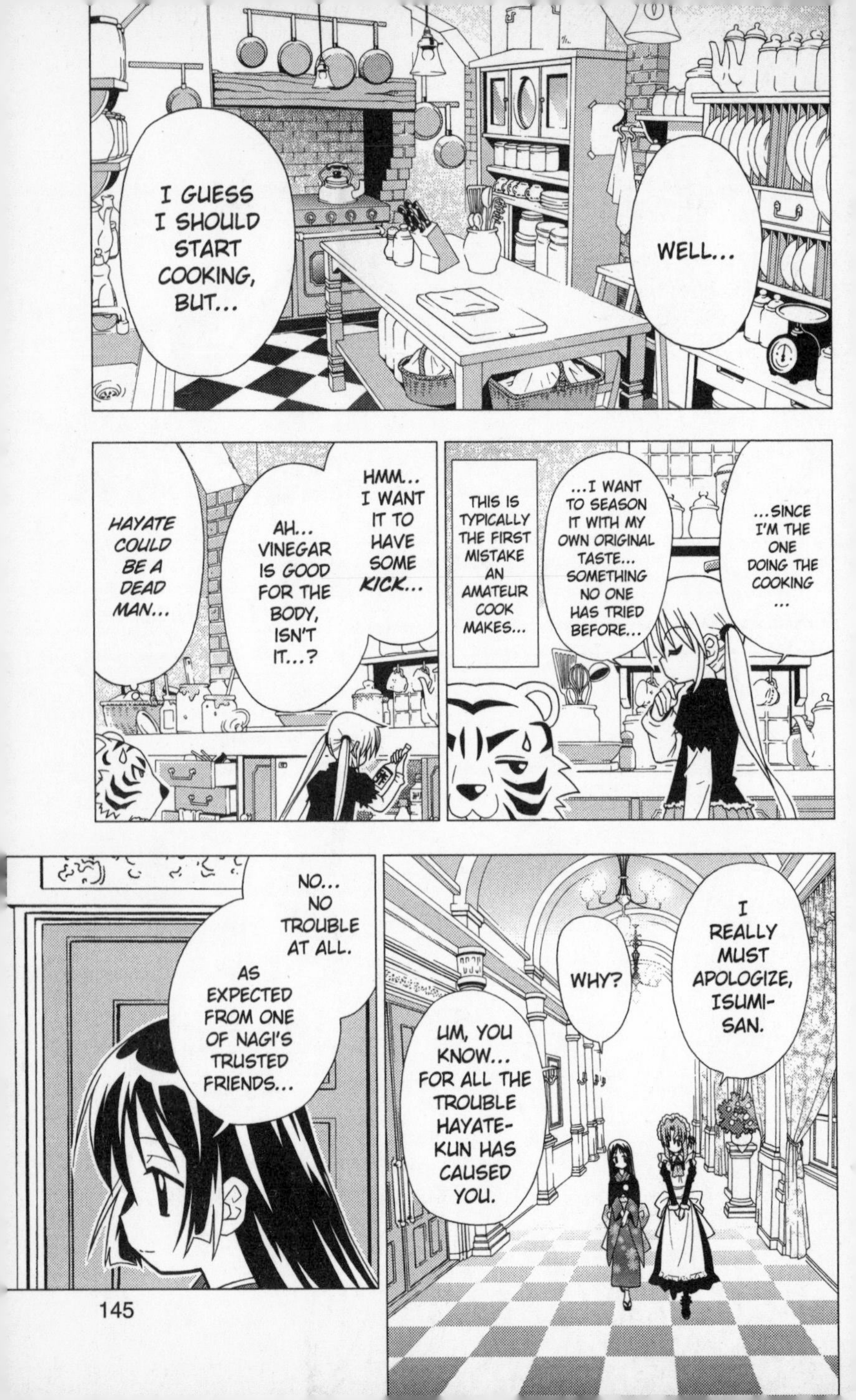
WELL...
I GUESS I SHOULD START COOKING, BUT...
...SINCE I'M THE ONE DOING THE COOKING...
...I WANT TO SEASON IT WITH MY OWN ORIGINAL TASTE... SOMETHING NO ONE HAS TRIED BEFORE...
THIS IS TYPICALLY THE FIRST MISTAKE AN AMATEUR COOK MAKES...
HMM... I WANT IT TO HAVE SOME *KICK*...
AH... VINEGAR IS GOOD FOR THE BODY, ISN'T IT...?
HAYATE COULD BE A DEAD MAN...
I REALLY MUST APOLOGIZE, ISUMI-SAN.
WHY?
UM, YOU KNOW... FOR ALL THE TROUBLE HAYATE-KUN HAS CAUSED YOU.
NO... NO TROUBLE AT ALL.
AS EXPECTED FROM ONE OF NAGI'S TRUSTED FRIENDS...

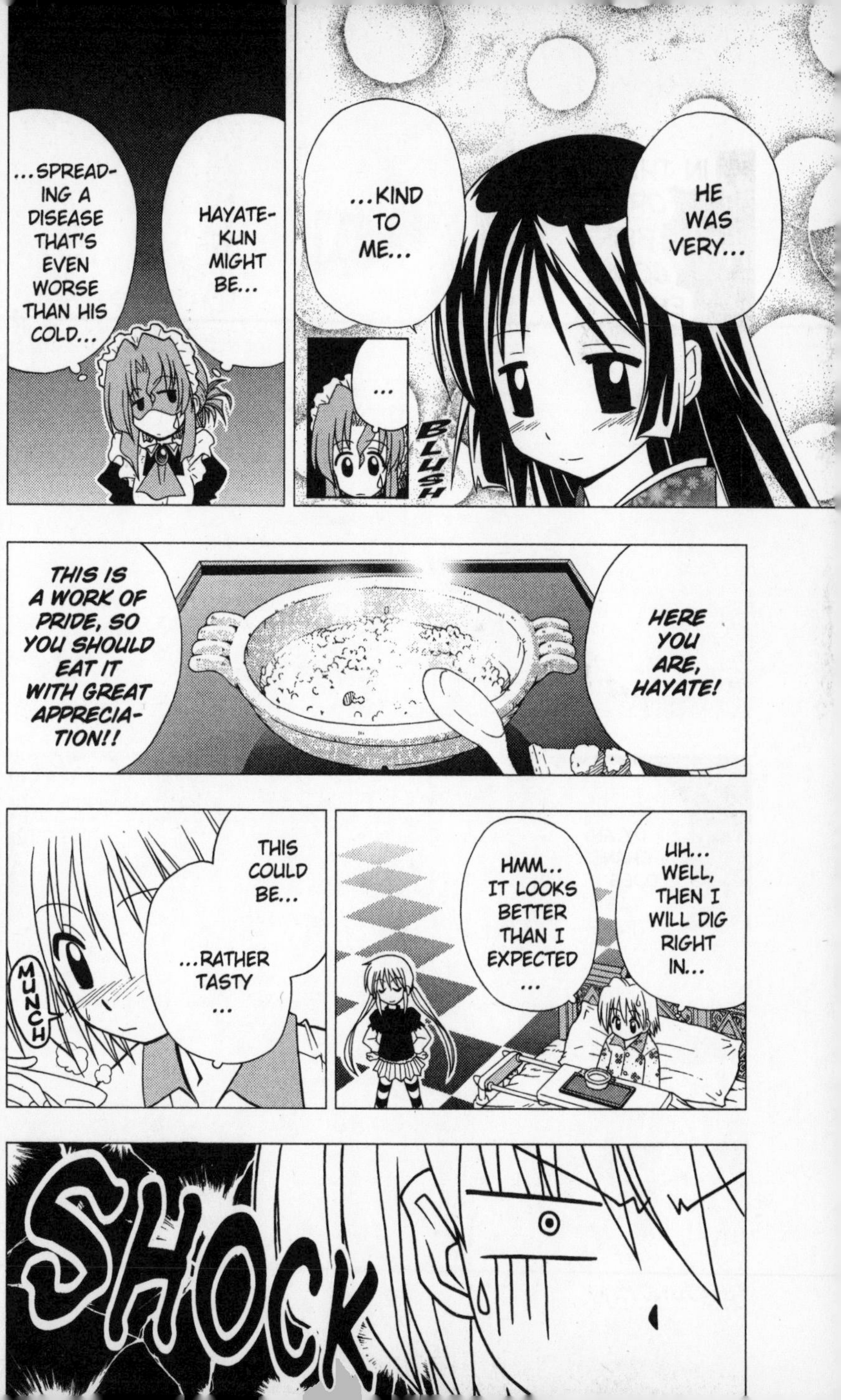
HE WAS VERY...
...KIND TO ME...
...
BLUSH
HAYATE-KUN MIGHT BE...
...SPREADING A DISEASE THAT'S EVEN WORSE THAN HIS COLD...
HERE YOU ARE, HAYATE!
THIS IS A WORK OF PRIDE, SO YOU SHOULD EAT IT WITH GREAT APPRECIATION!!
UH... WELL, THEN I WILL DIG RIGHT IN...
HMM... IT LOOKS BETTER THAN I EXPECTED ...
THIS COULD BE...
...RATHER TASTY ...
MUNCH
SHOCK

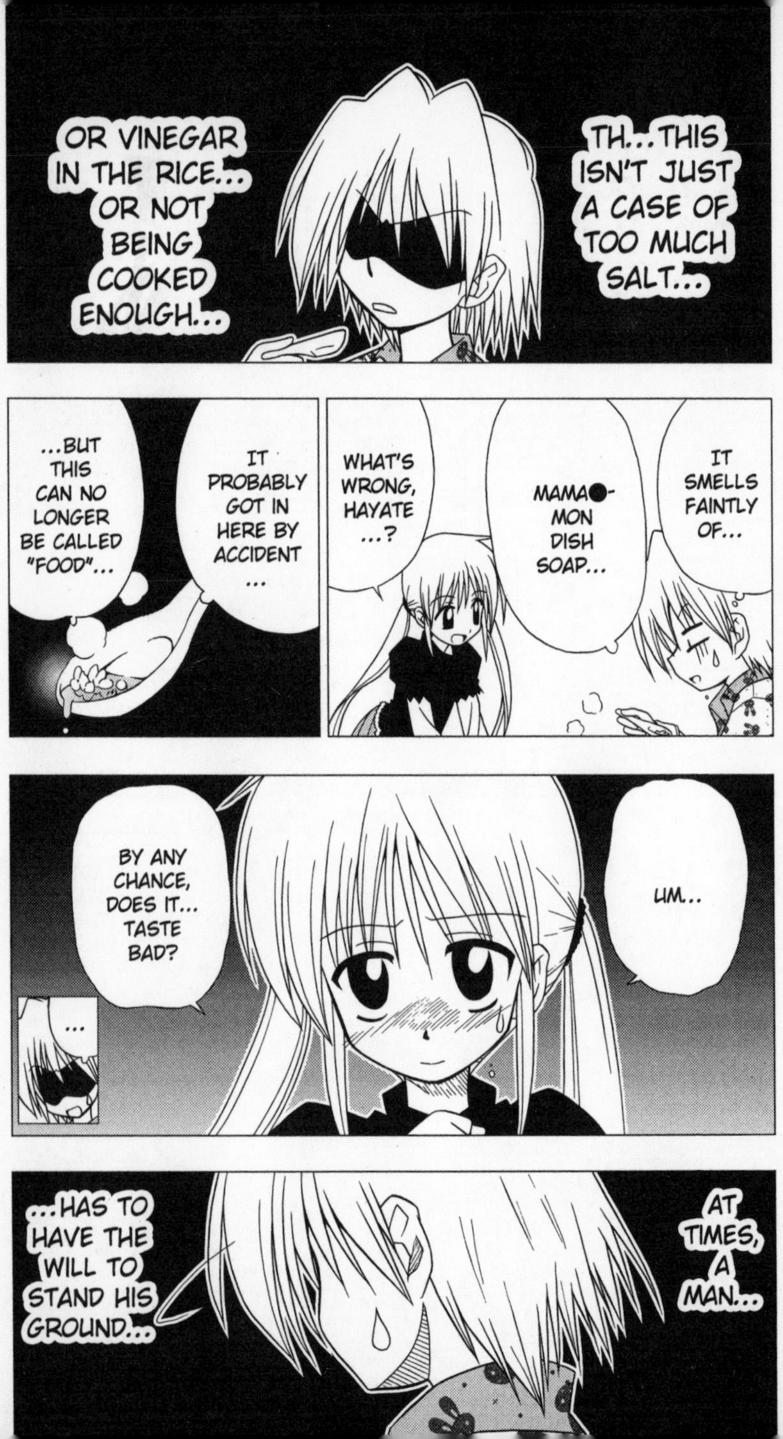
TH... THIS ISN'T JUST A CASE OF TOO MUCH SALT...
OR VINEGAR IN THE RICE... OR NOT BEING COOKED ENOUGH...
IT SMELLS FAINTLY OF...
MAMA●-MON DISH SOAP...
WHAT'S WRONG, HAYATE ...?
IT PROBABLY GOT IN HERE BY ACCIDENT ...
...BUT THIS CAN NO LONGER BE CALLED "FOOD"...
UM...
BY ANY CHANCE, DOES IT... TASTE BAD?
...
AT TIMES, A MAN...
...HAS TO HAVE THE WILL TO STAND HIS GROUND...

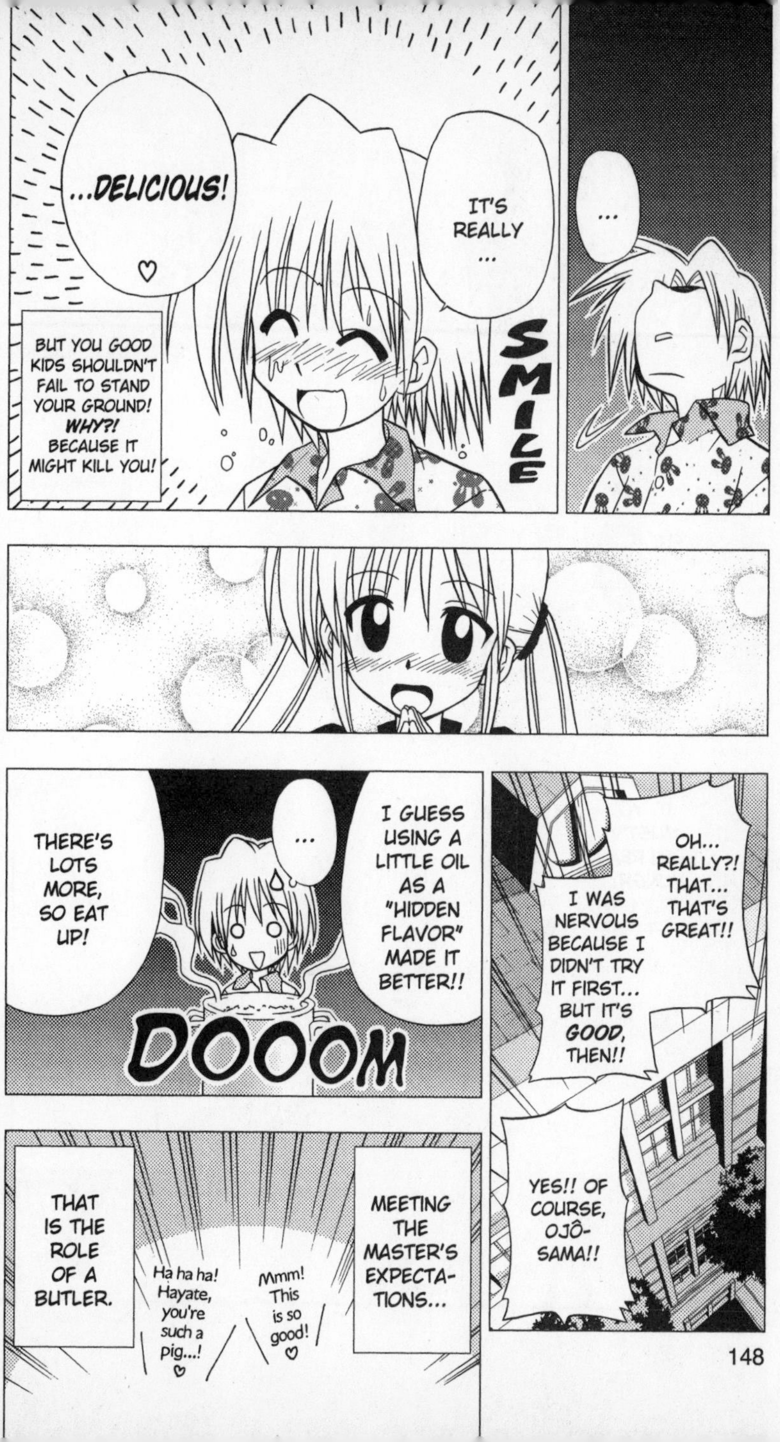
...
IT'S REALLY ...
SMILE
...DELICIOUS! ♡
BUT YOU GOOD KIDS SHOULDN'T FAIL TO STAND YOUR GROUND! WHY?! BECAUSE IT MIGHT KILL YOU!
OH... REALLY?! THAT... THAT'S GREAT!!
I WAS NERVOUS BECAUSE I DIDN'T TRY IT FIRST... BUT IT'S GOOD, THEN!!
YES!! OF COURSE, OJÔ-SAMA!!
I GUESS USING A LITTLE OIL AS A "HIDDEN FLAVOR" MADE IT BETTER!!
...
THERE'S LOTS MORE, SO EAT UP!
DOOOM
MEETING THE MASTER'S EXPECTA-TIONS...
Mmm! This is so good! ♡
Ha ha ha! Hayate, you're such a pig...! ♡
THAT IS THE ROLE OF A BUTLER.

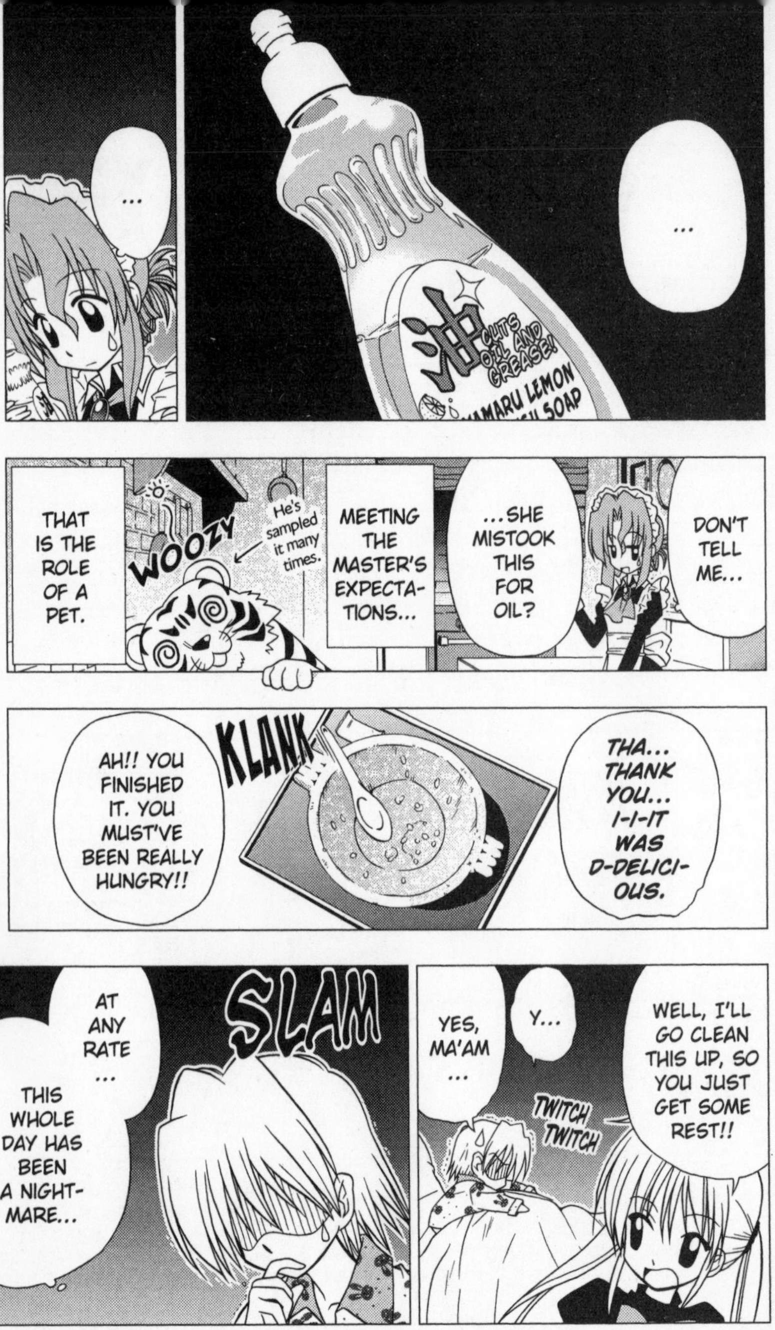
...
CUTS OIL AND GREASE!
...
DON'T TELL ME...
...SHE MISTOOK THIS FOR OIL?
MEETING THE MASTER'S EXPECTATIONS...
He's sampled it many times.
WOOZY
THAT IS THE ROLE OF A PET.
THA... THANK YOU... I-I-IT WAS D-DELICIOUS.
KLANK
AH!! YOU FINISHED IT. YOU MUST'VE BEEN REALLY HUNGRY!!
WELL, I'LL GO CLEAN THIS UP, SO YOU JUST GET SOME REST!!
Y...
YES, MA'AM ...
TWITCH TWITCH
SLAM
AT ANY RATE ...
THIS WHOLE DAY HAS BEEN A NIGHTMARE...

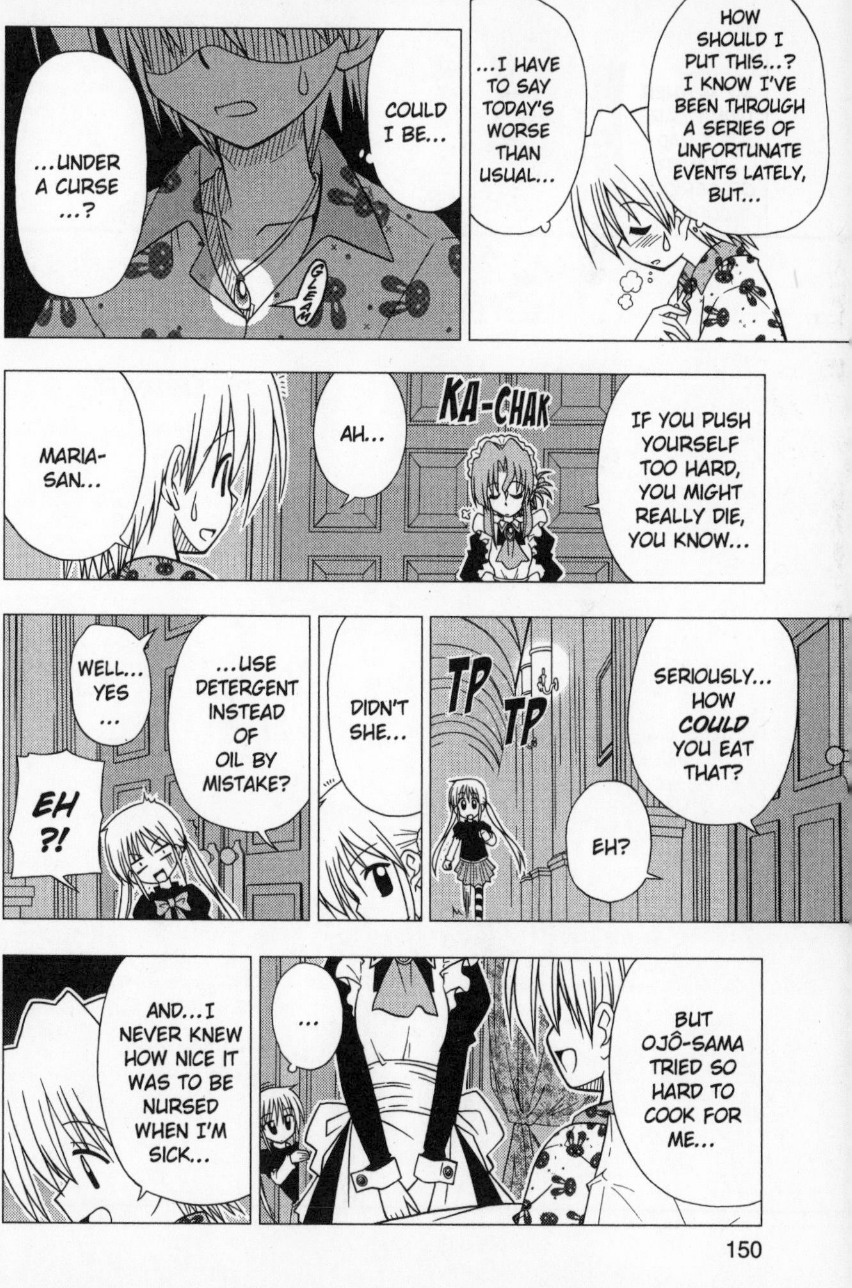
HOW SHOULD I PUT THIS...? I KNOW I'VE BEEN THROUGH A SERIES OF UNFORTUNATE EVENTS LATELY, BUT...
...I HAVE TO SAY TODAY'S WORSE THAN USUAL...
COULD I BE...
...UNDER A CURSE ...?
GLEAM
IF YOU PUSH YOURSELF TOO HARD, YOU MIGHT REALLY DIE, YOU KNOW...
KA-CHAK
AH...
MARIA-SAN...
SERIOUSLY... HOW **COULD** YOU EAT THAT?
TP TP
EH?
DIDN'T SHE...
...USE DETERGENT INSTEAD OF OIL BY MISTAKE?
WELL... YES ...
EH ?!
BUT OJÔ-SAMA TRIED SO HARD TO COOK FOR ME...
...
AND...I NEVER KNEW HOW NICE IT WAS TO BE NURSED WHEN I'M SICK...

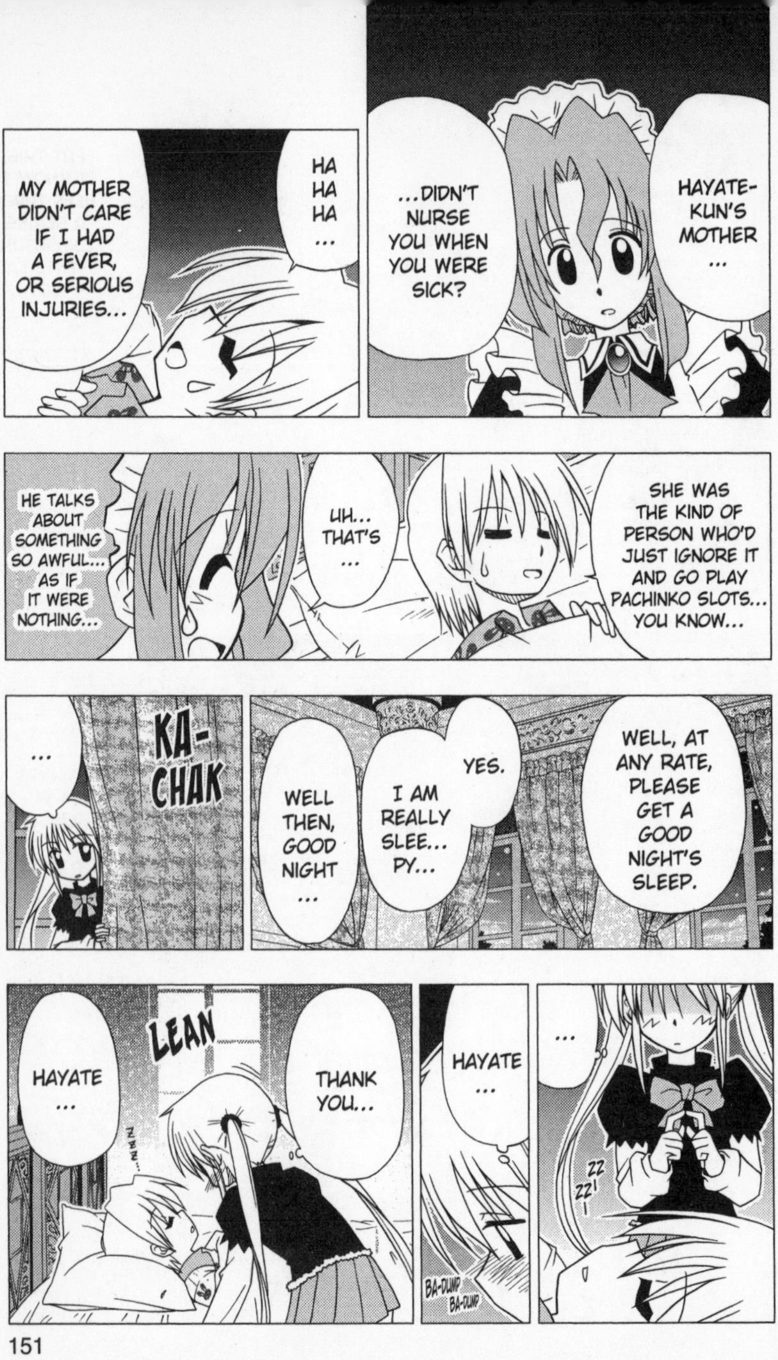
HAYATE-KUN'S MOTHER ...
...DIDN'T NURSE YOU WHEN YOU WERE SICK?
HA HA HA ...
MY MOTHER DIDN'T CARE IF I HAD A FEVER, OR SERIOUS INJURIES...
SHE WAS THE KIND OF PERSON WHO'D JUST IGNORE IT AND GO PLAY PACHINKO SLOTS... YOU KNOW...
UH... THAT'S ...
HE TALKS ABOUT SOMETHING SO AWFUL... AS IF IT WERE NOTHING...
WELL, AT ANY RATE, PLEASE GET A GOOD NIGHT'S SLEEP.
YES.
I AM REALLY SLEE... PY...
WELL THEN, GOOD NIGHT ...
KA-CHAK
...
...
ZZ ZZ!
HAYATE ...
BA-DUMP BA-DUMP
LEAN
THANK YOU...
HAYATE ...

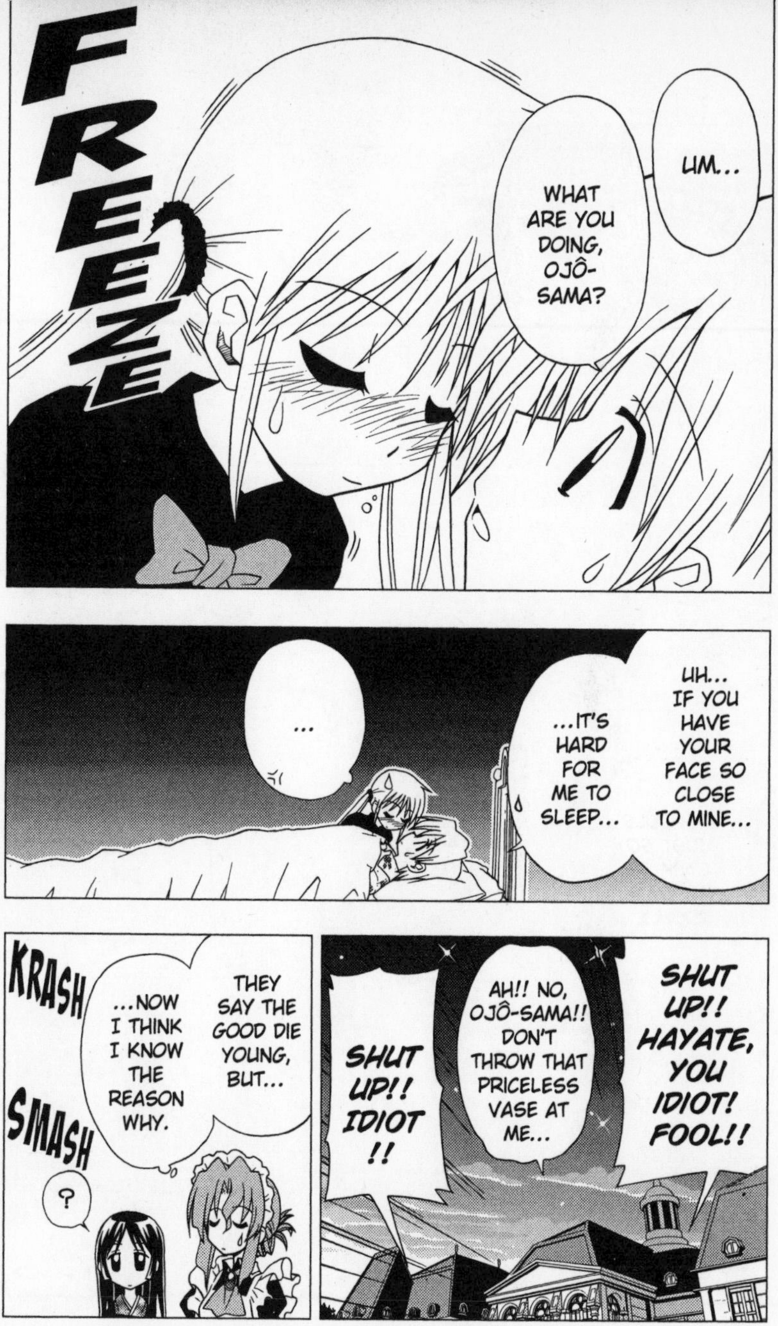
UM...
WHAT ARE YOU DOING, OJÔ-SAMA?
FREEZE
UH... IF YOU HAVE YOUR FACE SO CLOSE TO MINE...
...IT'S HARD FOR ME TO SLEEP...
...
SHUT UP!! HAYATE, YOU IDIOT! FOOL!!
AH!! NO, OJÔ-SAMA!! DON'T THROW THAT PRICELESS VASE AT ME...
SHUT UP!! IDIOT!!
KRASH
SMASH
THEY SAY THE GOOD DIE YOUNG, BUT...
...NOW I THINK I KNOW THE REASON WHY.
?

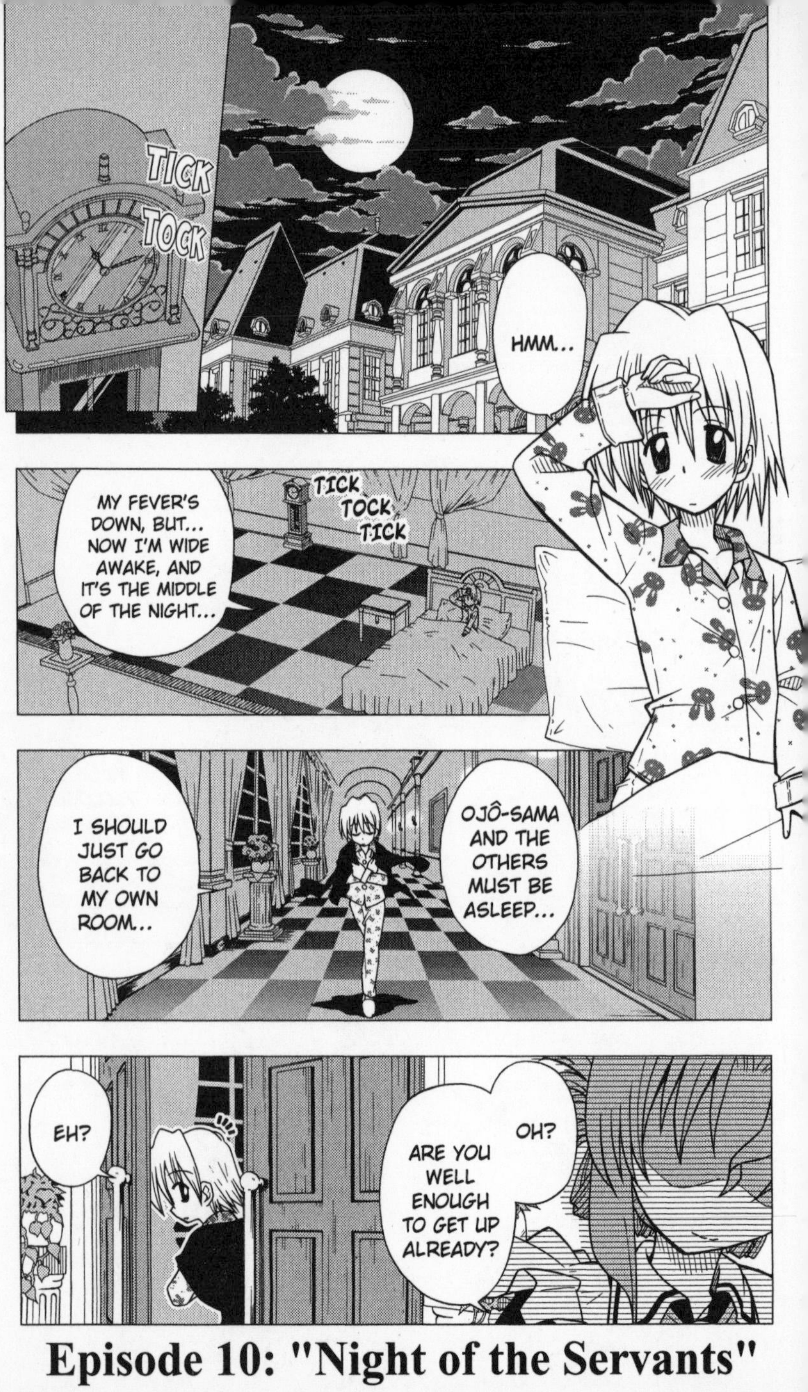
TICK
TOCK
HMM...
MY FEVER'S DOWN, BUT... NOW I'M WIDE AWAKE, AND IT'S THE MIDDLE OF THE NIGHT...
TICK TOCK TICK
OJÔ-SAMA AND THE OTHERS MUST BE ASLEEP...
I SHOULD JUST GO BACK TO MY OWN ROOM...
OH?
ARE YOU WELL ENOUGH TO GET UP ALREADY?
EH?

Episode 10: "Night of the Servants"

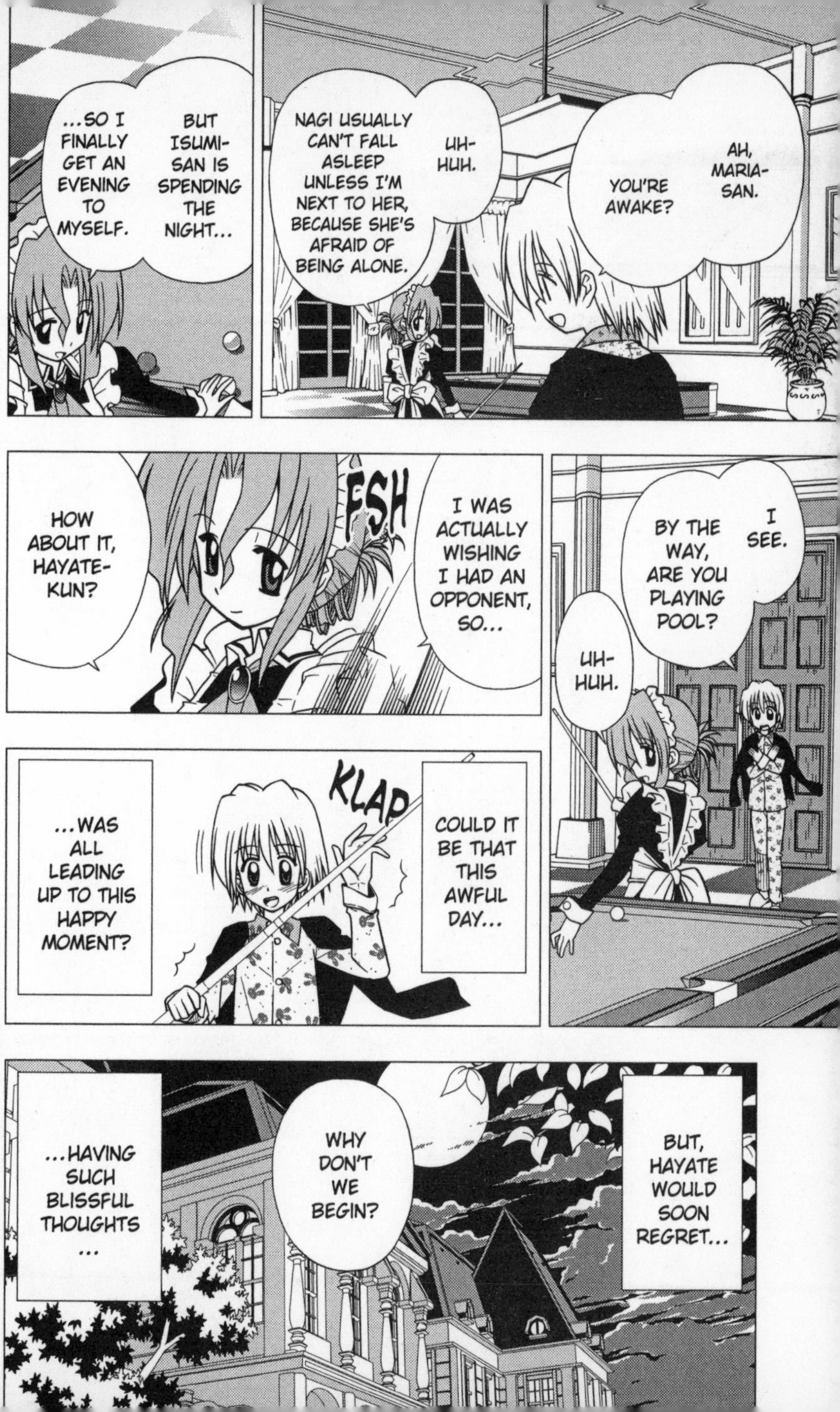
AH, MARIA-SAN.
YOU'RE AWAKE?
UH-HUH.
NAGI USUALLY CAN'T FALL ASLEEP UNLESS I'M NEXT TO HER, BECAUSE SHE'S AFRAID OF BEING ALONE.
BUT ISUMI-SAN IS SPENDING THE NIGHT...
...SO I FINALLY GET AN EVENING TO MYSELF.
I SEE.
BY THE WAY, ARE YOU PLAYING POOL?
UH-HUH.
I WAS ACTUALLY WISHING I HAD AN OPPONENT, SO...
FSH
HOW ABOUT IT, HAYATE-KUN?
COULD IT BE THAT THIS AWFUL DAY...
KLAP
...WAS ALL LEADING UP TO THIS HAPPY MOMENT?
BUT, HAYATE WOULD SOON REGRET...
WHY DON'T WE BEGIN?
...HAVING SUCH BLISSFUL THOUGHTS...

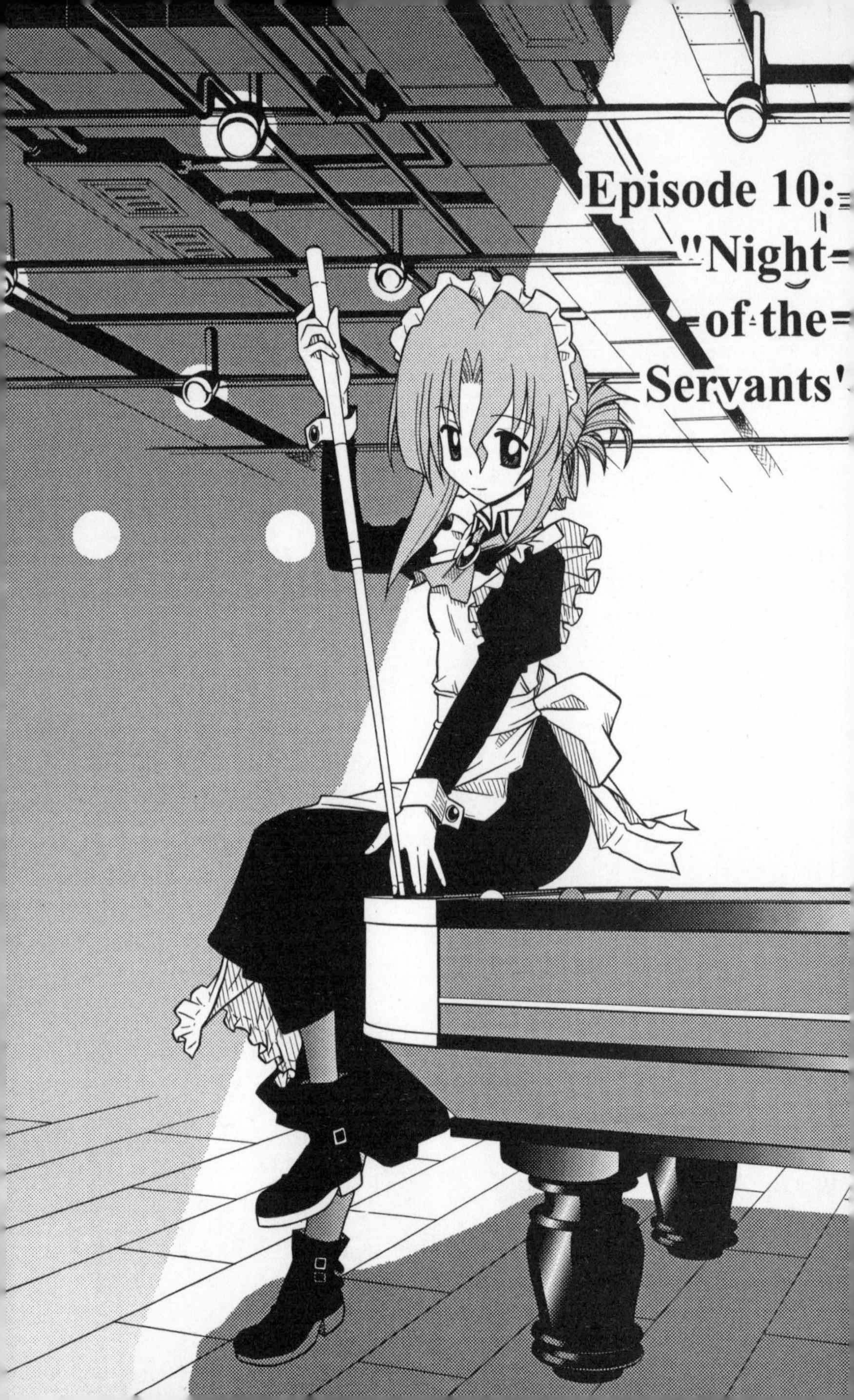
Episode 10:
"Night of the Servants"

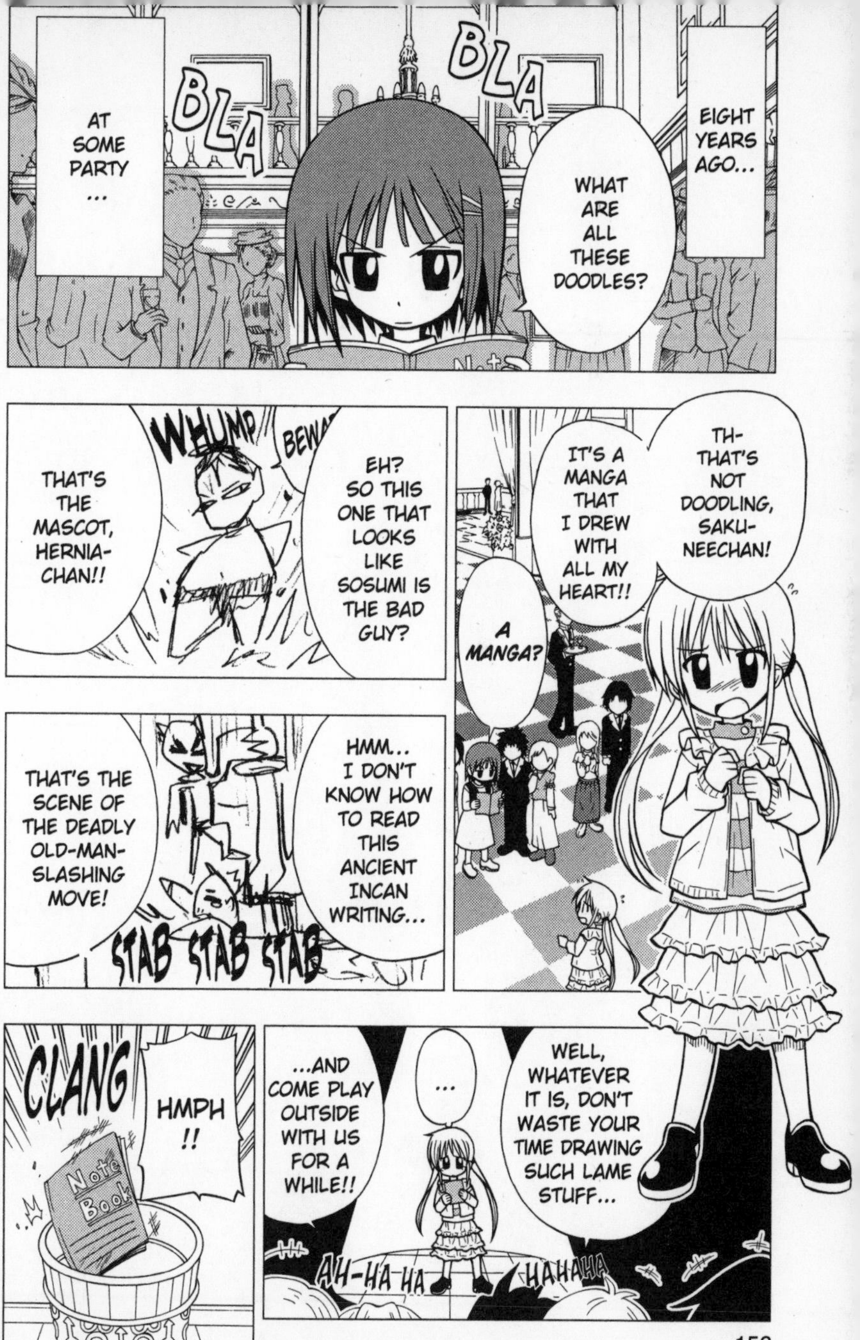
EIGHT YEARS AGO...
BLA
WHAT ARE ALL THESE DOODLES?
BLA
AT SOME PARTY...
TH-THAT'S NOT DOODLING, SAKU-NEECHAN!
IT'S A MANGA THAT I DREW WITH ALL MY HEART!!
A MANGA?
EH? SO THIS ONE THAT LOOKS LIKE SOSUMI IS THE BAD GUY?
WHUMP
THAT'S THE MASCOT, HERNIA-CHAN!!
HMM... I DON'T KNOW HOW TO READ THIS ANCIENT INCAN WRITING...
THAT'S THE SCENE OF THE DEADLY OLD-MAN-SLASHING MOVE!
STAB STAB STAB
WELL, WHATEVER IT IS, DON'T WASTE YOUR TIME DRAWING SUCH LAME STUFF...
...
...AND COME PLAY OUTSIDE WITH US FOR A WHILE!!
AH-HA HA
HAHAHA
HMPH!!
CLANG
Note Book

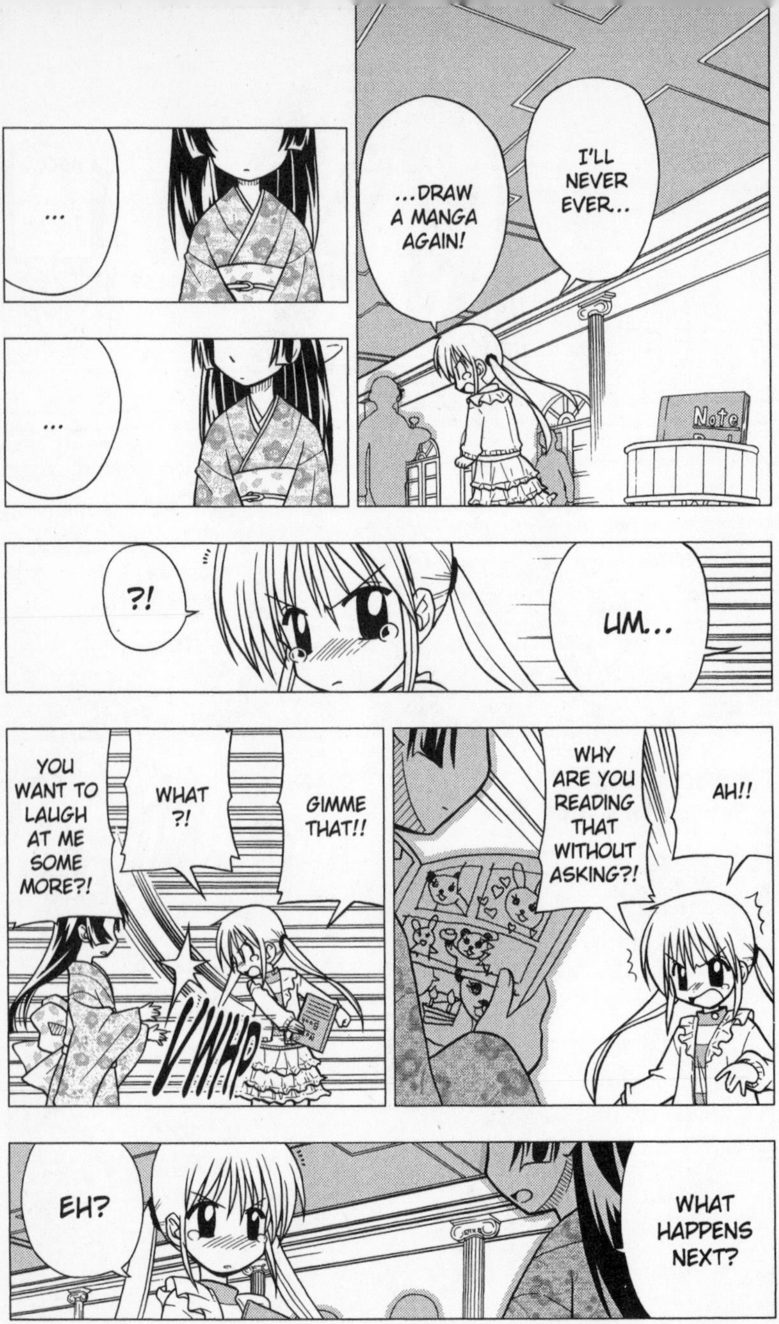
I'LL NEVER EVER..
...DRAW A MANGA AGAIN!
Note
...
...
UM...
?!
AH!!
WHY ARE YOU READING THAT WITHOUT ASKING?!
GIMME THAT!!
WHAT ?!
YOU WANT TO LAUGH AT ME SOME MORE?!
WHAP
WHAT HAPPENS NEXT?
EH?

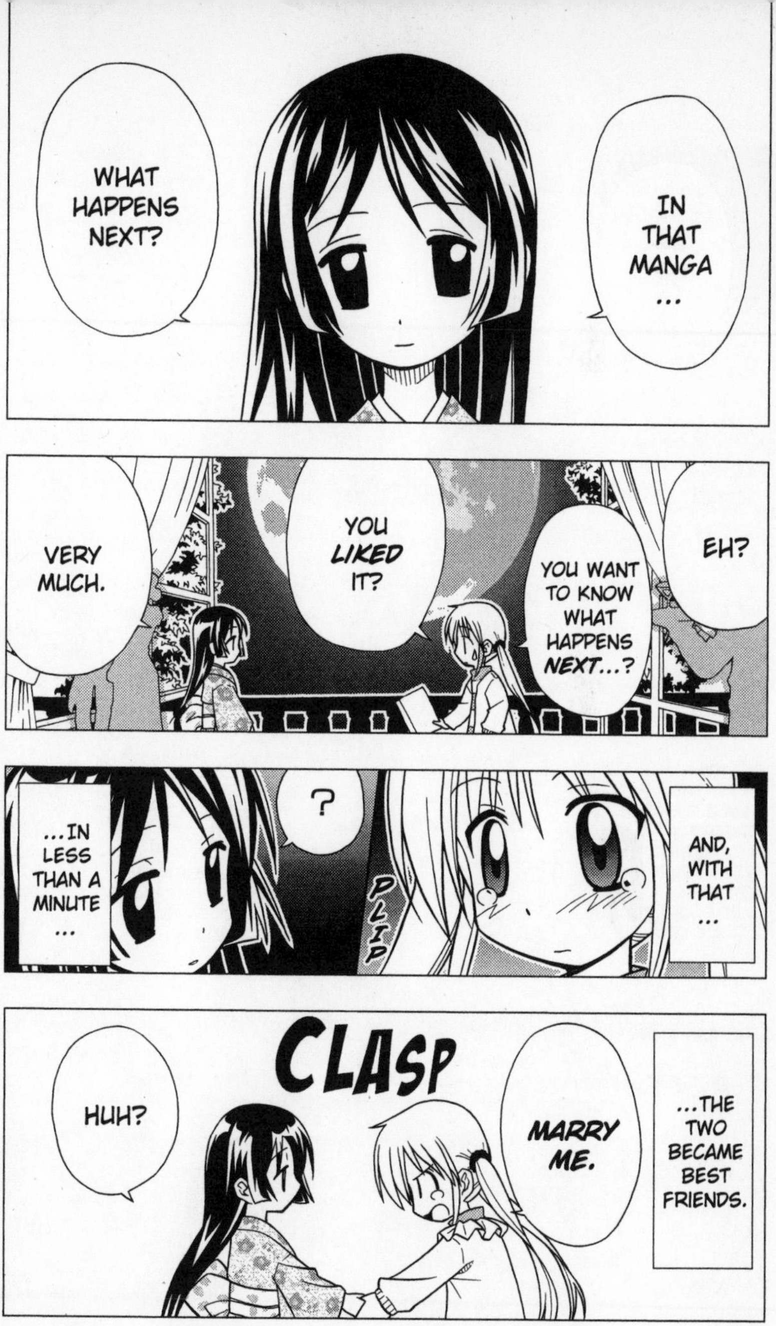
IN THAT MANGA ...
WHAT HAPPENS NEXT?
EH?
YOU WANT TO KNOW WHAT HAPPENS NEXT...?
YOU LIKED IT?
VERY MUCH.
AND, WITH THAT ...
PLIP
?
...IN LESS THAN A MINUTE ...
...THE TWO BECAME BEST FRIENDS.
MARRY ME.
CLASP
HUH?

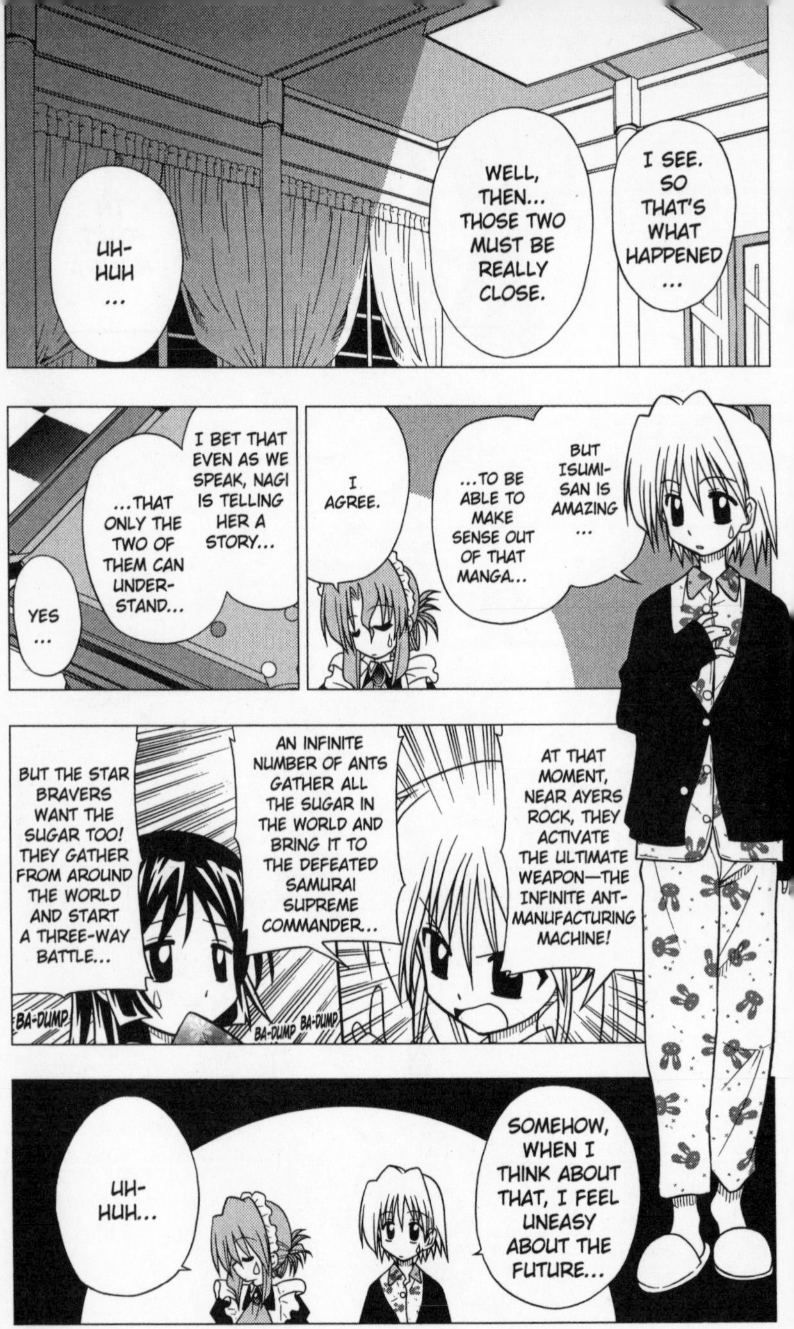
I SEE. SO THAT'S WHAT HAPPENED...
WELL, THEN... THOSE TWO MUST BE REALLY CLOSE.
UH-HUH...
BUT ISUMI-SAN IS AMAZING...
...TO BE ABLE TO MAKE SENSE OUT OF THAT MANGA...
I AGREE.
I BET THAT EVEN AS WE SPEAK, NAGI IS TELLING HER A STORY...
...THAT ONLY THE TWO OF THEM CAN UNDERSTAND...
YES...
AT THAT MOMENT, NEAR AYERS ROCK, THEY ACTIVATE THE ULTIMATE WEAPON—THE INFINITE ANT-MANUFACTURING MACHINE!
AN INFINITE NUMBER OF ANTS GATHER ALL THE SUGAR IN THE WORLD AND BRING IT TO THE DEFEATED SAMURAI SUPREME COMMANDER...
BUT THE STAR BRAVERS WANT THE SUGAR TOO! THEY GATHER FROM AROUND THE WORLD AND START A THREE-WAY BATTLE...
BA-DUMP
BA-DUMP
BA-DUMP
SOMEHOW, WHEN I THINK ABOUT THAT, I FEEL UNEASY ABOUT THE FUTURE...
UH-HUH...

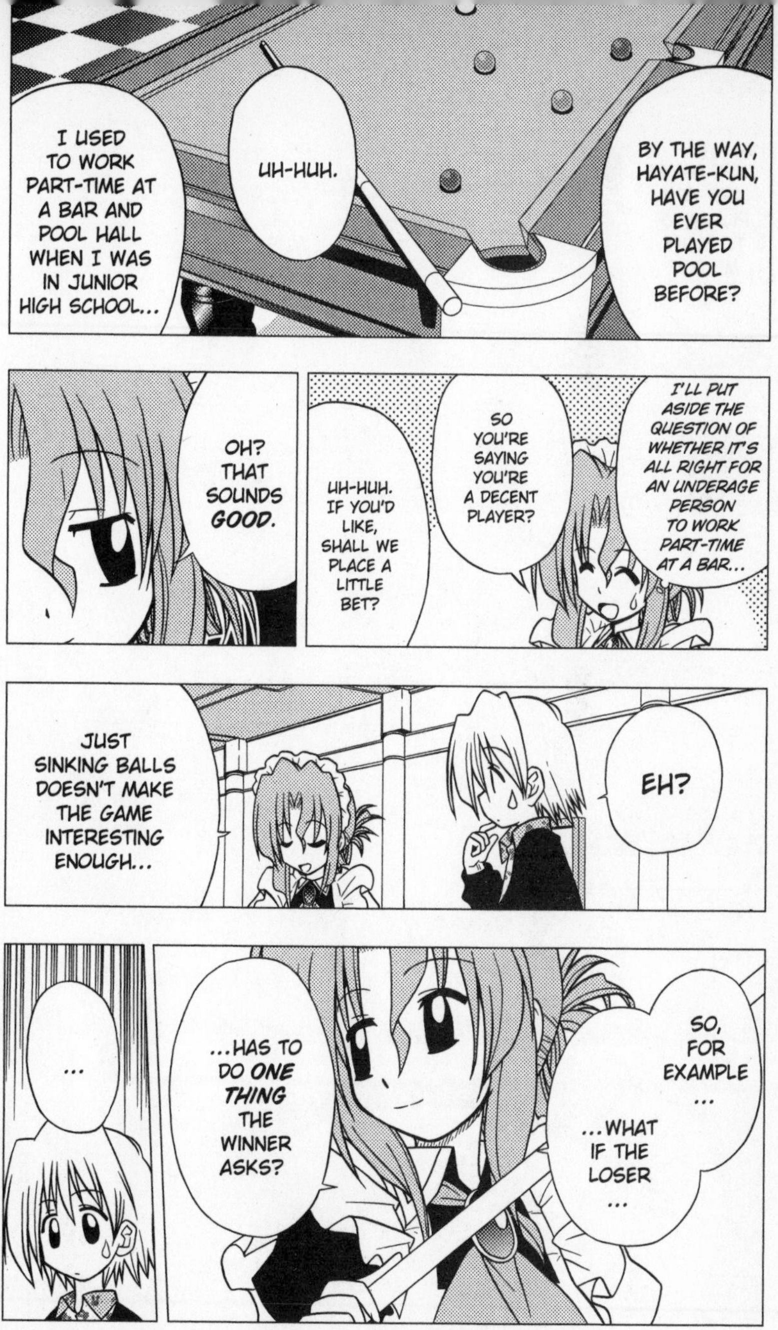
BY THE WAY, HAYATE-KUN, HAVE YOU EVER PLAYED POOL BEFORE?
UH-HUH.
I USED TO WORK PART-TIME AT A BAR AND POOL HALL WHEN I WAS IN JUNIOR HIGH SCHOOL...
I'LL PUT ASIDE THE QUESTION OF WHETHER IT'S ALL RIGHT FOR AN UNDERAGE PERSON TO WORK PART-TIME AT A BAR...
SO YOU'RE SAYING YOU'RE A DECENT PLAYER?
UH-HUH. IF YOU'D LIKE, SHALL WE PLACE A LITTLE BET?
OH? THAT SOUNDS GOOD.
EH?
JUST SINKING BALLS DOESN'T MAKE THE GAME INTERESTING ENOUGH...
SO, FOR EXAMPLE...
...WHAT IF THE LOSER...
...HAS TO DO ONE THING THE WINNER ASKS?
...

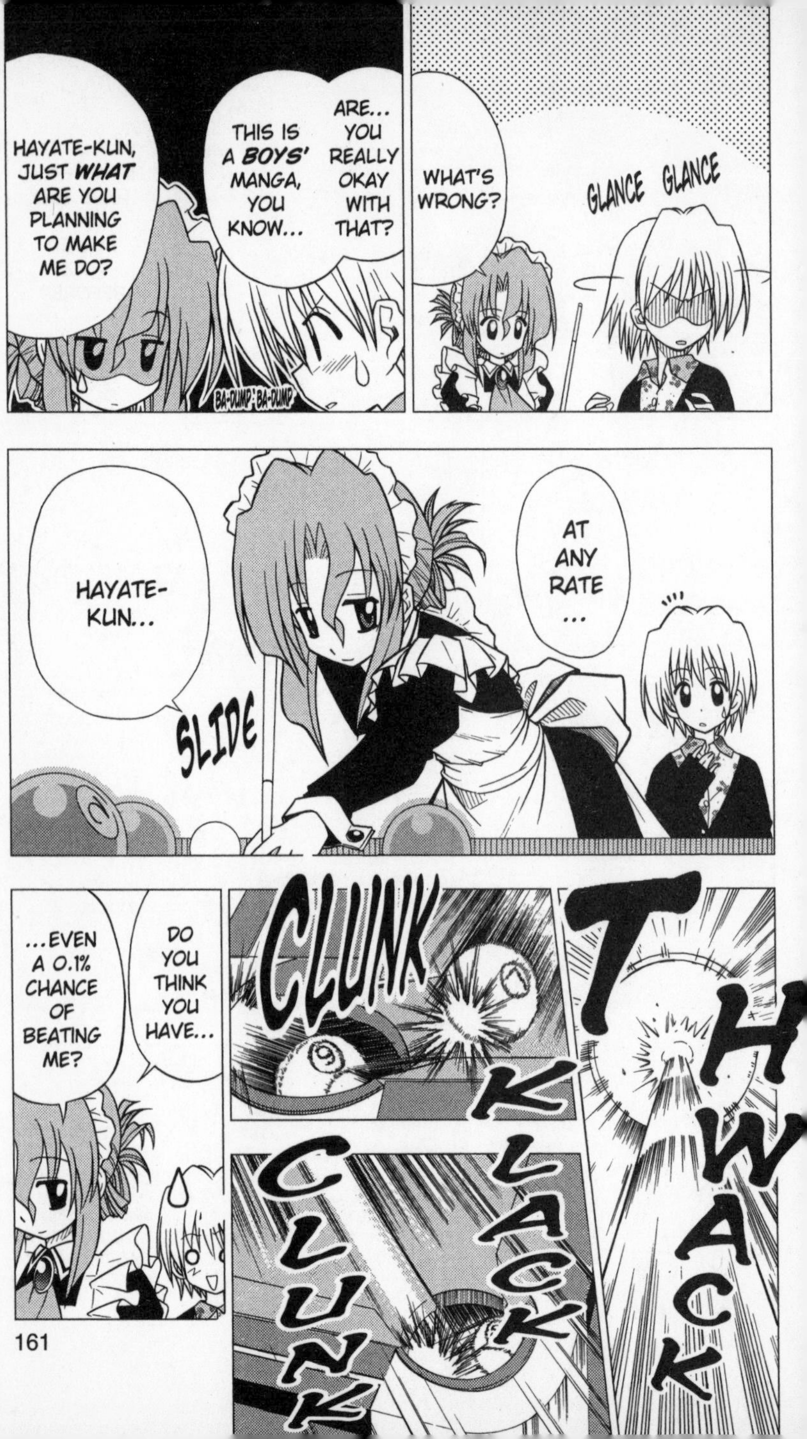
GLANCE GLANCE
WHAT'S WRONG?
ARE... YOU REALLY OKAY WITH THAT?
THIS IS A **BOYS'** MANGA, YOU KNOW...
BA-DUMP BA-DUMP
HAYATE-KUN, JUST **WHAT** ARE YOU PLANNING TO MAKE ME DO?
AT ANY RATE...
HAYATE-KUN...
SLIDE
THWACK
CLUNK
KLACK
CLUNK
DO YOU THINK YOU HAVE...
...EVEN A 0.1% CHANCE OF BEATING ME?

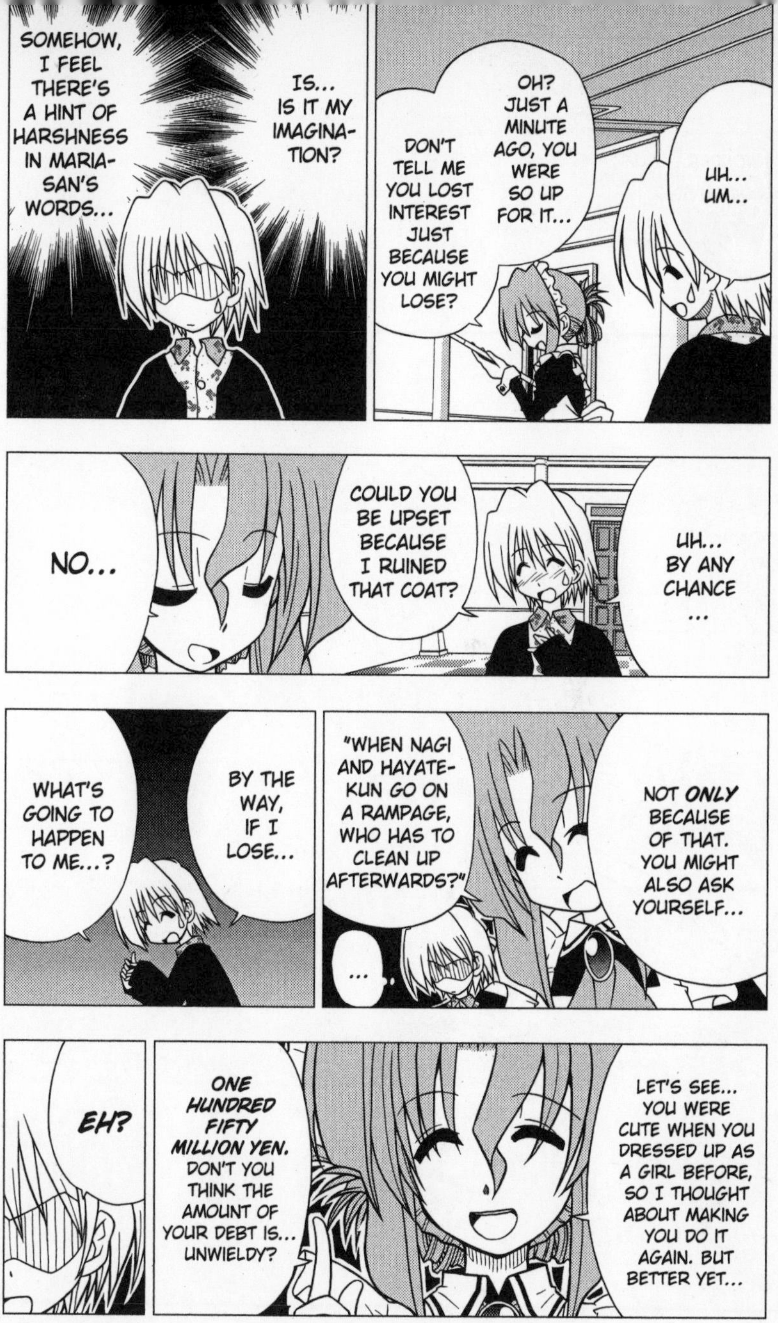
UH... UM...
OH? JUST A MINUTE AGO, YOU WERE SO UP FOR IT...
DON'T TELL ME YOU LOST INTEREST JUST BECAUSE YOU MIGHT LOSE?
IS... IS IT MY IMAGINA-TION?
SOMEHOW, I FEEL THERE'S A HINT OF HARSHNESS IN MARIA-SAN'S WORDS...
UH... BY ANY CHANCE...
COULD YOU BE UPSET BECAUSE I RUINED THAT COAT?
NO...
NOT *ONLY* BECAUSE OF THAT. YOU MIGHT ALSO ASK YOURSELF...
"WHEN NAGI AND HAYATE-KUN GO ON A RAMPAGE, WHO HAS TO CLEAN UP AFTERWARDS?"
...
BY THE WAY, IF I LOSE...
WHAT'S GOING TO HAPPEN TO ME...?
LET'S SEE... YOU WERE CUTE WHEN YOU DRESSED UP AS A GIRL BEFORE, SO I THOUGHT ABOUT MAKING YOU DO IT AGAIN. BUT BETTER YET...
ONE HUNDRED FIFTY MILLION YEN. DON'T YOU THINK THE AMOUNT OF YOUR DEBT IS... UNWIELDY?
EH?

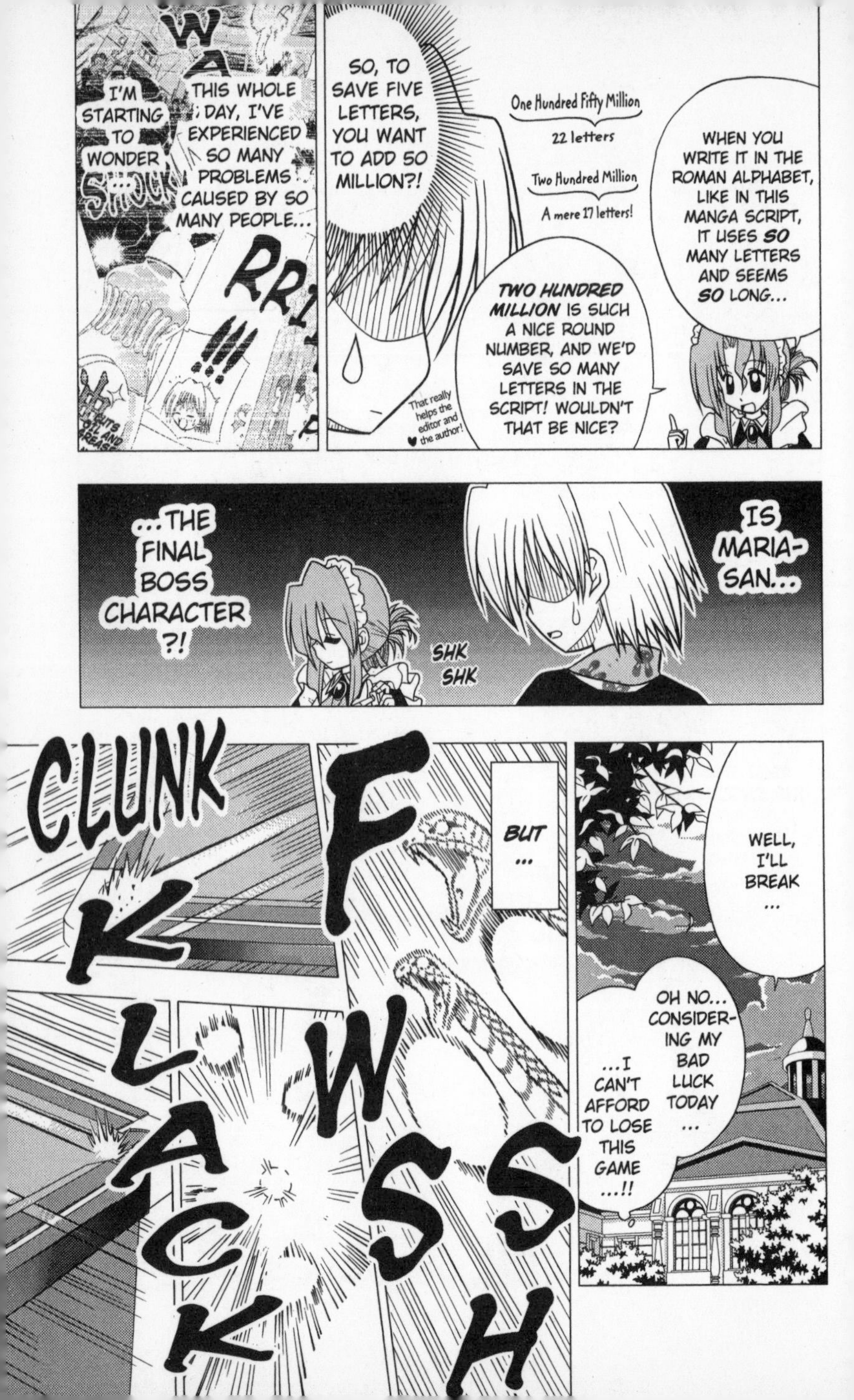
WHEN YOU WRITE IT IN THE ROMAN ALPHABET, LIKE IN THIS MANGA SCRIPT, IT USES **SO** MANY LETTERS AND SEEMS **SO** LONG...
TWO HUNDRED MILLION IS SUCH A NICE ROUND NUMBER, AND WE'D SAVE SO MANY LETTERS IN THE SCRIPT! WOULDN'T THAT BE NICE?
One Hundred Fifty Million
22 letters
Two Hundred Million
A mere 17 letters!
SO, TO SAVE FIVE LETTERS, YOU WANT TO ADD 50 MILLION?!
That really helps the editor and the author!
WA
THIS WHOLE DAY, I'VE EXPERIENCED SO MANY PROBLEMS CAUSED BY SO MANY PEOPLE...
I'M STARTING TO WONDER...
SHOCK
RRI
!!!
IS MARIA-SAN...
...THE FINAL BOSS CHARACTER?!
SHK SHK
WELL, I'LL BREAK...
OH NO... CONSIDERING MY BAD LUCK TODAY...
...I CAN'T AFFORD TO LOSE THIS GAME...!!
BUT...
FWSSH
CLUNK
KLACK

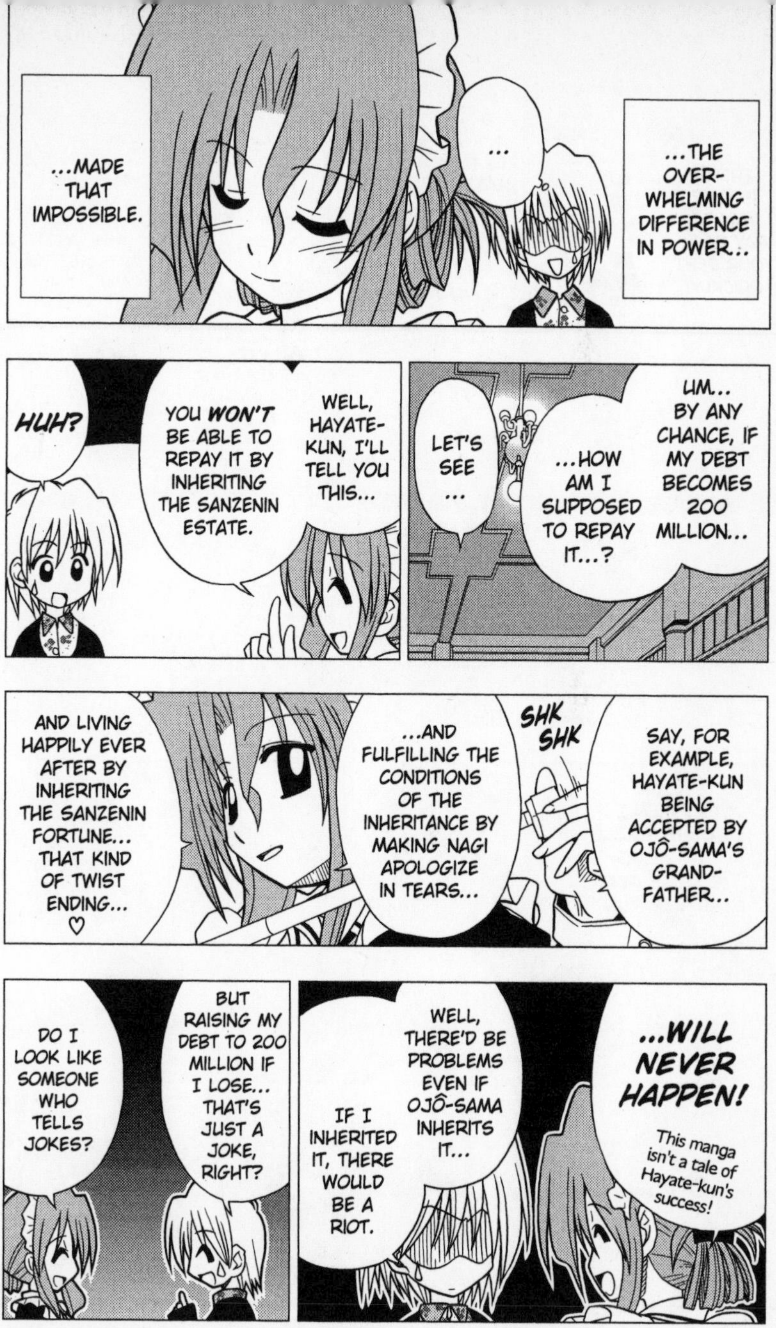
...THE OVERWHELMING DIFFERENCE IN POWER...
...
...MADE THAT IMPOSSIBLE.
UM... BY ANY CHANCE, IF MY DEBT BECOMES 200 MILLION...
...HOW AM I SUPPOSED TO REPAY IT...?
LET'S SEE ...
WELL, HAYATE-KUN, I'LL TELL YOU THIS...
YOU **WON'T** BE ABLE TO REPAY IT BY INHERITING THE SANZENIN ESTATE.
HUH?
SAY, FOR EXAMPLE, HAYATE-KUN BEING ACCEPTED BY OJÔ-SAMA'S GRANDFATHER...
SHK SHK
...AND FULFILLING THE CONDITIONS OF THE INHERITANCE BY MAKING NAGI APOLOGIZE IN TEARS...
AND LIVING HAPPILY EVER AFTER BY INHERITING THE SANZENIN FORTUNE... THAT KIND OF TWIST ENDING... ♡
...WILL NEVER HAPPEN!
This manga isn't a tale of Hayate-kun's success!
WELL, THERE'D BE PROBLEMS EVEN IF OJÔ-SAMA INHERITS IT...
IF I INHERITED IT, THERE WOULD BE A RIOT.
BUT RAISING MY DEBT TO 200 MILLION IF I LOSE... THAT'S JUST A JOKE, RIGHT?
DO I LOOK LIKE SOMEONE WHO TELLS JOKES?

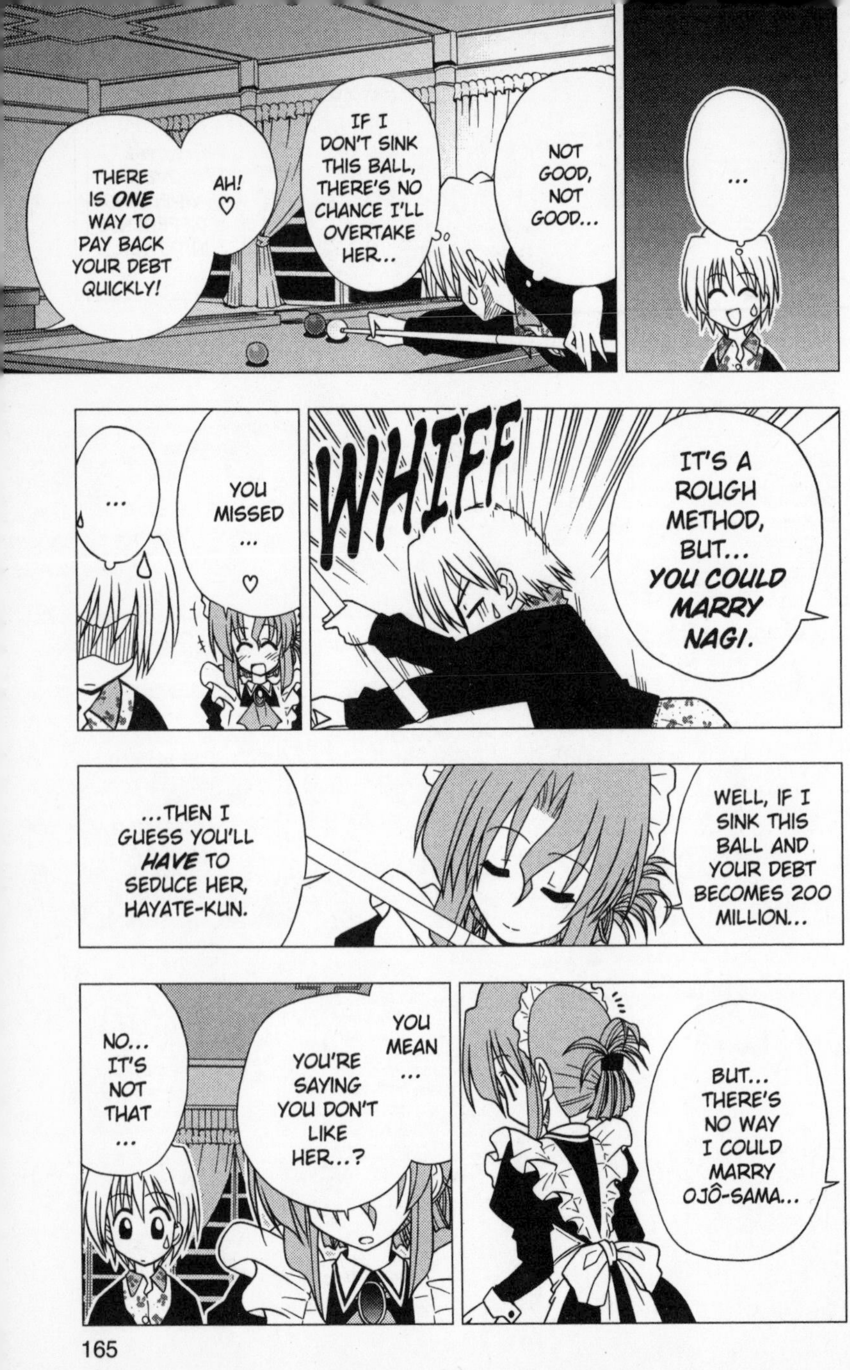
...
NOT GOOD, NOT GOOD...
IF I DON'T SINK THIS BALL, THERE'S NO CHANCE I'LL OVERTAKE HER...
AH! ♡
THERE IS ONE WAY TO PAY BACK YOUR DEBT QUICKLY!
IT'S A ROUGH METHOD, BUT... YOU COULD MARRY NAGI.
WHIFF
YOU MISSED ... ♡
...
WELL, IF I SINK THIS BALL AND YOUR DEBT BECOMES 200 MILLION...
...THEN I GUESS YOU'LL HAVE TO SEDUCE HER, HAYATE-KUN.
BUT... THERE'S NO WAY I COULD MARRY OJÔ-SAMA...
YOU MEAN ...
YOU'RE SAYING YOU DON'T LIKE HER...?
NO... IT'S NOT THAT ...

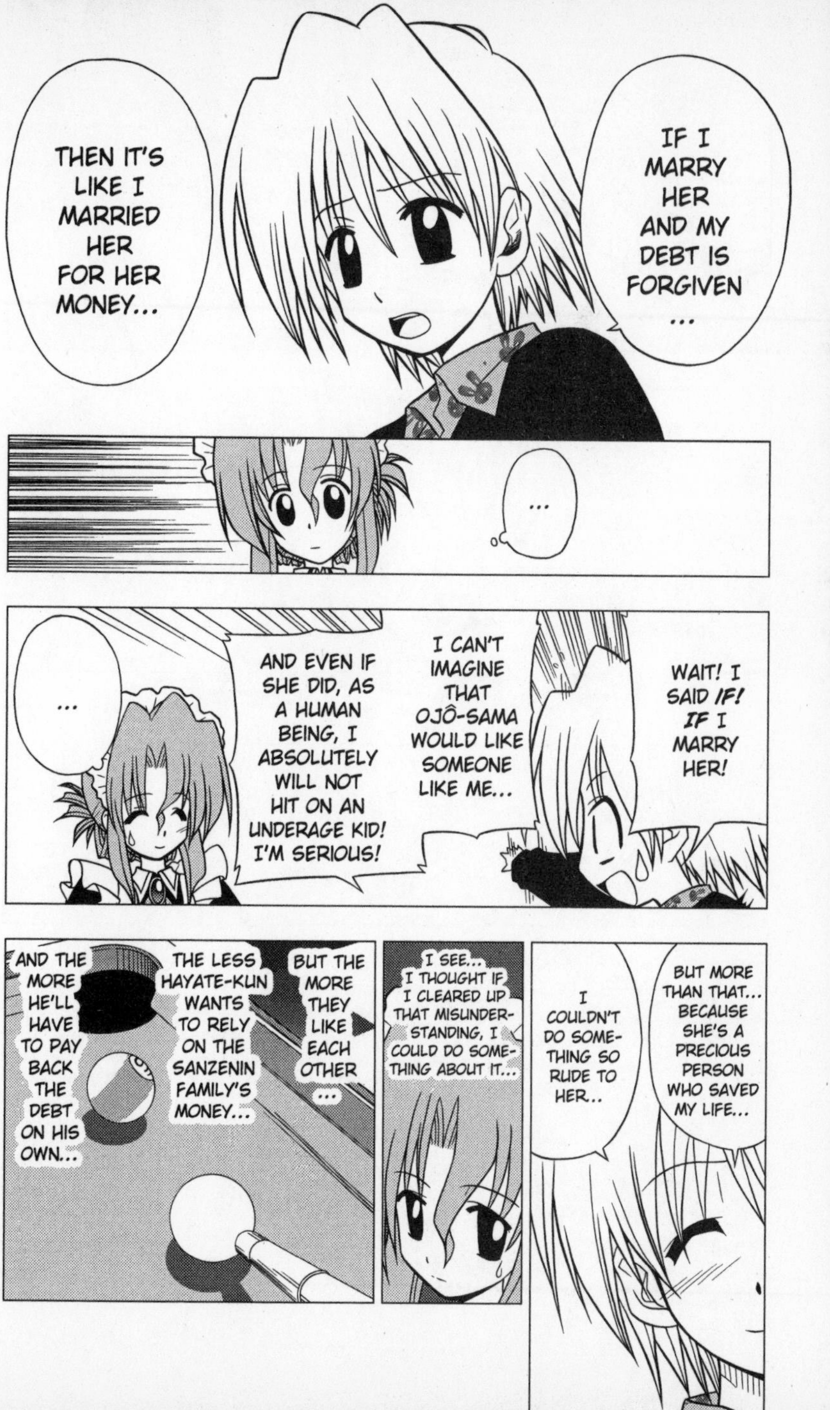
IF I MARRY HER AND MY DEBT IS FORGIVEN...
THEN IT'S LIKE I MARRIED HER FOR HER MONEY...
...
WAIT! I SAID *IF!* *IF* I MARRY HER!
I CAN'T IMAGINE THAT OJÔ-SAMA WOULD LIKE SOMEONE LIKE ME...
AND EVEN IF SHE DID, AS A HUMAN BEING, I ABSOLUTELY WILL NOT HIT ON AN UNDERAGE KID! I'M SERIOUS!
...
BUT MORE THAN THAT... BECAUSE SHE'S A PRECIOUS PERSON WHO SAVED MY LIFE...
I COULDN'T DO SOMETHING SO RUDE TO HER...
I SEE... I THOUGHT IF I CLEARED UP THAT MISUNDERSTANDING, I COULD DO SOMETHING ABOUT IT...
BUT THE MORE THEY LIKE EACH OTHER...
THE LESS HAYATE-KUN WANTS TO RELY ON THE SANZENIN FAMILY'S MONEY...
AND THE MORE HE'LL HAVE TO PAY BACK THE DEBT ON HIS OWN...

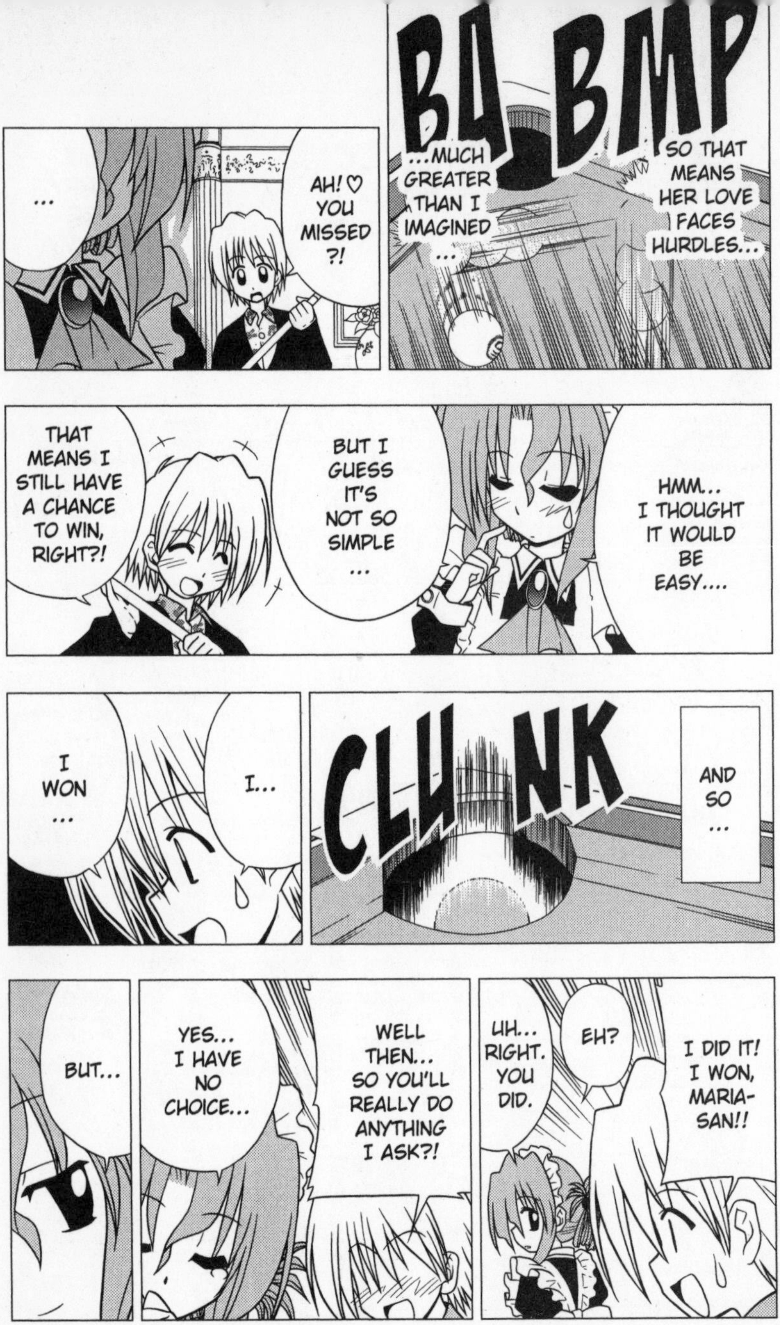
BA-BMP
SO THAT MEANS HER LOVE FACES HURDLES...
...MUCH GREATER THAN I IMAGINED ...
AH! ♡ YOU MISSED ?!
...
HMM... I THOUGHT IT WOULD BE EASY....
BUT I GUESS IT'S NOT SO SIMPLE ...
THAT MEANS I STILL HAVE A CHANCE TO WIN, RIGHT?!
AND SO ...
CLUNK
I...
I WON ...
I DID IT! I WON, MARIA-SAN!!
EH?
UH... RIGHT. YOU DID.
WELL THEN... SO YOU'LL REALLY DO ANYTHING I ASK?!
YES... I HAVE NO CHOICE...
BUT...

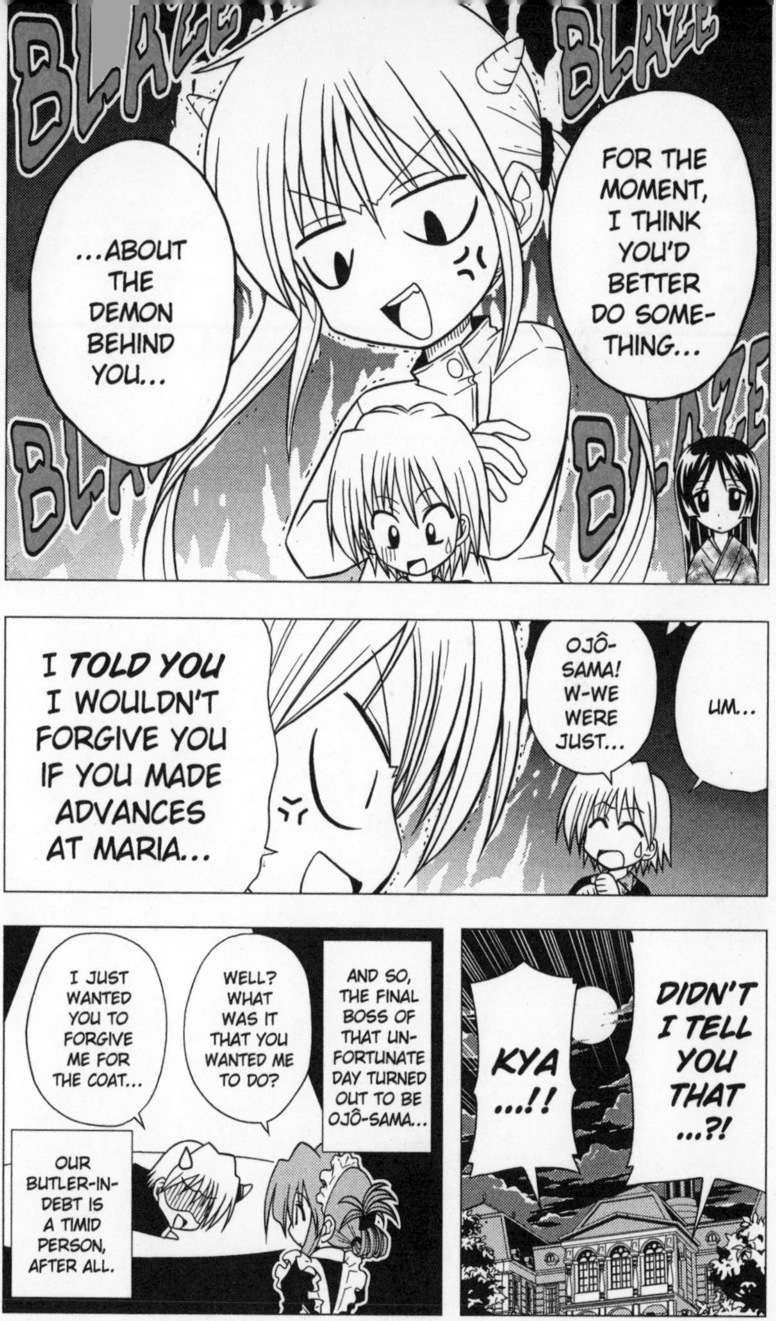
BLAZE
BLAZE
FOR THE MOMENT, I THINK YOU'D BETTER DO SOME-THING...
...ABOUT THE DEMON BEHIND YOU...
UM...
OJÔ-SAMA! W-WE WERE JUST...
I TOLD YOU I WOULDN'T FORGIVE YOU IF YOU MADE ADVANCES AT MARIA...
DIDN'T I TELL YOU THAT...?!
KYA...!!
AND SO, THE FINAL BOSS OF THAT UN-FORTUNATE DAY TURNED OUT TO BE OJÔ-SAMA...
WELL? WHAT WAS IT THAT YOU WANTED ME TO DO?
I JUST WANTED YOU TO FORGIVE ME FOR THE COAT...
OUR BUTLER-IN-DEBT IS A TIMID PERSON, AFTER ALL.

Episode 11: "When I Turned, I Remembered That Was the Beginning of Unhappiness"

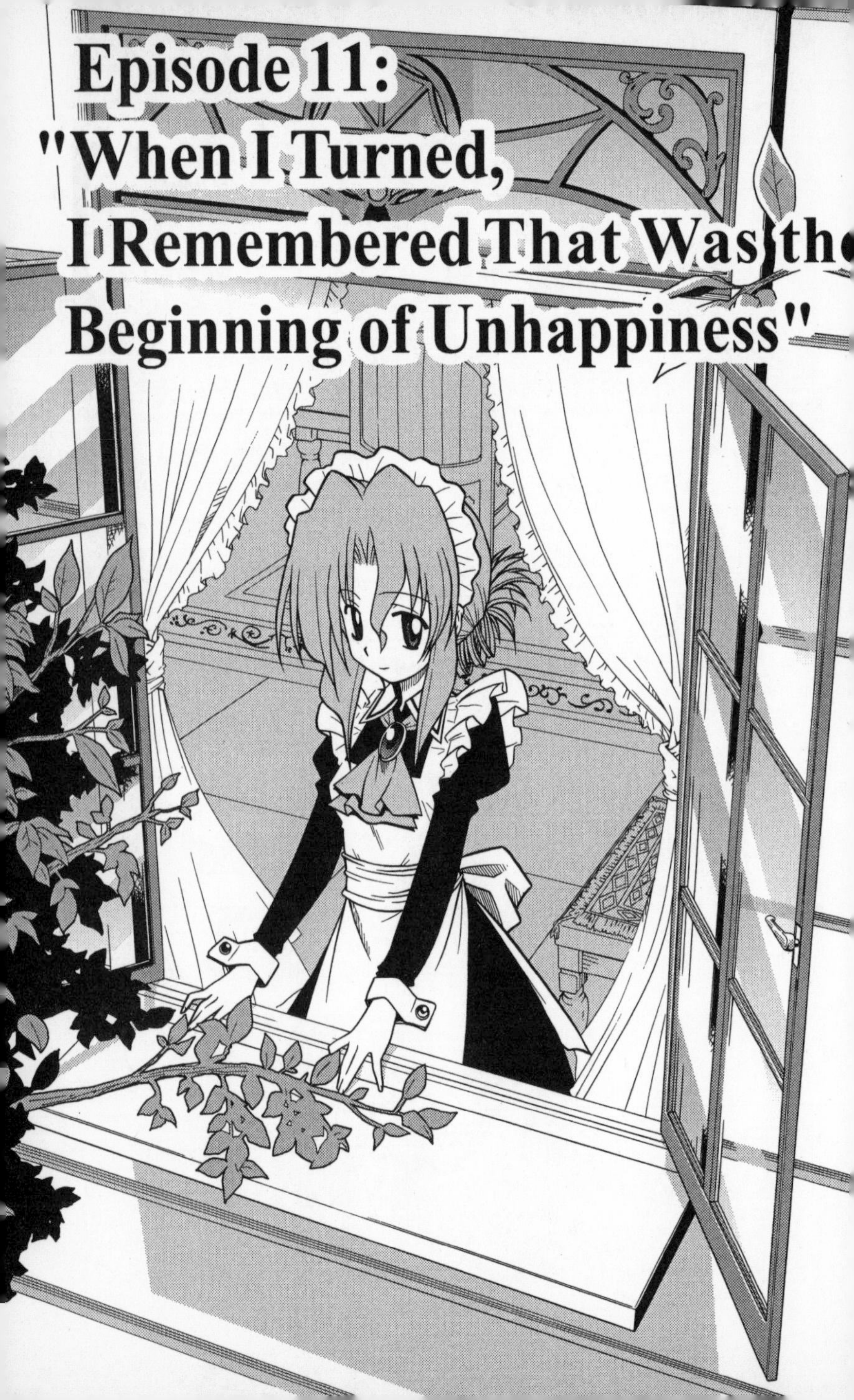

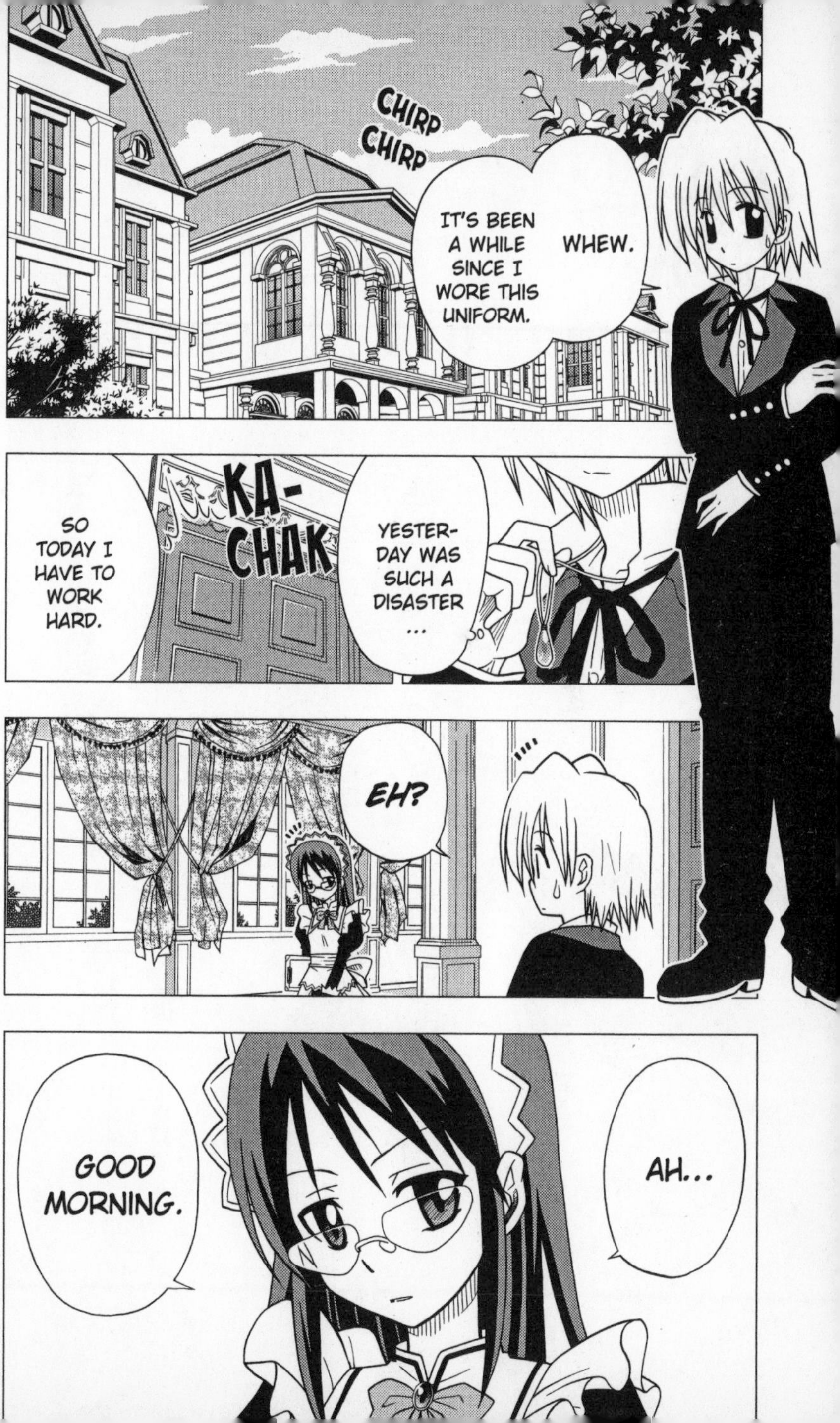
WHEW.
IT'S BEEN A WHILE SINCE I WORE THIS UNIFORM.
CHIRP CHIRP
YESTER-DAY WAS SUCH A DISASTER ...
KA-CHAK
SO TODAY I HAVE TO WORK HARD.
EH?
AH...
GOOD MORNING.

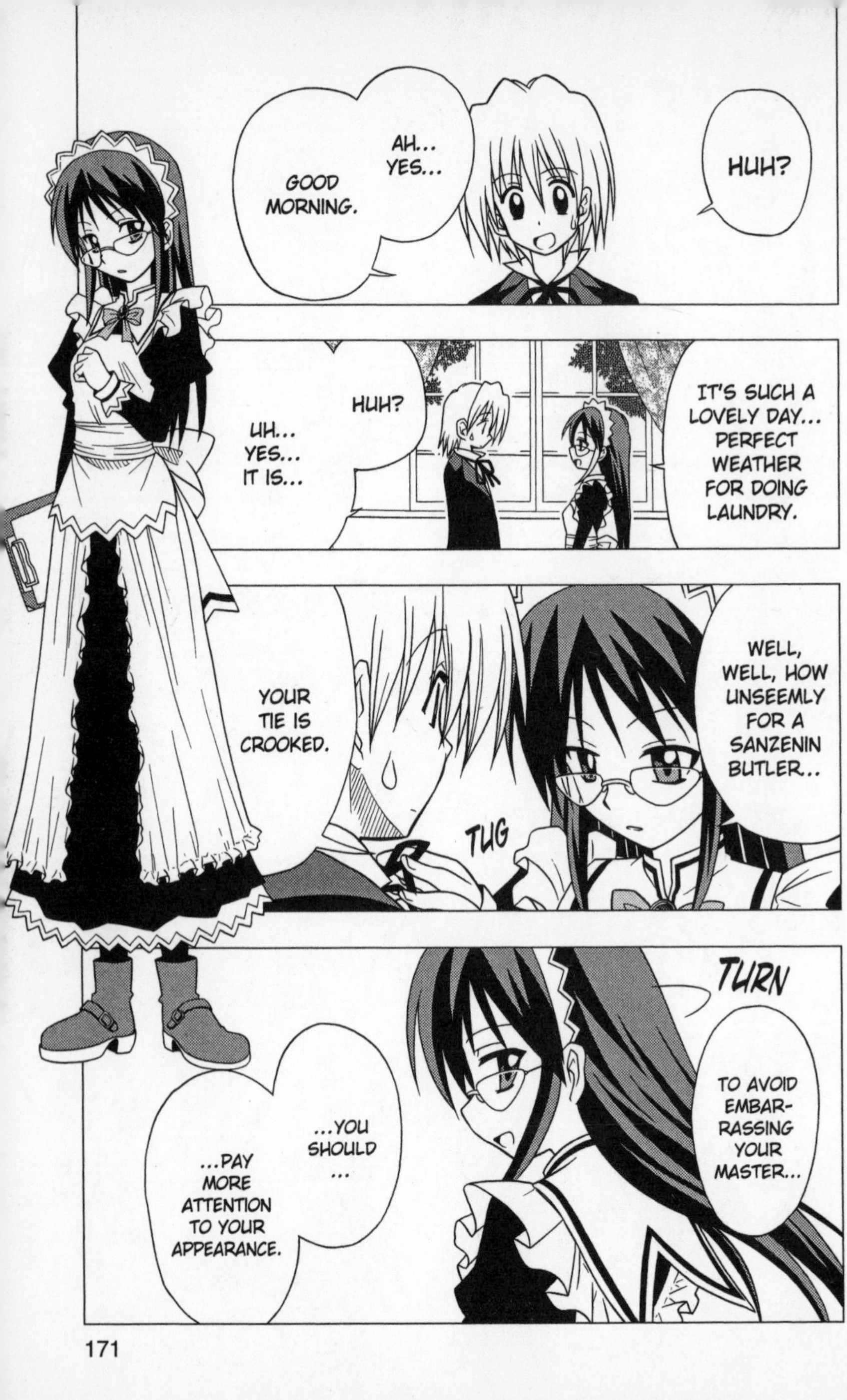
HUH?
AH... YES...
GOOD MORNING.
IT'S SUCH A LOVELY DAY... PERFECT WEATHER FOR DOING LAUNDRY.
HUH?
UH... YES... IT IS...
WELL, WELL, HOW UNSEEMLY FOR A SANZENIN BUTLER...
TUG
YOUR TIE IS CROOKED.
TURN
TO AVOID EMBAR-RASSING YOUR MASTER...
...YOU SHOULD ...
...PAY MORE ATTENTION TO YOUR APPEARANCE.

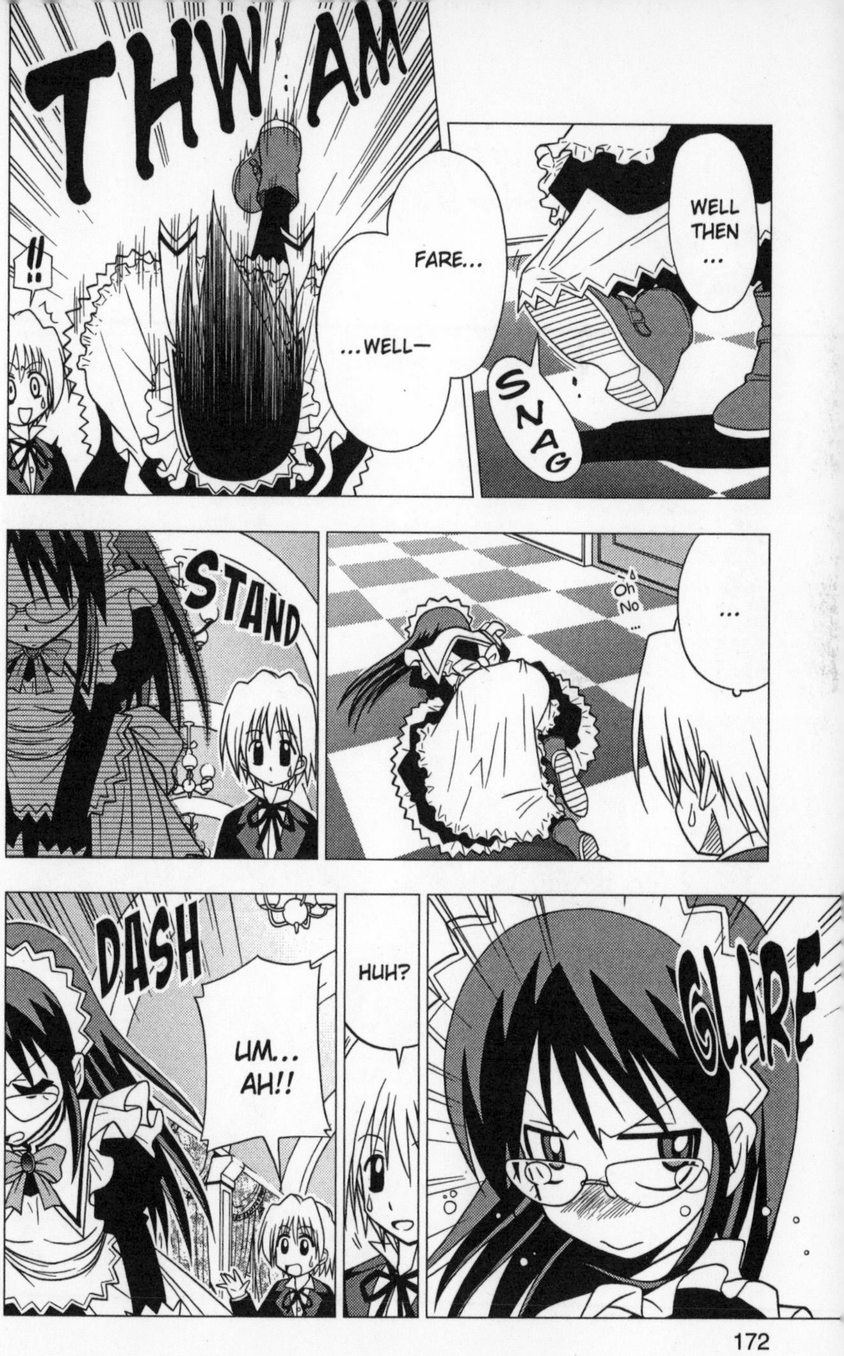
WELL THEN ...
SNAG
FARE...
...WELL—
THW AM
!!
...
Oh No ...
STAND
GLARE
HUH?
DASH
UM... AH!!

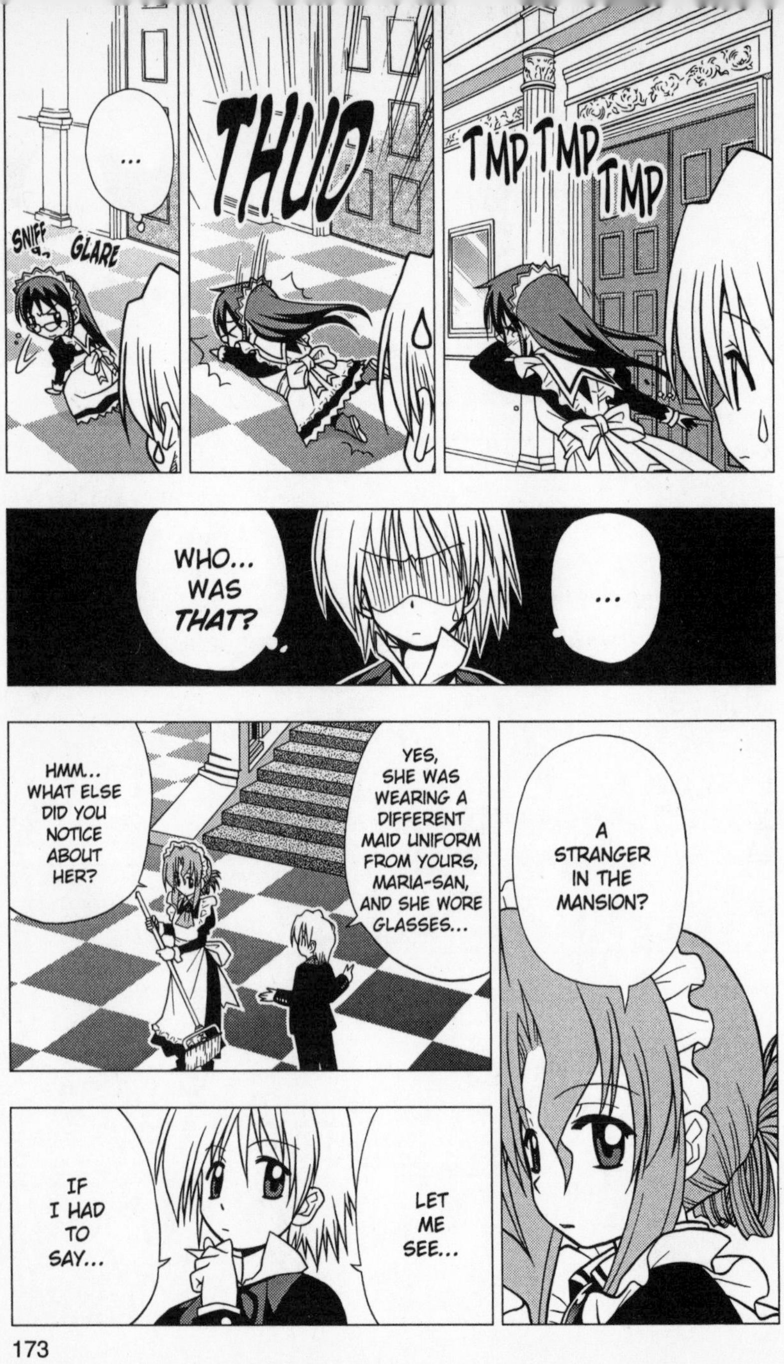
TMP TMP TMP
THUD
...
SNIFF
GLARE
...
WHO... WAS THAT?
A STRANGER IN THE MANSION?
YES, SHE WAS WEARING A DIFFERENT MAID UNIFORM FROM YOURS, MARIA-SAN, AND SHE WORE GLASSES...
HMM.. WHAT ELSE DID YOU NOTICE ABOUT HER?
LET ME SEE...
IF I HAD TO SAY...

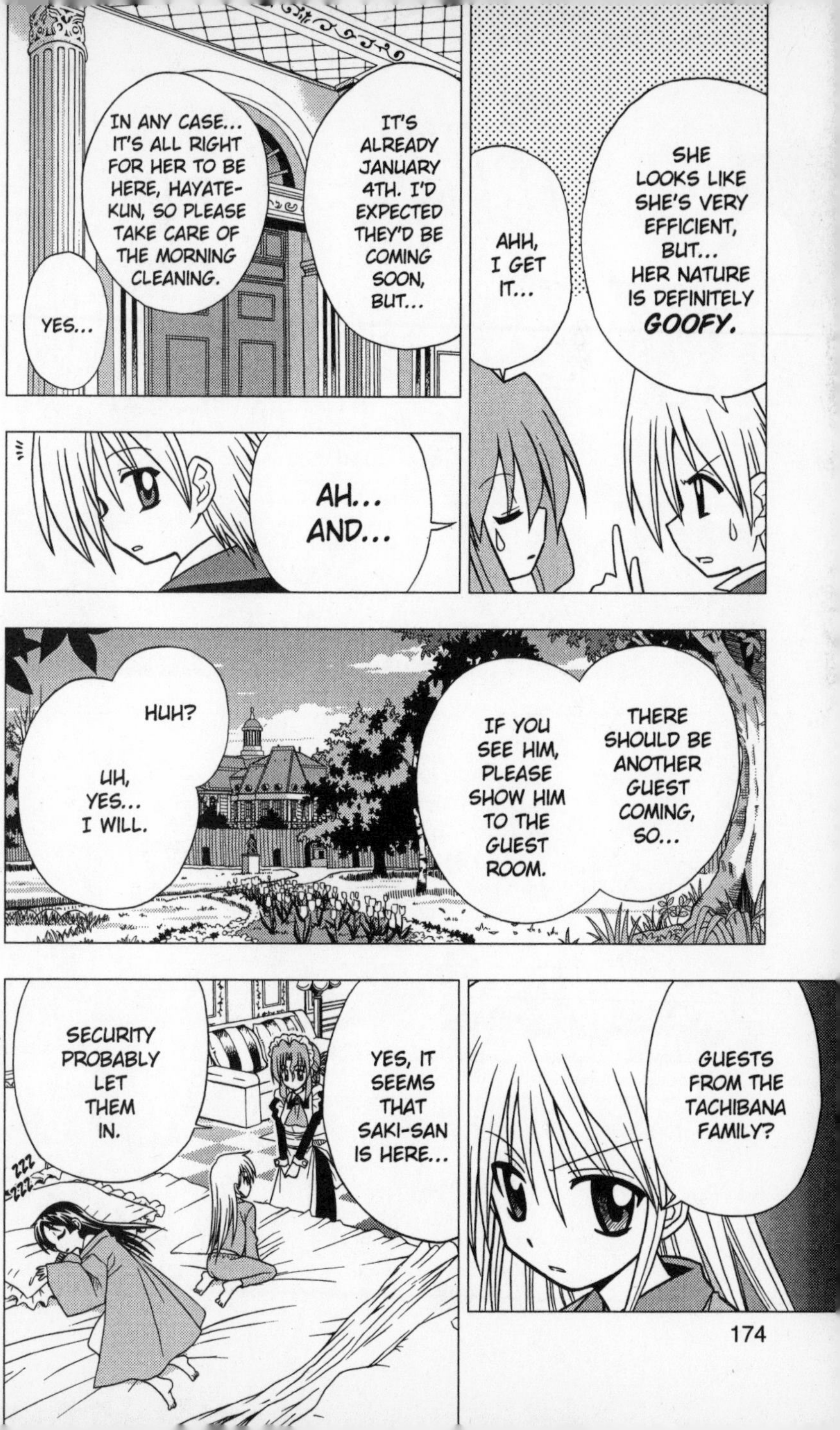
SHE LOOKS LIKE SHE'S VERY EFFICIENT, BUT... HER NATURE IS DEFINITELY **GOOFY.**
AHH, I GET IT...
IT'S ALREADY JANUARY 4TH. I'D EXPECTED THEY'D BE COMING SOON, BUT...
IN ANY CASE... IT'S ALL RIGHT FOR HER TO BE HERE, HAYATE-KUN, SO PLEASE TAKE CARE OF THE MORNING CLEANING.
YES...
AH... AND...
THERE SHOULD BE ANOTHER GUEST COMING, SO...
IF YOU SEE HIM, PLEASE SHOW HIM TO THE GUEST ROOM.
HUH?
UH, YES... I WILL.
GUESTS FROM THE TACHIBANA FAMILY?
YES, IT SEEMS THAT SAKI-SAN IS HERE...
SECURITY PROBABLY LET THEM IN.
ZZZ
ZZZ

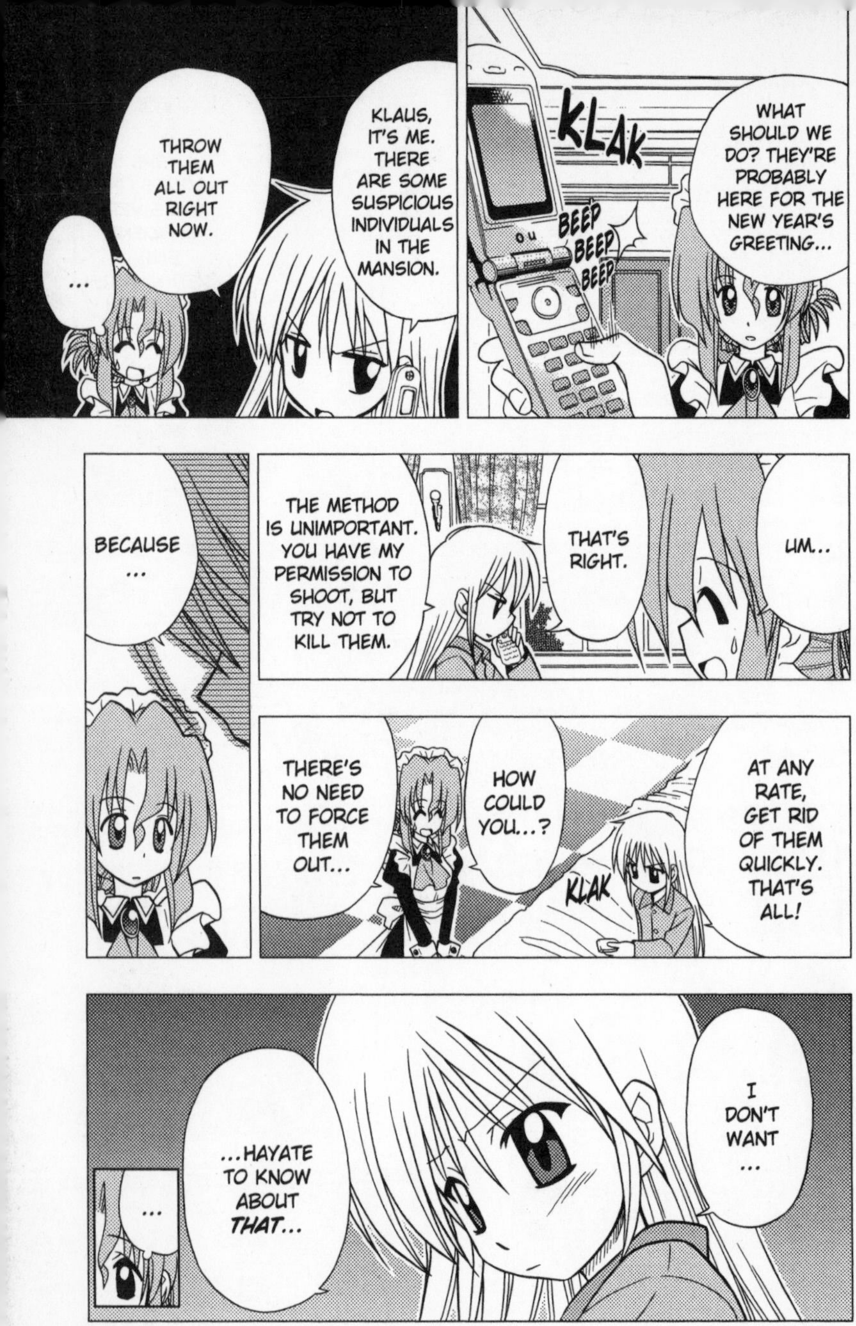
WHAT SHOULD WE DO? THEY'RE PROBABLY HERE FOR THE NEW YEAR'S GREETING...
KLAK
BEEP BEEP BEEP
KLAUS, IT'S ME. THERE ARE SOME SUSPICIOUS INDIVIDUALS IN THE MANSION.
THROW THEM ALL OUT RIGHT NOW.
...
UM...
THAT'S RIGHT.
THE METHOD IS UNIMPORTANT. YOU HAVE MY PERMISSION TO SHOOT, BUT TRY NOT TO KILL THEM.
AT ANY RATE, GET RID OF THEM QUICKLY. THAT'S ALL!
KLAK
HOW COULD YOU...?
THERE'S NO NEED TO FORCE THEM OUT...
BECAUSE...
I DON'T WANT...
...HAYATE TO KNOW ABOUT *THAT*...
...

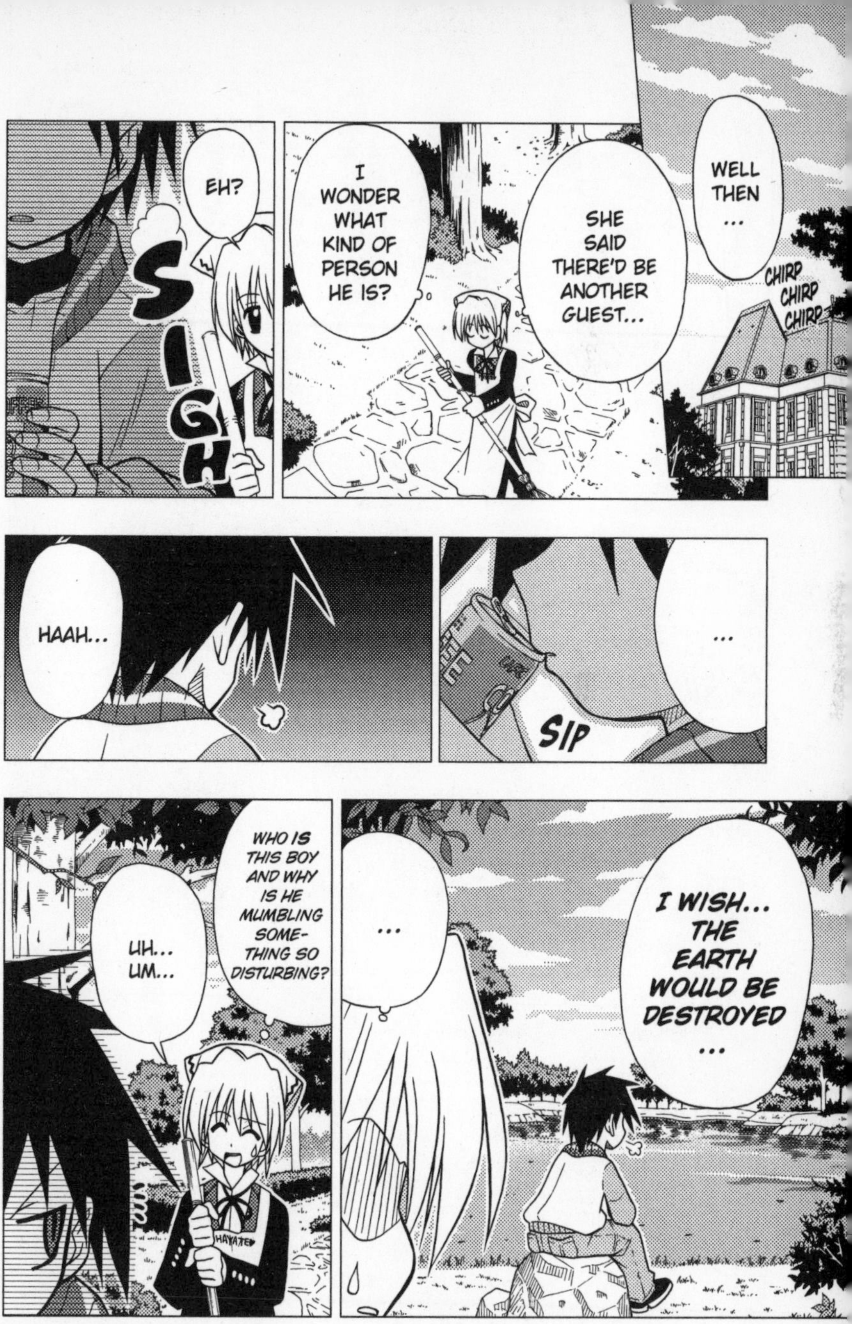
WELL THEN ...
CHIRP CHIRP CHIRP
SHE SAID THERE'D BE ANOTHER GUEST...
I WONDER WHAT KIND OF PERSON HE IS?
EH?
SIGH
...
SIP
HAAH...
I WISH... THE EARTH WOULD BE DESTROYED ...
...
WHO IS THIS BOY AND WHY IS HE MUMBLING SOME-THING SO DISTURBING?
UH... UM...

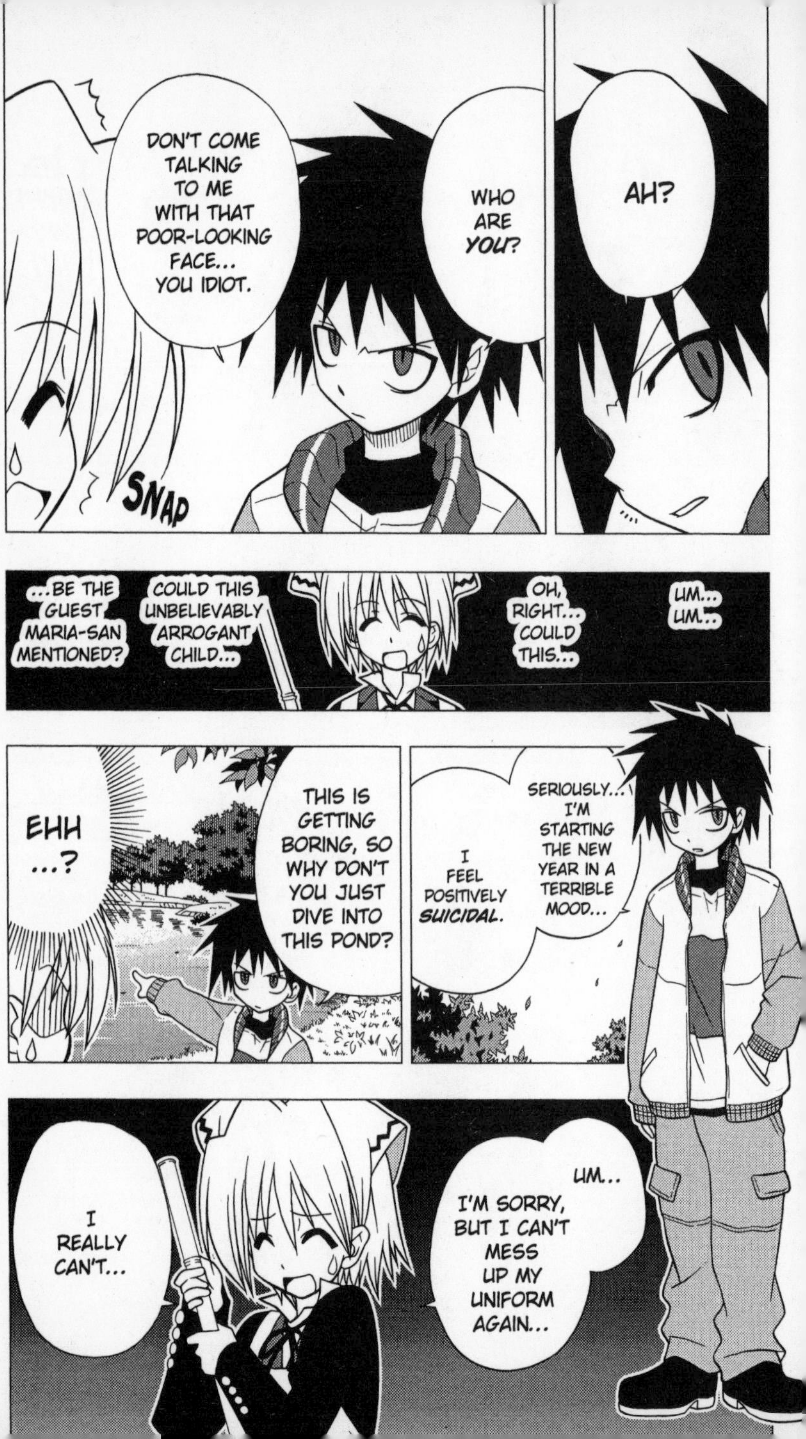
AH?
WHO ARE YOU?
DON'T COME TALKING TO ME WITH THAT POOR-LOOKING FACE... YOU IDIOT.
SNAP
UM... UM...
OH, RIGHT... COULD THIS...
COULD THIS UNBELIEVABLY ARROGANT CHILD...
...BE THE GUEST MARIA-SAN MENTIONED?
SERIOUSLY... I'M STARTING THE NEW YEAR IN A TERRIBLE MOOD...
I FEEL POSITIVELY SUICIDAL.
THIS IS GETTING BORING, SO WHY DON'T YOU JUST DIVE INTO THIS POND?
EHH ...?
UM...
I'M SORRY, BUT I CAN'T MESS UP MY UNIFORM AGAIN...
I REALLY CAN'T...

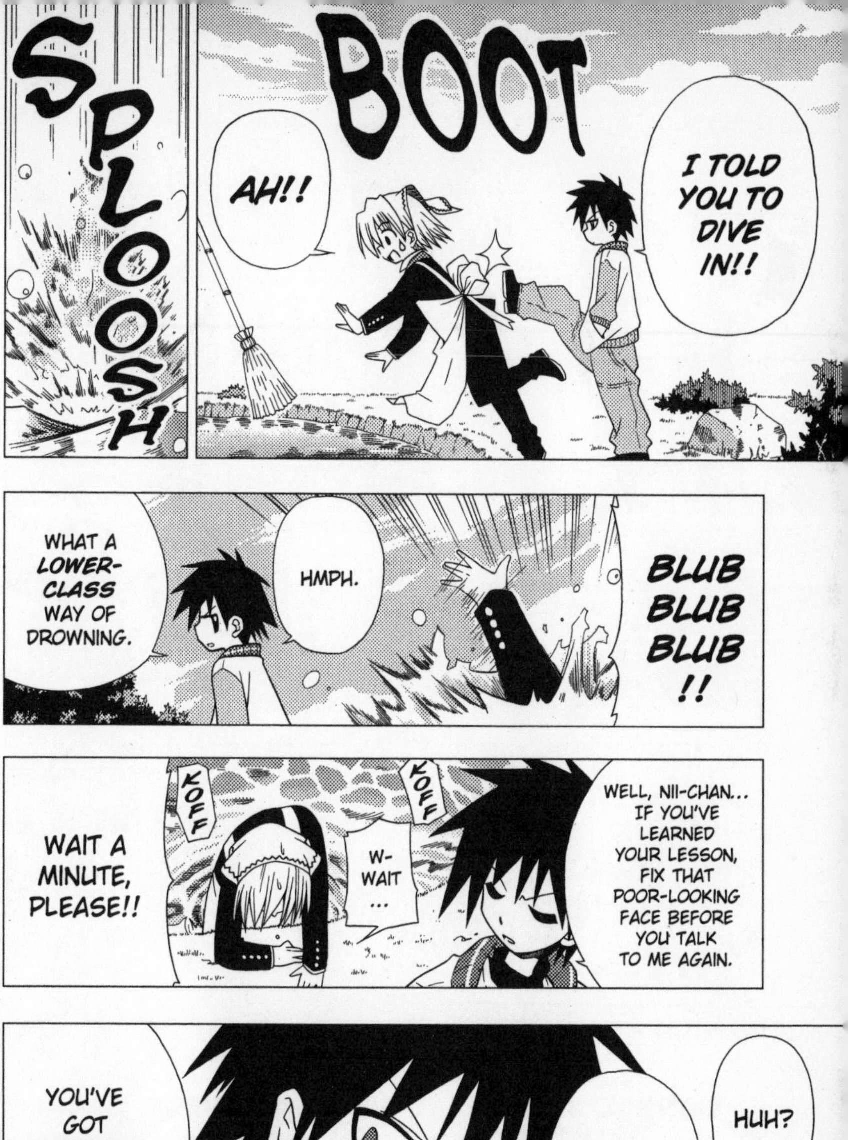
I TOLD YOU TO DIVE IN!!
BOOT
AH!!
SPLOOSH
BLUB BLUB BLUB!!
HMPH.
WHAT A LOWER-CLASS WAY OF DROWNING.
WELL, NII-CHAN... IF YOU'VE LEARNED YOUR LESSON, FIX THAT POOR-LOOKING FACE BEFORE YOU TALK TO ME AGAIN.
KOFF
W-WAIT...
KOFF
WAIT A MINUTE, PLEASE!!
HUH?
WHAT IS IT?
YOU'VE GOT SOMETHING TO SAY TO ME?

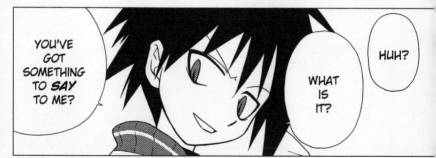

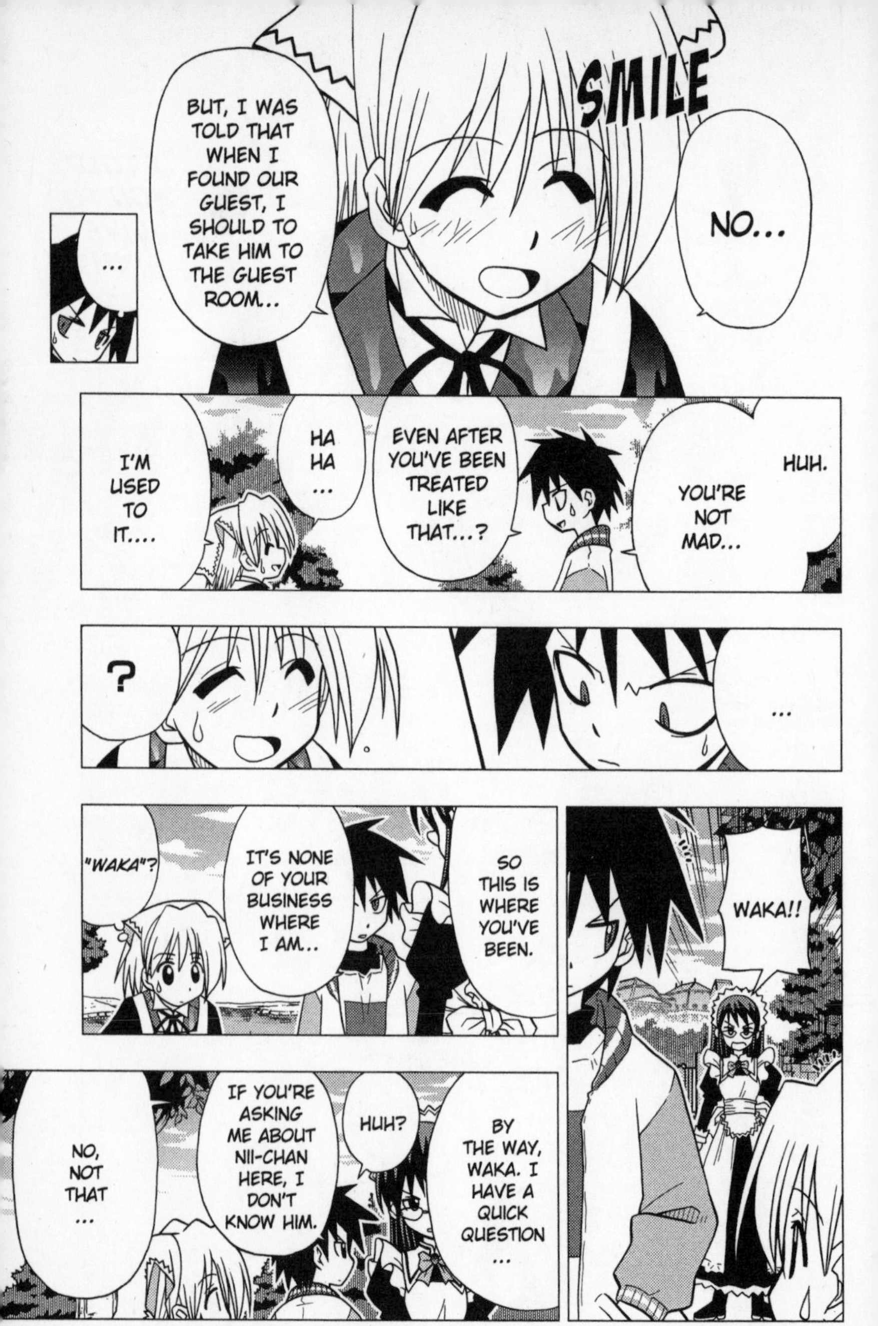
SMILE
NO...
BUT, I WAS TOLD THAT WHEN I FOUND OUR GUEST, I SHOULD TO TAKE HIM TO THE GUEST ROOM...
...
HUH. YOU'RE NOT MAD...
EVEN AFTER YOU'VE BEEN TREATED LIKE THAT...?
HA HA ...
I'M USED TO IT....
...
?
WAKA!!
SO THIS IS WHERE YOU'VE BEEN.
IT'S NONE OF YOUR BUSINESS WHERE I AM...
"WAKA"?
BY THE WAY, WAKA. I HAVE A QUICK QUESTION ...
HUH?
IF YOU'RE ASKING ME ABOUT NII-CHAN HERE, I DON'T KNOW HIM.
NO, NOT THAT ...

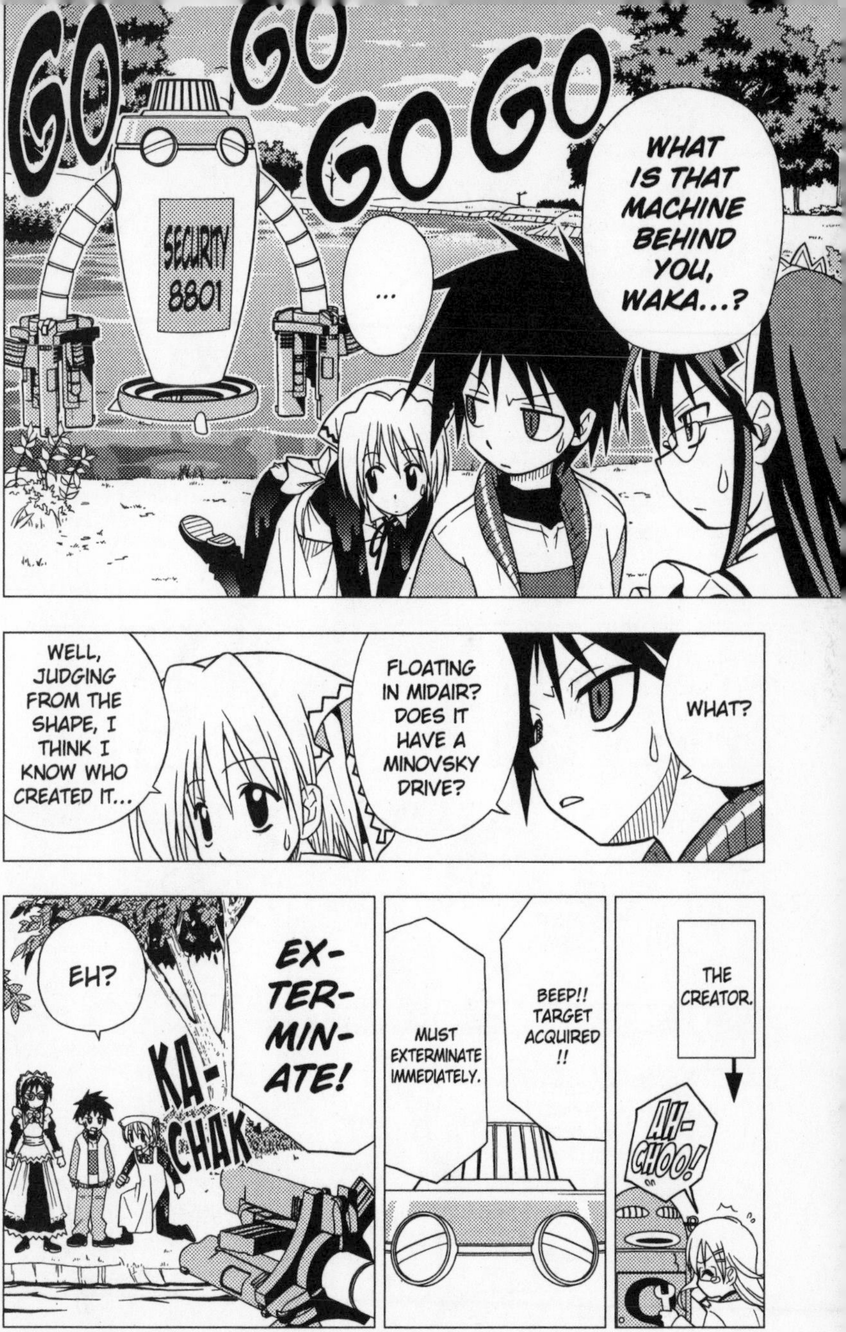
GO GO GO GO
SECURITY 8801
WHAT IS THAT MACHINE BEHIND YOU, WAKA...?
...
WHAT?
FLOATING IN MIDAIR? DOES IT HAVE A MINOVSKY DRIVE?
WELL, JUDGING FROM THE SHAPE, I THINK I KNOW WHO CREATED IT...
THE CREATOR.
AH-CHOO!
BEEP!! TARGET ACQUIRED !!
MUST EXTERMINATE IMMEDIATELY.
EX-TER-MIN-ATE!
KA-CHAK
EH?

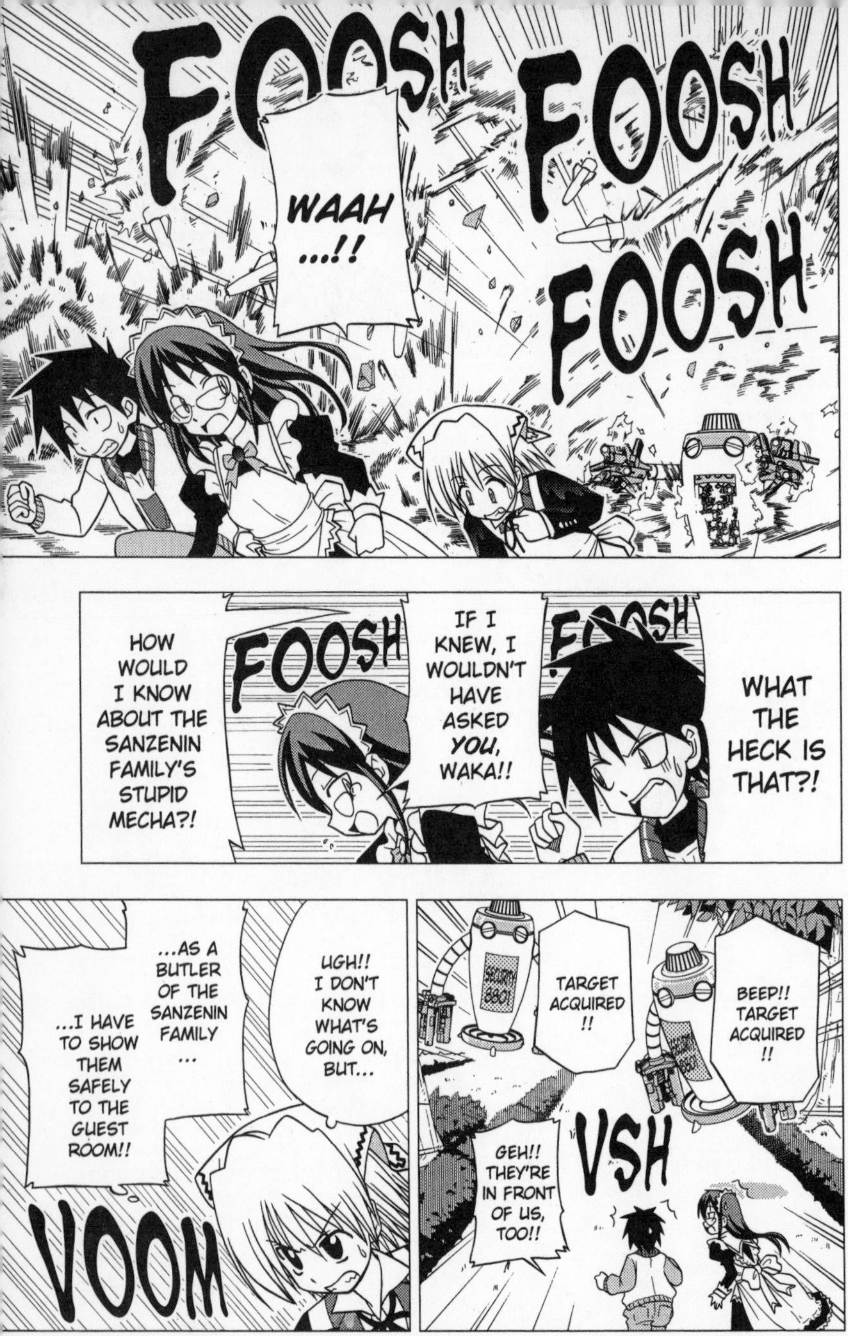
FOOSH
FOOSH
FOOSH
WAAH ...!!
FOOSH
WHAT THE HECK IS THAT?!
FOOSH
IF I KNEW, I WOULDN'T HAVE ASKED *YOU*, WAKA!!
FOOSH
HOW WOULD I KNOW ABOUT THE SANZENIN FAMILY'S STUPID MECHA?!
BEEP!! TARGET ACQUIRED !!
TARGET ACQUIRED !!
VSH
GEH!! THEY'RE IN FRONT OF US, TOO!!
UGH!! I DON'T KNOW WHAT'S GOING ON, BUT...
...AS A BUTLER OF THE SANZENIN FAMILY ...
...I HAVE TO SHOW THEM SAFELY TO THE GUEST ROOM!!
VOOM

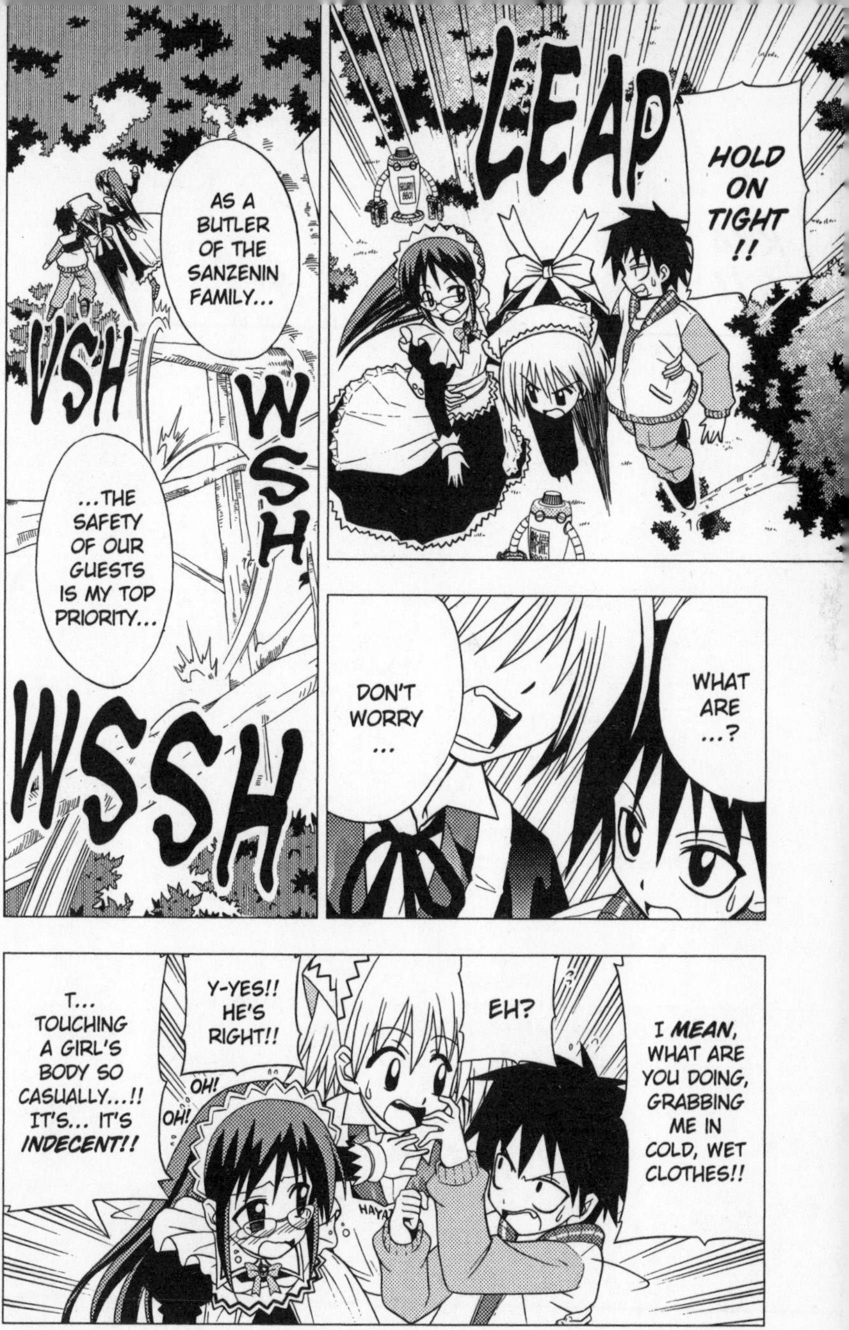
HOLD ON TIGHT!!
LEAP
WHAT ARE ...?
DON'T WORRY ...
AS A BUTLER OF THE SANZENIN FAMILY...
VSH
WSH
...THE SAFETY OF OUR GUESTS IS MY TOP PRIORITY...
WSSH
I *MEAN*, WHAT ARE YOU DOING, GRABBING ME IN COLD, WET CLOTHES!!
EH?
Y-YES!! HE'S RIGHT!!
OH!
OH!
T... TOUCHING A GIRL'S BODY SO CASUALLY...!! IT'S... IT'S *INDECENT*!!

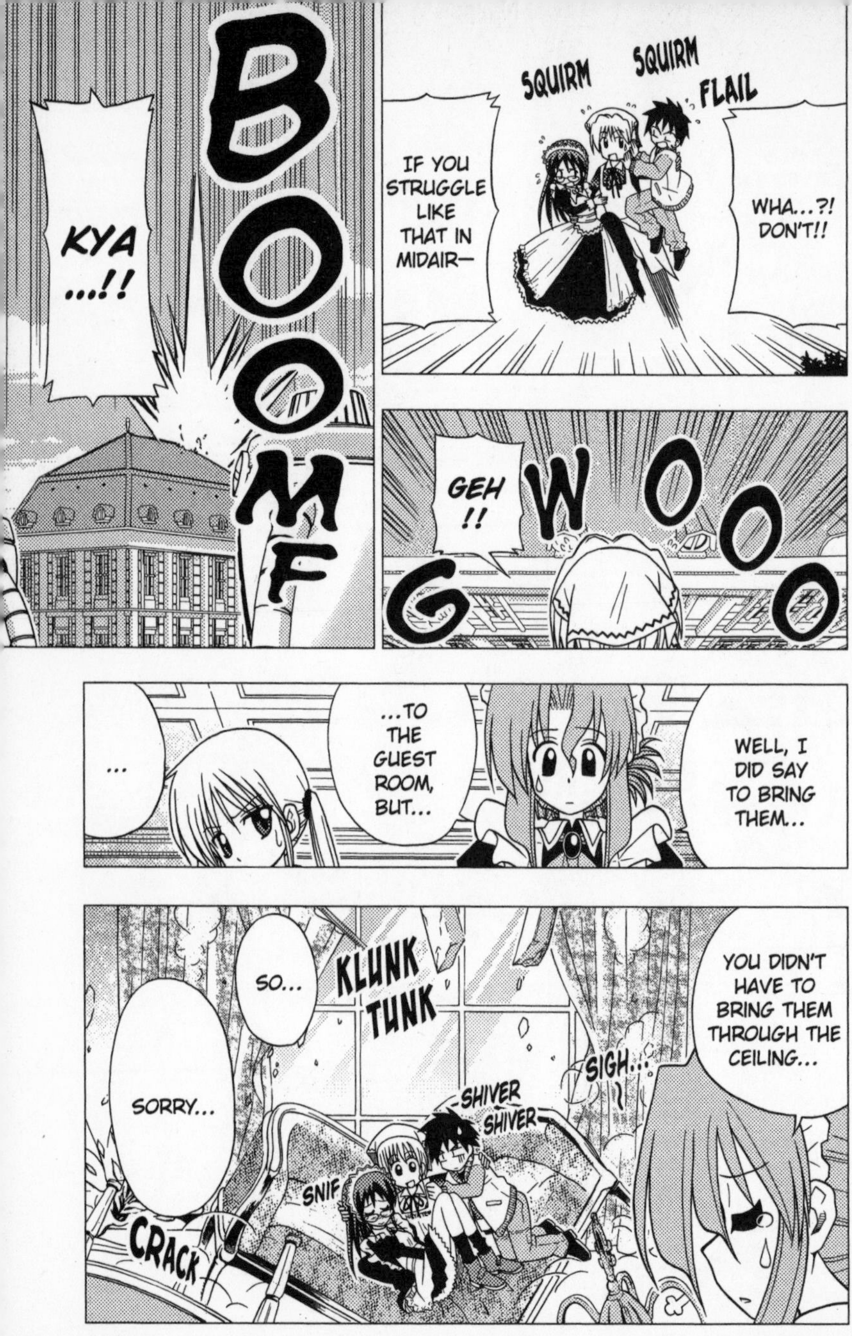

FLAIL
SQUIRM
SQUIRM
WHA...?! DON'T!!
IF YOU STRUGGLE LIKE THAT IN MIDAIR—
WOOOG
GEH!!
BOOMF
KYA...!!
WELL, I DID SAY TO BRING THEM...
...TO THE GUEST ROOM, BUT...
...
YOU DIDN'T HAVE TO BRING THEM THROUGH THE CEILING...
SIGH...
KLUNK
TUNK
SO...
SHIVER
SHIVER
SNIF
SORRY...
CRACK

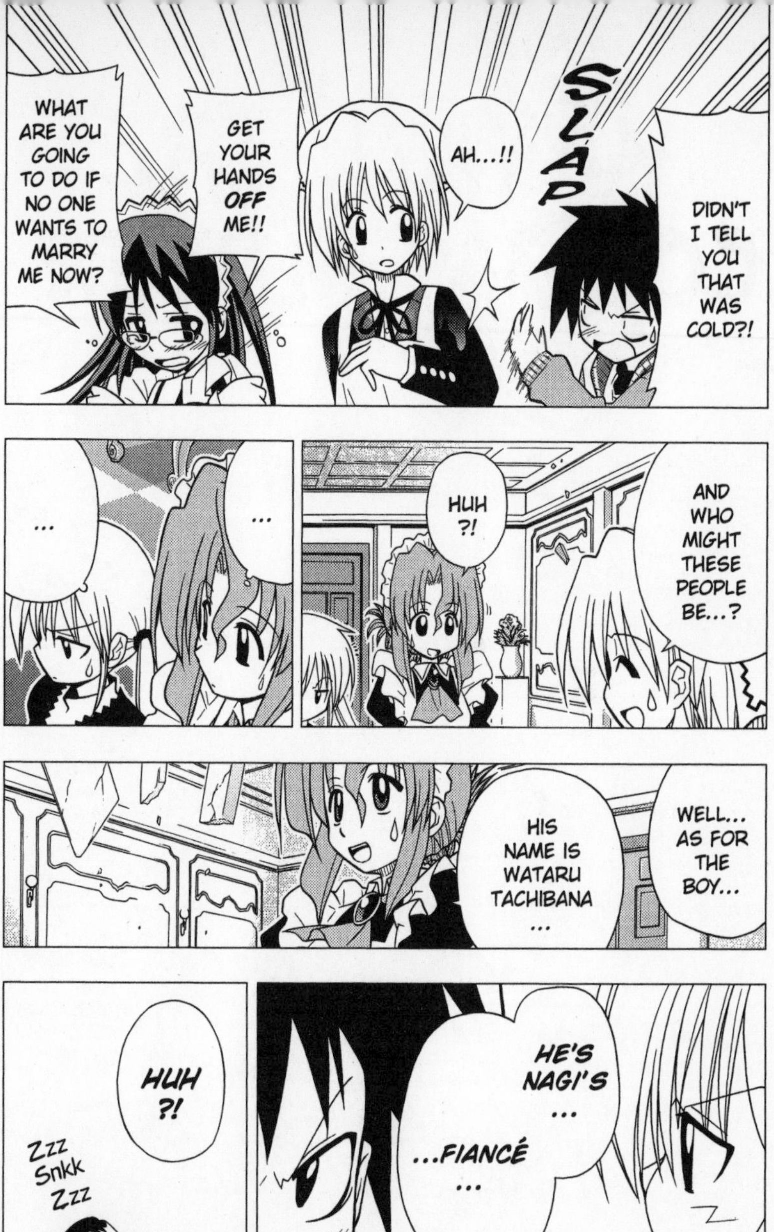
SLAP
DIDN'T I TELL YOU THAT WAS COLD?!
AH...!!
GET YOUR HANDS OFF ME!!
WHAT ARE YOU GOING TO DO IF NO ONE WANTS TO MARRY ME NOW?
AND WHO MIGHT THESE PEOPLE BE...?
HUH ?!
...
...
WELL... AS FOR THE BOY...
HIS NAME IS WATARU TACHIBANA ...
HE'S NAGI'S ...
...FIANCÉ ...
HMPH
HUH ?!
Zzz Snkk Zzz

TO BE CONTINUED

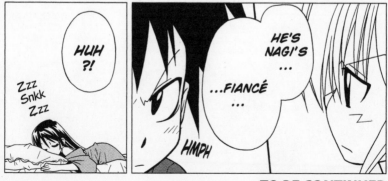

HAYATE THE COMBAT BUTLER

BONUS PAGE

CALLIGRAPHY/RITSUKO HATA (TEA MASTER)

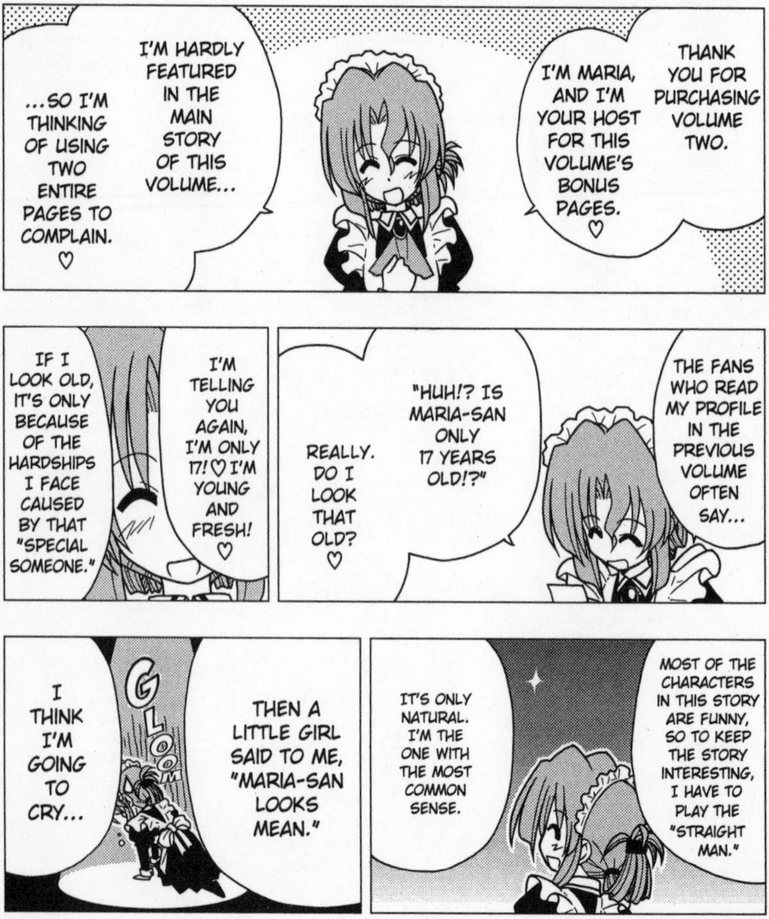
THANK YOU FOR PURCHASING VOLUME TWO.
I'M MARIA, AND I'M YOUR HOST FOR THIS VOLUME'S BONUS PAGES. ♡
I'M HARDLY FEATURED IN THE MAIN STORY OF THIS VOLUME...
...SO I'M THINKING OF USING TWO ENTIRE PAGES TO COMPLAIN. ♡
THE FANS WHO READ MY PROFILE IN THE PREVIOUS VOLUME OFTEN SAY...
"HUH!? IS MARIA-SAN ONLY 17 YEARS OLD!?"
REALLY. DO I LOOK THAT OLD? ♡
I'M TELLING YOU AGAIN, I'M ONLY 17! ♡ I'M YOUNG AND FRESH! ♡
IF I LOOK OLD, IT'S ONLY BECAUSE OF THE HARDSHIPS I FACE CAUSED BY THAT "SPECIAL SOMEONE."
MOST OF THE CHARACTERS IN THIS STORY ARE FUNNY, SO TO KEEP THE STORY INTERESTING, I HAVE TO PLAY THE "STRAIGHT MAN."
IT'S ONLY NATURAL. I'M THE ONE WITH THE MOST COMMON SENSE.
THEN A LITTLE GIRL SAID TO ME, "MARIA-SAN LOOKS MEAN."
GLOOM
I THINK I'M GOING TO CRY...

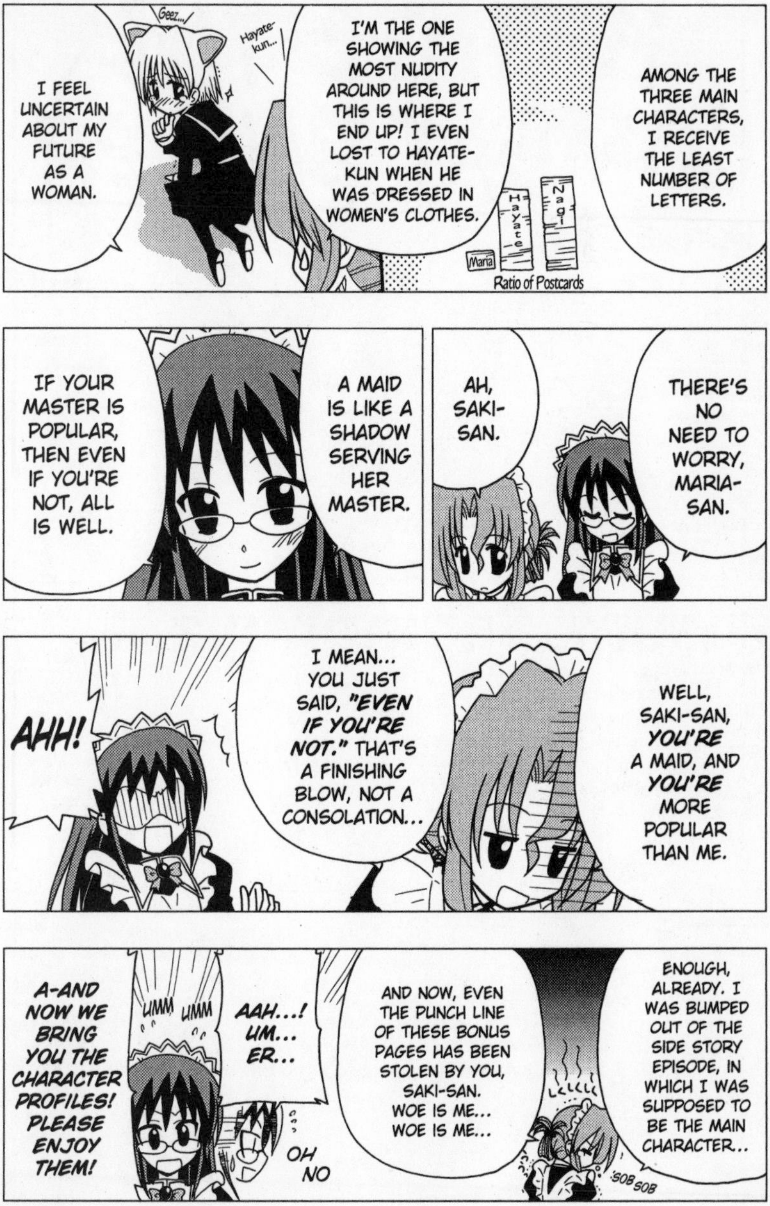
AMONG THE THREE MAIN CHARACTERS, I RECEIVE THE LEAST NUMBER OF LETTERS.
Nagi
Hayate
Maria
Ratio of Postcards
I'M THE ONE SHOWING THE MOST NUDITY AROUND HERE, BUT THIS IS WHERE I END UP! I EVEN LOST TO HAYATE-KUN WHEN HE WAS DRESSED IN WOMEN'S CLOTHES.
Hayate-kun...
Geez.../
I FEEL UNCERTAIN ABOUT MY FUTURE AS A WOMAN.
THERE'S NO NEED TO WORRY, MARIA-SAN.
AH, SAKI-SAN.
A MAID IS LIKE A SHADOW SERVING HER MASTER.
IF YOUR MASTER IS POPULAR, THEN EVEN IF YOU'RE NOT, ALL IS WELL.
WELL, SAKI-SAN, YOU'RE A MAID, AND YOU'RE MORE POPULAR THAN ME.
I MEAN... YOU JUST SAID, "EVEN IF YOU'RE NOT." THAT'S A FINISHING BLOW, NOT A CONSOLATION...
AHH!
ENOUGH, ALREADY. I WAS BUMPED OUT OF THE SIDE STORY EPISODE, IN WHICH I WAS SUPPOSED TO BE THE MAIN CHARACTER...
SOB SOB
AND NOW, EVEN THE PUNCH LINE OF THESE BONUS PAGES HAS BEEN STOLEN BY YOU, SAKI-SAN. WOE IS ME... WOE IS ME...
AAH...! UM... ER...
UMM UMM
OH NO
A-AND NOW WE BRING YOU THE CHARACTER PROFILES! PLEASE ENJOY THEM!

PROFILE

[Age] 13

[Birthday] September 24th

[Blood Type] O

[Family Structure]
Mother
Grandmother
Great-grandmother

[Height] 144 cm

[Weight] 30 kg

[Strengths/Likes]
Cooking, sewing, koto (Japanese harp),
tea ceremony, calligraphy, flower
arrangement, Nagi and Nagi's manga.

[Weaknesses/Dislikes]
Can't follow a fast-paced conversation.
Not good at riding the escalator.

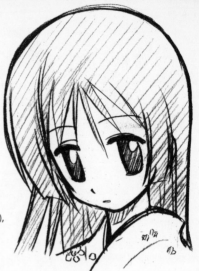

Isumi Saginomiya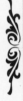

She hesitates all the time.
She always seems to get lost.
She is a priestess of the light who inherited the secret mystical power,
Jutsushiki Hachiyo, "the spell of the eight leaves," which has been handed
down to a chosen female child from generation to generation in the
Saginomiya family.
However, it's unknown whether this power will show up in the story.
If she were a character in a RPG, she would be a sage or a white magician.
Among all the characters in the story, she's probably the one most suited
to the title "ojô-sama," and compared to Nagi, she has less knowledge of
the world in general.
She's barely capable of anger, one of the four basic emotions.
Naturally, she's an honest person.
Sakuya not only talks too fast for her, she also talks in a Kansai accent.
Isumi doesn't understand half of what Sakuya is saying.
She's the only person who can understand Nagi's manga.
She's Nagi's best friend, and understands her better than Maria does.

PROFILE

[Age] 13

[Birthday] April 3rd

[Blood Type] AB

[Family Structure]
Father
Brother (illegitimate)
Sister Hinata (10)
Brother Asato (10)
Sister Yuuka (8)
Sister Haori (4)

[Height] 142 cm

[Weight] 31 kg

[Strengths/Likes]
Comedy, babysitting, horseback riding

[Weaknesses/Dislikes]
Dislikes people who don't get her jokes. Also dislikes
any life forms that eat natto (fermented soybeans).

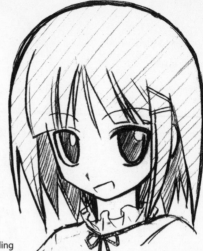

Sakuya Aizawa

Unlike Nagi and Isumi, Sakuya is an ojô-sama
who acts most like a normal person.
Probably because she has younger brothers and sisters,
she is good at taking care of others.
She's a responsible big sister.
That may be why she can't leave Nagi alone.
Because of her style, wit and distinctive personality,
she is very popular among both boys and girls,
and her teachers are also fond of her.
However, she tends to get carried away easily,
which gets her into dangerous situations.
The reason why Nagi used to call Sakuya "onee-chan" is
because that's what Sakuya's younger siblings called her.
For that matter, she has known Nagi longer than any of the
other characters, and has been responsible for many of the
events that messed up Nagi's personality.
Her two closest butlers are Makita (the guy with white hair)
and Kunieda (the guy with black hair).
Currently, she goes to an all-girls' school,
but she is very popular with boys.

THAT'S ALL FOR NOW. SO HOW DID YOU LIKE
HAYATE THE COMBAT BUTLER VOLUME TWO?

IT MIGHT SEEM LIKE I INTENTIONALLY HAD FEWER BONUS PAGES
THAN LAST TIME, BUT NO! THAT'S NOT TRUE! THE BONUS PAGES
ARE ONLY INTENDED TO MAKE EFFECTIVE USE OF EXTRA PAGES
RESULTING FROM THE BOOK BINDING PROCESS, SO I'M NOT THE
ONE WHO DECIDES THE NUMBER OF BONUS PAGES.

SO, PLEASE UNDERSTAND AND FORGIVE ME...

TO TELL YOU THE TRUTH, I WANTED TO INCLUDE COMMENTARIES
BY ROBO EIGHT, GRANDPA MIKADO, AND MAKIMURA-SAN, AS WELL AS
THE MANGA FROM THE *HAYATE THE COMBAT BUTLER* POSTER I MADE
FOR THE BOOKSTORES, BUT I JUST COULDN'T FIT THEM IN. I'LL
TRY TO HAVE THEM SHOW UP IN A FUTURE VOLUME.

WELL, ACTUALLY...I DON'T KNOW IF ANYBODY WANTS
COMMENTARIES BY THE ROBOT AND THE OLD MAN, ANYWAY...

AT ANY RATE, SINCE THIS IS VOLUME TWO, THERE ARE
MORE CHARACTERS APPEARING IN THE STORY. I THINK
IT'S GETTING LIVELIER THAN BEFORE. I HOPE YOU
LIKE THE NEW CHARACTERS IN THIS VOLUME.

AS I WRITE THIS, THE SERIES IS STARTING ITS NINTH MONTH
IN *WEEKLY SHÔNEN SUNDAY*. THANK YOU! IT'S ALL BECAUSE
OF YOUR SUPPORT! I WOULD LIKE TO KEEP GOING AS LONG AS
POSSIBLE, SO PLEASE KEEP SUPPORTING ME. AND OF COURSE,
PLEASE TELL ME WHERE TO GO WITH THE STORY WITH
AS SPECIFIC COMMENTS AS POSSIBLE (HA HA)!

ALSO, I AM UPDATING MY COLUMN ON THE *WEEKLY
SHÔNEN SUNDAY* WEBSITE EVERY WEEK AS USUAL
(HTTP://WEBSUNDAY.NET/RENSAI/SET HAYATE.HTML),
SO WHEN YOU HAVE TIME, PLEASE VISIT!

WELL, EVERYONE, I'LL SEE YOU AGAIN IN VOLUME THREE!

YOU *WILL* SEE ME, RIGHT? RIGHT? OKAY? P...PROMISE?

WELL, SEE YOU LATER! ~☆

One who laughs at one yen won't cry over one yen

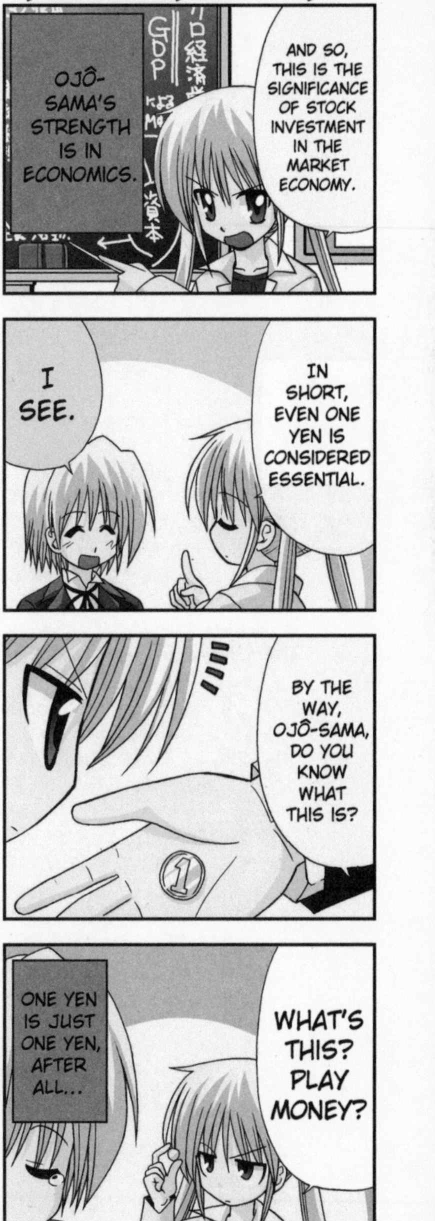
AND SO, THIS IS THE SIGNIFICANCE OF STOCK INVESTMENT IN THE MARKET ECONOMY.
OJÔ-SAMA'S STRENGTH IS IN ECONOMICS.
GDP
IN SHORT, EVEN ONE YEN IS CONSIDERED ESSENTIAL.
I SEE.
BY THE WAY, OJÔ-SAMA, DO YOU KNOW WHAT THIS IS?
1
WHAT'S THIS? PLAY MONEY?
ONE YEN IS JUST ONE YEN, AFTER ALL...

That's one thing, but this is another!!

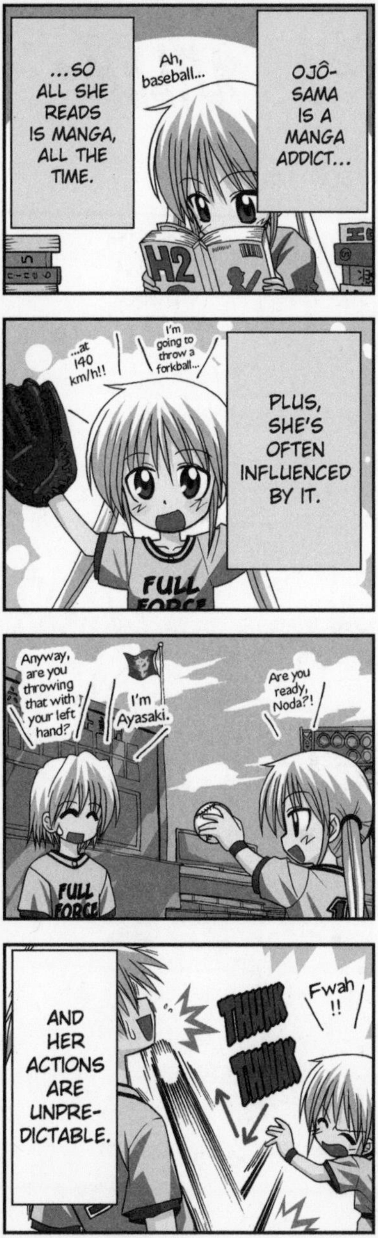
OJÔ-SAMA IS A MANGA ADDICT...
Ah, baseball...
...SO ALL SHE READS IS MANGA, ALL THE TIME.
H2
PLUS, SHE'S OFTEN INFLUENCED BY IT.
I'm going to throw a forkball...
...at 140 km/h!!
FULL FORCE
Are you ready, Noda?!
I'm Ayasaki.
Anyway, are you throwing that with your left hand?
FULL FORCE
Fwah !!
THWAK
THWAK
AND HER ACTIONS ARE UNPREDICTABLE.

- HAYATE THE COMBAT BUTLER -
[BAD ENDING (2)]

IF YOU SELECT "DON'T AVOID SAKUYA'S ATTACK," THEN THE GAME ENDS. "INCIDENTALLY, IN THE SECOND ROUND, IN THE SAKUYA ROUTE, THERE'S A FLAG CALLED "PERFORM THE 'RAKUGO TOKISOBA' ACT AND GAIN SAKUYA'S FAVOR"!

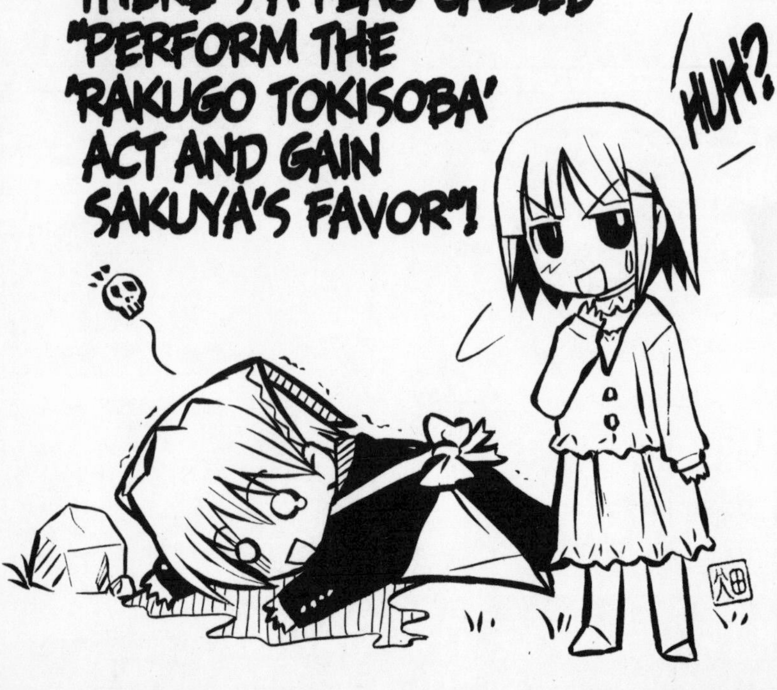
HUH?

LOVE MANGA!
LET US KNOW WHAT YOU THINK!

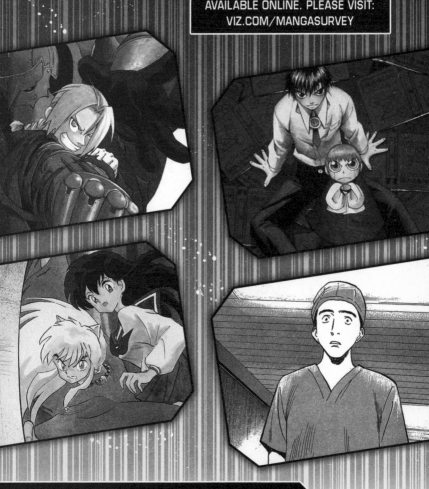

HELP US MAKE THE MANGA
YOU LOVE BETTER!